Modern Scholarship on European History

HENRY A. TURNER, JR.

General Editor

RUSSIAN ECONOMIC DEVELOPMENT *from* PETER THE GREAT *to* STALIN

RUS

SIAN

ECO

NOMIC

DEVELO

PMENT *from*

PETER

the

GREAT

to

edited with an introduction by

WILLIAM L. BLACKWELL

New Viewpoints · *New York* · *1974*

A Division of Franklin Watts, Inc.

Library of Congress Cataloging in Publication Data

Blackwell, William L   comp.
    Russian economic development from Peter the Great
to Stalin.

    (Modern scholarship on European history)
    CONTENTS: Baykov, A.   The economic development of
Russia.—Blanc, S.   The economic policy of Peter the
Great.—Kahan, A.   Continuity in economic activity and
policy during the post-Petrine period in Russia.   [etc.]
    1. Russia—Economic conditions—Addresses, essays,
lectures.   2. Russia—Economic policy—Addresses,
essays, lectures.   3. Russia—Industries—History—
Addresses, essays, lectures.   I. Title.
HC333.B543   330.9'47   73-11162
ISBN 0-531-06363-1
ISBN 0-531-06492-1 (pbk.)

Acknowledgments

The editor wishes to acknowledge with appreciation the work of Mr. Michael Markoff in the translation from the Russian of the two articles by V. K. Yatsunsky, of Stuart Brent's translation of the article by Roger Portal, and of Michel Bensadon's translation of the essay by Simone Blanc.

Alexander Baykov, "The Economic Development of Russia," *Economic History Review,* 2nd Series, Vol. VII, 137–49. By permission.

Simone Blanc, "The Economic Policy of Peter the Great," *Cahiers du monde Russe et Sovietique III,* 122–39. By permission of the École Pratique des Hautes Etudes and Mouton & Co.

Arcadius Kahan, "Continuity in Economic Activity and Policy During the Post-Petrine Period in Russia," *Journal of Economic History,* XXV (1965), 61–85. By permission of the author and the Economic History Association.

William L. Blackwell, "The Old Believers and the Rise of Private Industrial Enterprise in Early Nineteenth-Century Moscow," *Slavic Review,* XXIV, 407–24. By permission.

Roger Portal, "Muscovite Industrialists: The Cotton Sector (1861–1914)," *Cahiers du monde Russe et Sovietique IV,* 5–40. By permission of the École Pratique des Hautes Etudes and Mouton & Co.

Theodore H. Von Laue, "The State and the Economy," Cyril E. Black, ed., *The Transformation of Russian Society,* pp. 209–55. Copyright © 1960 by the President and Fellows of Harvard College. By permission of Harvard University Press and the author.

Alexander Erlich, "Stalin's Views on Soviet Economic Development," Ernest J. Simmons, ed., *Continuity and Change in Russian and Soviet Thought,* pp. 81–99. Copyright © 1955 by the President and Fellows of Harvard College. By permission of Harvard University Press and the author.

Herbert J. Ellison, "The Decision to Collectivize Agriculture," *American Slavic and East European Review,* XX, 2 (1961), 189–202. By permission of the *Review* and the author.

F. D. Holzman, "Financing Soviet Economic Development," from *Capital Formation and Economic Growth* (Princeton University Press for the National Bureau of Economic Research). By permission of the Bureau and the author.

Stanislaw Swianiewicz, "The Main Features of Soviet Forced Labor," *Forced Labour and Economic Development* (Oxford University Press, under the auspices of the Royal Institute of International Affairs). By permission.

Naum Jasny, "The Great Industrialization Drive," *Soviet Industrialization 1928–1952* (1961), pp. 1–21. By permission of the University of Chicago Press.

Stanley H. Cohn, "The Soviet Economy: Performance and Growth," V. G. Treml, ed., *The Development of the Soviet Economy, Plan and Performance* (Praeger, for the Institute for the Study of the USSR), pp. 24–50. By permission of the author and the Institute.

Contents

Introduction

The subject of Russian economic development, particularly that of the tsarist period, was for many years largely ignored by scholars. Most were drawn to the study of political movements. After the dramatic events of 1917, it became more important for historians, both within and outside the Soviet Union, to seek an explanation of the Russian Revolution, rather than to discover the contours of Russia's economic and social evolution in modern times. This made it difficult to understand both tsarist and Soviet economic development. Soviet economic progress attracted more interest; but the tendency was to explain the Bolshevik regime's policies in ideological terms, obscuring the other factors which determined economic developments in the USSR. The industrial advances which were achieved under the last tsars also were generally ignored. The same disinterest resulted in a passing over of the similarities of the tsarist and Soviet methods of industrialization.

Recently, scholars in the United States, Western Europe, and the Soviet Union have reexamined this subject and its interpretations. Most of the research is still embedded in monographs and in articles published in scholarly journals. No major work of synthesis embracing the economic development of Russia since Peter the Great has yet appeared. Hence, there has come to be an immediate and very practical need, for scholars and students alike, to have available the best of this recent scholarship in a relatively complete and coherent form.

The primary criteria in the selection of the works here presented have been quality and freshness. A secondary editorial aim has been to provide historical continuity and to illuminate specific problems that deserve attention. The collection is essentially historical in genre, although many of the authors represented are economists. However, their contributions focus not only on problems of the contemporary Soviet economy, but also range far into the past to deal with fundamental problems of Russian economic development. Among those contributions authored by historians, one obtains not only the time dimension, but also social and political perspectives without which Russian economic development can scarcely be understood. Obviously, much of the background, some significant larger trends, and a number of problems have not been discussed by scholars recently, or could not be included in a collection as short and highly selective as this. Reference to relevant materials not reproduced will be made in the concluding bibliography. It will be the purpose of the introductory essay to fill in the historical background in briefest fashion, and to provide a general historiographical context in which the relation of each section to the whole can more clearly be seen.

I

The economic development of Russia, particularly from the Petrine period to the era of the Great Reforms, must be considered largely as a history of economic backwardness. The first five articles in the collection are, in one way or another, concerned with the forces which held the Russian economy in check during this time.

The premodern Russian society prior to Peter the Great is a vast subject in itself, which reaches down the centuries to the formative period of the Muscovite state. Such a complex and wide-ranging topic has understandably provoked controversy among historians, although they have also arrived at a number of conclusions for which there is substantial agreement.

Many scholars—most notably in recent publications, Alexander Baykov, Roger Portal, V. K. Yatsunsky, Jerome Blum, and Holland Hunter—have concurred on the importance of geographic and strategic factors in impeding the economic development of Russia, particularly as these came into play in the crucial transitional period of the Mongol Yoke (thirteenth to sixteenth centuries). Fewer nations in the history of mankind were more poorly endowed by nature for economic growth and prosperity. Muscovite Russia began her modern history isolated from the main currents of world trade by centuries of Asian nomadic incursions, and besieged on a vast expanse of flat, frozen plain and forest. The scattering of resources, markets, and ports in remote and peripheral areas posed a fundamental problem for Russian economic development: until a modern system of rapid transport could be built to bind Russia's granaries and ports, as well as her minerals and fuels, domestic and foreign trade would remain stagnant, prices for Russian goods would be fixed at uncompetitively high levels, and industrial growth would be thwarted. This stagnation did not in fact end until the building of railroads in the late nineteenth century.

Alexander Baykov, in the opening article, is the first scholar in recent times to reevaluate the role of poor endowment in natural resources and inadequate transport facilities as opposed to institutional factors, such as serfdom, in retarding the development of Russian heavy industry and agriculture. Baykov's interpretation places these problems in the perspective of the nineteenth and twentieth centuries, and thus provides a useful approach to the subject as a whole. The late Soviet historian V. K. Yatsunsky, in the fourth article, has illuminated in a descriptive way the transport problem just prior to the railroad era by tracing the movement and prices of iron as this product inched its way across the vastness of the Russian Empire. Floods produced by the rapid thaw of snow-encrusted plains, and blocked rivers and ports frozen over for long parts of the year, are other examples of the depressing impact of climate and terrain on both the commercial and agricultural development of Russia.

More crucial, the same geographic conditions deprived the nation of defensible frontiers during a period of aggressive expansion on the part of bordering powers and migrating enemies. This exposure, which was most acute during the centuries of Mongol occupation, created not only formidable obstacles to Russian economic development, but also a framework for this development. The Mongol Yoke, not unlike the half-millennium of Turkish domination of the Balkans, or the centuries of Spanish misrule of Sicily, seriously retarded the development of Russia, and at the same time created institutions and habits which characterized the subsequent history of that area. War became a constant occupation, and one of the major factors in perpetuating backwardness. Out of centuries of war came not only the impoverishment of the people and the state, but also the creation of a sluggish and weighty military despotism.

Muscovite Russia was a land of thousands of isolated peasant villages, whose rude inhabitants scratched the land for its grain and food. Poor in natural resources, and scarce of labor, the nation had to meet its overwhelming military necessities by heavy taxation of the peasantry. Demanding such extravagant sacrifices of so disorganized a society, to say nothing of governing it, was a task that could only be executed by a powerful and centralized state apparatus. The same persistent military and economic needs demanded in time the disciplining of the nobility, the church, and all other elements of the society whose disobedience might weaken state power. This straitjacketing of Russian society was a slow and painful process which consumed the better part of three centuries, an age characterized by peasant riots, religious heresies, political dissent, expropriations of property, civil wars, brigandage, palace revolutions, and assassinations—many of frequent occurrence and unusually violent proportions. In this whirlwind of domestic turmoil and war were forged by 1725, either in mature or embryo form, the main institutions of Russian despotism, institutions which were to persist throughout modern times: autocracy, serfdom, bureaucracy, militarism, and the state control of religion and culture through an elaborately developed police apparatus.[1]

Such a society was no more conducive than was Russia's poor physical and geographic endowment to the kind of dynamic growth that was already making its appearance in Western Europe by the early eighteenth century. A formless social structure and undifferentiated economic conditions were little stimulative of the expansion of a middle class which could accumulate capital and assume leadership in commercial and industrial development. So long as the peasantry remained physically and psychologically immobilized in rural servitude, they could not be transformed to any significant degree into an industrial labor force, nor had they either the initiative or the freedom to engage in trade or other business enterprises. Serfdom pushed its masters into indolence; and in the eighteenth century, intensifying Western influences prompted the nobility to dissipate their wealth unproductively in the attempt to imitate European modes of luxury and pomp.

The military and civil bureaucracy, which by the eighteenth century had evolved into a sprawling apparatus, was available as an instrument of economic policy, but unsuited for the novel tasks of reform and development. Cumbersome and irrational organization, deeply embedded traditions of corruption, and brutal methods for coercing rural slaves and military conscripts were little suited for efficient management of factories and the productive employment of an industrial labor force. Even more crucial, neither the political system nor the culture of Old Russia were hospitable for the nurturing of science and technology. The church, like the bureaucracy, harbored a deep conservatism which was hostile to innovation, to foreign ideas, and very largely to education itself, beyond the realm of religious instruction and ritual. The result of such conditions was that Russia lacked the capacity for self-sustained technological improvement. This, combined with the absence of both a private and state impulse to apply or develop technology or foster technical education, forced Russia into an almost total reliance on foreign technology. This dependence endured until almost the middle of the twentieth century. Perhaps the most profound impediment to Russian economic development in modern times was the persistence of technological backwardness.

Despite these grave shortcomings, Russia was forced by the beginning of the eighteenth century to engage in a major modernization effort. By this time, she was becoming increasingly involved in European power politics. Postponement of reform now ran contrary to fundamental state interests and threatened the very independence of the nation. The lack of resources for such reforms necessitated an intense mobilization of the economy and society, which was, however, a partial or defensive kind of modernization. It was designed to provide the bare essentials of national defense, but did not fundamentally change the society or release the dynamisms necessary for comprehensive economic growth. This compromise reform was essentially a military and administrative modernization. It served to secure Russia's position as a great power for a while. However, such a system was costly for an underdeveloped country to maintain. It increasingly crippled the effort to develop the Russian economy, at a time when imperial expansion and involvement in wars with the European great powers intensified, and the gap between the respective rates of economic growth broadened. The sharpening competition brought on crises, new, more comprehensive mobilizations, and, in turn, more expansion and foreign conflict. However, because of Russia's limited resources, and the inertias of her society, each successive modernization drive remained inadequate and partial. This pattern, which characterized imperial Russian history, and which continues until today, was first instituted by Peter the Great.

II

Controversy over the economic policies of Peter the Great among leading Russian historians, both before and after the 1917 Revolution, as well as the interest this subject has aroused outside of Russia, is reflected in the articles included here by Simone Blanc and Arcadius Kahan. Peter's industrialization program was seen by some of the most accomplished historians of late tsarist times as both dynamic and premature.[2] More recently, the tendency among scholars has been to move away from the view of Peter's policies as a revolutionary parenthesis, and to attempt to integrate them into a more organic concept of Russian economic development in early modern times. Thus, increasing attention has been paid to continuities, in both the seventeenth century and the immediate post-Petrine era. The former period has been studied intensively by Soviet historians—most notably L. G. Beskrovny, V. N. Yakovtsevsky, and F. Ya. Polyansky—for evidence of Marx's concept of the "original accumulation of capital" (the emergence in the "feudal" period of workers and entrepreneurs, and an investment fund which could provide a basis for industrialization). Capital was derived, in their view, primarily from commerce, moneylending, and some primitive extractive and manufacturing industries. Factory workers were hired on a small scale in commercial and industrial enterprises, but impressment of peasant labor was the increasingly prevailing tendency. Craftsmen and petty traders also emerged from the rural masses to provide a cadre from which industrial entrepreneurs could be drawn. Russia was thus ripe for the dramatic mobilization of her resources performed by Peter the Great.

Few scholars have denied the dynamic and charismatic character of Peter's reforms. On the other hand, there has been little support among recent scholarship of the older view that Peter designed a grand strategy for the comprehensive modernization of Russian society—that he was acting as either a "mercantilist" or a revolutionary. The Petrine reforms, heroic and portentous as they were, nevertheless remained expedient and limited to the pressing military and economic exigencies of the hour.

Peter worked essentially to uphold Russia's national interests, as did those who ruled Russia in the thirty years following his death. What the latter lacked were not Peter's goals, but his stature and drive. Thus, there were continuities in state industrial policy in the post-Petrine period, as the Soviet scholar, F. Ya. Polyansky, has suggested recently, because, with Russia's deeper involvement in European power politics, it had become a vital interest of the state to maintain Peter's war machine.

Private industrial enterprise, encouraged by the state, also maintained the Petrine tempo of economic activity in the second quarter of the eighteenth century, as is shown by Arcadius Kahan's article. The geographical focus of Russia's industrial growth until the 1760s was the Urals region, which in the production of iron by the reign of Catherine the Great both rivaled and supplied England. The transformation of the Urals into one of the major heavy industrial centers of the world was in part the work of dynamic officials who consolidated the work of Peter the Great. Foremost among these was Vasily Tatishchev. A similar feat was accomplished by Russian private entrepreneurs, notably the Demidov and Stroganov families.

For a number of reasons to which historians attribute varying emphases—ranging from a declining foreign market and the depletion of resources (N. I. Pavlenko) to transport problems, bad management, and the Pugachov uprising (Roger Portal)—the Urals industries fell into a stagnation in the late eighteenth century from which they did not fully recover until the 1930s. Nevertheless, Russia experienced a new surge of industrial growth during the early nineteenth century. This occurred, not in the provincial interior, but at the very heart and brain of the empire, Moscow and St. Petersburg, and in the textile rather than in heavy industry. Industrial expansion was particularly rapid in the cotton industry during the reign of Nicholas I—enough to prompt Soviet historians, after some discussion, to conclude that the "Industrial Revolution" in Russia began about 1830. They were able to accept such a periodization by very largely ignoring quantitative criteria bearing on the Russian economy as a whole. Instead, they based their definitions on the more qualitative Marxist formulae of the factory system, machine technology, and wage labor, as these made their appearance in the infant industries of prereform Russia. Although the conclusions were thus limited in application and somewhat misleading, this lengthy debate among Soviet historians brought forth a substantial fund of useful materials from archives within the Soviet Union. The article here included by V. K. Yatsunsky is a good example of this kind of research. It also summarizes the main conclusions of leading Soviet scholars—S. G. Strumilin, K. A. Pazhitnov, and others—involved in the discussions.

Historians outside of the Soviet Union have taken issue with these conclusions. Although rejecting the long-standing view of the early nineteenth century in Russia as a period of economic stagnation, they contend that, in the building of railroads, the spread of the cotton industry, the emergence of capitalist enterprise, and other social and cultural changes, there is evidence for defining the half century before the emancipation of the serfs as one of necessary preparation for more rapid economic growth, although not as an overt industrial revolution (William L. Blackwell). Other Western historians, most notably Alexander Gerschenkron, would see less dynamism in the Russian economy until after the emancipation of the serfs.

Certainly, it was only after the Great Reforms that capitalistic enterprise—both domestic and foreign—assumed major proportions in the Russian economy. However, the uniqueness of Russian industrial capitalism and the reasons for its tardy appearance can only be fully grasped by a study of Russian society during the preceding century. Most of Russia's first industrial entrepreneurs, like Peter the Great's industrialists—most notably the Demidovs—were drawn from the small merchant-artisan class. Few capitalists, until the early nineteenth century, came from the peasantry or the religious minorities; and many of Peter's industrialist families soon married into the nobility.

The eighteenth century has been recognized as the "golden age" of the Russian nobility, in terms of privilege and influence, and indeed it was at this time that they sought to utilize their enhanced power and prestige to transform their resources into money through industrial enterprise. They needed additional cash to meet the debts that Westernization had accumulated. This could be done most conveniently by converting resources at hand—the labor, produce, and primitive technology of their estates could be utilized in simple industrial enterprises. These estate factories manufactured goods for local consumption or for purchase by the state—most notably vodka and woolen cloth for the army. Protected and subsidized by the government, these factories were more a side product of the manorial economy than true prototypes of capitalist enterprise. Although the largest ones persisted until the emancipation of the serfs, many of the smaller *votchinal* factories, costly and inefficient, slipped quickly into bankruptcy. The primitive natural economy of the average Russian estate could not sustain the costly, moneyed way of life of its Westernized master; while the few hundred aristocratic latifundists, into whose hands were concentrated most of Russia's rural wealth, lived lives of hopeless extravagance.

An authentic industrial, capitalist middle class began to appear in the cities of European Russia in the first quarter of the nineteenth century. Some of these were serfs—a few very innovative serf craftsmen actually became millionaires while still in bondage. Others came from a growing class of merchants and urban petit bourgeois who were being differentiated out of the peasantry. Many came from outcast religious minorities, for whom persecution and segregation acted as a stimulant to self-identity, group cooperation, pooling of capital, parsimony, profit-making, and business ventures. How this worked to mobilize capital and labor for the industrial enterprises of the Moscow Old Believers is described in the article by William L. Blackwell. A similar process was at work among Russia's submerged millions of Jews, from whom evolved a small but significant class of bankers, railroad magnates, and textile, sugar, and petroleum manufacturers. Foreign entrepreneurs also helped to develop Russian industry during the early nineteenth century. They brought with them not so much capital—massive foreign investment in Russia had to await several decades of economic growth in Europe and the United States—as technical and managerial skill, which was not yet to be found in Russia, and upon which they could place a large price tag.

The foundations thus had already been built for capitalism in Russia as it would mature in the late nineteenth century: a Russian industrial bourgeoisie descended from the Old Believers and the merchants of Moscow, largely controlling the textile industry there (whose development and composition have been summarized in the article by Roger Portal), and a more cosmopolitan capitalist society in St. Petersburg, which, as the administrative hub of the empire, as well as one of its chief ports and a center for the machine industry, naturally attracted many foreign bankers, merchants, and industrialists. Germans and English predominated, seconded by Belgians, Swedes, French, and Americans. During the last two decades of the old regime, foreign capital and technology found another profitable outlet in the development of heavy industry in the Ukraine, South Russia, and the Caucasus. This has frequently been cited as evidence of the growing intrusion of Western imperialism in Russia, although the recent study by John McKay has indicated that the tsars were not as generous in the dispensation of concessions and guarantees as formerly believed. What made Russia attractive to the foreign entrepreneur was the prospect of good profits, which could be made by the introduction of superior organization and technology. Advanced technique was worth money, for the Russians could not duplicate it, except at much higher cost.

The importation of foreign capital and technology was the keystone of the industrialization program developed by the tsarist ministers of finance—Reutern, Bunge, Vyshnegradsky, and, most notably, Sergei Witte—in the late nineteenth century. Its spring was the urgent problem of Russia's growing military inadequacies, and the economic and political strains caused by wars and defeats. Russia did not have the funds or the tools to effect the rapid industrialization essential to her national security: her limited resources had to be marshaled to bring in investment and machinery from abroad. The empire's meager wealth was very largely concentrated in grain and peasant labor. But the countryside, after the conservative and inadequate land reforms of the 1860s, was overpopulated, immobilized, and technologically backward. Such a rigid and poorly organized society could not provide the base for a prosperous agriculture, large-scale rural markets, the mobilization of industrial labor, and the growth of capital. However, with the construction of railroads from the grain markets to the ports, and the appropriate tax policy toward the peasantry, a commercial crop large enough to cover the costs of Russia's exports could be grown each year. The resulting favorable balance of trade would produce the fiscal stability essential for attracting foreign loans and investments. It was a harsh method of industrialization, based essentially on the exploitation of the peasantry, whose betterment was postponed for decades and whose marginal standard of living dropped even lower with the fall of grain prices on the international market. It was an economic strategy precariously exposed to the quirks of nature and the follies of man: famine or war could bring starvation to millions and the collapse of state finances.

Although this "Witte System" (detailed in the article by Theodore H. Von Laue) worked—Russia's industrial growth rate after 1885 was one of the highest in modern history—the cost was great. There was not only the expensive bill presented by foreign technology and capital, which controlled a third of Russian industry by 1900, but also the striking deterioration of the peasantry, which resulted not only in vast economic waste, but also more dangerous, growing political instability. The countryside exploded in 1905 and 1906, a whirlwind of violence which alarmed authorities sufficiently to produce fundamental land reforms. These reforms, identified with the statesman who implemented them, Peter Stolypin, sought to create a class of productive, landowning peasants loyal to the government, as well as to alleviate the shortage of land through the removal of restrictions on peasant migration and the settlement of fertile areas of Siberia. Well conceived and administered, the Stolypin reforms had begun to produce some of the most far-reaching social-economic changes in Russian history—the real breakdown of centuries of communalized slavery of the rural masses who had only been half freed in the emancipation of 1861. War and revolution intervened to disrupt these reforms and to change the course of Russian economic development.

III

A new period of Russian economic history began, not in 1917, but at the beginning of World War I. From the extensive studies of the tsarist economy during the war prepared in the 1920s for the Carnegie Endowment for International Peace, it is clear that Russian economic development was set back for many years by the 1914 involvement in total conflict with Germany and Austria-Hungary. It was then that Russia entered into the economic, political, and cultural isolation from which she has yet fully to emerge: the stage was set for the Russian Revolution, not in Petrograd, but in Sarajevo and Tannenberg. The war put a strain on the Russian economy and the tsarist state that could not be borne. In 1917, the old regime collapsed, soon followed by the demise of the caretaker Provisional Government, which possessed neither the power nor the will to sustain itself in the growing anarchy of Russian life.

Its successor, the more determined and ruthless Bolshevik regime, was able to cling on for three more years of devastating civil war and foreign intervention. During this holocaust, Russian industry and transport were practically destroyed, while the commercial and financial structure of the nation disintegrated. A social revolution swept the countryside, where massive peasant property seizures atomized the former pattern of estate and kulak land tenure into 24 million dwarf holdings. Fighting merely to survive, the Bolsheviks could give little more than lip service to problems of economic development or to their professed goals of creating a socialist society.[3] With the promulgation of the New Economic Policy (NEP) in 1921, it was clear that what they did would be determined not by ideology, but by the peasants. The Red Army easily crushed peasant rebellions with force; but passive resistance to forced requisitions of grain by the refusal to cultivate beyond personal needs, when this reached the ominous proportions of a 50-percent curtailment of production, could only be met with mass coercion, as in 1929, or mass concessions. At the end of an exhausting Civil War, Lenin had not the power, and probably not the inclination to force the peasants to produce. This meant the end of requisitions, and the guarantee that they could sell all that they could harvest, above and beyond the payment of a produce tax. As a consequence, the countryside, the largest part of the Soviet economy, soon reverted to capitalism, with free markets, retail trade, and small, rural industry in the hands of private entrepreneurs. Large industries, banks, and railroads—the "commanding heights," as Soviet leaders termed them at the time—remained under state control, although with considerable decentralization.

The NEP was essentially a policy of recovery through concession. It was not a program for economic development, because it did not envision the expansion or replacement of the existing industrial plant inherited from tsarist times, and it depended on a primitive and underproductive agricultural system. Once recovery had been achieved, such a makeshift remedy became unworkable. It was clear even earlier than the grain shortages of 1926 that not only stagnation, but also an intensifying agricultural crisis were Russia's lot unless a comprehensive program for economic development could be formulated and implemented.

Alexander Erlich's article summarizes the alternative programs that Soviet economists developed at this time, and traces Stalin's gradual acceptance, after many twists and turns, of the idea of collectivization and taxation of the peasantry to provide the capital necessary for a crash industrialization program. There is a wide range of disagreement among historians and economists about collectivization. The official explanation, which was frequently repeated outside of the Soviet Union, emphasized political and ideological factors—peasant grain hoarding, the deviation of the Rightist faction in the Party, and the restoration of capitalism by hostile powers from without and the kulak class from within. These interpretations are reviewed and criticized in the article by Herbert J. Ellison. Recently, other scholars have taken a closer look at the background of collectivization, but have achieved no close agreement as a result. Some, like Alec Nove, have emphasized the economic necessity of collectivization: it provided the only escape from an impasse that Russian agriculture had drifted into by the late 1920s, if the Bolsheviks were to retain power and achieve their aims. Moshe Lewin, in the most detailed and recent account we have of the administrative background of the collectivization drive, conversely emphasizes the factors of Stalin's character and power as these were reflected in decisions made during the grain crises in 1928 and 1929.[4]

The whirlwind of collectivization, in which ten millions of Russian lives were by Stalin's own admission disrupted or destroyed, was both the dynamism that activated the Soviet industrialization drive of the 1930s and the first forewarning of its brutal and exploitative nature. It assured Soviet planners of both the food necessary to feed Russia's burgeoning industrial cities and the capital essential for creating heavy industry. The counterpart of collectivization in the cities, as Naum Jasny has pointed out, was the rigorous restriction of consumption. The fiscal mechanism by which grain taxed from the peasants and inflated prices which resulted from the sharp curtailment of consumer industries were transformed into investment funds for heavy industry was the turnover tax. The secret of Stalinist capital accumulation, a concept which was soon applied everywhere, even in Soviet trade relations with Eastern European countries immediately after the Second World War, was, stated simply, to buy cheap and sell dear, pocketing the difference for industrial investment. The role of indirect and other forms of taxation in financing Soviet economic development is described in the article by Franklyn Holzman. In addition, the drastic reduction of the real income of urban workers, through inflated prices, longer working hours, and curtailment of housing construction, funneled vast wealth out of the pockets of consumers into the industrialization drive.

The machinery through which priorities and income were so massively reordered after 1929 was the planning system. The long-range plans (usually five or more years) were not, as originally advertised and believed, the "law of the land," in the sense of being concrete, operative programs. Scholars have increasingly come to conclude that the long-range plans, with their fantastic objectives, served largely propagandistic ends. As the economists, Naum Jasny and Eugene Zaleski have observed, the real planning, more modest in its ambitions, functioned on a year-to-year basis, or even for shorter terms. These plans were not so much strategic projections for economic growth as they were statistical expressions of a totally bureaucratized economy. The operative plan was a combination of party objectives and quotas, assessments of Russia's material and technological resources, reports on the previous performance of the economy, the results of negotiation with industrial management at all levels, the state budget, and vast computations of requisitions and allocations. All major economic activities in the Soviet Union were coordinated in one sprawling administrative apparatus. This machine was moved by a primitive system of quantitative quotas: the amount produced, measured in various ways, determined the rewards (or punishments) of the producers, be they factory managers, workers, peasants, or forced laborers. Such a combination of complexity, crudity, and control sorely tested the moral and intellectual capacities of its administrators. Inefficiency and corruption, inaccuracy and deception, wastefulness and shoddiness flourished on a vast scale. These in their turn bred a large, costly, and stifling bureaucracy of expedition, inspection, and control. Whim and political pressure at the top injected elements of irrationality into the direction of the system, much the same as the eccentricities of the consumer market brought glut and waste to capitalist economies. Like the latter in its own environment, the planning system, native to the Russian bureaucratic tradition, was a viable, if wasteful, method of economic growth.

However, the reorganization of the economy and the rechanneling of investment, as drastic and effective as these moves were, could not solve the problem of shortages. There were two essential ingredients of a productive economy of which the Soviet Union was in critically short supply in the 1930s, as so often before in Russian history: labor and technology. The industrial labor shortage was caused by the tremendous pool of underproductive labor which remained in the countryside. Collectivization drove millions of these peasants into the cities, although for a while large numbers of urban dwellers returned to their villages in hopes of protecting their own or gaining from the dispossession of others. However, the intensifying misery of the countryside, the rapid growth of industries and cities, and measures (such as the internal passport system) taken to bind workers to their jobs soon turned the tide. In less than a decade, the urban working force of the Soviet Union was swollen by the phenomenal migration off the land of 25 million people. Labor shortages were also met by a utilization of female labor in industry on a scale unprecedented in modern history. Forced labor also served the purpose of meeting the labor shortage by employing underutilized rural labor, and by providing a labor force for heavy construction work and the development of remote areas. As is pointed out in the essay by Stanislaw Swianiewicz, it also helped to depress consumption by removing several millions of consumers from the market. The slave camp system, however, was not created with these economic goals foremost in mind, but was a by-product of the politically motivated mass arrests of the Great Purge. The forced labor system paid in full for its armies of prisoners and guards, and gradually came to assume an economic importance of its own.

Both idealism and material incentives also played a role in increasing labor productivity during the industrialization drive of the 1930s. The arts and the media were mobilized to propagandize on behalf of government policy in farm and factory alike. A class of Shock Workers and Stakhanovites, workers rewarded for higher productivity on the basis of exemplary effort and efficient organization of work, came into being in the middle of the decade.

Despite heroic efforts in the educational field, the government was not able to produce the numbers or quality of technicians required for a major industrialization push. A relative technological independence was not achieved until the end of the Stalin era. Meanwhile, Soviet Russia, like its tsarist predecessor, had to look to foreign firms and engineers. This time it was the turn of the Americans more than the British or Germans. Several thousand foreign experts in all came to Russia in the early plan era, not to establish privately owned enterprises, as their fathers had done before the Revolution, but to fulfill contracts, which, however, were highly lucrative, when jobs were scarce in the depression-bound West.

It was clear by the time of the death of Stalin that the Soviet Union, despite decimations of the ranks of industrial management in the purges, and massive destruction of factories, transport facilities, and homes in the Second World War, had achieved an industrial revolution of major proportions. However, in the secrecy which veiled Russia in the last years of the Stalin period, little was known about many aspects of this revolution, and the statistics which the Soviet government made public seemed incredible. In the decade following the war, a number of economists in Europe and the United States attempted to make an accurate measurement of the Soviet economic achievement of the 1930s and 1940s on the basis of a critique of Soviet statistics, and any reliable information that could be found. A number of methodologies were developed, and, although there was wide disagreement among the several conclusions, it was clear that the official Soviet figures were grossly inflated. This was in part deliberate, an obvious propagandistic distortion, and in part unintentional, a product of exaggerative tendencies built into the planning system. It was also evident, however, that, during the Stalin era, the Soviet Union had achieved one of the most rapid economic growth rates in history—at least a sixfold expansion of industry and unchallenged status as the second industrial power of the world.[5] It was also possible to estimate the costs of this achievement, which were high. The Russian people paid for the building of one of the most formidable industrial war machines yet created by man, not only with millions of lives lost in the Great Purges, a decline of population growth practically to zero in the winter of 1932–1933, and a loss of half of the nation's livestock in the collectivization, but also with a catastrophic drop in agricultural and industrial real wages to almost the lowest level in Europe, and a per capita income which even today trails far behind those of most of the leading capitalist powers, and countries who are militarily far inferior to the Soviet Union.

The disproportionate economic development characteristic of the Stalinist industrialization, a policy favoring heavy industry and armaments, while depressing agriculture and consumption, was viable in the initial spurt of growth of the 1930s and the postwar recovery of the 1940s. However, just as the NEP of the 1920s, although effective for simulating recovery from the Civil War, impeded growth once that recovery was achieved, so the Stalinist policy of coercive and disproportionate development, workable for a period of "primary accumulation" and initial growth, became increasingly unsuitable for a more mature industrial economy. This is the burden that the successors of Stalin have borne. Protégés and pupils of Stalin, they inherited his system and have perpetuated it essentially intact. But a backward Soviet agriculture, neglected for a generation, can no longer sustain a disproportionately modernized industrial economy. At the same time, the long-deprived Soviet consumer can no longer—as a political as well as an economic matter —be rebuffed. The present condition and the future prospects of the contemporary Soviet economy constitute in themselves an important subject with an extensive literature, and are beyond the scope of this collection. The articles here reproduced deal essentially with the foundations of the present system, created under the tsars and re-created under Stalin, which perseveres with a changelessness and yet a capacity for regeneration that is remarkable.

William L. Blackwell

RUSSIAN ECONOMIC DEVELOPMENT *from* PETER THE GREAT *to* STALIN

I

The economic backwardness of tsarist Russia most frequently has been attributed to deficiencies in the political and social system, the implication being that the change or the demise of that system removed the impediments to growth, and released the dynamisms for rapid modernization. In the article that is here reprinted, Alexander Baykov argues that the "institutional" interpretation of Russia's backwardness, although valid, has been overstated. In a survey of tsarist and Soviet economic development, he emphasizes the decisive influence of natural resources and transport, particularly in the last century. Born in Russia, Alexander Baykov was one of the foremost Western economists in the immediate postwar era specializing in problems of the Soviet Union. He was the author of Soviet Foreign Trade (*Oxford, 1946*) *and* The Development of the Soviet Economic System (*Cambridge, 1947*), *and was a member of the Department of Economics and Institutions of the USSR at the Uni-*

3

versity of Birmingham, England. This article first appeared in The Economic History Review, *2nd ser.,* VII *(1954), 137–49. It is reprinted by permission of the author's heirs and the publisher, the* Economic History Society.

ALEXANDER BAYKOV

The Economic Development
of Russia

The purpose of these reflections is to reexamine current explanations of the course of Russian economic development, both with a view to provoking further thought and research on these problems and to providing a speculative hypothesis in an attempt to understand present problems. It should be emphasized that limitations of space demand that only a few main theses can be stated and some of the major problems indicated. Similarly, the arguments cannot be fully developed nor can supporting statistical material be provided; instead, references are given to well-known and easily accessible sources bearing on the matters under discussion.

I

The main difference in economic development as between Russia and the West European countries, from the middle of the eighteenth century to the second quarter of the twentieth century, was that Russia's industrial development was much slower, while the growth of her population was much more rapid than in the West: a difference which found its reflection in the standard of life of the population of Russia. The population of Russia increased from 14 million in 1722 to 129 million in 1897. Even if we exclude the population of the new territories which were incorporated into the Russian state during this period, the population increased from 13 million to 65 million in the basic territory.[1] In reality, the increase here was even greater, because several millions migrated from the older parts of Russia to newly conquered territories. Population thus increased much more rapidly in Russia than in the West European countries, and this growth of the population took place on an agricultural basis. The total urban population during the nineteenth century only increased from approximately 1.5 million at the beginning of the century to 16.5 million at the end; whereas total population in the meantime increased by 97 million.

The Russian urban population in 1800 was only approximately 3.5 percent of the whole—one-half of the ratio of urban to total population of France—not to mention England, in which, already by 1800, more than one-fifth of the population lived in towns.[2] During the nineteenth century, this difference in the degree of urbanization constantly increased, and, at the end of the nineteenth century, Russia with 12.8 percent urban population, as against over 40 percent in France and Germany and over 70 percent in England, was the most rural of the main European countries.

This prevalence of rural population in Russia was so striking that it is no wonder that most of the explanations for the retardation of Russia's economic development have been centered on the analysis of agricultural processes. The most generally accepted explanation is that Russia's economic retardation, especially the slow development of industry, was due, first, to Tatar invasion and the long maintenance of serfdom and, after its long-overdue abolition, to the preservation of certain features of a serf economy up to the beginning of the twentieth century. Among these factors were the continued system of repartitional tenure; the trammels of the village commune; the continued restrictions on civil and economic rights and on freedom of movement by the peasantry; the preservation of the strong social and political position of estate owners; the continued government by autocracy, together with an administration based on the landowning class without the participation of other classes. They also included the intervention of state power in economic activities to a much greater degree than in other countries (with its tendency to sponsor noncompetitive enterprises, by the creation of primitive monopolies, by bulk government purchases of certain industrial supplies for the army and navy at high assured prices and by the protectionist policy of excessive tariffs). These and other similar *institutional* explanations of the causes of economic retardation of Russia have now become generally current.

It would be foolish to deny the influence of Tatar invasion or of the long duration of serfdom or the influence of other institutional factors on the economic development of Russia. However, the importance of these institutional causes of the retardation of Russia's economic development is largely overstated. For example, the existence of serfdom cannot answer such problems as why England, where serfdom had to all intents and purposes ended as early as in the fourteenth century, and which had abundant iron and coal deposits, produced less cast iron than Russia in the eighteenth century, and even imported it (along with linen) from Russia and Sweden, while in the second half of the nineteenth century, when serfdom had been abolished in Russia, Russia produced much less coal and iron than England and imported both from England. Why, in the eighteenth century, when serfdom in Russia had been strengthened in comparison with the previous period, when the serf-owning classes were the actual rulers of the country, when the autocratic rule of the state was more prominent than before, was not Russia even further behind the leading European nations than in fact she was? For at that time in some branches of industrial production, such as in iron and linen, Russia was ahead of England, France, and Germany. In 1740 Russia produced 31,975 metric tons of cast iron, England 20,017, France 25,979 and Germany only 17,691 metric tons. It was only from 1805 that Russia, in the production of cast iron, fell behind England, from 1828 behind France and the United States, and from 1855 behind Austria and Germany.[3] Why, also, in the second half of the nineteenth century, when serfdom had been abolished, did Russia fall more and more behind the leading West European countries in industrial and, to some extent, agricultural development? It is asserted that this was caused by the maintenance of serfdom up to 1861, as a consequence of which industry suffered from a shortage of labor and capital for its development. However, all available evidence points out that the shortage of labor (and even of hired labor) was not the limiting factor in the development of industry. In industries which had economic possibilities for development, the amount of labor employed during the first half of the nineteenth century increased very rapidly, and *hired* labor was predominant in most of them. Besides, the serf population *itself* cannot be treated as a homogeneous group. Only as regards estate-owned serfs can we speak of "serfs" in the proper meaning of the term, but these comprised only a quarter of the total population on the eve of the abolition of serfdom.[4] Even if we take all the varieties of serf status, we find that, on the eve of the abolition of serfdom, they only accounted for just a little over half the total population (57.7 percent). In 1858 out of the total population of 74 million, they amounted to 42,717,000.[5] Thus, even on the eve of the abolition of serfdom there were in the country nearly 32 million people free of any kind of serf status, a nonserf population greater than the total population of contemporary England or France. Why was it not possible for 32 million free people to accumulate capital and participate in the development of industry to the same degree in Russia as in the other European countries?

For these and many other reasons it is not possible to accept institutional theories as the main explanations of the economic backwardness of Russia. Historians traditionally pay much attention to the institutional framework, to political institutions, social structure and social-philosophical views of society, to religious institutions, to relations with other states, and so on. Economic historians, too, mostly concentrate on forms of economic organization, on the institutions of production, distribution, and finance. Much less attention has been paid to, and very little research has been done to examine, the influence of natural resources, including transport, in their interrelations with the population trends and changes in technique. Research in this direction might necessitate the correction of many accepted explanations of economic development of different countries.

In this field one stock assumption, uncritically accepted as a working concept, has done much harm to realistic research into the causes of Russia's economic retardation, that is, the assumption that Russia is a "very rich country" as regards natural resources. But in reality European Russia viewed in historical perspective was worse endowed in natural resources than most of the leading West European countries. In order to utilize Russia's natural resources, the Russian people had to overcome more handicaps than the populations of most of the leading West European countries.

Up to the beginning of the eighteenth century the Russian state developed on a territory the European part of which was very poorly endowed with natural resources and transport possibilities. The soil of Moscow and the adjacent regions is very poor in comparison with that of most of the land in France, Germany, and England proper. Climatic conditions presented greater difficulties for the introduction of proper crop rotation, for the breeding of livestock and the full utilization of labor in agricultural occupations than in West European countries.[6] Given the same level of agricultural technique, the Russian peasant of Central and North European Russian regions had to overcome more natural handicaps than his counterpart in West European countries.

The agricultural resources of European Russia on the territory of the Russian state within the frontiers of 1700 were very limited, and if the Russian state had continued to develop on this territory alone it would soon have suffered from agrarian overpopulation, and its population would have been unable to grow at the pace at which it actually grew during the eighteenth and nineteenth centuries. In the same territories, during the eighteenth century, the Russian population increased by approximately 70 percent, but, during the nineteenth century it increased approximately three times. Such an expansion was possible only because the population of the older territory of the Russian state of the eighteenth century received a great deal of its agricultural supplies from the newly conquered territories of Southern Russia. As early as the end of the eighteenth century, most of Central and North European Russia (especially Moscow and the areas around Moscow) became consuming regions with deficiences in the balance of agricultural production and consumption. At the same time this territory had no industrial resources which could be compared with the industrial resources of the West European countries. The Central and Northwestern regions of Russia have only very poor deposits of iron ore, and these could only be worked by primitive methods of production, and were uneconomic to work with more advanced techniques of smelting.[7] When Peter the Great initiated a new drive for expanding the production of iron, these old Russian regions could not provide sufficient supplies of ore, and it was necessary to go over to the mountains of the Urals—1000 miles away from the historical centers of the population, from possible sources of labor supply and from the established centers of administration and trade of the country. It is enough to compare the location of Urals iron ore in relation to the historically established distribution of the population in Russia with the location of iron-ore deposits and the distribution of the population in England, Germany, and France, and with corresponding transport possibilities, to understand why Russia was handicapped in this respect too. In addition the Urals lack deposits of coking coal conveniently located near to iron ore. In England, coal found near the surface was used as a fuel as early as the sixteenth century. Experiments in the use of coal for smelting iron ore started as early as 1612 and coal was finally adopted for industrial use by 1735. But Russia had only poor deposits of brown coal (not suitable for coking and not easily accessible) in the Moscow region. Coal of very poor quality, which would not burn without an admixture of charcoal and was not suitable for coking, was discovered in the Urals only in 1797. Even then its mining was not undertaken because it was found uneconomical.

It would therefore be no exaggeration to say that it was the invention of smelting iron ore with coke that gave England (and afterward the other West European countries) the power rapidly to develop their iron production. This invention could not have been made in Russia, whatever institutional framework had existed at that time, because neither in the old center of Russian metallurgy in the central regions and Olonetsk region nor in the Urals were there available together the raw materials needed (that is, iron ore and coking coal). This invention could not be industrially used in Russia until the second half of the nineteenth century. Only then did it become possible economically to interconnect old centers of Russian population in the central regions with the deposits of iron ore in Krivoi Rog and coking coal in the Donets Basin. This invention allowed England immediately to increase the production of iron by leaps and bounds, while Russia, with only one region with iron-ore deposits which was unprovided with coking coal, needed sixty years (from the middle of the eighteenth century to the first quarter of the nineteenth century) to double her production of iron. England was able, in the same period, to increase her production of iron more than thirty times.[8]

Until the invention of the coke smelting of iron was realized, the Urals iron industry had some initial advantage. The region had easily mined, rich iron ore, an abundant supply of wood for charcoal, supplies of waterpower and cheap serf labor. However, its industry suffered from a very high, and constantly increasing, cost of transport, of charcoal from areas farther and farther away, and the high cost of transport of finished goods from the Urals to the markets. Besides, smelting on charcoal imposed certain limitations on the size of furnaces and on their productive cycle. The initial advantages of the Urals put Russia in the forefront of all West European countries as producers of cast iron in the eighteenth century, but after the application of coke smelting, Urals iron could not compete in cost with European, especially English production. It was the absence of suitably located coking coal and the high cost of transport that was the main cause of the slow development of iron production in the Urals—not difficulty in obtaining labor.[9]

It should also be remembered that territory on which the Krivoi Rog iron-ore basin (that is, the main iron-ore basin of European Russia) was situated was conquered by Russia from Turkey as late as 1733–1774 and part of the Donets Basin territory in 1739, that is, at the time when, in England, the Industrial Revolution was already being launched. These regions to the south of the Donets and the Dnieper rivers had been the stage for centuries of struggle between the centralized Russian state, the Tatars, Turkey, and Poland and were consequently very sparsely populated. Catherine II went so far as to promote the colonization of these regions with Germans, Bulgarians, and Greeks, and many thousands of them actually settled there. It was economically impossible to connect these two basins, Krivoi Rog and the Donets, with the historically evolved main centers of population of the Russian state until rail-

way connections were built. The Urals, in spite of their enormous
distance from the Moscow and Petersburg regions, were connected
with these markets by a system of rivers and canals; but often it
still required two navigational seasons to bring a load from the
Urals to Petersburg with intermediate wintering in Tver. In certain
favorable water and weather conditions, it was possible to reduce
transport time to six months, but it is very interesting to note that,
owing to nearly double costs of hiring horses and labor for towing,
loading and unloading operations in the summer months compared
with those of winter, the famous Demidov firm of ironmasters often
preferred to spread navigation over two seasons rather than shoul-
der the higher costs of transportation within a single season. On the
other hand Krivoi Rog and the Donets Basin could not be linked
with the Central region (distance from Krivoi Rog to Makeevka in
the Donets region 463 kilometers and to Moscow over 1000 kilometers) by the river system because, unfortunately, the rivers of
that region flow in the wrong direction, and could not economically
be connected by canals owing to great technical difficulties of construction. It was because Russian rivers flowed in the wrong directions that, up to the end of the eighteenth century, Russia had at
her disposal only the Volga River system and Northern Dvina
water system. This played an enormous part in determining the
direction and development of Russian trade and also (in the early
period of Russian history) of her cultural development. Had the
Krivoi Rog iron-ore basin and the Donets coal basin been located
in the Moscow region, and the Volga flowed from the Moscow region to the Black Sea instead of the Caspian, the history of Russia's
economy, and her political and cultural history, would have been
very different from what they in fact were.

II

Many more well-known facts support the thesis that historically Russia was much handicapped by a deficiency in the location
of her natural resources. Owing to this location of natural resources
and lines of communication, until railways could be built, it was
only possible to develop agricultural production in the southern re-

gions of Russia and to use it for supplying food to the central and northern regions of Russia and (later on) for export. When railways began to be built, the Urals industry could not even provide sufficient iron and steel, not to speak of engines and rolling stock. Between 1870 and 1879 Russia imported more than half (59 percent) of the iron and steel she consumed, and even in 1890–1899, by which time the southern regions were supplying more iron than the Urals, Russia still imported more than a quarter (27 percent) of her consumption of iron and steel.[10] The cause of this was that, up to the middle of the nineteenth century, Russia produced practically no coal. Until it became possible to develop the Donets and Krivoi Rog basins coal and iron ore, the Russian economy was built on grain and timber as its main natural resources. Even at the end of the nineteenth century, in 1886–1890, with a total consumption of coal still very low in comparison with West European countries, Russia imported a quarter of her coal consumption; and, up to the Revolution of 1917, the industry of the Petersburg region depended on imported English coal, which was cheaper (owing to lower transport costs) than coal brought from the Donets Basin.[11]

The turning point in Russian industrial history came when, for the first time in her history, it was possible to join the coal of the Donets Basin and the iron ore of Krivoi Rog with the old central regions of Russia. But the cost of building this new basis for the future development of Russian industry was borne, in the main, by the peasantry. In the last analysis, it was the Russian peasantry who paid for the foreign loans contracted for the building of the Russian railway system and for the foreign investments in mining and the iron and steel industries of the southern regions. Of the fifty-three years from 1860 to 1913, Russia had only twelve years with a negative balance of trade, and over this period taken as a whole, her exports were 6.5 billion (6,593,843,000) rubles higher than her imports, and all this export surplus was swallowed by the service on loans and payments for other invisible imports. At the outbreak of the Great War in 1914, Russia's total indebtedness (public and private) amounted to 7.5 billion rubles or about 3,750 million dollars.[12] Throughout the period 1860–1913, over three-quarters of Russia's exports were agricultural exports. It was in this period that Russia was nicknamed "the granary of Europe" and the Russian Finance Minister Vyshnegradsky coined the phrase, "Let us eat less, and export."

Yet Russia was a poor granary. Her sown area and her livestock grew very slowly.[13] The standard of living of her peasantry was much below that of the farmers of the countries to which Russian exports went. She was a granary which, at the beginning of the twentieth century, suffered an agrarian overpopulation to the extent of about 20 million.

III

If we turn now to the Soviet period, we see two distinct processes: a very rapid trend of increase in industrial output and a very uneven and slow development of agricultural production. The main results of Soviet economic development are well known. In spite of some disagreements among West European scholars as regards Soviet methods of statistical measurement, and consequently about actual rates of growth of industrial output and the extent of fluctuations in agricultural production, all agree that in the last twenty peaceful years in the Soviet Union a tempo of development of industrial production unprecedented in Russian history has been achieved.[14] I shall not attempt here to summarize the well-known facts of industrial and agricultural developments in the Soviet Union, but shall try to suggest some explanations of why such developments became possible and, in fact, took place.

In the first place, I shall put here the temporary influence of the Soviet economic policy aimed at the concentration of the economic activity on raising the productive capacity of the national economy and not on increasing consumption. By planned distribution of the total consumers' goods produced in the country it was possible, during the thirteen years from 1926 to 1939, not only to absorb 23.5 million of the natural increase of the population into the towns but to turn an additional 6.1 million rural inhabitants into urban dwellers. In this way for the first time in Russian history, the natural increase in population was absorbed by the towns. This permitted an increase in the numbers of workers employed in the national economy (excluding agriculture) by nearly 20 millions between 1928 and 1940 as well as an increase in the technical qualifications and general educational level of town dwellers as a whole. This in its turn not only made it possible to devote additional labor to the expansion of the productive capacity of industry in the southern regions (in the development of whose resources only a start had been made in the last twenty-five years before the Revolution), but also made possible the building of a new metallurgical and coal base for the further development of industry in the Urals and Siberia—Magnitogorsk, Kuznetsk, the Karaganda coal-iron combines [15]—and the development of nonferrous metallurgy in Kazakhstan, especially copper production. It would be no exaggeration to say that, when the coal of Kuznetsk and Karaganda was linked with the iron ore of the Urals, and when the copper of Dzhezkazgan and Kounrad in Kazakhstan was linked (by the newly built Turkestan-Siberian railway) with the engineering industry of the Moscow region, a new stage in Russian industrial history began. This application of the labor force also permitted the creation of a modern engineering industry. Thereby Soviet industry, for the first time in the history of Russia, was able to build machines which make other machines. This maturer stage of industrial development had been the weakest link in Russian industry in prerevolutionary times.

The application of modern technique has made it possible to overcome many of the handicaps imposed by the location of Russian natural resources.[16] In general it is very improbable that private enterprise would have undertaken to build a Volga-Don Canal or a Urals-Kuznetsk-Karaganda combine, even at the present level of technique, since it would have required not only enormous capital investment but the coordination of the interests of investors in many branches of economic activity. Even in the United States, the Tennessee Valley project was carried out by the government and not by private enterprise. In order to link the Urals iron ore with Central Russia, Peter the Great was forced to take this task into the hands of the state and to impose certain hardships on the Russian peasantry and even to extend serfdom to industry. In order to create the Russian railway system and connect the iron ore and coal of Southern Russia with Central Russia it was necessary "to eat less, and to export," to use a protective tariff policy and to force the peasantry to bear the main cost of the investment.

The building of a modern industry, and the possibilities of further development were again paid for in the main by the peasantry. In this lay the cause of the slowness and the difficulties in the development of agricultural production.

This time, the industrial development was achieved on, so to speak, an internal basis. Foreign investment played no part, foreign trade played a much smaller role than in the prerevolutionary period, and agricultural exports in all the years of the Soviet period did not reach even half of the level of prerevolutionary exports. The exertions of the Russian peasantry this time made possible a rapid growth of industrial labor and of labor employed in the education, welfare, and cultural services and the administration of the country; a growth which has been reflected in the growth of the town population.

IV

What light do these past economic tendencies of Russian development throw on the economic prospects of Soviet Russia? Will the Soviet Union find it possible to continue this rapid industrial development? Will it be possible simultaneously to increase agricultural production so as not only to provide the same standard of living for an increased population, but even to raise it? Will it be possible to achieve further increase in the town population and in the numbers of the industrial population on the basis of internal industrial and agricultural resources—or will Russia follow the path of the West European countries in the development of her industry and in the growth of the town population—the path of great increases in foreign trade? [17]

In attempting to consider these questions, in the light of historical experience it is impossible to do more than to enumerate the problems to which a final answer cannot yet be given. Thus, as regards fuel and power resources, it is probable that they would impose no limit on the development of industry in the near future. The Soviet Union has potential deposits of coal and waterpower resources which can for a long time serve as a basis for much greater industrial development than at present. But four-fifths of the potential coal deposits are located in Asiatic Russia. Five-sixths of her resources of waterpower are also in the Asiatic part of the Soviet Union.[18] On the other hand most of the known iron-ore deposits are in the Urals, and in Central and Southern Russia. It must, however, be remembered that our information is based on 1936 data when only 60 percent of Soviet territory had been geologically mapped—and only very superficially prospected. Many discoveries have been made since, but no information is available. All the main discoveries of nonferrous metals have been made during the Soviet period, for before the Revolution Russia was considered a country poorly endowed with nonferrous metals. Now it is thought that with the exception of tin, tungsten, molybdenum, cobalt, and some other rare metals, the Soviet Union has already discovered deposits adequate to meet the requirements of her industrial production for a long time ahead. But here again, most of these deposits are located in the Asiatic part of the Soviet Union and in the Urals, as well as some in the Caucasian region. European Russia has practically no deposits of nonferrous metals. So, although in general it can be said that neither fuel nor minerals will be a limiting factor on the development of Soviet industry, the overcoming of economic obstacles to the exploitation of fuel and power and mineral resources would be necessary owing to the character of their location. In 1939, for example, the average length of a haul of coal on the railways was 709 kilometers as against 485 kilometers in 1913, that is, the length of haul was increased by nearly a half.[19] Britain used only one-third as high a proportion of its fuel and power for railway transportation, and the United States and Canada only two-thirds as high a proportion as the Soviet Union.[20] Russia cannot economically afford to go on increasing the length of haul of fuel and raw materials. The location of resources therefore necessitates an eastward movement of Russian industry. This movement has been initiated in the last twenty-five years, and will have to be continued in the future.

As regards food resources, great expansion (that is, increasing the area under crops) is also possible only in the Asiatic part of the Soviet Union. It has been estimated by a very competent agricultural economist (Prasolov) that the Soviet Union has approximately 80 million hectares of land suitable for agriculture which could be added to the arable area, that is, the present arable area could be increased by some 40 percent.[21] But this land is situated in zones climatically less favorable than the existing regions and, consequently, its cultivation will require more effort. Very recently the Soviet Government initiated a campaign for bringing into cultivation 13 million hectares of unused land in the Kazakh Republic, in Western Siberia, in the Urals, the Volga region, and to some extent in the North Caucasus.[22] But in regions more remote from the present centers of the population and industry, the development of new land would become possible only if local markets could be developed. And this would necessitate a simultaneous increase in both agricultural cultivation and industrial urban growth in new regions.

Very considerable untapped fish reserves are available in the Siberian rivers, in the Arctic Sea and on the Far Eastern seaboard, but their use is limited by the productive capacity of the canning industry, and by refrigeration and transport facilities. This, again, indicates the necessity for an eastward tendency in the future development of industry. As regards more intensive use of land, in the European part of the Soviet Union there are possibilities for much greater increases in the productivity of land, in yields and in the ratio of livestock to land.[23] The work recently started on afforestation and irrigation of the southern regions affected by drought should make possible the more intensive use of land over a large area.[24] But the results of some of these measures will be forthcoming only in twenty to thirty years.

Thus the possibility of substantially increasing agricultural production in the near future depends on a more and more intensive use of agricultural resources already in exploitation. This intensification will become possible only on the condition that investment in agriculture proceeds at a higher tempo than hitherto, and will depend on the extent to which the standard of living of the rural population is improved. This means that more industrial production would have to be allocated for capital investment in agriculture and for the supply of rural population, which still represents a majority of the inhabitants of the Soviet Union. Without some such policy, it is very doubtful whether a great increase in the productivity of agriculture can take place.

There are indications that the Soviet Government is aware of this problem and has started to introduce corresponding measures.

Probably this need to increase the supply of capital and consumers' goods to the agricultural sector of the national economy plus the need to increase the supply of consumers' goods to the town population would slow down temporarily the tempo of investment in heavy industry. Perhaps a temporary limitation of the supply of labor might also slow down the tempo of industrial development, because the main reserves created by agrarian overpopulation have already been absorbed in the earlier period, during which the rate of growth of the town population has been nearly twice as high as the natural increase. On the other hand, the greatly increased and constantly improving ratio of equipment to labor in industry and the constant improvement in the skill of labor should reduce the need for high annual additions to the labor force.

As far as markets for the increased industrial production are concerned, I consider that for our generation, at any rate, the Soviet Union's problem will be more that of an unsatisfied demand than of a search for external markets. The development of the transport system has been behind the development of the national economy in the last twenty-five years. Great investments will be needed to expand and improve the Soviet rail, coastal, sea, river, and road transport systems. The living standards of the masses of the population, as regards dwellings and amenities in the towns and per capita consumption of industrial goods, are still much behind that of the leading industrial countries. Besides, apart from current consumption, accumulated stocks of durable consumers' goods in the possession of the population are very low compared with those in the West European countries. In the Western countries, stocks of durable consumers' goods represent the main obstacles for sales of current production. In the Soviet Union (for this generation in any case), all goods of good quality should find their own demand.

To sum up, the foreseeable development of Soviet policy and the present distribution of potential resources justify the expectation that industrial development in the Soviet Union could still go on for say the next twenty years at a greater speed than in the West European countries, but perhaps with some slowing down of the rate of development of heavy industry, accompanied by a speeding up in the output of consumers' goods as compared with the preceding twenty-five years. The increase in the town population would continue, but at a lesser rate than in the period 1929–1939. This development is feasible on basically internal industrial and agricultural resources. Moreover, further increases in agricultural production in the next twenty years will probably be sufficient only to cover the natural increase in the population. It is very doubtful whether a substantial improvement in the supply of basic agricultural products per head of the population can be achieved and no return to agricultural exports of prerevolutionary magnitude can be expected.

II

What was the role played by Peter the Great's policies in Russian economic development? Soviet historians have had much that is interesting to say about this subject. In a critical review of Soviet historiography of the economic policies of Peter the Great, Simone Blanc discusses their recent contributions to the larger problems of the pre-Petrine economic foundations of his reforms, and of the relationship of Russian policies to European "mercantilism," as well as the numerous Soviet studies of private entrepreneurship, state industrial administration, and the recruitment of factory labor in the early eighteenth century. Simone Blanc teaches at Strasbourg University. Her essay first appeared in Cahiers du Monde Russe et Sovietique, III (1962), 122–39, and is reprinted with the permission of the publisher, Mouton and Co.

SIMONE BLANC

The Economic Policy of
Peter the Great

The secular process which, according to Soviet terminology, led "feudal" economic Russia into a capitalist economy began with the reign of Ivan the Terrible and ended only in the third quarter of the nineteenth century. But it was suddenly accelerated in Peter the Great's time.

One then speaks of "decisive turn" (*perelom*), of a leap forward, so much more spectacular because of the accumulated delay.[1] Stalin's formula about "Peter's efforts to flee from the frame of a backward economy" comes back as a leitmotiv. And, with a basically servile system based on agriculture and handcraft appearing as the background of the canvas, with a manorial social regime, where taxes were still extant, with a national market barely on the way to being established, new, unusual forms emerged sporadically but with great potential: large-scale industry appeared (large scale according to contemporary standards), Russian metallurgy was about to challenge England's metallurgy, new rapports were established among social groups complex in their formation, but of which one can say, in general, that they prefigured the bourgeoisie and the proletariat.

Nevertheless, in economic matters, there is no such thing as "Peter's miracle." Soviet historians pursue, here, a tenacious myth: that of artificial implantation, dictated by Peter's mere wish, armed as he was by a national "yardstick," by economic forms false or at least premature in nature. It matters little to know whether Peter's initiative, imposing upon Russia a type of economy borrowed from the West, was a dangerous error—as the populists pretended it to be—or a stroke of genius—as their contemporary Marxist adversaries affirmed along with Tugan-Baranovsky. Both of these theories, according to present historians, share the same error in perspective: [2] no statesman, even though it be Peter the Great, deserves either the praise or the blame of having strained the "organic" laws of economic evolution.

Insofar as such a stand of principle agrees with or stimulates the careful study of facts and the in-depth analysis of the documents, we cannot but congratulate ourselves; and such is the case that the effort necessary to delineate further Peter's policies is a result of the rejection of the "lazy" solution which attributes all the changes to the genius or the whims of the Reformer.

Our interest is focused upon two series of facts: the first series of these facts show proof that Peter did not create *ex nihilo* a new economy, that he didn't build on sand, that, in short, the transformation began before him; the second series of facts compel us to reexamine the long accepted point of view of a sudden rupture which would have followed Peter's death, thereby bringing about the destruction of an unsuccessful attempt, temporary because it was premature and artificial; the truth of the matter being that the impulse would have followed *after him*.[3]

Thus, beginning with the seventeenth century, the economic and the social foundations upon which Russian industry of the eighteenth century rested become apparent.

The first factories, private or subject to royal prerogative (owned by a few nobles enriched by feudal rents, or by foreigners),[4] were in operation previous to Peter I's reign. They were, in different senses, ancestors of the enterprises which existed under Peter the Great: on one hand, the distribution of factories in the eighteenth century modeled itself partly on that of the seventeenth century. On the other hand, skilled labor, concentrated in the central sectors (arms factories at Tula, for instance), abounded in regions endowed with a newly acquired importance. It is in this way that the young industry of the Urals can be called the "daughter" of the old metallurgy of the central industrial region.[5]

But these early accomplishments are not to divert our attention from other phenomena, more complex, and as important as the previous insofar as the future of Russian industry is concerned.

Little by little, estate and natural economies gave precedence, on one hand, to an open economy in which the area of exchanges expanded into the multinational state which Russia was becoming; [6] and, on the other hand, into a monetary economy whose impetus made the first accumulation of capital possible and more important than it is often believed to be.[7]

The study of prices undertaken by Strumilin allows us to trace them back to the origins of the crisis which, at the same time, threatened the "feudalities": the wave of inflation which affected the West in the sixteenth century went even as far as Russia. This inflation revealed itself by a price rise in agricultural products; attracted by increasing benefits, the principal owners looked for a negotiable surplus: thus they rushed into tillable fields, populated with enslaved peasants, burdened with the heaviest tasks. The balance of the manorial system, in which the demands of the *pomestye* coincided so to speak with its immediate consumer needs, was suddenly upset. The pressured peasant reacted by fleeing; it was a real agrarian crisis which revealed itself in an unprecedented expansion of fallow land. The deserters, considered henceforth as "fugitives" (*beglie*), colonized the vacant lands "beyond the mountains," in the Urals and in Siberia as early as the sixteenth century; they later supplied the industries which were settled there with provisions and labor.[8] In the meantime, other runaways had become increasingly numerous; the wanderers, the beggars, and all those living in misery, thrown on the roads by this first rural exodus, were assigned to factory work as well.[9]

Where the lands were poorer, the lord, subjected to increasing expenses and a rise in costs which augmented the needs for currency, demanded that rents be paid in cash (*obrok*); this the peasant was able to obtain more and more often by selling his working strength to the factory owners. Peasant "desertion"—which was illegal—and mere "departure" (*otkhod*)—which was legal—were, originally at least, the two elements which supplied labor to industrial enterprises.

At the same time, together with new forms of economy, a social differentiation appeared at the center of the working classes. If a number of the peasants were impoverished, others, using the earth's products and rural crafts, became wholesale dealers, well-to-do "monopolizers" (*skupshchiki*); in order to become rich, their descendants had used the peasants who worked in their own homes, and become, thus, what we define as "merchants" in the West. Elsewhere craftsmen registered at the service of the tsar (in the arms factory at Tula for instance) separated themselves from the group their companions formed, and had the poorer ones work for them; thus, the craftsman became a kind of vassal who submitted payments to the tsar from which he had already deducted sums thanks to these *skudnie lyudi:* one can recognize here the history of the most famous "head blacksmiths" of Tula, the future pioneers of industry in the Urals, the Demidovs. Everywhere, the development of exchanges made it possible for a certain class of merchants, who were, for the most part, destined to establish the patronage of future industry, to become rich.[10]

We can easily sense from this picture that in the politics of industrialization, disappointments were as numerous as successes. Let us limit ourselves to two examples: the desertion of lands dependent on serfdom constituted the sign of inevitable *manorial reaction,* which the state, whose fiscal interests were affected by repercussion, supported by abolishing the peasants' freedom to move to other areas, and by fighting fiercely against "escapes." At that particular time, when industrial labor needs were increasing, there followed a decrease in this kind of labor, which had become the object of ardent competition between landed lords and manufacturers, and an increasingly frequent recourse by the manufacturers to a *pliant* instrument, "forced" labor (*prinuditel'nii*), which thwarted technical progress.[11]

As far as keeping up the class of craftsmen and small businesses outside "big" industry is concerned, it represents for the domestic market the beginning of a lasting conflict. Even when manufactured products were not competing with those produced in the workshop—the latter remaining better adapted to the ordinary or traditional needs of the population—it often happens that the merchant-manufacturer (the holding of these two offices was customary then) was a fierce competitor of the small businessman. Using and taking advantage of his privileges, exemption from taxes and tolls, for instance, the merchant-manufacturer encroached upon a domain which the small businessman was lawfully entitled to, and devoted himself to retail business, using as intermediaries, when the need arose, clerks, who acted as kind of *straw men*. The state, then, whose main concern was to secure the development of industrial capital, very quickly gave up fighting for the wronged party, offering as the only possible alternative the adhesion to the privileged party.[12]

Pomeshchiki against manufacturers, merchant-contractors against merchant-craftsmen: this double conflict, which the state's "politics of balance" didn't succeed in solving, weighed on the future of young Russian industry.

On the other hand, there is no indication that this industry was declining once Peter disappeared. To study its impetus in the half century which followed would lead us away from the framework of this article. Let us simply state that neither the reaction of the nobles, which actually hindered the "free" manual labor market and increased the participation of "forced" labor, nor the increasing number of "patrimonial" and "possessional" factories, in which productivity was hindered by the ties which the worker-serfs maintained with rural economy,[13] nor even the temporary slackening of protectionism in customhouses of the thirties, succeeded in stopping the impetus. If certain enterprises are jeopardized, others are born and become prosperous; the end result shows a progression more rapid than it was in Peter's time. Pavlenko believes that the great impetus of the metal industry of the Urals dates from the years 1730–1740. In 1725, the ratio of cast-iron production between Russia and England was 59 percent; and 150 percent in 1750; Russia continued leading and expanding until the beginning of the nineteenth century.[14]

Peter, then, probably gave Russia the economy it needed, not

the one he dreamed of. Soviet historians who emphasize the continuity of this economic stimulus wanted to prove that the plant was
strong and healthy, that Russian soil, in which the roots grew
deeply, supplied the elements necessary to its growth. A number of
these historians seem to dread the idea that one could believe that
the plant was "transplanted" (from the West) and that it soon de-
cayed; on the contrary, Russia herself bore the seed of great industry. This obsession prevents them from sufficiently emphasizing one
important factor which should be obvious to them: the economy of
the era of factories—as in Colbert's France or Frederick's Prussia
—developed in Russia thanks to vigilant concern and careful protection only, and, in that sense, was quite originally what Klyuchevsky called "a greenhouse plant." [15]

It is there that the entire problem of mercantilism in Peter the
Great's politics lies. It is rather strange to learn that Peter's pre-
dilection for mercantilism is disputed; nevertheless, in a book devoted to the study of Peter the Great's conceptions of economy,
Madame Spiridonova disputes Peter's practice of mercantilism.
More than of rectification, it is a question of "rehabilitation," as the
obsession we mentioned earlier reveals: Peter was falsely suspected
of practicing "a blind imitation" of Western mercantilism. Whatever the worth of the thesis, it allows Mme. Spiridonova the opportunity to make some useful observations; first of all, she reminds us
that Russia had a pleiad of economists, among whom one can read
such names as Ordin-Nashehokin and Pososhkov. [16] More conscious
of Russian reality and its concrete problems than of huge systems,
they all were connected with the movement of "literature of projects" which was so fruitful in Russia, and offered accurate solutions to limited questions. The fact that they were Russian did not
prevent these solutions from fitting the pattern of mercantilism; the
author would perhaps gladly admit this had she not seemed to wish
to ascribe the West with a monopoly on mercantilism: it is the
latter preliminaries which force her to "prove" that Russia did not
borrow mercantilism from the West.

From the same point of view, Mme. Spiridonova emphasizes
quite justly the national characteristics present in the politics of
Peter's economy, at a time when Peter was grappling with problems of a strictly Russian nature: the vital need to overcome a de-

lay which would prove catastrophic in case of war. He thereby acquired the necessary means for a "gently" imperialistic policy, since it satisfied itself by coveting what was strictly indispensable to the impetus of the economy, the basis for national greatness, such as the shores of the Baltic Sea and, though of a secondary nature, those of the Caspian Sea or the Black Sea. It was also appropriate to mention that the source of all wealth consisted, in the eyes of Peter and of many of his collaborators, in the improvement of a country whose exceptional wealth, especially in minerals, could already be felt, as well as the willingness by all to work, or at least to participate, from the humblest peasant to the courtier, in an effort necessary for a flourishing economy. So that Peter's attitude here resembles, after all, that of the great "mercantilists" of his time; it certainly doesn't differentiate him from them.

Peter, however, attached as great an importance on the monetary balance as his contemporary statesmen, and Madame Spiridonova herself—although she tries to free him from the accusation of "monetary fetishism"—provides us with proofs. The draconian prohibition to export precious metals, the obligation imposed upon foreign merchants to pay custom duties in foreign currency accepted by the Russian treasury, but with an interest rate inferior by 50 percent to the intrinsic value of the currency, are sound proof of an obvious desire to monopolize for Russia the greatest quantity of precious metals that was possible.

Peter was a convinced protectionist: to the extent that the merchant "beyond the seas" who brought his goods with himself threatened Russian merchants or goods, Peter's primary concern was to drive back the former so as to protect the latter: hence, the much higher interest rate on duties collected for goods imported by foreigners, and under foreign flags; the very harsh restrictions and even the prohibition which strongly affected foreign merchants who were forced to forward their merchandise through Russia; and, finally, the strongly protectionist tariffs established in 1724. On all these points, governments following Peter's reign were occasionally more liberal than his. The tariffs of 1731, or even the benefits granted the English following the treaty of 1734, mark a definite progress which brings out, by contrast, the indisputable "mercantilism" of Peter the Great.

Finally, even if we agree with Madame Spiridonova that "typical" mercantilism was more concerned with profits acquired in foreign trade than with managing and regulating an independent national economy, one cannot say, even in this case, that Peter did not practice "mercantilism." It is probably correct to say that the Reformer's choice to establish an "emergency order" among the industries to be created or expanded could have been dictated by the needs of the state, of the army, and, at times, by domestic trade, more than by prospects for foreign trade. At least, it was so in the beginning, when, in the middle of a war and deprived of Swedish iron, the survival of the country was at stake. On the other hand, commercial activities could not help remaining restricted as long as Russia did not have at its disposal a window on the Baltic Sea. One notices, however, that as soon as these mortgages were lifted, the possibilities for exporting were by no means neglected. The West couldn't possibly buy manufactured objects from Russia, which wasn't so eager to get rid of them anyway; on the other hand, the excellent quality of the iron she produced in increasing quantities could interest those European countries active in manufacturing as semifinished products; they would then transform the latter products and resell them at convenient prices. It is on these grounds that at the time when English metallurgy was threatened by forest exhaustion, the iron trade between England and Russia rested. Russia then, as early as 1720, tried to oust Sweden, her only competitor, by operating a real dumping: iron, which cost 66 kopecks in domestic trade, was exported at 56 kopecks, then at an increasingly higher cost, according to the number of clients acquired (60 kopecks in 1724). In 1724, Peter ordered the state factories, whose production was more and more geared toward exporting, to increase the iron sales "beyond the seas"; as for official deliveries, they were backed, paradoxically so, by the most powerful manufacturers (especially the Demidovs).[17]

In spite of the fact that Madame Spiridonova overdoes certain aspects of the thesis she defends, she, nevertheless, forces us to the useful task of evaluating more carefully the concrete context of Peter's "mercantilism"; she also induces us to write about and ponder over this "mercantilism." Peter was a Russian sovereign of the beginning of the eighteenth century, and he had the intelligence of his country and of his times; he was not obsessed with economic theories, even if they were Western. Solovyov has expressed this truth quite accurately by using a comparison which can allow us all to reach an agreement: "this tendency is so natural and so indispensable that it cannot be a matter of imitating or of borrowing: whether Colbert governed France or whether Peter governed Russia, they both acted the same way, for the same evident reason that two men, one in Europe and one in Asia, go under the sun to warm up or under the shade to cool off." [18] Peter's mercantilism is, in summary, nothing but a logical and spontaneous response directed to a given critical economic situation; his politics are by no means stripped of their importance when they are thought of as the Russian equivalent of Colbertism, for example (there is no question here of faithful imitation). Protectionism and the setting up of a favorable monetary or commercial balance were the result of a policy which, national in aim and mercantilistic in method, aimed at endowing Russia with an autonomous economy and with as varied an industry as possible. This political attitude was based on a small number of simple ideas, solidly anchored in Peter's mind and in that of his collaborators: European countries had reached a significant stage on the road to greatness when they entered the era of manufactures; but Russia had all the foundations necessary to follow their example; "she abounds in useful products"; in order to catch up with and surpass her competitors, she only needed to make an effort by exploring her resources further and by being better aware of her own worth. This effort is doubly fruitful: Russia would be esteemed the more because the other nations would not be able to do without certain of her products; she would be rich in the sense that a reestablishment of her productive forces would increase the financial capacities of the country; she would also become a vast workyard where everyone would engage in useful labor.[19] It is this meaning that one should ascribe to those expressions which Peter's ukases repeat ceaselessly, such as "the general good," and "the good of all the people." Here, the politics of "mercantilism" joins the enlightened despotism of which Peter is also a representative.

Nevertheless, Peter realized to the fullest that his subjects "had no experience and showed no enthusiasm in factory matters." It was possible to induce them by adopting two methods which seemed

quite acceptable: helping them or forcing them. Let us quickly note
that the latter amounted to very little. In Peter the Great's Russia,
work done in the "factories," by the owners as well as by the workmen, was probably considered as being at the "service of the state."

As we shall see later, the workers felt the strain at its fullest;
it was not so for the owners. One has, perhaps, insisted too much
on Peter's declarations of principles, or on some manifestations of
his temperament when he dealt with economic matters, or on his
authoritarian methods. For instance: when Peter recommended that
the College of Manufactures adopt constraint as a measure; when
Peter ordered by ukase the founding of an industrial "company" by
forcing the merchants to register; finally, when Peter compared his
nation to a child unable either to adapt himself rapidly to new activities, or to understand where his own self-interest lay; [20] such
were the traditional images which may have disguised a more complex, less fixed reality. If at the beginning of Peter's reign candidates for manufacturing enterprises were rare, they were numerous
in the twenties; the increasing number of applications for the granting of "privileges" addressed to the industrial colleges attests to this
rise. Those who considered themselves as being great captains of
industry, and who became the "giants" in the economy following
Peter's reign, launched out very early and deliberately in the manufacturing business. Such were the blacksmiths-owners of Tula, the
Demidovs. Thanks to the capital and the experience they had
amassed in the central industrial region, they were automatically
designated by the state, and perfectly willing to assume the tasks of
running a metal factory which the state had opened in the Urals,
and which it wished to give over to a private enterprise. Thus, as
early as 1702, the Demidovs settled down in this new sector to
which they later owed their fabulous fortune. From then on, the
state showed as much eagerness in supplying them with various
ways of expanding their enterprise as they did in adopting the new
means. They certainly did not need the funds: as far as investments
were concerned (since we are treating the industry of the Urals),
they were on a financial level almost equal to that of the state.
There is a popular legend which tells about the "humble" black-
smith of Tula, whom Peter defied by demanding that he emulate
the capabilities of German armorers, and who came out victorious;

this legend carries important information: the rapport between the Reformer and the industrial pioneer of the Urals focused on emulation not constraint.[21]

It is certainly this attitude which one must refer to when interpreting Peter's actions in economic matters. His aim was to treat with much care this "treasure" which the merchant class represented for him, this backbone of the industrial class of the future. It was also to concentrate the merchant's attention on the idea of investing capital in new activities. Finally, in a regime where fear often generated actions useful to the common interest, but where it hindered them even more often, Peter's goal was to reassure the merchant class, so that industrial property enjoyed a privileged status, and manufacturers were assured that under no pretext would theirs or their descendants' enterprise be confiscated, even in the case of bankruptcy.[22]

If it is true that industry was, in a sense, a "service of the state," it did not mean constraint so much; it rather implied a wish to rehabilitate it, and to tempt with honors, profits, and rewards those who were engaged in it, regardless of the social class they belonged to. The younger brother of a noble family who was not allowed to inherit his share could regain it if he chose to enter military or civil service, or, even if he went in for business and industry. The delay imposed upon him was longer in this case. But, Peter could in this way offer more than the laws promised; thus, the successful manufacturer could expect that Peter satisfy his ambitions: the Demidovs owed their access to hereditary nobility, with all the privileges that this involved, to "industrial" service to the tsar.

What were the means the state could make use of in order to apply the politics of which we have tried to define the principles?

Let us immediately note that in the area of economics as well as in many others, it is only at the end of his reign that those institutions [23] which would afterward be instruments of Peter the Great's policies were in fact slowly created. In the year 1718, the colleges were born, among which were the three colleges of "economics": the Business College, the College of Manufactures, and the College of Mines (or Berg-Collegium). The last two colleges, though they were conceived as separate institutions, functioned as

one institution due to a lack of staff members; they became autonomous only in 1722. The beginning was slow; qualified administrators were rare; foreigners had to be called in. The "Privilege of the
College of Mines" and the "Regulations of the College of Manufactures," which judged qualifications, decided upon functions, and
began drafting unified legislation on economic matters, were only
completed in 1719 and 1723 respectively.

In fact, all the economic policies of Peter's reign are contained
in these two precious documents: they reveal the principles which
inspired these policies, codify decisions taken at the mercy of circumstances, and, finally and above all, they denote, *in virtue of
collective privileges,* those privileges which were originally con-
ferred on an individual basis and in virtue of special decisions,
upon the most favored manufacturers. These documents represent
thereby "the official birth certificate" of a new class whose rights
were linked to the exercise of a function considered vital to the
state.

The lag one notices between the practice of principles and
their theoretical statements, the a posteriori creation of institutions
and the slow elaboration of "Regulations," indicates that the Reformer's politics tended toward improvisation, and that especially in
this area, at the beginning of his reign, Peter had no choice but to
innovate, grope, and act in the obsolete, inadequate frameworks
which were handed on to him by his predecessors.

Moreover, the inadequateness of these frameworks was quite
obvious in economic matters; the effectiveness of Peter's attitude in
such mediocre conditions calls for admiration. Up until the creation
of the Colleges, the *prikazes* divided control among themselves and,
even worse, passed on to each other for geographic or administrative reasons the control or direction of private or state manufacturing enterprises. Local administration (the *voivodas*) added to the
confusion: they increased irritation, interrupted the operation of
factories which they were theoretically supposed to favor, practiced
sanctions arbitrarily, refused to supply those peasants or recruits
who were headed for factory work, and demanded the traditional
bribes. But the state was distracted by one thing only: all these disputes hindered production. It also granted the manufacturers im-
munity vis-à-vis local tyrants, as well as the privilege to depend

strictly upon the central administration. The Demidovs were among the first to enjoy these privileges. However, the habit of independence and intractability remained. As a result, the representatives who were later sent to the Ural region by the College of Mines, and considered to be recognized specialists, experienced from these proud, powerful lords the same insolent refusal to obey which the incompetent, abusive *voivodas* had dealt with.[24]

Along with the "theoreticians" of the economy who sometimes acted as his counselors, Peter grew disturbed by the confusion. Plans accumulated and proclaimed the need for the centralization of economic matters by proposing the system of colleges which was then popular. Prior to this time, organizations came and went; their aim was to mitigate those gaps which disturbed the state, such as the *"prikaz* for matters pertaining to the mines," which from 1700 to 1711, then again from 1715 to 1718, served as a subsidiary to the Prikaz of the Treasury, and whose task was to stimulate the prospecting of precious metals. It was not by any means used to expand in its entirety the metal and the mining industry.[25]

The innovations of 1718 therefore mark not only a result, but also the inauguration of a new stage in the history of Russian economy. From then on, business and industry were considered as autonomous sectors participating in national activity; they were not conceived as supplements resulting from the activity produced by war, the navy, or by monetary activity. The ensuing problems which their growth might have brought about, be they administrative or technical, were the concern of specialized centralizing institutions which managed to continue the work of the Reformer tsar. One of these, the Berg-Collegium, relied on a remarkable network of local institutions at the center of which were excellent technicians and brilliant administrators who kept them constantly active. Their methods were infinitely more efficient than those adopted by the temporary inspectors of former times: they worked in shifts and without interruptions, often remaining for several years in the same immense new region, far away from the town, and to which they attributed such an importance that it seemed a personal matter to them. Thanks to the initiative, the broad vision, and the enthusiasm of Hennin and Tatishchev, the Bureau of Mines in Siberia and the Urals, which became successively Hennin's and Tatishchev's "thing," was transplanted to the very work sites, becoming, thus, a true Berg-Collegium worthy of continuing Peter the Great's tradition.[26]

The main aspects of the Berg-Privilege or the Regulations of the College of Manufactures were devoted, as we have already mentioned, to the enumeration of the privileges which the state granted the manufacturers. A careful study of the documents may allow historians to raise a number of problems caused by the practical application of these privileges.

What was, first of all, their field of application? Regulations as well as privileges extended the right to open a factory to all subjects, "regardless of their rank or their worthiness." In fact, the very diversified aspect of the class of manufacturers seems to confirm this stand on principle.

But we can already notice the inequality of proportion present in the different social categories which were represented: the peasants, whose fortunes always had commercial origins, made up a minute minority; the nobles developed a taste for new activities only later. Even so, they very often satisfied themselves by merely drawing the profits which their fat "feudal" income brought them by having the manufacturer serfs pay; the latter were themselves beneficiaries of the "capitalist" profit and became, at times, as wealthy as their lords. Finally, aside from a few representatives of bureaucracy, there were a few foreigners becoming less and less numerous, and a few famous but rare "artisan-owners," such as the Demidovs. The overwhelming majority consisted of turncoats of the merchant class, the *kupechestvo*.

When the Colleges of the Economy authorized the foundation of an enterprise provided with the privileges which were considered necessary to this foundation (such as shares of land, forests, and laborers; exemption of both temporary and renewable taxes and duties; liberation of the owner as well as of the supervisors and workmen under him, from "service to the state" or from recruitment; loans without interest rates, or, even, subsidies without reservations), they did not concern themselves with class differences. On the other hand, they were strict when examining the candidates' competence in technical matters and even stricter where their *financial* abilities were concerned. The only refusals of "Privileges" we know of were due to the supposed inability on the part of the recipient to assume factory responsibilities. Next to the privileged group of "approved manufacturers" (*ukaznye*), there was a class of manufacturers whose accumulated capital did not reach the required standards. They engaged in business or in small industry without any support from the state, and without the least fiscal statement, so that they could think of avoiding competition caused by the "great ones" only by raising their own standards through additional wealth.[27]

The kind of help which the happy minority of the "approved ones" could expect would nevertheless vary. Before the publication of the "Regulations" and after, and in spite of the "equality in privileges" they publicized, the state, concerned with efficiency, lent funds only to the rich. So that beginning with manual labor which was precious, and ending with protection from local administrators, Peter could refuse nothing to the Demidovs. Later, when the colleges didn't know where to turn for loans, because of a lack of an individual budget and because they were even reduced to meager sources of income (the sale of stamped paper), exceptions were made for the most "solid" enterprises, since they could expect to use fully the sums that were lent to them. Reimbursements were also expected on the shortest terms.[28] Finally, the state loathed the thought of securing "monopolies" to the manufacturers who were considered generators of "laisser-aller." In the framework of a "scarce" economy, this procedure might have appeared as the most secure of encouragements to Peter's predecessors. As for Peter, he wanted to strengthen Russian industry; slowly and prudently, he was concerned with withdrawing some of its "guardians." Thus, monopolies shrank in time and space, and, with some exceptions, from perpetual, national monopolies, they turned into temporary, regional ones.[29]

To conclude, one can say that the "State-Providence" proceeded in much the same rational and pitiless fashion as those competitors it seemed to want to eliminate, though perhaps with less brutality. National industry was well protected from industry abroad by custom tariffs; but, in the closed area which Russia was becoming, only those indicating their ability to set the country on its way to economic progress were supported. In this way, the state succeeded in rapidly stimulating the appearance of the real "magnates" of the industry. Once again, we think of the Demidovs who financially destroyed those competitors whom they did not favor; they appropriated the best sites to themselves and felt free of any punishment; they also dictated the laws for the iron market and set its prices. The part which competition played and the natural selection of it entailed indicates to us one of the essential characteristics of Peter's politics; namely, that, since it was definitely oriented toward the future, it was paving the way for the liberal economy which succeeded it. In other words, Peter's only aim was to create a current of activity strong enough for the state to be able one day to transfer the burden of economic growth to its subjects; Peter and his disciples, according to the famous formula, aimed at "manufacturing the manufacturers."

The outcome of "state enterprise" (*kazennye*) can serve to illustrate this idea. Why did the *state* turn itself into a *manufacturer,* in Russia as well as in many other European countries, especially in Central and Eastern Europe? In order for us to understand this better, let us think of those seventeenth-century manufacturing enterprises which existed under the tsar, and which at first could be considered as ancestors of the eighteenth-century state enterprise. Then, groupings of craftsmen were free as far as the law went, but had to remain in the area they lived in; most of the time, they worked at home, on a seasonal basis, and produced a fixed quantity of manufactured goods for the state from which they received in exchange, the "salary of the tsar." Aside from the goods they produced, they paid the state their peasant *obrok* (a rent which they owed the state for the land they were using). Once their obligations to the tsar were fulfilled, they could do a different type of work. Most of the time, however, state orders were attended to either by members of the peasant's family (for female work), or by other workers serving them (as was the case for the Demidovs). The enterprise lived in a closed circuit; the cost prices on its products were very high; since the owner was at the same time the only customer, the enterprise was much concerned with profits. The tsar, the "feudal" lord, had a number of his subjects work in these enterprises for his own benefit, in exchange for land and money. Strumilin refuses to compare these subjects to serfs and considers their status that of a "vassal." [30]

The state factories of the eighteenth century were essentially different. They were, most of the time, centralized enterprises. Their workers consisted of recruits of peasants from the treasury assigned to factory work, and also of specialized Russian or foreign workers freely recruited. Their products were used for export trade and also for the domestic market, not only for the needs of the court or the state. Finally, these enterprises were concerned with technical improvement which would generate more profits. They were part of one entity, the state, which showed all the characteristics of a *capitalist owner;* they did not belong to a master, the tsar, who was comparable to a lord.

It is more by their *raison d'être* than by their nature that they are in contrast with their seventeenth-century ancestors. By assuming the role of the manufacturer, the state meant, first, to share with its subjects a burden which was too heavy for their own shoulders, the industrialization of the country. The state's contribution consisted both of funds for personnel (whether they were workers or managers) and of capital. Secondly, the state transformed itself into a *pioneer* (this trait is characteristic of Russia's behavior) and hoped to signal the rise of faraway regions where either speculation with private capital was not practiced, or this capital was being engulfed by the unfriendly immensity in which it found itself and because of poor management. When the state anticipated the advent of private manufacturers, it had in mind to welcome and attract them by "handing over" to them factories which were already "rolling" (*v khodu*), and by continuing to assist them. It created a sort of fireside around which industrialization was considered an "oil spot." Such was the history of the Ural region where only the Stroganovs, who were landed lords as well as businessmen and manufacturers, had anticipated the state's action, and where the Demidovs themselves had settled only after the state had encouraged them to do so. Certain facts indicate that the government was perfectly conscious of the role it could thus play; with the exception of well-established manufacturers, the colleges had not much confidence in those factories which operated in areas far removed from the center, and where the state had not yet set the foundations for prosperous industry. In the latter case, therefore, the privilege requested was refused. Indeed the facts proved their decision correct: the percentage of "abortive" factories which had been granted the privilege, but which had not succeeded in functioning satisfactorily, had considerably increased in those regions where state industries were absent.

The state manufacture, which was considered a "guiding" manufacture, was conceived as a transitory stage, and intended for transfer to private manufacturers. *Private initiative* was, in Peter's eyes, *the real motor* of industrial development, and private capital was its true nourishment. As a matter of fact, circumstances were such that the transfer intended from the beginning was quite slow; nevertheless, the state, acting as a manufacturer, was less attracted by profits which could accrue to the treasury, than it was motivated by the desire to stimulate industrial development. In spite of the arguments in favor or against the *kazennye* factories, continuously brought forth during the eighteenth century in the disputes opposing those in favor of assigning these factories to the state which would support them, it seems that to their creators the fiscal aspect was less important than the economic and national interest.[31]

Whatever Peter's hopes for the future of Russian industry might have been, and whatever his wish to see its emancipation someday, he remained, nonetheless, *a very mistrustful guardian.* Peter feared, perhaps, Klyuchevsky's hypothesis that "the spirit of initiative in Russia did not emulate its hopes." [32] However, the state had more specific reasons for wanting to supervise those who benefited from its help. First, these reasons were opposed to each other by nature: when the treasury supplied funds, labor, and technical advisers, it intended to make sure, *de visu,* that its sums were not wasted. Second, in order to satisfy the needs of the army, the navy, the minting of coins, and the planning of new towns and enterprises, the state was closely dependent upon an industry of which it was the first customer, and of which it expected quantity, quality, and a cost price (therefore a sale price) which would have been as low as possible.

The supervision of private factories and of those which had been assigned to private owners assumed the classical traits of a guardianship oriented toward mercantilism, such as: regulations, inspections, the obligation to accept certain manufacturing procedures, investigations, interrogation of the workers, questionnaires handed to manufacturers, and interventions in the life inside the factories. This type of guardianship was often embarrassing, created worries, and paralyzed initiative as well as the normal pace of the enterprise. As a result, the manufacturers who were always willing to benefit from the state's help, but always wished to throw off their yoke, were ill-tempered. These are well-known traits which, nevertheless, are not typical of Russian industry. One should really go beyond the chronological framework of Peter's reign in order to witness the blooming of his policies of the thirties, which was marked by the temporary appointment of "factory inspectors" (*sikhtmeistery*). The latter had permanently settled near the factories of the Ural region and interfered in the most minute details of the social, administrative, financial, and technical aspects of their operations. As a result, they provoked violent reactions on the part of the manufacturers. The suppression of their activities by the Business College announced the evolution toward a liberalism which not only Russia enjoyed but other countries as well.[33]

It is the conditional aspects of the privileges the manufacturers were granted which were even more typically Russian: the social regime under which they operated decided upon the rights of the individual according to the duties he performed. We have already mentioned that the manufacturers who enjoyed these privileges had previously had access to the group of "approved manufacturers." However, this social promotion could be called in question again if its recipient proved himself unworthy of it. Thus, "false manufacturers" (*lzhefabrikanty*) who "made believe" that they were committed to the factories they owned (*dlya lisha, pod vidom*) were searched. They engaged in entirely different activities and used these fraudulently acquired privileges as precious sources of assistance (tax exemptions, and the right to exploit servile peasant labor). Thus, instead of making sure that these factories functioned efficiently, inspectors commissioned by the college were, in reality, being satisfied with the knowledge that these factories existed.[34]

Finally, one must ask oneself whether or not manufacturers profited from state customers, and if so to what extent. One could

assume that the purpose of the state factories was precisely to satisfy their customers' needs. We have shown, however, that this was
not the case, and that a significant quantity of the state factories'
products was used for the market, especially for the foreign market
(the iron metallurgy of the Ural region, for instance). Private factories, on the contrary, often supplied the state, which was an important consumer, with cloth, leather, cast iron, and copper. But the
state-customer attitude evolved during Peter the Great's reign. At
the beginning, he still seemed to be a demanding master who bade
ridiculously low prices in exchange for compulsory delivery which
took the place of real taxes. Moreover, payments were very long in
coming. As for other outlets, they must have been quite rare if one
is to accept, as Zaozerskaya [35] does, that the customers of the state
were considered, in the latter conditions, as a source of profit.

This supposition, nevertheless, gradually proves to be true:
around 1719, especially in the metallurgic sectors, the "fiscal" aspect of compulsory delivery was fading away. Price offers increased
slowly until they reached a level approximating that found on the
so-called "free" market. Prices were later uniformly established. At
any rate, the regularity of continuous benefits, the expectation of
massive sales which allowed the manufacturer to use to the fullest
the productive capacity of his plants (this was a rare privilege at the
time), and, finally, the possibility of maintaining an "account" with
the treasury for the payment of taxes, of advanced credit sums, and
of workers' rents, represented so many more advantages which were
appreciated by some of the powerful manufacturers such as the
Demidovs and the Millers. When one adds to this the privileges
and the massive appropriation of peasants which most of the time
went to the manufacturers supplying the state, it is then easy to understand that their resentment for these tasks was indeed very
low.[36]

In certain industrial sectors, however, the state had for a long
time been considered a dreaded customer. Thus copper deliveries
became veritable taxes, and extremely heavy ones, even well after
Peter's death (copper was a metal of coinage which the fisc coveted). Thus, the quantity of production which the manufacturer was
allowed for the free market sometimes reached the minute proportion of one-tenth; the remaining nine-tenths were either given over

to the state free of charge, or at arbitrary low prices. As a result, the copper industry stagnated. In spite of this stagnation, one notices, in the middle of the century, a desire to protect private interests and to establish a more liberal regime.

The interest vested in the new forms of the economy should not let us overlook the background from which they sprung. Hence, the Russia in which the Demidovs, Hennin, and Tatishchev lived is also the one in which the lords and their serfs, the peasants and their *kustary* (small rural craftsmen) lived, and where forced labor and *obrok* still existed. This "feudal" Russia disappeared only as late as 1861. However, if we go back to our Soviet historians, we realize that "Capitalist Russia" springs from the very center of feudal Russia in which it develops.

The unquestionable originality of the history of eighteenth- and nineteenth-century Russia can be ascribed to the coexistence of forms which would be excluded elsewhere and which here, on the contrary, seem to create mutual friction. All studies dealing with Petrovian society and economy focus on this particular problem. If we consider the tortuous road along which medieval Russian institutions passed as they evolved into modern ones, it is difficult to determine which of the historians are correct: is it those who, by strictly emphasizing the economy's mechanisms and by analyzing them according to Marxist dialectics, trace the appearance of "capitalism" very far back and deny the possibility of connecting the following antinomic terms, "factory" and "servile," without creating an absurdity? Or is it those others who are more interested in the concrete relationships existing between owner and worker, which they interpret as prolonged vestiges of "feudal" forms? [37] A detailed exposition of these two viewpoints and the arguments brought forth could become the object of much research, so that we shall limit ourselves to studying the role which the Petrovian state played when faced with the latter contradictions.

Marxist theory states that the absolutist state, *the state-arbiter,* draws its strength from the antagonism existing between two social classes which gradually became almost equally powerful. This statement undoubtedly provides a possible approach to the study of Peter's politics in economic matters. The state was caught up on one hand between the contradictory interests of a social class near its peak, that of "owners of inhabited lands," and a newly born group of manufacturers which was, nevertheless, fully expanding, on the other; so that the state tried to keep the scales almost at an equilibrium. Under Peter the Great's reign, it was the manufacturers who often benefited from this game of scales; the equilibrium was then reached in the interest of the *pomeshchiks* in the second quarter of the century. In fact, Peter, in his desire to hasten the country's development, boldly impaired the nobility's "fundamental rights." Thus, mining laws, which had been elaborated in 1719, appeared as some of the most modern laws of the times: the wealth which mines represented belonged to the tsar, and the proprietor of the area was only allowed precedence in the exploitation of the mine. If he refused it, he had no choice but to accept replacement by a patentee, and be satisifed with one thirty-second of the gains.[38]

But it was especially from labor matters that the conflict between "feudal" and "industrial" members derived its greatest meaning and acuteness.

Russian industry under Peter the Great had two categories of workers at its disposal: "freely hired ones" (*volnonaemnye*) who temporarily rented their working ability to their employer in exchange for a salary whose payments depended on a sort of "mobile capital" handled by the employer. As for the other category of workers, they were "forced to work" (*prinuditel'nye*) and could easily become the property of the master who used them (as it was the case for patrimonial manufacturers in which the *pomeshchik* turned into an entrepreneur, and transformed his serfs into workmen), or of the factory—regardless of the successive owners—in which they worked (as was the case for so-called factories of possession).

The first category is familiar to us, as it represented the equivalent of free labor which, at that time, could be found in all European factories. The second, on the other hand, had no Western counterpart, and Russian historians, who themselves had difficulty in defining the nature of the latter category, went from argument to argument without arriving at agreement. In the case of "forced workers," it is the person of the worker that was bought; the buying of his person was here replaced by the renting of his working ability and demanded a greater deposit of funds which jeopardized the amount of mobile capital at the expense of the "base capital." As a result, the freedom of movement and the ability to choose jobs which the worker used to enjoy disappeared; at the same time, *in spite of the fact that he was earning a salary,* the element of economic emulation *theoretically speaking* no longer played a part and gave way to the "extraeconomic" constraint which serfdom represented. On the whole, when compared with his "free" companion, the worker-serf appeared as an anomaly, as an artificial vestige, whose implantation and whose progress, stemming from the core of the capitalistic system which was symbolized by the factory, could only be accounted for if we attribute them to the abnormal prolongation of the servile regime. The role which the state had played in maintaining this anomaly has yet to be known. If we except the case of the "patrimonial" factory which was very rare under Peter's reign, free manual labor was the only kind of labor which the manufacturer could obtain without the state's intervention. The workers were of varied origins: escaped serfs; serfs equipped with a pass, whose salaries were used for the payment of dues to the lords; craftsmen, "inhabitants of the suburbs" who were dispossessed of their own means of production by the process of social stratification; soldiers' and churchmen's sons; foreigners who served as instructors; and children or adolescent orphans looking for a way of earning bread.[39] They were not all lawfully free, but vis-à-vis the employer they were voluntary workers.

Nevertheless, the tsar, along with factory administrators and theoreticians of the economy, were unanimous in their opinions: namely, that free labor was far more productive than forced labor. Peter's ukases all urged its adoption by industry. Such is the theory. It hardly seems applicable, though, because supply was from the very beginning inferior to demand, and the gap only kept widening as the industry expanded. Cities (2 percent of the population) were rapidly exhausted reservoirs. As for the country, the growing strictness of the *pomeshchik,* which became even more obvious after Peter disappeared, reduced the number of peasants who were headed for the factories. It was only at that point that the state interfered, in order to arbitrate the conflict between the *pomeshchiks* and the manufacturers. This caused the state much embarrassment and opposition. The state tided over the difficulty by continuously standing up for lords' rights, namely by criticizing the illegal hiring of "fugitives" and of *obrok* serfs whose pass had expired, and by prohibiting the return to such recourses "in the future." Actually, the state was serving as an accomplice of the manufacturers by approving their irregular hiring procedures [40] (by sometimes compensating the *pomeshchiks,* but especially by registering newcomers on tax rolls).

The role played by the state went even beyond these practices: the more productive industry was, the more it needed the permanent, the established, perhaps even the hereditary cooperation of its workers, mainly of its specialized workers. In Peter's times, a category of "apprentices" already appeared; they were trained at a very early age in the factory or sometimes in schools associated with the factory and were tied to their training grounds for seven years.[41] Later, in 1736, they were assigned to specific grounds for life, or according to a father-and-son procedure. And since the state was faithful to the wish of the manufacturers, it contributed to this real subjugation of formerly free workers. So that it all seemed as if the post-Petrovian state, unable to modify let alone abolish the slave system which threatened to choke industry, had had recourse *to the implantation of a system which was itself at the core of the threatened organism.* Had Peter foreseen this paradoxical situation? [42]

In any case, an exact prefiguration of this can certainly be found in his politics. His theory amounted to allowing manufacturers to use their own means in recruiting their workers, even if they had to give the approval themselves (in case it had not been already ratified). As for the application of this theory, it consisted in making available to the manufacturers the means by which they could obtain forced labor. As for the procedures, they are well known. Some of these were mere unoriginal means often found in the mercantilist Europe of the times, which did not transmit any specific social characteristics to those enterprises benefiting from them. Thus, convicts, wanderers, and loafers of all sorts were sent to factories.[43] There are other procedures which, on the contrary, pose the same typically Russian problem again: that of the *servile factory*. Thus, "peasants from the treasury" were assigned to village factories which supplied groups of workers at very low costs, since the technical processes of the times called for massive employment. A more important result was the privilege to buy serfs which had been granted the entrepreneurs in 1721, whether or not they owned land. It was, without a doubt, a conditional privilege, since peasants were acquired for the factory and not for its owner; nonetheless, this privilege indicates the insertion of factories in the servile system, and constitutes the legal foundation of this hybrid form of economy which the possessional factory represented in Russia.[44]

To assume that Peter was suddenly contradicting himself by *deliberately* endowing Russia, overnight, with factories founded on a servile basis would amount to a grave error. His decision rather seems to represent the result of a long struggle carried out since the beginning of the reign by the entrepreneurs and aimed at having at his disposal the labor reserve which the peasantry represented. This was made possible by means of the lords' manorial rights. The ukase of 1721 represents the ratification of a *fait accompli* (since the Demidovs had bought "villages" in 1720); but mainly it was a *confession of failure,* the official realization of an evolution which Peter probably would have liked to avoid since it had been, from that point on, adapted to the social structure of the country. It was, nevertheless, to this evolution which the industry owed its survival. The moment the manufacturers gave up their attempts at attacking the servile system surely meant that they intended to take advantage of it. As for the *pomeshchiks,* it would have been absurd for them to go through the trouble of keeping a privilege which already had been attacked; furthermore, the maintenance of this privilege would only have exacerbated the scarce industrial manpower, increased the temptation of escaping, and encouraged the desertion of lands. The ukase of 1721, which was intended to safeguard the interests of two antagonistic classes,[45] somehow managed to mix them partially, thereby causing the appearance in midcentury of "manufacturer-lords." One can rightly observe that it represents the perfect expression of this "scale politics" which characterizes the "state-arbiter."

Moreover, it should be pointed out that this ukase was probably more symptomatic than decisive. Soviet historians do not agree that the transfer of manpower that it initiated and more often ratified was all important. Pavlenko tends to elongate the list of beneficiaries, a great number of whom forgot to have their purchases registered. They have probably not caught the attention of researchers yet. The ukase of 1736, which limited for a very short period the rights of the bourgeoisie to the purchase of *peasants without land,* reflected, according to Pavlenko again, a desire to curb the entrepreneurs' freedom of acquisition. As a matter of fact, very few of these entrepreneurs had a fortune large enough to buy if not, say, a number of countryless individuals or families, then entire villages, and at the same time to own large domains. Even if this were possible, especially in the newly industrialized sectors where the population was rather small, was the available "merchandise" sufficient? Pavlenko himself accepts the fact that manufacturers from the Ural region often lacked the necessary funds, and even more often the opportunity to purchase. He also emphasizes the fact that only the newcomers were able to obtain servile manpower,[46] even in the center of the region. We can therefore assume that the supply on which industry fed for a long period of time increased in very small quantities following the ukase of 1721, and that it was composed, on the one hand, of the coveted mass of peasants from the state, and on the other, of a "mobile" labor force always available but forever unstable, represented by wanderers, fugitives, "newcomers," or workers abducted from the neighboring factory; in spite of all sorts of efforts and constraints, one could not count on their staying in the factory.

Let us retain from this rapid review that Soviet researchers attribute much importance to the economic history of Peter's reign: it is a field in which publications are most numerous, and discussions most passionate. They resuscitate, through the issue of servile or capitalistic manufacturing, the old quarrels of the periodization of Russian history.

Once the dogmatic apparatus has been put aside, one can draw a few conclusions: Peter's politics cannot but evoke in the eyes of a Western historian, not only in its grand lines but also in its smallest details,[47] the practice of mercantilism by the great European statesmen of the seventeenth century. Let us refrain, however, from exaggerating the role played by this politics; given the backward state of Russian economy, this politics represented a necessary complement that would not have been sufficient had growth not preceded alongside it.

Finally, Peter's real triumph does not consist in having invented a "Russian" mercantilism; the material assistance which he granted the young industry in his empire has nothing original about it. At most, it answered the needs of the particular structure of Russian society. However, few sovereigns, few statesmen would have been able to awake in their subjects the patriotic pride, and the faith in potentials until then unknown or neglected, needed for boosting the economy with such impetus, especially since he already seemed to care less about the quality of its products than about the grandiose importance of natural resources. It is through this enthusiasm which he succeeded in transferring to a pleiad of men capable of supporting and continuing his work that Peter gave Russia the psychological foundations on which its modern economy stands; and for that same reason he was its founder.

III

Recent historical scholarship, both in the Soviet Union and in the United States, has revised the traditional view, established by eminent Russian historians of the tsarist period, that Peter the Great's industries were a "hothouse" development, and that the period following his death witnessed a regression. Although Russia had less dynamic and capable leadership in the second quarter of the eighteenth century, the Petrine war machine was maintained as a matter of urgent national interest, and the industry which supported it was sufficiently rooted to continue to grow. This continuity is described by Professor Arcadius Kahan, Professor of Economics at the University of Chicago. Dr. Kahan is the author of numerous articles dealing with the economic history of Russia in the eighteenth century, and, with D. Gale Johnson, the book: Soviet Agricultural Progress: An Evaluation of the 1965 Goals (1967). The article reprinted appeared initially in the Journal of Economic History, XXV (1965), 61–85, and is reprinted here with the permission of the publisher, the Economic History Association, and the author.

ARCADIUS KAHAN

Continuity in Economic Activity and Policy During the Post-Petrine Period in Russia*

To discuss economic activity in the Russia of the eighteenth century is to deal with an economic and social order that antedates the age of industrialization. Industrial activity in Russia during the eighteenth century was carried on within the political framework of an autocratic state, with ill-defined norms of legal behavior, and against the background of a serf agriculture which reached its apogee during this very period. The state of the industrial arts was low in comparison with Western European standards, and the use of waterpower as a motive force in manufactories was introduced in Russia by foreign enterpreneurs only in the seventeenth century.

* Most of the data for this article were gathered during the tenure of a Research Fellowship at the Russian Research Center, Harvard University. My colleagues at the University of Chicago generously offered their comments. Michael Cherniavsky, Earl J. Hamilton, and Roger Weiss read an earlier draft. Ralph Lerner improved the organization and presentation.

Against this background, the efforts by Peter the Great (reigned 1682–1725) to modernize Russia appear genuinely heroic. The demands of his policy forced the government to engage directly in a vast program of establishing new industries, of converting small handicraft workshops into large-scale manufactories, and of encouraging private entrepreneurs to follow the government's example.

The Petrine policy of what we would now describe as forced economic or industrial development was marked by a relentless race against time, dictated by political reasons. This haste and urgency led to major disproportions in the structure and production pattern of the "Petrine manufactories" and caused their mode of operation to differ from that of any other industrial complex built up elsewhere over a longer time span. It is the fate of the manufacturing sector in the Russian economy during the post-Petrine period that concerns us in the following discussion.

The early development of manufactures in eighteenth-century Russia presents an interesting issue for the economic historian— namely, the problem of the continuity or discontinuity of the initial industrialization.

It will be argued that the economic process set in motion during the Petrine period continued during the post-Petrine period and that the policies that supported the early industrialization drive were not abandoned by Peter's successors. It will be assumed that the early development of a new branch of the economy is not necessarily marked by a smooth upward movement of its output curve. Such a development is in most instances a process by which the new branch asserts itself against various adverse social conditions, involving conflicts of economic interests and policies. However, when the general activity is being pursued and similar policies persist over a longer time span, the basic continuity is established.

The traditional concept of discontinuity in industrialization in Russia has given rise to two assertions voiced from diametrically opposed positions. The first concluded on the basis of this assumed experience that government intervention, so frequently undertaken during the period of early industrialization, is futile and unreliable as a factor in economic development. The second argued that this experience proves the dependence of continuing economic growth upon the continuity of an active governmental policy and hence that the government's direct involvement is the decisive element in the economic growth effort of a nation. Thus both the liberal school and the etatist school of Russian historians have assumed the discontinuity in economic growth during the post-Petrine period of the eighteenth century to be a fact and have used it as a historical example to lend added credibility to their respective positions.[1] The two outstanding authorities among the Russian historians who elaborated the concept of discontinuity and thereby helped to get their judgments and images of the post-Petrine period entrenched in the popular mind were V. O. Klyuchevsky and P. Milyukov, both representatives of the liberal school.

In the following essay, three problems are singled out for investigation: (1) How durable was the industrial development in Russia that occurred during the Petrine period? (2) How serious and of what nature was the slump in economic activity during the immediate post-Petrine period, and what was its impact upon the industrial sector of the Russian economy? (3) Could the post-Petrine period be considered as one of major discontinuity in the economic growth of Russia?

The theses of Milyukov and Klyuchevsky about economic discontinuity may be summarized as follows: The growth of manufactories under Peter the Great cannot be attributed to the increase of demand in the domestic market and is therefore not a "result of the organic development of the domestic industry";[2] it was created by an extraeconomic factor—the government—to serve its political ends.[3] The existence of the manufactories depended upon government protection and special privileges, hence their instability.[4] Periods of government inactivity in the economic sphere are therefore correlated with slumps or declines in industrial activity. Milyukov supports his argument about the lack of durability of the manufactories created during the Petrine period by the fact that by 1780 only twenty-two of them were in existence.[5] Klyuchevsky reaches the sweeping but obviously erroneous conclusion for the whole period 1725–1762 that "industry after Peter did not make any noticeable progress."[6]

Although one might agree with some of these conclusions, I would question most of them as being irrelevant as explanatory factors and some of them as being simply erroneous. The general impression of a feeble state of manufactories in Russia and of a lack in indigenous entrepreneurship is largely built upon statements made by Peter the Great himself and upon the choice of methods used by him in his attempts to introduce and develop manufactories in Russia. Such a view ignores the historical experience of other countries at a similar stage in their economic development.

In discussing the nature of the post-Petrine period, one cannot ignore some features of the Petrine period that most impressed contemporaries and posterity (historians included). The features of Petrine economic policy that made the most lasting impression were: (1) the scope of public works and the creation of social overhead, and (2) the effort to supply the army and navy. Certainly in terms of employment (not in efficiency), the public works of the Petrine period remained unrivaled throughout the entire eighteenth century.

Thousands of forced laborers (drafted serfs) were employed in the construction of the Voronezh wharves and of the Black Sea navy during the turn of the century; [7] many thousands were employed in the digging of a Volga-Don canal; thousands were mobilized yearly for the construction of the Taganrog harbor [8] and for the erection of fortifications in Azov and Troitsk.[9] All these projects were later discontinued and abandoned. For years, resources (human and capital) were squandered in the construction of the Vyshnevolotsk canal system, in harbor construction in Rogervik, etc.[10] They all were monuments to the ability of the Petrine administration to mobilize the labor effort of the nation. Of course, the crown of Peter's domestic projects was the construction of the new capital, St. Petersburg. We now have some notion of the magnitude of its drain on labor resources.[11]

The government's public works programs do not account for all of the redistribution of resources or forced savings that were channeled into construction. Government pressure forced both the nobility and the merchants to channel a part of their savings or wealth into housing construction in St. Petersburg, in addition to substantial government expenditures.[12] Such investments might have turned out to be profitable for the individuals in the long run, but within the time horizon of the people involved, they were considered as an inferior alternative to the ones existing elsewhere, as witnessed by the coercion applied by the government to enforce the investment in housing construction. Contemporaries regarded these involuntary investments as a form of additional taxation.

The channeling of labor and capital into construction and public works on such an unprecedented scale left its imprint both upon Peter's contemporaries and upon subsequent generations. None of the Russian historians has tried to find out what the real costs were, as though the mobilized labor force had zero opportunity costs. This is mentioned, not to question the economic rationale or political wisdom of the public works, but to call attention to the lack of elements of economic analysis in the works of the historians. Obviously, the awe and admiration of posterity for the labor mobilization policies of Peter were strengthened in view of the fact that they coincided with army recruitment carried out on an almost yearly basis.[13]

The volume of employment in manufactories is obviously dwarfed by the large numbers of the military draft and the forced labor mobilization in the Petrine period. Any increase in industrial employment in the post-Petrine period could not compensate, in terms of sheer numbers, for the decline in employment in public works.

The effort to supply the needs of the army and navy during the Petrine period was most impressive. Within fifteen to twenty years the newly established ironworks and munition factories were able to supply the needs of an army of about 220,000 men. In 1715, the Russian artillery already had about 13,000 domestically produced cannons of various sizes; by 1720, the yearly output of military rifles exceeded 20,000; a navy on the Baltic and Caspian seas was constructed and well equipped. The textile industries supplied an increasing portion of army cloth, all of the sailcloth, and so forth. This was the work of one generation.

Milyukov assumed the survival rate of manufacturing enterprises to be *the* criterion of the durability of entrepreneurial effort of a particular period. Leaving aside for the moment the validity of this assumption, it is necessary to point out certain pitfalls involved in Milyukov's procedure. The computation of a survival rate of enterprises that ignores the distribution of enterprises by size or by industry branches is a biased measure. Moreover, to ignore the distinction between one-owner firms, partnerships, and joint-stock companies tends to obscure a great deal of what we know about the various elements that determine the life structure of firms in general. These criticisms may be made without even raising considerations of the peculiar characteristics of turnover in ownership of enterprises or of the survival rate of firms in most European countries during the eighteenth century in general [14] and of the conditions of Russian manufactories in particular. But quite apart from all this, additional considerations make the survival rate a poor indicator of entrepreneurial activity.

Available evidence indicates that industrial plant and equipment were not the largest item in the total investment expenditures of particular firms; [15] hence, the continued existence of an industrial firm was only in part influenced by the desire to maintain the capital stock as a unit.[16] We have evidence that skilled labor frequently constituted a greater asset than the physical capital stock.[17] Therefore, transfers of capital stock and skilled labor from one firm to the other took place for entirely different reasons. Secondly, given the continuous engagement in domestic or foreign commerce, the occurrence of transfers, mergers, and so forth might not necessarily reflect upon the viability of the manufacturing enterprises themselves.[18] In addition, partnerships and joint-stock companies, organized to remedy the scarcity of capital, were frequently broken up, transformed, and replaced, thus distorting the purely numerical relationship between the number of firms and the stock of capital with which the firms were identified. By tracing the history of individual enterprises and the transfers of labor and equipment, it is possible to ascertain a much greater real continuity than Milyukov was able to observe. An additional fallacy of Milyukov's approach in making the survival rate of the firms *the* criterion of entrepreneurial efficiency lies in his total disregard of both general and specific conditions that affected the operations of enterprises during this period. He disregards such phenomena as the transition from war to peace and its impact upon the product mix—a transition that not all modern enterprises could survive; the relative insecurity of life and property; forced relocations; [19] and the risks of fire and floods, to mention just some items of a rather extensive list.

The survival rate for private ironworks for the period

1725–1745 was 86 percent.[20] A survival rate of 72 percent for the same period for enterprises in all branches of the textile industry further weakens the validity of Milyukov's assertion.[21] A closer scrutiny of the older surviving enterprises reveals that they were of larger average size and of somewhat higher productivity than the ones that were liquidated or the ones established during the immediate post-Petrine period.[22] Under conditions of an almost stable technology, the size of plant, output, and capital endowment was apparently among the most important factors determining the survival of the enterprises. Some advantage from an earlier start on a larger-than-average scale, from superior knowledge of the market, and from possible preferential or privileged treatment by the government should obviously not be dismissed. In result, the survival capacity of the Petrine manufactories was as great as that of any manufactories established during the later periods and certainly contradicts Milyukov's assertions.[23]

The impressive achievements of Petrine policies were identified with the personality of Peter himself. His death could not but leave a mark upon the economic life of the country. From the many historical descriptions of the Petrine and immediate post-Petrine periods, the following general picture can be reconstructed about the immediate effect of Peter's death: Previously pushed and strained almost to the limit of endurance by the "tsar-transformer," economic activity slowed down for a while. Entrepreneurs, hitherto conscious of a sense of direction, became uncertain whether the pressure in the same direction would be sustained by the new rulers before new directions were taken. The need for a reallocation of available resources, the accumulation and transfer of new resources, and the adjustment to a peace economy required time during which the pressures of the Petrine period had to abate. Consequently, some of the government projects were continued with diminished vigor (Ladoga canal), new projects were not embarked upon, and the conspicuous and massive government activity diminished markedly. The decrease in the scale of government economic activity, however, did not decrease the total activity of the various branches of the economy to the same degree. Not only was there a different effect upon various branches, but also the slackening of government economic activity was rapidly compensated for by increased activity in the private sector of the economy.

Let us consider the extent to which the contraction of government activity in the area of public works was accompanied by a general contraction of foreign and domestic trade. With respect to foreign trade, the only continuous data available pertain to trade with England, which was Russia's main trading partner.[24]

A few comments are in order with respect to the degree to which the British data are indicative of the pattern of trade in general and for the years under consideration in particular. The chief characteristic of Russian foreign trade was its positive trade balance, the excess of exports over imports. Although the excess of total Russian exports over imports was proportionally not as high as in the case of Russian-British trade, that excess can be estimated for the year 1726 as against the years 1717–1719 (including 1718—the peak year for Russian exports to England during Peter's reign). Exports amounted to 4,238,810 rubles and imports to 2,125,543 rubles in 1726,[25] while for 1717–1719, exports of 2,613,000 rubles and imports of 816,000 rubles were recorded.[26] Consequently, there was a substantial increase in exports for 1726 as against 1717–1719, which can be explained in part by a rise in exports of manufactured goods, both iron and textiles.[27] Thus, the estimates for total trade as well as the British data testify to an unchanged pattern of Russian exports during the post-Petrine period.

The pattern of change of the imports of English goods into Russia during the immediate post-Petrine period can rather easily be explained in terms of the substitution of Prussian wool cloth for the English ones [28] and is in general not typical for the growing tendency exhibited by Russian imports. To the extent that the foreign trade data for 1726 or for Russian exports to England can be used as indirect evidence of the state of the Russian economy after Peter's death, at least they indicate neither an interruption in Russia's economic development nor a decline in the industrial output.

The sources of information about changes in the value or the volume of internal trade are even scarcer than those about the changes in foreign trade. The only available series pertains to the volume of trade on the Makarievska Trade Fair, which was an important trading institution but probably not representative of the volume or composition of internal trade in general. But, since the Makarievska Trade Fair was the largest in Russia, it would be logical to expect that a serious economic disturbance would be reflected in the turnover at that fair. Although the figures suggest a general downward trend in the total taxes collected and show no evidence of growth in the custom-duty collections, which more directly reflect the turnover, on the whole the data do not point to a general stagnation in business after the death of Peter the Great.[29] Granted that there was a general slowdown in governmental economic activity, how strongly did it affect the industrial sector? Was there a slump in the output of Russian manufactories following Peter's death?

The normal expectation would be that the cessation of war operations against Sweden (1721) and Persia (1724) should bring about a contraction of military output during the reign of Peter. The most affected branches of manufacturing would be iron and textiles, since their output level depended to a large extent upon the volume of government contracts. An examination of those industries ought to provide the clue to the nature of the post-Petrine slump in industrial output.

The change in the output pattern of the iron industry can be derived from the yearly data on total output and on the two sectors, state and private.[30] The temporary decrease in output for 1726 and 1727 registered in the data can in part be explained by factors outside the general impact of postwar contraction. The decline in output was most clearly marked in the state sector of iron manufacturing. Documents pertaining to this sector point to two causes: replacement of worn-out equipment, and labor unrest in the ironworks.[31] The decrease of iron output is not explained by any inherent deficiencies of the industry. Of course, an adjustment period was involved during which some markets were expanded (notably foreign markets for state-produced iron) to compensate for the decreased military demand, and adjustments of the output mix had to be made.[32] But there is ample evidence that even during the years of the "post-Petrine slump," there was net investment in the iron industry.[33]

Further supporting evidence for the contention that the "post-

Petrine slump" had little effect upon manufacturing may be found in the data of copper output.[34] Not only had the output of copper almost doubled during 1725–1727, but by 1728 the rapid rise of private output had begun, a fact that indicates that private investments had been made during the preceding years, the "years of slump." [35]

The situation of the textile industry was not as clear cut as that of the metal industry. A large part of the linen-hemp manufactories was geared to the production of sailcloth, and the sharp decrease in domestic naval construction forced the manufactures to seek foreign markets for their output and to change the output mix of the industry. This accounts for the lack of new investment in this area during 1725–1727.

The wool industry, in turn, had to overcome an internal misallocation of resources with respect to the proportion of wool cloth to coarse wool lining material, previously established as a result of the demands of Peter's army quartermasters.[36] Nevertheless, new wool and silk manufactories were established during the years 1725–1728,[37] indicating that these branches of industry were not paralyzed by what has been called the post-Petrine slump.

Available evidence pertaining to other branches of manufacturing (chemical, leather, and so forth) points to a similar conclusion. The years immediately following the death of Peter were years of adjustment for the newly established branches of manufacturing and for the manufacturing enterprises. They were not years of slackening of total demand that, according to some historians, caused far-reaching decreases in output and in investment in the manufacturing sector.

Data on the total volume and rate of capital investment would throw light upon the existence of a hypothetical downward trend in manufacturing. Unfortunately, estimates of the total capital investment in manufacturing are not available.[38] The closest approximations to such data are estimates of capital in the ironworks for certain years. Although a number of objections could be raised about the accuracy of the estimates, they can nevertheless be used in such conjectures.

The cumulative estimates supplied by S. G. Strumilin for the period under consideration are the following:

CAPITAL INVESTMENT IN IRONWORKS
(*in 1000 silver rubles*)

Year	Private	State	Total
1700	22	n.a.	22
1725	124	46	170
1735	288	83	371
1745	870	232	1102

SOURCE: Strumilin (cited in n. 30), p. 240.

An approximate division of the total volume of capital invest-ment in the private sector during the period 1725–1735 (1726–1729 and 1730–1735), using the number of furnaces and of forge hammers installed as an approximate index of capital invest-ment, would indicate about 40 percent for the earlier and 60 per-cent for the later period. An equal distribution of state investment between the two periods appears to be plausible on the basis of available evidence.[39] Consequently, the distribution of the total 201,000 rubles of capital investment between the two periods yields 85,000 rubles for 1726–1729 and 116,000 rubles for 1730–1735. If we allocate the capital investment outlays for the period 1700–1725 not to the whole period but to about ten years of the most intensive capital construction of ironworks, we end with a yearly average of about 15,000 rubles, while the yearly average for the period 1726–1729 (excluding the outlays for capital repair) would reach the sum of over 20,000 rubles. In iron manufacturing, therefore, there is no apparent evidence of a decrease in the volume of capital investment during the years following the death of Peter the Great.[40]

Among the basic elements of government policy with regard to industry that indicate continuity of the two periods, there can be no doubt that foreign-trade policy was of utmost importance. The need to obtain foreign markets for some raw materials and for industrial products led to a reexamination of the Petrine foreign-trade and tariff policies. This took place during 1727–1731 and resulted in a new tariff in 1731.[41] Most of the Soviet historians have con-demned the 1731 tariff as a betrayal of Russian industrial interests to those of foreign countries and as a major deviation from the Petrine tariff policy of 1724. A more careful analysis of the two tariffs does not substantiate the charge of major liberalization of tariff policies. While the 1724 tariff was unabashedly protectionist, that of 1731 was much more selective in its discriminatory features. It was protective with respect to products manufactured within Russia, both by the new manufactories and by the craft or domestic industries. It was protective with regard to the export of manufactured goods and set high duties upon the export of raw materials used by domestic manufacturers. True, it deviated from the 1724 tariff with regard to the level of duties in a number of cases but was much more effective in enforcing them, whereas previous widespread smuggling had rendered many prohibitive duties of the Petrine tariff ineffective.[42] Built upon the reported market prices of Russian commodities, the new tariff resulted in continuous protection of the commodities produced for mass consumption and liberalized the import duties for so-called luxuries, the domestic production of which was clearly inadequate. The new tariff doubtless also resulted in more normal foreign-trade relations with other countries with which commercial treaties were subsequently concluded. While the desire to conclude long-run commercial treaties with some major partners was apparent, it must be realized that such an operation required concessions from both partners; therefore, commercial and tariff policies had to become more flexible. Although utterances were made about the desirability of Russian industries' becoming more competitive in the domestic and world markets, the calculations upon which the tariff legislation rested tended to provide at least a 30-percent margin for the Russian manufacturers (based upon the assumption that the transportation and other costs came up to 30 percent of the price of the imports in the country of origin). Therefore, it seems safe to conclude that the tariff policy of Peter's successors was not less effective in its features protective of Russian industry. In fact, it introduced corrections into some of Peter's typical short-run measures which were designed to achieve high rates of growth in some chosen areas to the detriment of others.[43]

Needless to say, even during the latter part of Elizabeth's reign —when the gentry won the first round against the *posad* (urban population) in the fight over the trading rights of the peasants, the abolition of internal duties, and the increase of foreign trade duties —the manufacturers were little, if at all, affected by the increased foreign-trade duties. They certainly gained from the inclusion of the south in the domestic market by eliminating some foreign competition from it.

As far as fiscal policy is concerned, no additional burdens were put directly upon the manufacturers. It is difficult to assess the effect upon the demand for manufactured goods which resulted from an increased burden of direct and indirect taxation placed upon the agricultural producers.

There was, however, a turn in government policy that is of considerable significance for our problem. The policy change concerning the transfer of state-owned industrial enterprises to private ownership actually did not contradict the basic tenets of the Petrine period. However, prior to the change in policy it was necessary to test what could only be conjectured by some observers during Peter's reign—namely, the question of the relative efficiency of state-owned and private enterprises. The discussion pertaining to this subject was intensified during the period 1732–1736.[44]

The policy accepted by the government may perhaps be summarized as follows: (1) The higher efficiency of the private enterprises was basically admitted. (2) The state interests, whenever involved in the form of volume of deliveries and prices for the output or tax revenues, ought to be safeguarded in any transaction involving the transfer of state-owned enterprises to private hands. (3) A major condition of such transfer remained the promise on the part of the entrepreneur to increase capital investment in, and the output of, the particular enterprises.[45]

While the private share in total output increased as a result of the various transfers of previously state-owned enterprises to private ownership, this result was accompanied by an increase in the degree of state control and regulation of the private enterprises. The more refined aspects of the mercantilist system replaced the crude mercantilist policies of the Petrine period. The policy makers apparently decided that state control might serve in lieu of state ownership and that state ownership in the absence of profits was more expensive than the administration of state controls. We can, therefore, observe the simultaneous development of two interrelated phenomena. A more firm establishment of private property rights, accepted as a basic precondition of private entrepreneurial activity, went hand in hand with a more rigid definition of the conditions of exercising ownership rights in the area of manufacturing.[46]

The major areas of government control over private enterprises (including information collection and interference) were defined as follows: (1) preservation of the system of licensing and control of entry into industry; (2) control of the size of operations and of some sources of raw materials and labor (principally when imports and serf labor were involved); (3) control to ensure continuous operation of the enterprise; (4) control and stimulation of capital investment. These policies or controls constituted a step forward in the direction of perfecting the mercantilist system in Russia and thereby could be considered as a continuation of the Petrine policies.[47]

However, my main contention would be that the basic economic continuity between the Petrine and post-Petrine periods in the manufacturing sector was not so much provided by government policy as by the existence of a "natural" link of an emerging distinct group of Russian manufacturers.

It has already been pointed out that the prevailing notion (especially among Russian historians) about the lack of indigenous entrepreneurship and "entrepreneurial spirit" in Russia is based largely upon the views expressed by Peter the Great. In this connection four factors should be borne in mind. (1) Peter, in appraising the entrepreneurial capabilities of the industrialist and merchant group, made the comparison with contemporary Western Europe. He underestimated the differences in property rights, risks, and investment returns in Western Europe and in Russia. Therefore, regardless of the many limitations imposed upon private enterprise previously (limitations among which Peter's fiscal policies were not inconspicuous), Peter's characterization of the Russian entrepreneur ought not to be taken as an unbiased observation. (2) Peter's view of Russian entrepreneurs was part and parcel of his political thought and of his ideas regarding his own calling and obligation. He considered himself the guardian of the welfare of his subjects who, because of their ignorance, had to be propelled into new conditions. Possessing superior awareness of new horizons and opportunities, he believed himself entitled to force his subjects to a rude awakening by a ruler who, by his own definition, placed the interest of the community above the interests of individuals. The rudeness of the treatment was justified, in his view, by the urgency of national interests as defined by him. (3) Command and outright coercion in social relations were not yet replaced in Russia by compromise and persuasion; therefore, imposing investment decisions upon entrepreneurs was almost perfectly consistent with methods generally employed in administering other areas of national activity. The impression given by Peter the Great is therefore a blend of "new" Western ideas and "old" Russian methods. (4) The Petrine period of development of manufactories was a period of almost uninterrupted war, with economic policies geared and tailored to the war effort. The largest investments were in the armament industries or those that supplied the army. The general pattern of resource use and the allocation of investment within industry differed from what would be considered optimal during a period of peace; the attitudes of entrepreneurs and the behavior of firms differed also. To understand the challenge and to evaluate the impact of a war lasting a quarter century upon a newly emerging entrepreneurial group were above even the very substantial analytical abilities and intellectual faculties of Peter the Great.

During the Petrine as well as during the post-Petrine period, this was a group still *in statu nascendi*, open to both gentry and the lower strata of merchants and even peasants, within the limits of government licensing.[48] Its structure was in large measure determined by the serf society in which it found itself, and very little effort was exerted by the entrepreneurial group to defy the norms of that society. The main problem for the manufacturers was to be able to perform their economic tasks within the limits prescribed by the social framework. It would, therefore, be a mistake to attribute to the eighteenth-century Russian entrepreneurs and manufacturers attitudes and concepts of liberal capitalism. While struggling for broader rights (to consolidate their position and to make more independent business decisions), they were quite willing to operate under an umbrella of basically paternalistic and protectionist government policies. Under the prevailing institutional arrangement, freedom of choice and decision for the entrepreneurs was limited. It was only through negotiations and pressures that the extension of freedom and greater independence from the government could be won, and at that the government was not always willing or able to understand the manufacturers' point of view. Peter seldom got involved in dialogues; his was the style of command. During the post-Petrine period, dialogues between the entrepreneurs and the government became more frequent. It is possible, therefore, to reconstruct some of the opinions and attitudes of the entrepreneurs and representatives of the government and to delineate and distinguish meaningful differences between their respective positions.

While the state officials would elevate the principles of output maximization and growth of investment as the chief criteria of success of manufacturing enterprises, the entrepreneurs would have the profit motive as their chief criterion. Therefore, once established in a particular branch of manufacturing, the owners of the enterprises would favor greater restrictions upon entry than the government would allow (in view of the slow growth in demand the possibility to benefit from quasi-monopoly profits would rapidly disappear with free entry).[49] The demands for exclusive monopoly privileges were perhaps less frequent during the post-Petrine period than during the preceding one.

The manufacturers were against government attempts to determine the product mix and to set quality standards of production. In the latter case the manufacturers exhibited a more intimate knowledge of the potentialities of the domestic market and the consumer demand.

The manufacturers resisted government measures that would impose upon them the financial responsibility of providing both social overhead (school buildings, roads, churches) and welfare measures for their labor force (accident and unemployment compensation, education, and so forth).

They also resisted government price setting, both because of the principle involved and because of their anticipation that the price would be below the market level. Another source of this resistance was the suspicion that price setting ultimately leads to wage setting, which they wanted to avoid. The latter attitude does not imply that the private manufacturers were necessarily paying lower wages than the state enterprises but only that they guarded their rights to set wage rates in a manner that would maximize profits for the enterprise and would establish wage scales more flexible and geared to the effectiveness of the labor performance.

Needless to say, one of the major aspirations of the manufacturers was to gain a share in the opportunity to employ serf labor wherever that was profitable. Therefore, the actual extent to which manufacturers were able to acquire serf labor for the manufactories might be used as a tentative test of their economic and political influence.

We ought to begin with the assumption that, prior to the decrees of March 21, 1762, and August 8, 1762, resistance to purchases of serfs by manufacturers was widespread among the landed gentry, as they had been urging for forty years that such purchases be prohibited or limited. Clearly, since it was not until 1762 that such pressures took the form of law, it might be assumed that the existence both of counterpressures on the part of the manufacturers and of some reasons of policy led the government during the reigns of Anna and Elizabeth to steer a middle course. That the government did in fact pursue such a middle course, even going back to Peter's reign, may be learned from an examination of relevant legislation and from the record of actual purchases of serfs by manufacturers. First, about the evidence in terms of legislation: the Petrine policy expressed by the decree of January 18, 1721, was a typical compromise policy. It allowed merchants to buy villages by permission of the Berg and Manufacture Collegiums under the condition that they remain forever attached to the plants. A similar compromise policy prevailed under Peter's successors.[50]

Second, about the record of purchases: although the data may be inaccurate and somewhat confusing, they point to permission given for purchases of more than 60,000 serfs.[51]

Thus the policies of the state, prior to 1762, allowed the owners of the manufactories to invest in serf labor, thereby enabling them to continue the operations of their enterprises in the absence of free labor. This measure lessened the dependency of the manufactories' owners upon the gentry serf owners and resulted in greater stability for the activities of the industrial entrepreneurs.

The data and observations presented above would indicate two general conclusions: first, that the process of development of manu-factures, started in the pre-Petrine period and gaining momentum under Peter, continued—at least in the private sector—into the post-Petrine period; second, that during the post-Petrine period the tendencies toward a strengthening of the entrepreneurial group were developing within a framework of government policy that was rather favorably inclined toward cooperation with this particular group. Thereby, continuity in policy and economic activity between the Petrine and the post-Petrine periods was essentially maintained.

IV

The slow and costly means of transport prior to the development of railroads and steam navigation on the waterways was a major factor in perpetuating the backwardness of Russia. This has been stated many times by scholars, including Alexander Baykov, in his article included earlier in this collection. What V. K. Yatsunsky does is to demonstrate this proposition with exhaustive scholarly research. He traces in great detail the movement and prices of iron from the mines and factories of the Urals, through the waterways and fairs of Central Russia, to local markets farther west. Yatsunsky's research draws upon an extensive and varied fund of Soviet archival materials. V. K. Yatsunsky was a prominent Soviet historian of the 1950s and early 1960s. He participated in many of the important scholarly debates taking place in the Soviet Union at that time, and published numerous studies on the industrial and commercial history of Russia in the early nineteenth century. The article here reprinted first appeared in Voprosy Geografii [Problems of Geography], 50 (1960), 110–45.

V. K. YATSUNSKY

Geography of the Iron Market in Prereform Russia[1]

The geography of the iron market in prereform Russia has not been a subject of study in our scientific literature. It is true that in B. B. Kafengauz's book, *The Demidov Estate* (Moscow, 1949), an excellent description is given of the transport of iron from the Demidov plants in the Urals to St. Petersburg, made on the basis of the Demidov archives. But this description is only of one way of iron transport, though the most important, until that time, and not of the totality of these ways; moreover it refers to the eighteenth century. In any case the geography of iron transport by water and over land, is not only an interesting page of the historical geography of Russia and of the history of prereform heavy metallurgy, but also shows quite objectively the impeding effect conditions of communication had on the national economy of prereform Russia.

At the very close of the 1840s, the Russian Geographical Society with the assistance of the Mining Industry Department (then called the Department of Mining Industry and Salt Production), undertook a special investigation of the geography of the iron market.[2] The assembled material remained unpublished almost in its entirety.[3] In addition, quite detailed data about the conditions of the iron market together with its geographical aspects in the first half of the fifties were collected by the government Commission for Raising Funds for the Development of Iron Production in Russia. These materials remained unpublished as well. Thanks to this research [4] the historian has at his disposal quite detailed and authentic sources to characterize the iron market in the middle of the nineteenth century. These sources are the basis of the present article. As a supplement, the author has made use of data from the Archives of the Mining Industry,[5] and from the Archives of the Ural Industrialists—the Demidovs,[6] the Stroganovs,[7] and the Golitsins.[8]

For the period preceding the two special investigations of the iron trade, the sources are much more scanty, but nevertheless they permit one to assert that the geography of this market, known from the data of the middle of the nineteenth century, was formed gradually during several decades, and its beginnings go back to the eighteenth century.

In the iron trade, fairs played a very important part. The leading role belonged to the Nizhnii Novgorod Fair. Its influence on the iron trade extended almost over all European Russia. The major part of the Ural iron ore, which constituted more than four-fifths of Russia's total production, passed through the Nizhnii Novgorod Fair and from there was distributed throughout the country.

Plants in Central Russia (they were then called "outside-of-Moscow") produced essentially for markets other than the Nizhnii Novgorod Fair.[9] The plants "outside-of-Moscow" produced only about one-seventh of the iron production in Russia.[10]

Prices for iron were fixed at the Nizhnii Novgorod Fair.

The basic market for Russian metallurgy in the middle of the nineteenth century was the domestic market. In 1845–1850 exports comprised only 8 percent of the production, and in 1851–1855, 6 percent.[11] Exports to Europe were about three-fourths of the total iron export.

Exports to Europe mainly went through St. Petersburg. Russian iron went to Great Britain, which then occupied first place in the purchase of this iron, and to the United States of America. Some iron was exported via the Black Sea and the Azov Sea ports to Turkey. Along the Asian border, exports went through Astrakhan from whence iron went to Iran and to the Transcaucasian Customs (also of Iran) via the city of Troitsk (to the Khanates of Central Asia). Iron was sold to foreign exporters almost exclusively by the plant owners themselves, without Russian middlemen.[12]

In the domestic market, at the head of the trade stood big wholesale merchants. They bought up almost all the iron brought by the producers to the Nizhnii Novgorod Fair. Numerous Ural producers in need of turnover capital for the upkeep of their plants concluded forward sale contracts with the wholesale merchants and received advances of these sales,[13] undertaking to deliver the iron to the purchaser either at the fair or at Laishev. Laishev was a landing place on the Kama River not far from its confluence with the Volga River. These producers lost much on the price of iron. At the forward sale of iron, the merchant usually paid the plant owner not with money, but with provisions and other merchandise necessary to the plants.[14]

Some plant owners, burdened with debts they had made, not for the upkeep of their plants, but for personal use, made forward sale agreements with the wholesale merchants a year in advance and even for longer periods, undertaking to deliver the iron on the production site. Thus, the owner of the Pozhev mining region, Alexander Vsevolozhsky, used to make forward sales of iron to the merchant Lyubimov a year in advance with the provision that the latter would pay his taxes and interest to the Board of Trustees with whom the Vsevolozhsky's mining plant property was mortgaged. Vsevolozhsky was forced, according to the statement he made to the above-mentioned government commission, to make a reduction in this deal of up to 20 percent.[15]

The iron of the plants outside-of-Moscow, as already stated, was sold almost exclusively outside the Nizhnii Novgorod Fair, and in most cases it passed through the hands of big wholesale merchants. From among the big plant owners of this district, the Shepelevs and the Batashovs made forward sale agreements on their products with Kasimov Trading House of the Barkovs and the Elatom Trading House of the Sorokins, with the delivery of iron at the plant.[16]

In the wholesale trade of iron, both at the Nizhnii Novgorod Fair as well as outside of it, credit sales were widely used.

The biggest wholesale merchants who played the leading part in the iron trade were few in number. There were considerably more small wholesale merchants who bought the iron in part directly from the plant owners and in part from the big wholesale merchants. Those who had at their disposal large turnover capital traveled to the Nizhnii Novgorod Fair, while those who had smaller turnover capital and wholesale merchants who traded in the Baltic region and in the northwestern provinces purchased the goods at the trade centers close to them.

The small number of big wholesale merchants who bought large lots of iron at the Nizhnii Novgorod Fair gave cause for the plant owners to accuse them of being monopolists of the iron trade, artifically reducing wholesale prices to the detriment of the interests of the plant owners. According to the data supplied by the above-mentioned investigation by the government, this allegation was not substantiated with facts.[17] Prices for iron were determined at the Nizhnii Novgorod Fair by the relationship between supply and demand, usual in the capitalist trade. The plant owners' volume of iron supply depended to a large degree upon factors of a meteorological character, namely the amount of water in the reservoirs of the plants in the preceding year.[18] The amount of water in the reservoirs was determined by the amount of atmospheric sediments and the tempo of the spring thaw. If there was much water, the production capability of the plants increased, the plant owners produced more metal, and, consequently, brought more metal to the fair. The demand situation was largely influenced by crops.[19]

Each wholesale merchant, having purchased the iron from the plant owners, took it to the region of Russia where he conducted a wholesale iron trade. The biggest wholesale merchants sold the greater part of the purchased iron at the fair itself and took the iron not sold there to their districts. The turnover of one of these merchants was quite considerable. The first place as regards the size of turnovers belonged to the Yaroslavl merchant, Pastukhov. He bought yearly about 900,000 poods of iron [20] (toward the end of the forties and the beginning of the fifties from 4.5 to 5.5 millions of poods were brought yearly to the Nizhnii Novgorod Fair). His base for trading activities was the ancient metal handicraft industry centers in Novgorod and Tver provinces, where nails were made which were distributed throughout Russia, and in Yaroslavl province, where various metal objects were made for the needs of the peasant economy and life. Nail makers received iron from merchants to whom they handed over the produce. Pastukhov resold the iron to these merchants and distributed to iron artisans through commission agents.[21] He also imported iron in Petersburg. Pastukhov purchased the Omut mining district in the Vyatka province together with two plants which produced annually about 150,000 poods of pig iron.

The second place in respect to turnover, was occupied by the Nizhnii Novgorod merchant Rukavishnikov.[22] He purchased from the plant owners a year in advance from 250,000 to 290,000 poods of pig iron; during the Nizhnii Novgorod Fair from 275,000 to 325,000 poods or more. He sold from 400,000 to 450,000 poods at the fair itself, and over 100,000 remained for sale at Nizhnii Novgorod in the course of the year and for distribution for processing to the artisans of this province, where metal processing industries were well developed and flourishing. In Nizhnii Novgorod, Rukavishnikov had a plant for processing steel.

In Moscow the wholesale trade in iron was led by merchants from Kasim, the Barkovs. They bought iron both at the Nizhnii Novgorod Fair and at the plants outside-of-Moscow owned by the Shepelevs and by the Batashovs. The size of their iron imports to Moscow alone, without taking into account other places of sale, they evaluated in their reply to a query from the Department of Mining, to amount to more than 300,000 poods.[23] Apart from the Barkovs, the wholesale trade in Moscow was conducted by several large wholesale merchants, namely Shelaputin, Korchagin, Sorokin, and by a number of small merchants.[24]

In Kiev the leading part in the iron trade was played by the House of Dekhterev,[25] which brought the goods from the Nizhnii

Novgorod Fair yearly, about 200,000 to 250,000 poods, and sold iron not only to the Kiev province, but also in the neighboring localities of the Right Bank Ukraine.

In Kharkov the largest iron merchant was Ryzhov,[26] who bought each year up to 175,000 poods. He bought the metal mainly at the Nizhnii Novgorod Fair from plant owners, and partly from wholesale merchants. Ryzhov also purchased iron outside the fair from owners in the Nizhnii Tagil mining district in the Urals and from the Kholunits district in Vyatka province, on condition that the plant owners would bring the goods to Rostov-on-Don or to the port of Dubov on the Lower Volga; he also bought iron from the plants "outside-of-Moscow." Ryzhov exported iron not only to the provinces of Kharkov, Poltava, Ekaterinoslav, and Tavrida, but also to the localities bordering on Kharkov in Voronezh and Kursk provinces. A Perm merchant, Lyubimov,[27] traded in iron on a large scale. But no characteristics of his trading operations with this merchandise could be found in the sources. Popov,[28] a Riga merchant, purchased yearly 80,000 poods of iron. The greater part of this merchandise he received from Finland; in addition, he made purchases in Petersburg from the Ural plant owners and some secondhand at the Nizhnii Novgorod Fair.

The majority of the plant owners sold their products in full to wholesale merchants. But some of them, in order to obtain more favorable prices, organized their own agencies for the sale of iron in different parts of Russia and made some use of commission agents. Among the Ural plant owners, it was the Demidovs, owners of the Nizhnii Tagil mining district, who displayed most energy in this respect.

In the eighteenth century the Demidovs already had agencies in St. Petersburg and in Moscow,[29] and also in Tver, Yaroslavl, Nizhnii Novgorod, Kazan, Laishev, Yagoshikha on the Kama, and at the port of Duben on the Volga. In the twenties of the nineteenth century [30] they had in addition agencies in Taganrog, Odessa, and Vilna. Systematically, they dispatched iron also to Kiev for export through commission agents.[31] The Taganrog and the Odessa agencies were very active. Iron was transported from Taganrog to Odessa by the Demidovs' own ships which accepted freight both from the government and from private individuals. The Vilna agency functioned sluggishly and was, later on, liquidated.[32] At the beginning of the 1850s [33] the Demidovs had agencies in Ekaterinburg, Perm, Kazan, Astrakhan, Nizhnii Novgorod, Moscow, Tula, Nakhichevan-on-Don,[34] Odessa, Kiev, and St. Petersburg. They also possessed warehouses for metals with commission agents in Norva and Riga.

The Kolunits plants of the Ponomarevs in the Vyatka province had permanent agencies in Vyatka, Spobodskoye, Kazan, Moscow, Yaroslavl, Rostov-on-Don, Odessa, and St. Petersburg.[35]

Apart from the Demidovs and the Ponomarevs, there were in St. Petersburg the following agencies: the Vekhiset plants, owned by the heirs of A. I. Yakovlev,[36] the Alapaev plants of S. S. Yakovlev's heirs, the Nevvan plants of P. S. Yakovlev's heirs,[37] the Suksun plants formerly owned by the Demidovs,[38] and the Katavsk plants owned by the heirs of Beloselsky-Belozersky.[39] These agencies in St. Petersburg were principally concerned with the export of iron and at the same time made use of the local Petersburg market. With the exception of the Katavsk and the Kholunits plants, all belonged in the eighteenth century to the Demidovs and inherited the export of iron abroad already well developed by the Demidovs in the eighteenth century. In Nizhnii Novgorod there existed for permanent trade outside the fair officers [40] of the plants owned by Countess Stroganov, by the Lazarevs (the Chernomoz mining district), and by the Golitsins (the Nytven mining district). In 1846, the Lazarevs began to export their iron to Rybinsk and Yaroslavl.

The iron from the Golitsins' plant appeared already in the eighteenth century in the Cherepovetz district of Novgorod province,[41] and began to displace iron made directly from the local ore. Beginning with the nineteenth century, the Golitsins organized a systematic dispatch of iron to this region. They established warehouses in the local centers of the industry, namely in the villages Pekhteev, Vanskaya, and Vakhnova, and from there sold iron to the domestic industry engaged in forging nails and to the local merchants who distributed iron among the blacksmiths for making nails.[42] According to an approximate estimate of the direction of Nizhnii Tagil plants and the Demidovs,[43] 7.5 million poods of iron from the Ural private plants were distributed in the trade from the end of the forties to the beginning of the fifties [44] as follows:

(a) sold at the plants and in
    the vicinity   about   300,000 poods
(b) went to Siberia   "   500,000   "
(c) sold at departure of fleets   "   200,000   "
(d) received at the Nizhnii Novgorod
    Fair (I)   "   4,500,000   "
(e) sold by plant owners through
    commission agents and to
    their own agencies in different
    parts of Russia   "   1,300,000   "
(f) exported by them   "   700,000   "

According to government statistics, the following amounts were brought to the Nizhnii Novgorod Fair:

in 1847	4,993,000	poods
1848	4,506,000	"
1849	4,531,000	"
1850	4,909,000	"
1851	5,400,000	"
1852	6,000,000	"

SOURCE: Ts.G.I.A.L., Folio 46, Register I, File 15, p. 175 (back).

It is obvious that the Demidov administration was guided by the 1848 and 1849 data.

The iron which was sold in Laishev and the iron which was shipped to Rostov and Nakhichevan by the Demidovs and the Ponomarevs, as well as some part of the iron from the Nizhnii Novgorod Fair, went down the Volga. Iron from the government plants in the Urals, which produced in the early fifties a little under a million poods, was mainly designated for government war plants and for other needs of the state. About 1.5 million poods of government iron, whose quality did not satisfy the requirements of the war plants (so called unpurchasable according to the current terminology), was sold at the Nizhnii Novgorod Fair.[45]

Metal from other government plants, with a few exceptions,

was used entirely for the needs of the state. Maltzev organized with the owners of the plants outside-of-Moscow a whole network of warehouses for the export of iron.[46] Among the feudal plant owners of that time, he was about the only energetic and talented organizer of industry. He organized a series of warehouses along the Desna and the Dnieper from Bryansk to Kherson (in Trubchevsk, Korop, Kolotkova, Kiev, Cherkassy, Kremenchug, Ekaterinoslav, and Nikolaev) on the southern coast of Crimea; at Redut-Kaleh, Maran, and Tiflis in the Caucasus; at Ismail in Bessarabia, along the Western Dvina, starting from Porechier, a port on the Kaspla River, one of the former's tributaries, and continuing to the mouth of the same river (at Vitebsk, Polotsk, Dinaburg, and Riga); at Zubtscv on the Volga; in St. Petersburg, Kursk, Byelgorod, and Kharkov. Apart from the main center of the iron trade, Nizhnii Novgorod, which was of importance to all Russia, there were centers of local importance which varied with the volume of the trade. Some were principal points of transit while others were trade centers from which iron was shipped over a large territory.

The principal transit points were the settlement Dubovka on the Lower Volga and Kaluga. Through each of these points about half a million poods of iron passed yearly.[47] At these points iron was transferred from water transport to cartage.

Laishev too should be regarded as a transport center. At the Laishev stop, a part of the iron changed not its mode of transport, but owners of the cargo. The iron sold there was not overloaded. In accordance with the trading custom, the buyer who purchased an entire cargo received as a bonus an entire ship.[48] The largest local distribution centers were Moscow [49] and St. Petersburg.[50]

Very important centers in the iron trade were the following: Rostov-on-Don, together with Nakhichevan, adjacent to it,[51] Kharkov,[52] Kiev,[53] Astrakhan,[54] Yaroslavl,[55] and Rybinsk.

Iron went to Siberia through the Irbit Fair and Ekaterinburg [56] in considerable amounts. The turnover of Odessa, Saratov, and Tula, which played a noticeable part in the iron trade, was smaller. Iron is heavy merchandise. During transportation, owners endeavored to use waterways as much as possible, and used the services of cartage transport only in the absence of transportation by water.

The journey of the iron started at the plant. A description of this journey is, therefore, best begun with a sketch of the situation of the plants in relation to the transportation routes. Choice of location for the construction of a metallurgical plant was determined in the eighteenth century and during the first half of the nineteenth century by a combination of three basic conditions: in the vicinity of the iron ore the presence of forest and a river which could supply enough energy for operating the blowers and mallets. To construct a dam on a large river was a task beyond the capability of the technology of the day, and building it on a small river was much too unprofitable. Plants were constructed along the rivers neither too big nor too small. Especially profitable from the point of view of transportation was to build plants close to the mouths of small rivers, and not far from the place of their confluence with large water arteries. It was precisely in this way that plants built along the Kama and certain plants (Revdinsky, Bilimbaevsky, and others) in the vicinity of the Chusovaya were situated.

Frequently the power of the river on which a plant was constructed was insufficient for servicing the whole cycle of production. In such cases, either pig iron alone was smelted or it was smelted and parts of it were converted into iron. The mallets, either all of them or only those for which there was not sufficient energy, were set up on a separate converter plant (termed in those days "the mallet plant"). Such plants were constructed either up or down the same river nearest to the blast furnace plant. Pig iron for conversion was transported either in full or in part to the mallet plant. Usually the distance between the furnace plants and mallet plants connected with them in respect of production was not great.

Transportation of pig iron for processing over a long distance by cartage was, comparatively speaking, rare. With suitable water communications, such a distance could be a few hundred versts.

Proximity to big waterways, that is, to the Kama or the Oka, was desirable: it made export of the product cheaper, but it was not an indispensable condition of the construction of a plant. Distance could be overcome with cartage.

Only the plants situated in the vicinity of the Kama were able to ship iron to the market by water. Of the thirteen plants situated there, eleven were for redistribution, and only two had blast furnaces: these two had, in addition, enough of their own pig iron to satisfy over one-third of their needs,[57] and they forged the bulk of their iron from imported pig iron. The pig iron was brought to the Kama plants partly from the plants situated along the tributaries of the Yaiva (about 15 percent of the total needed),[58] but mainly from the plants which shipped the metal down the Chusovaya (over three-fourths of the total amount needed). The pig iron had to be transported over a few hundred versts.[59]

It follows then that the Kama plants actually only to a very small degree could make use of the advantages of their situation with regard to the export market.

With the exception of the Kama, all the rivers along which the shipping of the Ural metal began were navigable only early in the spring, in full flood, and for a very short interval of time. During the summer it was either nearly or completely impossible on account of shallow water to ship the metal down the small rivers where shipping started.[60] On the Chusovaya at this time of the year, it was very difficult. The Chusovaya, too, was used mainly in the spring during the floods. Shipping by the Demidovs from their plants in the Nizhnii Tagil mining district is significant. From 1844 to 1850 they shipped down the Chusovaya in the spring, yearly, on the average of 274,000 poods of iron, and in the summer, 15,000 poods.[61] It was on account of such transportation conditions that almost all the iron was shipped from the Urals to the markets of European Russia and to the sea for export once a year only, early in the spring.[62]

In winter, iron and pig iron earmarked for redistribution at the Kama plants was brought gradually by sled to the landing places of the plants. Some plant owners did this through feudal obligations exacted from serfs, while others did it with hired labor. Some plant owners hired their own peasants. In the sources there is no evidence of this for individual plants. But the evidence we have makes one think that hiring of free labor obviously dominated.

The distance the iron had to be transported and, consequently, the cost of transportation varied. For the majority of plants this distance was not great. A whole series of plants had landings directly near the plant, at a distance of a few versts or a little farther. But the plants situated to the east of the Urals which separated the waterways were in a different position: they shipped the metal down the Chusovaya or the Ufa. There, the distance from the landings was not only very considerable, but, in addition, the carts in which the metal was transported were forced to cross the Urals.

Fairly typical for the plants of this group were the distances between the trans-Ural plants of the Nizhnii Tagil district and the Ust-Utkin landing on the Chusovaya that belonged to them.[63]

TABLE 1

Plants	Versts	Transportation Fare per Pood, Kopecks
Nizhnii-Sladinsky	113	4.5
Verkhny-Sladinsky	103	4.5
Nizhnii-Tagilsky	65	3.8
Cherno-Stochensky	59	2.7

For the plants of the Alapaev district, situated farther away from the Chusovaya than the others, this distance was the greatest. The distance to the Kashkinsky landing on the Chusovaya owned by the plants of this district was as follows: [64]

TABLE 2

Plants	Versts	Transportation Fare per Pood, Kopecks
Irbitsky plant	275	5⁶/₇
Neyvo-Alapaevsky	200	5¹/₇
Neyvo-Shaitansky	163	4²/₇

The government-owned Goroblagodatsk plants were situated far from the Chusovaya. The distance between the government-owned Oslyansky landing and the most distant one among them, the Nizhnii-Turinsky plant, was 120 versts.[65] These plants shipped, apart from cast iron, about half a million poods of pig iron for processing into cast iron at the Votkinsky plant.[66]

Among the remaining plants of this group distant from the

Chusovaya was the Sysertsk plant situated at a distance of 120 versts from the landing.[67]

The plants situated in Trans-Uralia that shipped iron down the Ufa River were also compelled to send the merchandise to the landing a long way overland. The Kymshtamsk plants were at a distance of 90 to 120 versts from the landings on the Ufa River.[68] The transportation cost was 2.25 to 2.5 kopecks per pood.[69]

The Trans-Uralian plants which shipped down the Chusovaya and the Ufa forged a little more than one-quarter of all the iron produced, and it was they that shipped pig iron to the Kama region for processing.[70]

Among the plants near the western Urals situated in the majority of cases close to the landings, there were a few that were located at some considerable distance. For instance, the distance between the Seversky plant and the landing was 88 versts. Frequently the boats began the journey not fully loaded and, having reached deeper water, completed their loading on the way. This was accomplished in two ways. In some cases the number of boats, after additional loading, decreased, their voyage continued with a reduction in the number of boats, and the unloaded ones were sold; while in others, the additional freight of iron was brought to a more distant landing in carts. The necessity for an additional loading on the way frequently arose on rivers flowing into the Ufa and the Belaya. Thus, boats carrying the iron from the Yurezan-Ivanovsky plant to the confluence of the Yurezan and Ufa rivers sailed with incomplete cargoes and were loaded up to capacity at that point.[71]

At the landing place of the Avzyano-Petrovsky plants, each ship was loaded with 5500 poods of iron and, upon their arrival at the Tabynskaya landing on the Belaya River, up to 9000 poods were added.[72] From the Beloretzky plant,[73] situated in the upper regions of the Belaya River, boats were sent with a load of 5500 poods; at the Tabynskaya they were additionally loaded up to 8000 poods. At the landing of the Simsky plant, of the cargo of 80,000 poods of iron, only 45,000 were loaded on the boats; 35,000 previously, in winter, had been carted a distance of 100 versts to the Tekeevsky ferry where barges had been loaded.[74]

In spring, the moment the rivers were opened, almost all the yearly product of the Ural plants was loaded on boats and shipped to the export points. The shipping was done mainly in barges, large boats 122.5 feet long, 28 feet wide, with covered deck and a draft in water of 31.5 to 35 inches.[75] The barges took 10,000 to 10,500 poods of freight on their sailings down the Chusovaya. For shipping within the Belaya River system, they were constructed narrower (24.5 feet wide) and were loaded with 8000 to 9000 poods, sometimes up to 10,000 poods or more.[76] These barges were usually employed for shipping iron up the Volga, not farther than Rybinsk. Down the river, they went as far as Astrakhan. The cost of construction of such a barge at the beginning of the fifties amounted to 200 silver rubles, not inclusive of the cost of standing timber.

For transportation of iron to St. Petersburg down the Mariinsk canal system, without reloading at Rybinsk, the boats used a construction that assured extra durability—*Gibezh* boats, 84 feet long, 28 feet wide, with covered decks.[77] The loading capacity of the *Gibezh* boat was 7500 to 8000 poods and the cost 290 rubles.

In summertime, when the river was very shallow, semibarges were used. These were boats of a simple structure, with little iron used, 84 to 105 feet long, 24.5 to 28 feet wide, with an open deck. Semibarges lifted from 2500 to 4500 poods and rarely sailed farther than Perm. The cost of a semibarge was 90 rubles. As auxiliaries, when, in summertime, the Chusovaya became very shallow, rafts were used that cost 25 silver rubles and had a loading capacity of 500 to 700 poods.

Rafts, semibarges, barges, and *Gibezh* boats were used for one passage only. At the point of arrival of the iron, they were sold for a trifling sum of 30 to 80 rubles. These vessels were, as a rule, built by the plant personnel from the timber of the plant. For the transportation of the yearly product of large plants, several dozen boats sailing at the same time were needed. Such fleets, even in the eighteenth century, were named iron caravans.

The organization of shipping was usually the responsibility of the administration of the plant. At the head of the caravan went the manager who was called the caravan manager. Laborers were normally hired as free labor, but some plant owners used forced labor recruited from the mining plant population dependent on them. Such was the case in the fifties for the owners of the Lysvensky plant in Perm province [78] and some others. Among the crew the most highly qualified were the watermen and the pilots. The role played by the latter on such stormy rivers as the Chusovaya and the tributaries of the Belaya, as well as the Belaya itself in its upper course, was very important.[79]

The crewman, hired on the free labor market, were usually recruited from the peasants of Vyatsk province, and the pilots, from the population close to the rivers on which the metal was shipped. Sometimes the plant administration organized the shipping by contract.

At different parts of the route there were certain specific sailing peculiarities.

From the point of view of number of caravans sent out, the first place was occupied by the landing places on the Chusovaya and its tributaries. Evaluating the size of transportation of metal down the Chusovaya, one must take into consideration both the shipping of metal to the markets and the supply of pig iron to the Kama region plants. On the basis of the ratio between the smelting of pig iron and the smelting of iron in the plants of the Kama region, the amount of pig iron shipped to these plants down the Chusovaya may be estimated to be equal approximately to just less than 2 million poods. With the exception of the comparatively small part of the lower course of the river (after the confluence of the Tava and Lysva rivers) when the Chusovaya comes out into the plain, sailing down it was difficult and often dangerous not only for the freight, but also for the crew.

The Chusovaya is a mountain river with a swift current and a meandering course. Its bottom is stony with a multitude of underwater rocks; frequently, the shore cliffs cut into the river, wrecking the sailing boats. In order to avoid striking against them, great skill was necessary on the part of the pilots as well as coordinated precision on the part of the crew.

Each cliff that was dangerous to navigation was given a special name by the sailors: the Blue Rock, the Pool Rock, the Multyk Rock, the Gorchak Rock, the Bandit Rock, the Sleek Horse Rock, the Ornamented Rock, the Devil Rock, and so forth.[80]

To these difficulties was added the shallowness of the Chusovaya and its quickly changing waters. The administration of the Nizhnii Tagil plants of the Demidovs thus characterized this peculiarity of the Chusovaya: "The Chusovaya flows down the western slope of the Ural Mountains chain and, with its steep fall, water in it accumulates and runs off so fast, that caravans must reckon the periods favorable for shipping not only in days, but even in hours. Otherwise, to assist them, water must be let out of the plants' pools constructed on the rivers, tributaries to the Chusovaya, which, in it-self is harmful to the private interests of those plant owners to whom the pools belong, by reducing the water reserves for their needs in the operation of their plants." [81] The Chusovaya had many shoals called "partitions." Each one of them also had a special name with the raftsmen: Bogorodsky, Kashinsky, Dyravatovsky, Serebryansky, Oslyansky, Kosoi, and so on; and each had its own perculiarities which interfered with shipping. Bogorodsky "is wide and therefore shallow," Kashinsky "winds sharply"; Dyravatovsky "dove-tails and is shallow," and so forth. [82]

The navigability of the Chusovaya was summed up by the administration of the Nizhnii Tagil mining district in these words: "The Chusovaya in its present position and at high water presents so many difficulties and dangers for shipping caravans that not a year passes without a plant owner having several of his boats wrecked." [83] Sometimes the number of wrecked boats was fairly large. Thus, in 1858, eight boats out of the eighty-seven that comprised the caravan of the Nizhnii Tagil plants were wrecked. [84]

The sunken iron from boats wrecked on the Chusovaya was salvaged from the river by specially hired laborers at an extra cost.

Shipping on the Chusovaya required a much larger number of hands than on the Kama. In the caravan of the Bevdinsky plant to Perm, from thirty-six to forty hands worked on each barge and from Perm, on the Kama, twelve hands. [85] The caravan of the Sysertsky plants, when sailing on the Chusovaya, had forty hands on board each barge, and fifteen when going on the Kama. [86]

In the caravan of the Alapaevsky plants, [87] there were seventeen hands on each barge, but in the initial stages of the way from the plant's landing to Perm, nineteen hands of "additionals" joined them.

The cost of shipping from the plant's landing place to Perm was estimated by the administration of the Nizhnii Tagil district to be 7.5 kopecks per pood. [88] Out of this, 3 kopecks went toward the payment of wages to the hands, and the rest went mainly toward the cost of the boat and partly toward the payment of the tolls collected by the government from water transports.

Down the Sylva, which joined the Chusovaya in its lower portion close to its delta, and was notorious for its quiet course, shipping did not involve danger, as was the case on the Chusovaya. The major obstacle there was shallow water.

Down the Belaya system, less iron was shipped than down the Chusovaya, and the Kama region processing plants did not receive any pig iron from there. But, as the figures of Table 1 show, the volume of production of the plants situated there and, consequently, the volume of transportation on the rivers of that system were, nevertheless, very considerable. The plants of this region were situated principally along the banks of mountain rivers smaller than the Chusovaya, but often much more difficult for shipping. These rivers often had stony bottoms, meandering beds, high narrow banks with cliffs jutting into the river, and fast currents. The current of the Yerezan River was three times faster than that of the Chusovya.[89]

The small size and shallowness of the rivers used for shipping necessitated additional loading on the routes mentioned above. Barges were frequently wrecked. Salvaging the sunken iron cost "from 3 to 6 and even 10 kopecks per pood depending upon the depth of the cavity." [90]

The administration of the Serginsky and the Yufaleysky plants wrote in their reply to an inquiry from the Geographical Society that along the Ufa and in the upper regions of the Belaya, navigation was "dangerous on account of shoals and islands covered with water in the spring and because of the meandering course and the rocky banks, so that some boats are wrecked and perish." [91] In the caravans of these plants, for each barge, until the safer places on the Ufa River, there were thirty hands, then to the town of Ufa, twenty-four, and after Ufa, on the Belaya and the Kama, eighteen.[92] In the caravans of the Avsyanopetrovsky plants up to the Tabynsky landing, there had to be forty hands per barge,[93] and after it, eighteen. On the rapid current of the Yurezan to the place of its confluence with the Ufa, the administration of the Yerezansk mining plant put sixty hands on each barge.[94]

The rivers of the Vyatsk basin flowed, generally, across plains, and there were not any special dangers in navigation. Shallowness presented the basic difficulty. But there, too, at the beginning of the voyage, when the boats were sailing in shallow rivers, it became necessary to hire additional hands. Each barge of the Omutninsk plant [95] was assigned sixteen hands for the whole journey, for sailing down the Vyatka River to the town of Vyatka, seven hands were added, but when the boats were sailing down the Omutnaya River from the plant's landing place to the point of confluence of the Omutnaya and the Vyatka, twenty more hands were added.

Sailing on the deep Kama was considerably easier than on its tributaries. Naturally, this required a lesser number of hands, but it had its dangers. Strong winds capable of making a boat capsize were dangerous. When the wind was strong, the caravans stopped by the riverbank and remained there until the spell of bad weather was over. There were accidents when, with a large accumulation of boats, mistakes in control led to collisions between boats. Thus, in May 1853, one of the barges of the Stroganov caravans carrying iron on the Kama rammed into a merchant barge-carrying wheat. Not only did the iron sink, but the ferryman was drowned.

Having reached Laishev, which was situated 60 versts from the Kama's estuary, the caravans stopped in order to prepare for the journey up the Volga. Usually, buyers came to Laishev from places on the Volga below Nizhnii Novgorod. But, since at that time it was not yet clear what level the prices at the fair had reached, the plant owners were afraid to sell too cheaply and the merchants were afraid to pay too much. As a result, in Laishev the demand from provinces to the south was far from being fully satisfied. They received considerable amounts of iron from the Nizhnii Novgorod Fair despite the transportation of the goods over a greater distance. The journey up the Volga was effected from ancient times by means of towing by barge haulers. The norm was 3.5 barge haulers per thousand poods. Consequently, each barge was tugged with ropes by thirty-five hands. In the 1850s and 1860s, the so-called horse-towing machines [96] were widely used on the Volga, and it was with their help that the caravans of iron mainly moved.[97] Furthermore, in the 1850s the practice of towing by tugboat steamers in the transportation of iron began to spread.

On the Volga, apart from the winds, serious obstacles to the movement of caravans were presented by shoals and sandbanks. They were numerous. Some of them enjoyed wide notoriety. One such was the shoal "The Calf Ford" not far from Nizhnii Novgorod. Boats that came up the river to the Nizhnii Novgorod Fair accumulated at this shoal. In 1859, a caravan of the Stroganovs spent several days there because the caravan leader never thought of giving a bribe to the government official who controlled the movements of ships.[98]

The movement of caravans along the waterways from the Urals to Nizhnii Novgorod was performed at varying speeds in different parts of the route. Along the Chusovaya, the shipping took about eight days,[99] that is, the caravans traveled a little over 60 versts a day. On the Kama, they traveled at a speed of about 50 versts a day. On the Volga, the boats traveled considerably more slowly.

The speed of traveling was greatly affected by route conditions and weather. In the absence of obstacles, and with favorable wind, distances several times greater were traversed than with an adverse wind. When the wind was strong, it was necessary to stop.[100] On an average, the journey from the plant's landing place to Nizhnii Novgorod took two months, more often two and a half. The caravans started from landings on the Chusovaya at the end of April, from landings on the Kama and on the tributaries of the Vyatka at the beginning of May, and from landings in the Belaya system in the middle of April. The caravans arrived in Nizhnii Novgorod from the end of June to the first half of July.

The transportation cost of a pood of iron from the plant to Nizhnii Novgorod, inclusive of transportation to the landing construction of barges, the administration of the Nizhnii Tagil mining district evaluated at 21 kopecks (inclusive of costs from Perm to Nizhnii Novgorod, 10 kopecks).[101] Other plant owners give a slightly smaller figure. This is accounted for partly by a more favorable geographical situation of these plants and partly, apparently, by the fact that certain factories did not take into account the cost of the barges.

The sale of iron at the Nizhnii Novgorod Fair, which continued from July 25 to August 25, usually went slowly at the beginning of the fair. Both the sellers and the buyers temporized. The bulk of the iron deals were made toward the end of the fair. This limited considerably the possibility of bringing the iron to the place of consumption by water in the same year. The merchandise of a few plant owners who had offices in different parts of Russia was brought by caravans directly to these places, bypassing the fair.[102]

From Nizhnii Novgorod there were two basic water routes by which iron was shipped: (1) up the Volga and then to St. Petersburg, and (2) up the Oka. The third route, less important, was down the Volga. As has already been said, the demand for iron in the territory favoring from the point of view of transportation the Lower Volga ports was not fully satisfied with the quantity shipped down the Volga from Laishev. The iron from the Nizhnii Novgorod Fair went there too.

From Nizhnii Novgorod, a very large quantity of iron was shipped up the Volga. The transportation of iron from Nizhnii Novgorod to Yaroslavl, the largest center of the iron trade on the Upper Volga, cost, with the use of the "horse-powered machines," 4 to 5 kopecks per pood.[103] Transportation of iron from the plants directly to Yaroslavl, without unloading, and with a second loading at Nizhnii Novgorod, cost a little less. The administration of the Golitsin plants informed the Geographical Society that the transportation of iron from the plants to Yaroslavl cost 15.5 kopecks per pood, with a cost of transportation to Nizhnii Novgorod of 12.5 kopecks.[104] The administration of the Nizhnii Tagil district evaluated the difference in the cost of transportation to Nizhnii Novgorod and to Rybinsk (second in importance in the iron trade of the region) as 4 kopecks per pood.[105] Transportation from Nizhnii to Tver where up to 200,000 poods of iron were distributed, according to the report of the governor of Tver to the Department of Mining, amounted to 10 to 13 kopecks per pood.[106]

Yaroslavl, Rybinsk, and Tver played the leading role in supplying iron to the cottage industry of one of the three original, ancient regions of the metal-working industry in Russia.[107] Within this region there were iron-trading centers of lesser importance. The route to them was along the water systems which joined the Volga with St. Petersburg. These centers were Vesegonsk, Ostashkov, and, partly, Novgorod. An important role in local iron trade was played by the villages of Vakhnova and Pekhteeva situated on the Sheksna about 200 versts from Rybinsk. Iron was brought to Vesegonsk from Yaroslavl.[108] The transportation cost amounted to 10 to 15 kopecks. It was brought from Nizhnii Novgorod, Moscow, and partly from Tver.[109] Transportation from Nizhnii Novgorod to Ostashkov by water cost 15 to 20 kopecks per pood, and from Tver in winter, overland, 8 to 9 kopecks.

Iron was transported to St. Petersburg in the 1850s, mainly along the Mariinsk canal system. The journey from Rybinsk to St. Petersburg took about sixty-five days. Transportation cost was 11 kopecks per pood. Along the Tikhvinsk canal system, the time required for transportation was less by almost half—thirty-five days —but the transportation cost was higher—15 kopecks, and, as a result, little iron was shipped along this system. The Vyshnii Volochek canal system in the 1850s was hardly used at all for the transportation of iron, since boats carrying iron did not take it as far as St. Petersburg in a single trip.[110]

The traveling time from the landings of the plants and St. Petersburg varied depending upon weather conditions and the geographical location of the plants. The administration of the Kholunits mining district calculated the average length of the trip to be from 125 to 135 days; [111] that of the Revdinsk plant from 150 to 168 days; [112] and that of the Yurezan-Ivanovsk plant as five and a half months or more.[113] The caravans carrying iron, having left the landings of the plants in the early spring, reached St. Petersburg in September, or even in October. Sometimes they did not have time to reach St. Petersburg in a single trip and were forced to winter on the way.[114] Thus, the length of the trip approximated that of the eighteenth century.[115]

Iron was also sent from St. Petersburg to the Baltic provinces for export. A considerable amount of it was used by the capital itself.

For the transportation of iron along the Mariinsk canal system, boats of various types were used. The most convenient ones were the *tikhvinska,* which had a loading capacity of about 5000 poods. For shipping directly from the plants, the *Gibezh* type of boat was used, and in such case there was no necessity for reloading at Rybinsk. Along the Tikhvinsk canal system, small *tikhvinskas,* with a loading capacity of 2500 poods were used.[116] Along the

Sheksna, boats were tugged by horses, then boatmen were used; and on the Svir and Neva rivers they were rowed.[117]

Much iron was shipped up the Oka River, where boats were tugged by horses. When iron was shipped to localities along the upper regions of this river, it was loaded in *gusyanki*—flat-bottomed boats up to 210 feet long and up to 49 feet wide, with a loading capacity of up to 30,000 poods. When water was high in the river, they could reach Kaluga with such a load; with water low, they transferred part of the load to boats held in reserve. Above Kaluga, the freight was transported in smaller crafts.[118] The transportation of iron from Nizhnii Novgorod to Kaluga cost from 12 to 15 kopecks per pood.[119]

On the Oka, besides Urals iron, products of the plants beyond Moscow situated along the lower regions of the river were shipped.

Near Kolomna, a considerable part of boats carrying iron up the Moscow River toward Moscow changed course. Because of the shallowness of the Moscow River at Kolomna, the *gusyanki* transferred their freight to boats in reserve, and frequently repeated the operation on the way. Sailing on the Moscow River, as a result of its shallowness, was very slow and, although the distance between Kolomna and Moscow was short (only 38 versts), the trip took from four to six weeks. Frequently, iron from the Nizhnii Novgorod Fair failed to reach Moscow before the end of the navigation season, and the rest of the trip had to be completed by cartage.[120] The expenses for bringing iron from Nizhnii Novgorod to Moscow by water amounted on an average to 10 kopecks per pood.[121] When the rivers froze early, there was an additional charge of 7 to 15 kopecks per pood for transportation by cartage, depending upon the location of the point where transportation by water was interrupted and on the condition of the roads at the time of transport.[122]

The expenses for bringing iron to Moscow from the plants beyond Moscow of the Shepelevs and the Batashovs amounted to 8 to 10 kopecks per pood by water, and from 15 to 20 kopecks by cartage, in winter, and 25 to 35 kopecks in summertime.[123] Moscow played a prominent role in the iron trade. Loginov, an official of the Department of Mining, sent to make a study of trade conditions at the Nizhnii Novgorod Fair, wrote in his report to the minister of finance as follows: "After the Nizhnii Novgorod Fair, Moscow constitutes one of the important points for the export of iron to the provinces in the interior." [124] From Moscow, Moscow province received its iron, as well as the adjacent parts of Tula, Kaluga, and Smolensk provinces; Eastern Byelorussia also received part of its iron from Moscow. Much iron was used also in Moscow itself. The amount of iron coming to Moscow, according to incomplete data, exceeded 600,000 poods.

Part of the iron transported up the Oka was unloaded at Aleksin, and was then sent to Tula in carts. The transportation of iron from the Nizhnii Novgorod Fair to Tula, according to the statistics of the administration of the Nizhnii Tagil district, cost 10 kopecks per pood. [125] The mayor of Tula reported to the Department of Mining somewhat higher figures: for transportation by water to Aleksin, 10 to 15 kopecks per pood, and from Aleksin to Tula overland, 2 kopecks in winter, and 5 kopecks or more in the fall when the iron arrived from the fair. [126]

Tula was one of the secondary centers of the iron trade, but nevertheless its turnover in this trade was considerable. The iron supplied the needs of the metal-working industry of this region, and was distributed to the cartage points and to towns and localities commercially dependent on Tula. The import of iron to Tula was estimated by the mayor to amount to 90,000 poods a year. [127]

The iron brought along the Oka to Kaluga was stored there to await the opening of the sled route, at which time the bulk was transported to Bryansk at a fee of 12 to 15 kopecks per pood. [128] In the spring, it was shipped from Bryansk down the Desna and then down the Dnieper; the same route was followed by the bulk of the product of the Maltsevs' plants situated at a distance of two to six versts from the Bolva, a tributary of the Desna. [129] The part of the iron shipped down the Desna was sold on the way in Chernigov province, where the centers of the iron trade were Nezhin (yearly import of iron was 23,000 poods), and Chernigov (yearly import, 19,000 poods), [130] while the major part of the iron was earmarked for Kiev. The import of iron to Kiev province exceeded half a million poods; the major part went through Kiev, and only a comparatively small portion was shipped at once below Kiev. This iron was brought only a year after its dispatch from the Nizhnii Novgorod Fair to Kiev, a former big center of the iron trade in the Ukraine, and its transportation from the fair cost 30 kopecks per pood.[131]

The iron that was shipped down the Volga from Laishev and from the Nizhnii Novgorod Fair went mainly to two points: Dubovka and Astrakhan. A part of it was sold from the boats along the way. Among these landings, an iron trade of considerable size was conducted at Simbirsk and especially at Saratov. About 60,000 poods of iron arrived annually at Simbirsk, and was from there distributed by cartage throughout the territory commercially dependent on Simbirsk. Shipping on the Volga was cheap and cost 5 kopecks per pood from the Nizhnii Novgorod Fair, and 3 kopecks per pood from Laishev.[132]

Saratov imported annually about 125,000 poods of iron,[133] mainly from the Nizhnii Novgorod Fair. The transport cost was 5 kopecks per pood. From Saratov, iron was distributed in carts throughout the Saratov province and part of it went to Penza and Tambov provinces which imported iron from plants beyond Moscow.

Kazan, although situated close to Laishev, imported iron, mainly from the Nizhnii Novgorod Fair, and only partially from Laishev.[134] Transportation from Kazan to Laishev was cheaper than from Nizhnii Novgorod by 2 kopecks per pood.[135] The insignificant difference in the transport costs and the hopes of the buyers to buy cheaper and of the merchants to sell dearer at the Nizhnii Novgorod Fair explain why the merchants of the Volga region preferred buying iron from the Nizhnii Novgorod Fair to buying at Laishev.

Astrakhan imported yearly about 250,000 poods of iron. In Astrakhan province itself, less than one-tenth of this amount remained; about 180,000 poods was exported to Iran and to the Khanates of Central Asia, and about 140,000 poods by way of the Caspian Sea to Transcaucasia.[136]

The greater part of the iron that was shipped down the Volga was unloaded at Dubovka. Almost all of this iron was transported by oxen in the summer or at the beginning of the fall to the landing of Kachalinsk on the Don. As a result of the shortage of timber on the Don, disassembled boats were also brought there, where they were reassembled, and then, loaded with iron, they went to Rostov-on-Don and the adjacent Nakhichevan.[137] At the beginning of the 1850s, about 475,000 poods [138] were imported there yearly, and the transportation from Laishev cost 15 kopecks per pood.[139] Thus these two towns, which economically constituted one whole, were one of the largest centers in the iron trade. From there iron was distributed in the south and the southeast of Russia, and was shipped to Transcaucasia for export.

Of the total amount of iron imported by Rostov-on-Don and Nakhichevan, about one-seventh remained within the boundaries of the Don Army District,[140] and of the remaining amount, one-third was exported to Turkey and the Levant, and two-thirds was distributed by sea to the ports of the Black and the Azov seas and were sent in carts to Kharkov, Ekaterinoslav province, and the steppe north of the Caucacus. The export was done entirely by sea. More than one-half of the iron traded by Rostov and Nakhichevan in the domestic market was transported by sea.[141]

Cartage was usually done with oxen and, in contradistinction to Central and North Russia, it very often cost much less in summer than in winter, because in summer the oxen fed mainly on pasture in the spacious, virgin steppes, across which the oxcarts traveled with iron; and short winter and frequent thaws often interfered with the making of good sled roads.

On the Left Bank Ukraine, together with the adjacent regions of the Ukrainian steppe and the central black-earth provinces, Kharkov was the main center of iron trade.[142]

Kharkov imported yearly about 150,000 to 200,000 poods of iron.[143] The greater part (approximately three-fourths to four-fifths) was brought from the Nizhnii Novgorod Fair and partly from the plants beyond Moscow.[144] The rest came from Rostov-on-Don, from which oxen did the transporting.

The iron from Nizhnii Novgorod was shipped down the Oka and the Zusha and reached the city of Mtsensk in Orlov province in October. There, it was necessary to wait for the opening of the sled road, and then the iron was transported to Kharkov, a distance of several hundred versts by horses.[145] Transportation from Nizhnii Novgorod to Kharkov cost 25 to 32 kopecks per pood; from the plants beyond Moscow, 26 to 30 kopecks,[146] and from Rostov-on-Don, 15 to 20 kopecks.[147]

Kharkov served as a wholesale market for Kharkov province and for the major part of Poltava, Kursk, and Tavrida provinces.[148] Ekaterinoslav and Kherson provinces were supplied principally from Rostov-on-Don. But a part of the merchandise was imported from Kharkov, and all transportation was effected by cartage.

Among the Black Sea ports it was Odessa, a fairly large local center in iron trading, that imported most iron. The amount of yearly import was about 100,000 poods.[149] Nine-tenths was brought by sea from Rostov-on-Don and the rest was brought from Kharkov, and was also shipped down the Dnieper as far as Kherson, from where it went by sea to Odessa. Shipping down the Dnieper over the rapids often entailed great difficulties. It was transported from Kharkov and Kherson when and if the supplies of iron brought from Rostov were exhausted and the prices rose.[150]

Transportation of iron from Rostov cost 1 to 5 kopecks per pood; from Kharkov in the summer, 30 to 35 kopecks, and in the winter, 60 kopecks.[151] From Odessa, a small quantity of iron was exported to Turkey,[152] and a considerable amount went to Bessarabia,[153] partly by sea to its coastal localities, but mainly by cartage. The main part of the iron that came to Odessa was distributed within Kherson province.

The western provinces of European Russia, from the point of view of transportation costs of iron, were in an especially unfavorable situation. They not only were situated far from the Urals, but —with the exception of the Baltic provinces—had almost no waterways which could be used for the transportation of iron.

In the Baltic provinces, Riga was the center of the iron trade. It imported yearly about 140,000 poods.[154] The iron came mainly from St. Petersburg, from where the transportation was made by sea and cost 4 to 5 kopecks per pood. Apart from this, iron was brought from the Nizhnii Novgorod Fair along a fairly complicated route. The iron was shipped up the Oka as far as Kaluga, from where in winter it was transported to the town of Bely in the province of Smolensk, on a landing on the Obsha River, which flowed into the Mezhya River (a tributary of the Western Dvina), and was then shipped to Riga. Transportation from Nizhnii Novgorod to Bely cost 15 to 20 kopecks per pood and from there to Riga, 10 to 15 kopecks. From the Maltsevs' plants in winter, iron was brought to the landing of Porechia on the Kasplya River, a tributary of the Western Dvina, and even in spring it was shipped to Riga by water.

The Riga merchants purchased part of the iron in Finland. Before the abolition of the customs frontier between the Kingdom of Poland and Russia, iron from Riga was imported in considerable quantities by Kurland and Kovno, Grodno and Vilna provinces. After the abolition of the customs frontier in 1851, these provinces began to import Polish iron. Its quality was inferior to that of the Urals, but it was much cheaper. It was imported by cartage. This competition cut down the size of the region that was supplied with iron from Riga.

Byelorussia imported its iron mainly from the Ural plants. It was purchased in Nizhnii Novgorod and transported by water to Kaluga, from where it was taken on sleds in winter at a cost of 35 to 60 kopecks per pood (depending upon the road conditions and the cost of oats), to Minsk,[155] and at 50 kopecks to Bobruisk.[156] The iron from the Maltsevs' plants came there by sled routes. Transportation to Broisovo cost 35 kopecks per pood.[157] The iron went to Pinsk by water, and the cost of transportation was 15 kopecks per pood.[158] Upon the liquidation of the customs line between the Kingdom of Poland and Russia, Polish iron began to be imported to Western Byelorussia by cartage. The transportation cost 30 kopecks per pood to Minsk and 70 kopecks to Bobruisk.

Eastern Byelorussia imported part of the iron from Moscow as well. The cost of transportation of one pood of iron from Moscow to Mogilev amounted in winter to 40 kopecks, and in summer, to 75 kopecks.[159]

As we have said, the Right Bank Ukraine imported iron from Kiev by cartage. The transportation cost amounted to 2 to 20 kopecks per pood for each 100 versts.[160] After 1851, Polish iron too began to penetrate there.

The north of European Russia had its own metallurgy. There were plants which shipped iron down the Sysol and the Vychegda. They supplied metal to the eastern parts of Vologda and Archangel provinces. Transportation from landing places of the plants to Velikii-Ustyug cost 6 kopecks and to Archangel 10 kopecks per pood.[161] From Archangel a small quantity of iron was exported. Transportation from Archangel to the district towns of the same province was effected by sea, along the rivers, and by cartage. The cost of transportation of one pood of iron was as follows: to Kema in summer, by water, 12 kopecks, in winter on sleds, 48.5 kopecks; to Mezen in summer, by sea, 10 kopecks, in winter by cartage, 25 kopecks.[162]

The western part of Vologoda province imported metal in the winter from Yaroslavl. Transportation to Vologoda cost 10 to 15 kopecks per pood.[163] Especially expensive was the transport of iron to Transcaucasia and to Siberia.

Eastern Transcaucasia imported iron from the Nizhnii Novgorod Fair. Transportation from Nizhnii Novgorod to Astrakhan cost 8 to 10 kopecks per pood, from Astrakhan to Baku by sea, 6 to 10 kopecks more. From Baku, the iron was distributed by sea to coastal points. This was comparatively inexpensive, for example to Lenkoran it was 8 to 10 kopecks. But transportation to the interior of the country was extremely expensive. The merchandise was transported up the Kura River to Mingchaur. Then one had to use carts. The cost of transportation was as follows: to Shusha, 35 to 45 kopecks; to Tiflis, 40 to 50 kopecks; [164] and to Telava, 50 to 70 kopecks per pood.[165] The Erivan merchants purchased iron in Tiflis and paid 45 kopecks per pood for transportation.[166]

Western Transcaucasia was supplied with iron from Rostov-on-Don. The merchandise was shipped by sea to Redut-Kala in September and October, then it was distributed in Abkhasia and western Georgia. In western Transcaucasia, land transport was also expensive, especially in mountainous regions. Transportation from Redut-Kala to the city of Akhaltsi cost 50 to 60 kopecks per pood.[167]

In Siberia, there were small government plants; their production supplied principally the needs of the state, and only a small portion of it was marketed. Thus, the demand for iron of the population of Siberia was satisfied by the Ural plants. The merchandise was transported partly from Ekaterinburg, a trade center in the Urals, from which the annual import was up to 150,000 poods, but more came from the Irbit Fair (the yearly import was about 350,000 poods).[168] The iron had to be transported over very long distances, and, naturally, the transportation cost frequently exceeded the price of iron in the Urals. According to the reports of the local administration, transportation from Irbit to Tumen was

10 kopecks; to Tobolsk, 15 to 17 kopecks; to Omsk, 25 to 30 kopecks; to Krasnoyarsk from 1 ruble, 30 kopecks to 1 ruble, 50 kopecks. Transportation from Ekaterinburg to Irkutsk cost from 1 ruble, 50 kopecks to 3 rubles per pood.[169]

Thus, the transportation costs in the iron trade for the greater part of the localities of Russia were very considerable, while the turnover was very slow. In the best instances, there was a capital turnover once a year, but very often only once in two years. With the rising cost of credit, there was a steep rise in prices.

Both the geography of prices for iron and a comparison between the transportation expenses and the selling price of iron at the production sites are significant. Local administration, upon request from the commission mentioned above, sent in much material pertaining to local prices for iron. Analyzing the data on prices, it must be taken into account that this information is far from being always accurate, and is frequently inaccurate, of course, in the numerous reports on the transportation expenses cited above. An exception, apparently, are the figures of the transportation costs given by the administration of the Nizhnii Tagil plants, based on the data from their books. Furthermore, one must not forget that the same kind of iron, even from the Ural plants, often had a different market price, since some plants produced a better quality metal than others, and this depended mainly upon the quality of the ore.

Iron manufactured from the ore of the famous Vysokii Mountain always had a higher value than that obtained from the ores of the majority of other localities. In Moscow, in September 1851, bar iron from the Nizhnii Tagil district of the Demidovs cost 1 ruble, 50 kopecks per pood, that from the plants of the heirs of Yakovlev, 1 ruble, 25 kopecks, and that from the rest of the plants cost from 1 ruble to 1 ruble, 20 kopecks. Furthermore, the Ural iron was priced higher than that from other regions. In Vokna, in September 1851, the Maltsevs' iron was sold at 1 ruble, 70 kopecks per pood, Polish iron for 1 ruble, 80 kopecks, and Urals iron at 2 rubles, 10 kopecks per pood.[170]

The local administration, reporting prices for iron, only occasionally indicated exactly the plant whose prices were being quoted. It is very possible that, in many cases, average prices were quoted, but, apparently, they were the prices of iron of those plants whose production was sold mainly at a given locality. Distinction is not always made between the original and the resale price. On the other hand, the lowest and the highest prices are often indicated: for example, from 1 ruble, 20 kopecks to 1 ruble, 30 kopecks. All this makes one consider information on the sale price of iron only approximate.

Data on the sale price of iron at the plants are scarce in the sources. Apart from this, the price level was determined at the Nizhnii Novgorod Fair. It was not by accident that the administration of the Nizhnii Tagil plants, in order to determine the sale price of iron, at the plant, omitted consideration of the actual price which it obtained selling the iron of the plant, but calculated it by subtracting from the price obtained at the Nizhnii Novgorod Fair, the transportation and other expenses connected with the sale of merchandise at the fair.[171]

It is to be regretted that the price of iron at the Nizhnii Tagil plants cannot be considered the average price for iron in the Urals since the iron there was known to be more expensive. The most practical method to determine the average selling price of iron at the plants of the Urals is to calculate it according to the method used by the administration of the Nizhnii Tagil district. According to the reports of the Nizhnii Novgorod governor, the average price for bar iron at the Nizhnii Novgorod Fair at the beginning of the 1850s was 1 ruble, 10 kopecks.[172] The administration of the Nizhnii Tagil plants determined the cost of transportation of iron from their plants to Nizhnii Novgorod to be 21 kopecks. This gives a conditional average selling price in the Urals of 80 kopecks.

In Ekaterinburg the price per pood of bar iron was 1 ruble.[173] The transportation of iron here from the Nizhnii Tagil plants cost 8 kopecks per pood;[174] from the Alapaevsk and the Kyshtymak plants, 6 kopecks; and from the Verkhne-Isetsk, 1 kopeck.[175] It follows that, according to this data, the conditional, average price at the plant was 92 to 99 kopecks a pood. But it must be taken into consideration that the price of iron at the Nizhnii Tagil, the Alapaevsk, and the Verkhne-Isetsk plants was considerably higher on the market than the average price of Urals iron. This permits one to make an assertion that the selling price of the Urals bar iron at the place of production, on an average, did not exceed 90 kopecks a pood.[176]

Table 3 shows clearly the dependence of iron prices on the

distance of the point of export from the Urals and on transportation conditions. Even at the Nizhnii Novgorod Fair, which was connected with the Urals by a continuous waterway, the price exceeded the price in the Urals by 22 percent. The price in St. Petersburg, where the iron was brought over a very long but nevertheless continuous waterway, was higher by 35 percent that that of the Urals. In Kiev, where iron was brought first by water, then by cartage, and then again by water, and where it arrived only the following year, its price exceeded the price of the place of production by 78 percent.

TABLE 3

AVERAGE SELLING PRICES OF BAR IRON IN DIFFERENT LOCALITIES
IN RUSSIA IN SEPTEMBER 1851

Nizhnii Novgorod	1 rb., 10 kop.	Khotin	2 rbs.
Yaroslavl	1 rb., 15 kop.	Velikii-Ustyug	1 rb., 7 kop.
Tver	1 rb., 28 kop.	Baku	1 rb., 30 kop.
	1 rb., 35 kop.	Tiflis	2 rbs.
St. Petersburg	1 rb., 25 kop.	Erivan	2 rb., 50 kop.
Moscow	1 rb., 20 kop.	Telav	2 rb., 60 kop.
Kaluga	1 rb., 20 kop.	Redut-Kala	1 rb., 50 kop.
Tula	1 rb., 18 kop.	Akhalitzikh	2 rb., 20 kop.
Kiev	1 rb., 60 kop.	Irbit	1 rb., 20 kop.
Saratov	1 rb., 15 kop.	Tumen	1 rb., 30 kop.
Rostov-on-Don	1 rb., 20 kop.	Tomsk	1 rb., 75 kop.
Kharkov	1 rb., 45 kop.	Krasnoyarsk	2 rb., 80 kop.
Ekateroslav	1 rb., 85 kop.	Irkutsk	2 rb., 95 kop.
Stavropol (Caucasus)	1 rb., 70 kop.	Kursk	1 rb., 57 kop.
Pyatigorsk	1 rb., 90 kop.	Pskov	1 rb., 50 kop.
Odessa	1 rb., 50 kop.	Bely (Smolensk	
Minsk	1 rb., 60 kop.	province)	1 rb., 43 kop.
Kamenetz-Podolsk	2 rbs.	Vyatka	1 rb., 4 kop.

SOURCE: Ts.G.I.A.L., Folio 46, Register 1, File 1, pp. 224–33.

In Western Byelorussia, the Right Bank Ukraine, and in Bessarabia, where the iron, after a lengthy journey by water, was taken a long distance by carts, the prices were two or more times higher than in the Urals. The role of cartage transportation in the rise in the price for iron is well shown by prices in the Caucasus and also in Krasnoyarsk and Irkutsk. In Irkutsk the price of bar iron sometimes reached 5 rubles per pood.[177]

The price for iron in the localities that were distant from the Urals was determined not only by the cost of transportation, but also by the length of time necessary for the transportation of the merchandise. Furthermore, in localities far from the Urals and from Nizhnii Novgorod, wholesale prices were often those of the first or the second sale and, at times, even of the third sale. The influence these factors exercised is clearly shown in Table 3. It shows that, for Moscow, St. Petersburg, Tula, Kaluga, and Rostov-on-Don, the difference between the sale price and the cost of transportation of iron from the Urals was approximately equal to the selling price of iron at the Ural plants. A small deviation of 1 or 2 kopecks per pood is explained by the inexactness of the data on the prices from which the table was constructed. For Bobruisk, Kiev, Kharkov, Odessa, Tiflis, and Erivan, this difference is greater, and it cannot be regarded as the result of inaccuracies in statistics. It shows the role played by the above-mentioned factors.

B. B. Kafengauz, in his valuable work, *History of the Demidov Economy,* cites the data supplied by the Demidovs on the cost of iron in the eighteenth century from Nizhnii Tagil to Kazan, Nizhnii Novgorod, Yaroslavl, Tver, Moscow, and St. Petersburg, on the selling price of the Demidovs' bar iron in these places, and calculates the ratio between the two figures.

It is of interest to compare the data supplied by Kafengauz with the relevant figures of the 1850s in the Nizhnii Tagil mining district which continued to be Demidov property.

In the 1850s, the Demidovs did not export iron [178] to Yaroslavl and Tver. Furthermore, I have not found any information [179] concerning the price at which Moscow and St. Petersburg provide the data for a full comparison, while Moscow and Kazan do that for a partial comparison only. This ratio is shown in Table 4. It indicates that, in the course of a hundred years, both the price of iron and the transportation costs increased considerably.[180]

The transportation costs increased more than the price of iron, despite the use in the 1850s of horse-powered machines, which did

TABLE 4

Place of Export	Wholesale Price of Bar Iron per Pood	Cost of Transportation from the Urals *	Percent Above the Selling Price	The Difference Between the Wholesale Price and the Cost of Transportation
Nizhnii Novgorod	1 rb., 10 kop.	20 kop.	18	90 kop.
Moscow	1 rb., 20 kop.	30 kop.	25	90 kop.
St. Petersburg	1 rb., 25 kop.	35 kop.	28	90 kop.
Tula	1 rb., 18 kop.	30 kop.	25	88 kop.
Kaluga	1 rb., 20 kop.	32 kop.	27	88 kop.
Rostov-on-Don	1 rb., 20 kop.	29 kop.	24	91 kop.
Bobruisk	1 rb., 80 kop.	83 kop.	46	97 kop.
Kiev	1 rb., 50 kop.	50 kop.	33	1 rb.
Kharkov	1 rb., 45 kop.	44 kop.	30	1 rb., 1 kop.
Odessa	1 rb., 50 kop.	41 kop.	27	1 rb., 9 kop.
Tiflis	2 rbs.	74/92 kop.	37/46	1 rb., 8 kop.
Erivan	2 rbs., 50 kop.	1 rb., 19 kop.	48/54	1 rb., 24 kop.
				1 rb., 14 kop.

* The transportation cost from the Urals to Nizhnii Novgorod is taken, for the sake of greater precision, to be 1 kopeck lower than that supplied by the Nizhnii Tagil plants, since the majority of the Ural plants were situated somewhat closer to the ports than those plants.

TABLE 5

Points of Export	Transportation Cost of a Pood of Iron from Nizhnii Tagil (in kopecks)		Transportation Cost in the Nineteenth Century, Taking into Account the Eighteenth-Century Data for 100 Years.	Selling Price of a Pood of Bar Iron (in kopecks)		Selling Prices in the Nineteenth Century, Taking into Account the Data of the Eighteenth Century for 100 Years.	Transportation Percentage of the Selling Price	
	In the 1740s	In the 1850s		In the 1740s	In the 1850s		In the 1740s	In the 1850s
Kazan	2.75	16	580	50	?	?	5,5	?
Nizhnii Novgorod	3.5	21	600	50	1,37	274	7,0	15,3
Moscow	8.25	31	375	52	?	?	16,0	?
St. Petersburg	11.5	36	313	60	1,50	250	19,0	24,0

not exist in the eighteenth century, and despite the beginning of the use of steamships. The transportation costs were basically determined by the expenditure for wages of the hands and of shipbuilders. This expenditure depended upon the prices of agricultural products. Prices for the agricultural products rose faster than the prices for industrial products.

Thus, in prereform Russia, the role played by transportation costs in the formation of local prices for iron had a tendency to grow in importance. Only the development of steam navigation and the building of railways in the postreform period changed the situation radically. The extremely high price of iron in the western parts of Russia and in the Caucasus and in Siberia made possible the preservation there of a primitive way of making iron in archaic furnaces directly from the ore, without passing it through the pig-iron stage. This was how Russia obtained iron prior to the appearance in the first half of the seventeenth century of metallurgical manufacturing plants. In the eighteenth century, with the burgeoning of Russian metallurgy, these archaic furnaces were very nearly liquidated. However, in the above-mentioned localities, they survived almost until the fall of serfdom. In the 1850s, these archaic furnaces still existed in Volynia,[181] in the province of Grodno,[182] in the Rachinsk region of Western Georgia,[183] in Dagestan,[184] in Yeniseysk,[185] and in Yakutia.[186] It is true that the total quantity of iron obtained in this way in the 1850s amounted only to 15 percent of the total of forged iron in Russia.

Transportation conditions clearly underlined the question of the necessity for organizing ferrous metallurgy in the Donets Basin. Attempts to organize it were made more than once by the government as early as the end of the eighteenth century, and throughout the first half of the nineteenth century.

The geography of the iron market shows very clearly the role played by transportation in the economic backwardness of prereform Russia.

V

In the early 1950s Soviet historical scholars engaged in debates on the nature and timing of the Industrial Revolution in Russia. The concluding consensus was that it began not in Stalin's 1930s or Witte's 1890s or even at the time of the 1861 serf emancipation (when capitalism began in Russia, according to the Soviet view), but in the early years of the reign of Nicholas I. They were able to justify their claims by avoiding quantitative data, and by adhering to a very circumscribed and qualitative Marxian definition of the Industrial Revolution—not the transformation of the Russian economy from an agricultural to an industrial base, but rather the appearance of new forms of industrial organization and technology in the "feudal" agrarian society of prereform Russia. This was an important discovery in itself, which revealed new facts from the archives. Yatsunsky's article summarizes the main conclusions of this debate, and presents his own thesis, based on the same type of re-

search. It first was published in Voprosy Istorii [*Problems of History*] *1952, no. 12, pp. 48–70, and is reprinted here minus the ritualistic incantations to Stalin required of Soviet historians at the time.*

V. K. YATSUNSKY

The Industrial Revolution in Russia

M. F. Zlotnikov touches upon the question of the Industrial Revolution in Russia in his article, "From the Manufacturing Enterprise to the Factory." [1] This article is devoted, basically, to criticism of the industrial statistics before the reforms. Only a few pages are devoted to the question of the Industrial Revolution in Russia; the author could not have made a study of this question, but could only touch upon it. Zlotnikov believed that "the Industrial Revolution continued for several decades and made very slow progress, especially before the period of the reforms."

Zlotnikov attempted to trace the history of the mechanization of Russian industry from the 1830s to the 1850s. He traced the dynamics of the importation of machinery into Russia from 1824 to 1860 on the basis of the customs statistics, cited a few instances of the construction of machinery in Russian enterprises, and made a table of the increase in the number of mechanized factories and plants, of the workmen employed there, and of the total of the production during the period 1851–1865. Finally, Zlotnikov attempted to total the power potential of industry of Moscow province in 1842 and 1857.

S. G. Strumilin published in 1944 a small (48 pages) book entitled *The Industrial Revolution in Russia*. He begins this study with a short characterization of the Industrial Revolution in England. Then, the author analyzes the mechanization of industry in Russia before the reforms. He draws a statistical comparison between the import of cotton in England from 1750 to 1820 and in Russia from 1819 to 1869. He considers weaving in Russia of cotton textiles by hand and with machinery in 1866 and compares the import dynamics with the home production of machinery in Russia. On the basis of these facts, Strumilin arrives at the conclusion that "Whichever way we date the initial and the final moments of the Industrial Revolution in England and in Russia, the *turning points* are approximately the years 1770–1800 in England and, in Russia, very approximately, the years 1830–1860." [2] This lagging behind England, in the opinion of Strumilin, "took place, no doubt, because of the prevalence of serfdom in Russia but, as it disintegrated, the tempo of the transformation grew and took place here, despite serfdom, on a much greater scale. But such retarded transformation was only instrumental in making it work on a larger scale than was possible in English conditions of the eighteenth century, but, in any case, not less violently." [3] Thus, contrary to the opinion of Zlotnikov, who stresses the slow progress of the transformation of manufacturing plants before the reforms into factories, Strumilin believes that this transformation developed very fast.

S. G. Strumilin also analyzes the economic conditions in which industry was developing before the reforms and considers, partly, certain aspects of the dynamics of this industry. In addition, he investigates the disintegration of manufacturing and the dynamics of productivity of labor in Russia before the reforms. The rapid growth of the productivity of labor in the years 1845–1863 proves, in the opinion of Strumilin, that it was in those years that the Industrial Revolution in Russia was taking place.

Strumilin indicated in his work that the history of the Industrial Revolution had to be studied branch by branch. However, he limited himself to a brief consideration of the industrial question as a whole, and a fleeting excursion into the history of cotton spinning and weaving.

A detailed analysis of the works of S. G. Strumilin has already been made by me and there is no need to repeat it here.[4] Two remarks will suffice. Strumilin, on the basis of significantly richer material than Zlotnikov and, to be sure, to a fully sufficiently convincing degree, showed that the Industrial Revolution in Russia began as early as the period of serfdom. But the extent of the organizational changes that took place in Russian industry in the 1840s and 1850s is overestimated by him.

Strumilin, as he himself points out in the introduction,[5] was not aiming at making a study, even in outline, of the whole history of the Industrial Revolution in Russia. He wished only to put this problem before scholars on the basis of factual material; and that he has achieved. His work, abundant in facts and ideas, attracted the attention of wide circles of Soviet historians and economists. But, despite the fact that Strumilin's book attracted attention, nonetheless, after its publication, there came out only a few short articles on individual aspects of the subject.[6]

Thus, the question of the Industrial Revolution in Russia has been posed in our scientific literature, but very little has been done as yet to solve it. Actually, only the fact that the Industrial Revolution began before the reforms and ended in the postreform period can be considered firmly established.

I now pass on to a concrete study of the history of the Industrial Revolution in Russia. For this purpose, I shall have to make a study which applies to Russia the characteristics cited above typical for the technical and social aspects of the Industrial Revolution. I shall confine myself to but a brief analysis of the course of the Industrial Revolution in the two large branches of industry that had a great significance for the national economy: one, progressive, the cotton industry, and one that was backward, ferrous metallurgy. In this way I wish to give at least a very general idea of my proposed method of branch-by-branch investigation. In addition, I will present a sketch of the possible solution of the question.

A systematic and not just sporadic use of machinery in Russian industry began even before the period of reforms in different branches of industry and at different times. It was the development of manufacturing enterprises which applied fairly widely the division of labor principle that paved the way for the introduction of machinery.

It is interesting to note the wide use in manufacturing plants, before the reforms, of the waterwheel and horsepower for the operation of various mechanisms in several branches of the manufacturing industry.

For metallurgy, both ferrous and nonferrous, the mechanization of certain industrial processes by means of the waterwheel had been in use for some time and had had wide application long before the nineteenth century. But the application of horsepower in the wool, linen, cotton print, and sugar industries is typical precisely of the decades before the reforms. Archive material permits one to form a fairly clear picture of these initial steps of the Industrial Revolution.

During the period before the reforms, the steam engine began to take root as a motive power. Mechanization took root more readily with free labor than with the enterprises which employed forced labor. In the first case, more progressive industrial relationship made the progress of the productive forces more rapid, while, in the second case, the backward industrial relationships retarded it. There were individual exceptions to this rule. For instance, Volkov, an estate owner, contrived to organize, with serf labor, a model cotton factory, from the technical point of view, in Gorenki in the district of Moscow that became widely known. But there were not many such cases.

In Russian industry before the reforms, a leading role was played by the technically progressive cotton industry, which employed almost exclusively free labor. Despite this, its history has not been studied extensively by the historians of our national economy. In this branch of industry it was the technical reorganization that began first. But it started in different stages of the industrial process. As is generally known, the cotton industry consists of three basic parts: spinning, weaving, and printing and decoration.

The development of the cotton industry in Russia began as

early as the eighteenth century with printing of imported calico. In the eighteenth century, cotton weaving from imported calico came into existence also. Both processes, weaving and printing, with decoration, had existed for a long time in the form of small-scale merchandise production and manufacturing plants.

Cotton spinning was the last to appear. It came to Russia in the form of a mechanized factory industry [7] without having previously passed through the stages of the small merchandise industry and manufacturing enterprise. It is generally known that the first cotton spinning factory in Russia was the government-controlled Alexandrovsk manufacturing plant. It played an important part in the history of Russian cotton spinning. But this role has hardly been studied yet; and its rich archives have not interested researchers with the exception of E. A. Zeitlin who, however, studied not cotton but linen spinning in this plant.

The Alexandrovsk plant came into being in 1798. It expanded its activities in the first half of the first decade of the nineteenth century. This plant at first used the so-called "jenny," which was put in motion with horsepower and waterwheel. But very soon it went on to more perfected steam-operated spinning machines.

At first, the yarn was of an inferior quality, and merchants, trading in yarn in the central industrial region, did not want to buy it. But gradually, matters improved. In the archives there has been preserved an interesting table which sums up the dynamics of the productivity of labor in cotton spinning at the Alexandrovsk plant. According to this data, taking one-man productivity per day in 1805 as a unit, in 1810 productivity already expanded by the figure 2.5, in 1820 by the figure 7, in 1830 with 14, and in 1841 with 22. Parallel with this grew the production of thread per pood of cotton. [8]

Even before the Great Patriotic War of 1812 there appeared, principally in Moscow, a series of private mechanical cotton mills. [9] During the Moscow fire in 1812, the Moscow cotton mills perished. After the Great Patriotic War of 1812, for a whole decade there exists no data in our archives on cotton-mill enterprises.

In the 1820s, private cotton mills reappear anew. Data concerning their production in 1828 has been preserved. The nine cotton mills in existence in that year together produced less yarn than the Alexandrovsk plant alone. Without a doubt, the latter was superior to them as regards quality of the product. All these enterprises also turned out to be short-lived.

Thus, before the 1830s, cotton spinning in Russia was done mainly by the Alexandrovsk plant. In the 1830s, the Volkov factory, already mentioned, which was built in 1828, began to develop its work, but it did not actually change the situation. Only in the second half of the 1830s did things change: in St. Petersburg three large, private cotton mills were established. The largest of them was the Russian cotton-spinning plant with a capital of 3.5 million paper rubles. In the Leningrad district archive, a fairly rich deposit for this factory has been preserved. This joint-stock enterprise was founded by the manager of the Alexandrovsk plant and several St. Petersburg merchants.[10] Among the stockholders, there were prominent representatives of St. Petersburg's bourgeoisie and high-ranking bureaucrats (for example, Nesselrode). Of the two other cotton mills, one inferior in size to the above-mentioned factory, was founded by Baron Stieglitz,[11] a well-known banker and businessman of that time, and the other one by Maltsev, also a well-known businessman and estate owner, who soon sold it to merchants.[12]

These three factories existed until the time of the Great October Socialist Revolution, when they were nationalized.

New cotton mills also appeared in Moscow province. The most important of them was established in 1835 in the Dmitrievsk district: it was the factory of Lepyoshkin which was named, later on, "the Voznesensk plant." Thus, in the second half of the 1830s, the Alexandrovsk plant retreats far into the background.

In the 1840s, especially beginning in the second half, a new stage in the history of the Russian cotton-spinning industry begins. The owners of the weaving and printing enterprises in the central industrial region began to build cotton-spinning factories: the Khlyudovs, the Morozovs, the Malyutins, and the Konshins in the Moscow district, and the Garelins in Ivanovo. A series of new cotton-spinning factories appear at the same time in St. Petersburg.

Beginning with 1846, the import of thread rapidly decreased. The import of cotton, which exceeded the import of thread for the first time in 1845, was rapidly growing. Already in the 1850s, the cotton-weaving enterprises in Russia used mostly Russian thread.

Thus, the birth of mechanical cotton spinning took place at the very beginning of the nineteenth century in the form of government enterprises. Mechanical cotton spinning acquired a great significance for the national economy beginning with the second half of the 1830s. Even ten years before the peasant reforms, it had begun, basically, to supply the needs of Russian industry.

In the cotton-printing business that began to develop in Russia in the form of manufacturing plants and small merchandise production, mechanization began at the enterprises of the St. Petersburg capitalists Weber and Bethpage where, in the second half of the first decade of the nineteenth century, cotton-printing machines were installed. These enterprises were considered to be, technically, the most accomplished cotton-printing enterprises in Russia in those days. At the end of the 1820s, cotton-printing machines began to spread at the chintz manufacturing plants of the Moscow region, whose products were slightly inferior to those from St. Petersburg, but were superior to those of Ivanovo. At Ivanovo the first cotton-printing machine was installed in 1828 at the manufacturing plant of Spridonov. In the 1830s, cotton printing spread, comparatively slowly. An Alsatian, Steinback, one of the founders of the Moscow firm Tsindel, which later became widely known, characterized, in the *Bulletins of the Industrial Society of Mulhouse,* cotton production in Russia in the end of the 1830s with these words: "Printing of cotton by hand and its engraving have achieved great perfection, but the author was astonished by the slow diffusion of printing machines." [13]

Printing by hand began to diminish beginning with the second half of the 1830s, but it still existed in the middle of the 1850s, not only in a series of small, technically backward manufacturing plants, but also in certain large, technically well-equipped enterprises, for example in the joint-stock Tsarevsk cotton manufactury, which used steam machinery and had an output worth about half a million silver rubles. In 1856 it had 170 printing tables. [14]

Nevertheless, on the eve of the reforms, cotton printing began, obviously, to displace printing by hand. Cotton-printing machinery was powered before the reforms mainly by horses. Steam-powered machinery was used only in large and technically better-equipped enterprises. Horsepower was displaced by the steam-driven machinery only after the reforms.

The mechanical loom made its appearance in the cotton industry long before the reforms. But its spread was slow. Before the reforms, the farming-out system, in combination with weaving by hand, dominated weaving manufacture. According to an evaluation by a specialist of that time, Sherer, in 1859 only one-fifth of the total production was mechanized. The application of the farming-out system was considerably reduced only in the 1870s. In this respect archive statistics on Ivanovo [15] are revealing. In the 1860s, in the Ivanovo industry, twice as many weavers worked at home as on the premises of enterprises. In the 1870s, the number of laborers who worked at home was three times less than that of those working on the premises of enterprises. In 1880, the farming-out system at Ivanovo was reduced to almost nothing. In the production of certain woven goods, the farming-out system existed until the Great October Socialist Revolution, but it had no great weight in the total production of weaving enterprises.

In 1867, cotton production was the branch of industry which was hit worst by economic crisis. In 1873, the general picture of the crisis was more complicated than in 1867. But in this case, too, the cotton industry was severely shaken. A contemporary, a well-known factory owner from Ivanovo and, at the same time, a historian of the city of Ivanovo, Ya. P. Garelin, noting the difficulties in the cotton textile trade at the end of 1872 and in 1873, wrote: "The way the trade went cannot be explained by competition with foreign manufacturers. The main reason for bad trade was that there was a great overproduction in cotton textiles and they had to be put on the market at all costs." [16] Indeed, cotton production in a quantity which exceeds the market demand was not the main reason for the crisis which was born of the capitalist character of the industry, but was only one of its manifestations.

Even before the reforms of 1861, there began to be formed in the cotton industry cadres of permanent workmen, hired as free laborers for whom their wages constituted the basic, and often the only, means of sustenance. They were recruited mainly from serfs and were objects of double exploitation: capitalistic on the part of the businessmen, and feudal on the part of the estate owner, to whom they gave part of their wages by way of a tax. Because of this, they must be considered still pre-proletarians. But after 1861 they became proletarians. Links that many of them had with agriculture even before the reforms of 1861 were either weak or altogether absent. Ivanovo may serve as a fair example: it had, on the eve of the reforms of 1861, 9,000 inhabitants practically not connected with agriculture and employed exclusively in the cotton industry.

The role of mechanized production in the estrangement of peasant labor from agriculture is well known from the data of the first half of the 1880s collected by municipal statisticians. In Moscow province, the number of laborers of peasant origin who had come away from fieldwork were as follows: [17]

Spinning department of cotton-spinning factories	3%
Mechanically powered weaving factories	10%
Hand-powered weaving factories	78%
Cotton-printing departments of cotton factories	4%

The significance of the mechanization of the cotton industry for the estrangement of peasant laborers from agriculture is clearly shown by these figures.[18]

In the other branches of the textile industry, the transition from the manufacturing plant into the factory began later than in the cotton industry. In the wool and the linen industries, this transition began even before the reforms, but on a comparatively small scale, and was completed during the period following the reforms, that is, largely approximately toward the beginning of the 1880s. Manual production of linen, and partly of broadcloth by the peasantry, mainly for home consumption, remained until the Great October Socialist Revolution.

Of the other branches of industry I shall discuss two: the sugar and the paper industries. In these branches a fairly large technical reorganization took place even before the peasant reforms. The beet sugar industry appeared in Russia at the very beginning of the nineteenth century in Tula province in the form of manufacturing enterprise. At first, it developed very slowly. During the second half of the 1830s, when there began the construction of sugar factories in the Ukraine, this industry entered a new stage of development. Its history during the time before the reforms has been fairly well studied in the book by the Ukrainian academician, K. G. Vobly.[19] Vobly devoted considerable attention to questions of the technical development of the sugar industry, but his work needs, nevertheless, material additions.

In 1848–1849, steam-powered factories (the first was founded in 1840) already contributed 44 percent of the total production; in 1853–1854, their share already was 56 percent, that is, over one-half; [20] in 1860–1861, that is, on the eve of the fall of serfdom, steam-powered factories yielded 85 percent of the total production of granulated sugar.[21]

The history of the mechanization of the paper industry presents considerable interest. In paper production, before 1861, mechanized enterprises already supplied over one-half of the production.

The branches I have enumerated were the leading ones on the eve of the peasant reforms, and included about three-fourths of all the labor in the manufacturing industry that have been taken into account by government statistics. I have not studied in detail the rest of the branches of the processing industry. I can only say that with regard to their technological development, the majority of them did not lag behind the ones enumerated by me above.

I shall now pass on to the history of the Industrial Revolution in ferrous metallurgy (I shall not dwell on nonferrous metallurgy because of its considerable resemblance in the technical-organizational respect to ferrous metallurgy).

First of all, what is to be considered the beginning of the technological revolution in a given branch of industry? Smelting with mineral fuel cannot be chosen as a criterion, since, in such a case, the metallurgy of not only the Urals of tsarist Russia before the reforms, but also that of Sweden of today will have to be considered, technologically, as one which has not yet passed through the stage of the Industrial Revolution. I am taking, as a criterion, the replacement of the Bloom furnace with a puddling oven, with other more perfected equipment, and the substitution for the waterwheel of a steam engine and a water turbine.

In our archives there has accumulated a considerable amount of material on the history of metallurgy. The published source material also yields much. Before the reforms, ferrous metallurgy was served by forced labor. Serfdom exercised on it that retarding effect which V. I. Lenin noted.

Puddling in the Urals was first established on the Kamenko-Votkinsk state plant where proper experiments began to be conducted in 1837.[22] In the 1840s, puddling furnaces were already in operation in eleven plants of the Urals.[23] In the 1850s, further progress in this respect was made. The leading plants of the Shepelevs and the Maltsevs had already been converted to puddling in the 1840s. On the eve of the reforms, in Russia as a whole, according to the calculations of S. G. Strumilin, puddling furnaces supplied about one-half of the metal. In the south of Russia, ferrous metallurgy, without taking into consideration minor enterprises in the province of Volynia, came into being, all of a sudden, on the foundations of the new, capitalistic technology.

In 1882, the share of the furnaces was only about one-ninth of all the metal.[24]

The successes in the field of power were much smaller. On the eve of the reforms in Russia, on the whole, 88 percent of the power equipment for ferrous metallurgy was supplied by the waterwheel. The rest was powered by steam-driven machinery and water turbines. In 1882,[25] only 37 percent of the machinery was powered by the waterwheel. But in the Urals, even in that year, waterwheel power constituted more than one-half of the total power.

Cadres of permanent laborers, who worked in the plants from generation to generation, were formed in the metallurgical plants of the Urals and of the central industrial region as early as the eighteenth century. Craftsmen who performed basic operations at the plants were fully employed in the industry. Nevertheless, they possessed small farms of an auxiliary character: meadows which made it possible for them to keep cows, vegetable gardens, and, at times, tiny little bits of arable land.

During the haymaking season, plants stopped work. Laborers had farms with houses and outbuildings. Free labor in the ferrous metallurgical plants was hardly used. Clearly, the laborers in the ferrous metallurgy industry before the reforms might be called only a pre-proletariat.

The reforms of 1861 granted the laborers of metallurgical plants personal freedom, and they began to hire themselves out for work. Because of the considerable number of Urals laborers, which exceeded the needs of the plants before the reforms, there was no inflow of new labor power into the Urals plants. On the contrary, there was not sufficient work for the permanent personnel. A similar situation existed in the metallurgical plants of the central industrial region. Cadres of laborers in metallurgy in Southern Russia had been formed between the 1870s and the 1880s on a purely capitalist basis.

On the basis of what has been said, it is possible to arrive at a general conclusion concerning the industry as a whole. On the whole, in Russian heavy industry, machine technology forced manual labor to a position of secondary importance toward the beginning of the 1880s. However, alongside heavy industry, there was preserved a light industry which utilized many laborers. Home industry was preserved mainly in backwater localities still not separated from agriculture.

The period of technical reorganization of heavy industry is a time interval of a little less than fifty years, from the middle of the 1830s to the beginning of the 1880s. The backbone of the railway network was created in the 1860s and 1870s. This is well known and it is not necessary to dwell on it. The history of the mechanization of water transport is of great interest. It developed before the creation of the railway network. This area has been little studied by historians and economists; and the transportation experts have provided very few works. The most interesting of these is a book by I. A. Shubin,[26] published a quarter of a century ago. The original material, archival and published, is quite significant and interesting.

The extensive development of steamships was preceded by a primitive mechanization utilizing horsepower. I am referring in this case not to horse towing which is similar to hauling by manpower, but to the so-called horse-powered machines which appeared in the second half of the first decade of the century and spread in the 1840s.

Steamers came to us early, but their spread on the Volga began only in the second half of the 1840s. On the eve of the reforms of 1861, over two hundred steamers were sailing on the Volga and its tributaries. In the 1850s, important works were undertaken to improve the routes in the Mariinsk system and partly on the Volga. This made the spread of steamer navigation easier.

After the reforms of 1861, river transport continued to develop. In the 1870s, double-decked ships appeared on the Volga.

Thus, the period of the technical reorganization of transportation is with us closer chronologically to the time of the technical reorganization of industry than was the case in Western Europe.

In the area of the supply of industries that were being mechanized, and of transport with metal, fuel, and machines, our Industrial Revolution had a series of special features, born, mainly, of social causes, and partly of natural conditions, which also should not be forgotten.

Russia before the reforms satisfied her very limited needs in metal with home production. But, when the government began to build the railway between Moscow and St. Petersburg, the Urals, under serfdom, were unable to supple the rails. It was necessary to have recourse to imports. The railway building of the 1860s and the 1870s developed considerably using imported metal. In the 1860s and the 1870s, metal was also imported for the construction of machinery. Only at the end of the 1880s were radical changes in the supply of metal beginning to be made. This was because of the growth of industry in the south.

In this way, in the process of the mechanization of industry and of transportation, imported metal played an important role. The causes consist of the survival of serfdom, which retarded the development of the Urals after the reforms, and of the belated solution to the problems of metallurgy in the south.

The peculiarities of Russia's fuel balance in the years of the Industrial Revolution were, on the one hand, the continued importance of wood fuel in the central industrial region and, on the other hand, utilization of imported coal in the industry of St. Petersburg and in other ports of the Baltic Sea. This, to a great degree, was the result of the remoteness of the Donets Basin from the main regions of the country's manufacturing industry and the inability of capitalism to overcome this remoteness. But, of course, our coal and oil industries were created by the Industrial Revolution.

Machine building was born in Russia even before the reforms of 1861. Independent machine construction enterprises did not appear all of a sudden. Their predecessors were mechanical workshops at the metallurgical plants of light industry and foundries. Even in the eighteenth century in the plants for ferrous and nonferrous metallurgy, there were often found special workshops which prepared the equipment for these plants. Usually, these workshops did not take orders from outside but worked to supply the needs of their own enterprise.

It was precisely in this type of workshop that our first steam-powered machines were constructed as early as the eighteenth century. I. I. Polzunov, a genius, constructed his first steam-powered machine on the Kolyvano-Voskresensky plants in the Altai for the needs of these plants. A little later, in 1790, at the Alexandrovsk plant in Petrozavodsk, the first steam-driven plant made for sluicing down water at the Vonsk gold mine was constructed and remained in use for a number of years.

In the first half of the nineteenth century, some of these workshops accepted private orders and sometimes played a fairly important part in the technical equipping of Russian industry. The mechanical workshop of the state Alexandrovsk manufacturing plant must be given precedence among them.

The activities of this manufacturing plant in supplying equipment to Russian cotton mills during the initial stages of the development of cotton spinning in Russia, at the time when the export of looms was forbidden in England, was of a very great significance. In this respect one must stress the important role the Alexandrovsk manufacturing plant played [27] in supplying looms and other equipment to those three large private cotton mills which were established in Petersburg in the second half of the 1830s and whose establishment constituted one of the most important stages in the development of the cotton-spinning industry in Russia.

Mechanized workshops at the sugar refineries of Yakhnenko and Simerenko, and at the Bobrinsky refinery, produced in the 1840s and 1850s certain types of equipment both for their own refineries and for certain other sugar refineries on order. Apart from this, some sugar refineries had attached mechanized workshops to supply the needs of their own plants. The role these workshops played in the history of the Russian sugar-refining industry is by far more modest than the role played by the Alexandrovsk manufacturing plant in the history of cotton spinning.

In the middle of the nineteenth century, the mechanized workshops of the government Kamsk-Votkinsk plant in the province of Vyatka, the Snovetsk plant of the Shepelevs,[28] and the plants of the Maltsevs developed their business on a very wide scale. The Kamsk-Votkinsk plant was, for many years, a pioneer of the new techniques in ferrous metallurgy. The activities of its mechanized workshops, which produced part of the equipment necessary for mastering these new techniques, had some connection with it. The mechanized workshops at the plant were considerably enlarged beginning in 1837, when experiments for the introduction of puddling were started at the plants. They were enlarged still more in 1847 when the Votkinsk plant began to build steamers.[29] After the reforms, this plant also produced steam engines. Technologically the plants of the Shepelevs were in the first rank of the metallurgical plants east of Moscow.

The mechanized workshop of the Snovetsk plant of the Shepelevs began, in the second half of the 1830s, to produce steam-operated machinery. In the 1850s, the plant developed shipbuilding. The Maltsev plants, where mechanized production had developed in the 1840s, undertook the same kind of work on a smaller scale.

The oldest foundries in Russia, which grew into large machine construction enterprises, were the plants of Baird and the government Alexandrovsk plant in St. Petersburg. These two plants laid the foundations for the development of St. Petersburg as a center of Russian machinery construction.

The Baird plant was founded as early as 1792 as a foundry. At first, the plant produced kitchen and oven appliances, galleys, axes, hammers, various tools, and castings of all sorts, mainly for the government. In 1811, the plant constructed a steam-powered machine and lathes for the government armaments factory in Tula.

In 1815, the first steamer in Russia was built at this plant. After that the adjoining plant with casting works, which constituted its principal occupation until the 1830s, also developed machinery construction. In the 1830s, machinery construction at the Baird plant increased, but the casting work continued, too. The plant operated on the basis of free labor. On orders from the government at the beginning of the century, it accepted for training workers from government plants. The plant brought up the first generation of Russian machine-construction workers.

The Alexandrovsk plant was built in 1825–1828 after another government plant, a foundry, established in 1801, had sustained great damages from the flood in 1824. The new plant was to replace its predecessor.[30] Like the Baird plant, the Alexandrovsk plant combined casting with the construction of steam-powered machinery and steamers. When the construction of the Moscow-Petersburg railway began, the Alexandrovsk plant, leased to Harrison and Winans, was reorganized. It began to produce movable components for that railway.

Other foundries, established later, also combined casting with machinery construction. From a small foundry, established in the 1850s, grew the well known Neva plant in St. Petersburg.

Even before the reforms of 1861, there were also established in Russia independent machine-construction plants. In 1839, in Ekaterinburg, a mechanized government factory was founded. This enterprise was built to supply the needs of the Ural government plants, but later it began to take private orders as well. The Ekaterinburg mechanized factory produced certain kinds of equipment for the Ural plants, as well as steam-powered machinery and boilers for steamers.

In 1849, in the vicinity of Nizhnii Novgorod, the Sormovsk plant for shipbuilding was founded. At the beginning of the 1850s, a machine construction plant was established in Kostransa by Shipov. This plant began operations with the manufacture of copper shafts for cotton-printing factories, but, basically, produced steam engines and steamships.

In Moscow, in 1847, with the help of government subsidies, the Rigley machine construction plant was founded; in 1853, it passed into the hands of Alekseev, a Moscow textile factory owner. The plant produced equipment for textile enterprises, constructed steam engines, and repaired machinery. From a workshop for the repair of steamships, founded in St. Petersburg by MacPherson in the 1850s, the Baltic plant developed later on.

Basically, the development of Russian machine construction declined in the years after the reforms. The various branches of machine construction did not develop uniformly in Russia. The construction of transport machinery was developed much better than for industry. The first to stand firmly on its own feet was the building of river steamboats. In this area imports played an essential role only during the initial stage of steam navigation. About two-thirds of the steamers on the rivers and lakes of Russia in 1878 were built within the country.

The construction of steam engines and railway carriages developed a little later than the building of steamships. It is true that the first steam engine in Russia was built as early as the first half of the 1830s in the Urals by technicians who were serfs of the Demidovs, the Cherepanovs, father and son; but in the second half of the 1840s, the Alexandrovsk plant was already producing steam engines and railway cars. Nevertheless, in supplying Russian railways with movable components, both before the reforms and in the 1860s, and the first half of the 1870s, imports played the leading role. In the second half of the 1870s, when the construction of railways was curtailed and the construction of steam engines and railway carriages was on the increase, domestic machine construction became the principal supplier of movable components for the Russian railways.

Machine production for industry was, by far, less successful. Russian industry, both during the years of the Industrial Revolution and after it, used mainly imported machinery. As is generally known, the slow development of the industrial machine construction remained a characteristic trait of Russian industry up to the Great October Socialist Revolution.

Thus, foreign technology was widely used in Russia during the period of the Industrial Revolution, but, nevertheless, the role which domestic technology played, even in the early stages, was more important than it is generally believed to be. Evaluating the roles played by foreign and Russian technology in the Industrial Revolution in Russia, one must take into account the discrepancy between the achievements of the Russian technological thinking which had a worldwide significance, and the social environment that hindered them from taking root in industrial practice. Backward industrial relationships in this case impeded the development of the creative forces of the country.

The process of original accumulation of capital in Russia differed considerably from its "classical" English form. Russia in this respect was closer to the countries of continental Europe, but, in comparison with them, this process had in Russia notable peculiarities.

The similarity of the process of the original accumulation in Russia and in the countries of continental Western Europe can be seen in the absence both in Russia and in these countries of the mass deprivation of peasantry of land which is so characteristic of England and led to the disappearance there of the peasant class. The existence in Russia of original accumulation during the period of serfdom was a characteristic feature, compared both with England and with other leading countries of capitalist Western Europe.

Groups of the population, deprived of the means to produce, and living on their wages, existed in Russia as early as the seventeenth century. In the eighteenth century, and during the first half of the nineteenth century, their numbers grew considerably. But to a large degree and especially in the eighteenth century, these groups consisted of serfs. It must be noted that, as early as the beginning of the nineteenth century, the majority of laborers in heavy industry were not only serfs, but also worked in the enterprises of their owners not as free wage earners, but doing forced labor.

The laborers of the mining plants in the eighteenth century were recruited to a large extent by forcibly transferring "registered" peasants to workshops as craftsmen and, also, through the purchase of peasants by plant owners in different Russian provinces, and by transferring peasants from estates to the plants. The growth of the manufacturing industry, based on forced labor, entailed also in a large measure either a complete or partial liquidation of their farms by the peasants employed in the plants.

Additional labor cadres in government enterprises were effected by turning recruits into laborers. In this way, peasants, too, were torn away from agriculture. At the beginning of the nineteenth century, in the Urals, registered peasants were replaced with so-called permanent laborers (at the rate of fifty-eight permanent laborers per one thousand registered souls). This detached the permanent laborer from agriculture.

During the first half of the nineteenth century, the purchase of peasants by the gentry and owners of industrial enterprises for the purpose of turning them into laborers, or the transfer of serfs to enterprises, also took place, although, it appears, on a noticeably smaller scale than previously. Thus in Russia the deprivation of land, typical of the original accumulation, affected some portion of the peasantry long before the reforms of 1861. But in the eighteenth century, this deprivation of land turned the peasant serf not into a capitalistically employed laborer, who worked on the basis of free hire, but into an estate laborer or a workman at a "possessional" manufacturing plant.

The reforms of 1861 which V. I. Lenin called "clean up of the lands by the estate-owners" for capitalism not only reduced, as is generally known, the allotments of the majority of the peasants, but it also created large cadres of landless peasantry.[31] To these landless cadres was given an opportunity to look for work on a capitalistic basis.

The original accumulation, as was established by Marx, constituted not only a deprivation of the small producer of the means of production, but also an accumulation of capital for subsequent investment in capitalistic enterprises. The sources of this accumulation, typical of Western Europe of the manufacturing period, in the majority of cases were also found in Russia during the corresponding period of her history. The exploitation of border regions by colonial methods began in tsarist Russia in the seventeenth century. The role played by precious metals from the colonies which enriched the Western Europe of the manufacturing period was played in seventeenth-century Russia by the Siberian fur trade. Its significance diminished considerably in the following century, but it was in the same Siberia that the processing of precious metal began.

Supplying the government, primarily to satisfy the needs of the army and the navy, became an important means for making money beginning in the eighteenth century. It was then that such an important source of original accumulation as liquor leasing gained prominence. Vast fortunes were made on leases. Part of these fortunes went to industry as early as the eighteenth century, being invested exactly in the form that was typical of that century in Russia, namely in manufacturing plants operated by forced labor. As an example, one may cite the case of Savva Yakovlev who made his fortune in liquor leases and became a plant owner in the Urals, as well as the owner of the Bolshoi Yaroslav manufacturing plant.

Thus, the original accumulation in Russia, which possessed very special features, chronologically coincided, as was the case in other countries, with a period of manufacturing and preceded the Industrial Revolution. Capital accumulation, separation of the small producer from the means to produce, and an increase in the number of laborers living on wages took place in Russia, as everywhere else, of course, both at the time of the Industrial Revolution and after it. But these processes then took a slightly different course; they were not a "prehistory of capital" but characteristic symptoms of the development of capitalism in a country.

The Industrial Revolution provoked in Russia, as in other countries, a growth of industrial production. The basic market for the capitalist industry of Russia at the time of the Industrial Revolution and after it was the home market. The export of iron and linen to Western Europe and America, which had great significance in the eighteenth century, at first decreased sharply and then petered out during the years of the Industrial Revolution and following it. The export of textiles and of certain other industrial products to Asia acquired a comparatively limited importance.

But the home market in Russia is not wholly comparable in its character with the home markets of the leading capitalist countries of nineteenth-century Western Europe. The Russian Empire, as is generally known, included territories of the colonial type, such as, for example, Kazakhstan and Central Asia, or Transcaucasia. Such territories did not exist, for example, in the German Zollverein. However, it would be a serious error to consider as colonies all the parts of the Russian Empire with non-Russian populations. There were in the Russian Empire territories that were oppressed as nations, but were developed economically. Latvia and Estonia might serve as good examples.

Beginning with the second half of the 1840s, the export of wheat increased. The growth of the export of agricultural products increased the purchasing power of the exporting regions and boosted the demand for products of Russian industry protected from foreign competition by high customs tariffs. Thus, the growth of agricultural exports stimulated the growth of industrial production.

The Industrial Revolution in Russia created technological preconditions for the appearance of capitalist crises. The cotton industry cited above serves as a good example. The development of railway construction at the end of the 1860s and the beginning of 1870, coinciding with the concluding stages of the technical reorganization of industry, laid the foundations for increasing the role of heavy industry in the capitalist cycles in Russia.

The Industrial Revolution in Russia, as in other countries, helped the growth of cities and other industrial centers and the formation of industrial regions. Closely linked to the Industrial Revolution was the transformation of St. Petersburg into an industrial center. St. Petersburg was a pioneer of new technology in the cotton industry. It was there that cotton printing was first developed in Russia. St. Petersburg became the first center of cotton spinning in Russia. It first took root there and then began to spread into the central industrial region.

St. Petersburg acquired an especially great importance as the center of machine construction in Russia. The machine-construction industry appeared there at the beginning of the nineteenth century in the Baird plant and in the state Alexandrovsk plant. Its development saw markedly good progress in the 1850s, and spread especially widely after the peasant reforms of 1861. In St. Petersburg the earliest cadre of the Russian proletariat was formed, and the strike movement developed earlier than in other centers of Russian industry.

The formation of industrial centers in Latvia and Estonia— Riga, Tallin, Narva, and Lepaya—was closely linked with the Industrial Revolution in Russia. The type of industry and the role played in Russia's economy in Riga, Tallin, and Lepaya were very much like that of St. Petersburg, but, of course, these cities were greatly inferior to it in the extent of production. The linking of the

Baltic states with the inner provinces in Russia by means of railways made it easier for the industrial centers of Latvia and Estonia to work in the Russian market, and assisted, thereby, their capitalistic development. The Krenholm manufacturing plant in Narva was founded in 1857 by capitalists of the central industrial region (Knoop, Soldatenkov, and Khlyudov) and became, later, the largest cotton factory not only in Russia, but also in the whole of Europe. In 1870, Riga occupied, on the basis of the number of laborers in heavy industry, third place in European Russia (excluding Poland) and was inferior in this respect only to Moscow and St. Petersburg.

Enterprises in the Baltic provinces grew, working for the Russian market. When, later, many years after the completion of the Industrial Revolution, Latvia and Estonia became bourgeois republics, and local industry lost the Russian market, their industrial production entered a stage of lengthy and sharp decline.

The Industrial Revolution in Russia brought to life the industrial development of the Donets Basin and Baku.

The industrial geography of the central industrial region took shape before the Industrial Revolution. But there, too, the concentration of industry in centers, situated in localities which were developed earlier industrially, was brought about by the Industrial Revolution. The growth of Sormov, Orekhovo-Zuev, and of other similar centers, not to mention industrial cities, was conditioned by the Industrial Revolution. Thanks to this Industrial Revolution, Moscow's industry, already well developed, grew especially markedly.

However, despite the significant growth of heavy industry in connection with the Industrial Revolution, the proportion of industry in the national economy of the country was smaller by far than in the leading countries of Western Europe. The causes must be sought first of all in the retarding effects of serfdom and its postreform vestiges which held back the growth of the productive forces of the country.

The technological revolution in industry had already begun in the time of serfdom. It was completed after its liquidation. The peasant reforms of 1861 took place in the middle of that interval of time that encompassed the Revolution. Before 1861, the technological transformation of industry strengthened the capitalist structure and was one of the forces that were undermining serfdom. The abolition of serfdom, in its turn, affected the course of the Industrial Revolution, speeding it up and facilitating its completion.

Cadres of laborers who lived on their wages had begun to form already in the manufacturing period. But at first they consisted mainly of laborers of manufacturing enterprises which employed forced labor. At the end of the eighteenth century, the number of laborers at the capitalist manufacturing enterprises began to grow. These laborers were mainly peasants who paid *obrok* to the estate owners. They were marketing their work power and in this way were different from laborers on the estates and at the "possessional" manufacturing plants. But the peasants who paid *obrok* were not free personally, and, as a result, it is impossible to call them as yet proletarians in the proper sense of this word. Nevertheless, among the laborers of the capitalist manufacturing enterprises were free men. These were, first of all, members of the lower middle class in the city. State peasants who worked in capitalist enterprises should be included in this latter grouping.

The transition of the manufacturing plant into the factory added impetus to the formation of cadres of permanent industrial laborers and increased the numbers of these cadres by including a part which consisted of free men. It is, therefore, possible to speak about the presence of small proletarian cadres within the ranks of industrial labor even before 1861. From the point of view of numbers, these cadres become noticeable beginning in the 1840s.

After the reforms of 1861, both the above-mentioned proletarian cadres and laborers from among the former *obrok*-paying peasants, and, to a certain extent, laborers who had been freed but were now forced to work in industry [32] became the first significant groupings of the emerging Russian proletariat.

After 1861, when the mechanization of the industrial production increased, when the peasant reforms cast on the labor market large cadres of men either without land or with very little land, and the disintegration of the peasant class began to push laborers with plots of land out of agriculture, the process of the formation of the proletariat gathered momentum. A statistical survey of the 1880s showed the presence in Russia of fully formed cadres of the proletariat; thus, according to the statistics of 1881 [33] in Moscow, 42 percent of all textile laborers were already hereditary laborers. More-over, among the spinners, 88.1 percent were such a type, and among the manual laborers, 21 percent. Not less suggestive is the data on the enterprises of Moscow province for the years 1884–1885, given by E. M. Dementiev. Out of the total of these la-borers investigated, 55 percent were sons of factory workers. More-over, 70.4 percent of fathers of laborers engaged in processing fiber were workers.[34]

The Industrial Revolution in Russia altered, as was the case in other countries, the structure of labor cadres and lowered the wages. The facts given by Ya. P. Garelin are typical in this respect. He writes: "The time of high wages was over for the Ivanov laborer with the introduction of machinery." [35] Ya. P. Garelin cites statisti-cal data on changes in wages and in prices for rye flour at Ivanovo during the period from 1810 to 1880.[36] From this data one can see that the earnings of an average manual weaver decreased several times over between the end of the 1850s and the beginning of the 1880s; the earnings of the weaver working on a mechanical loom increased by 15 percent, the price of rye flour increased by 102 percent, and the earnings of a cotton finisher were halved between the beginning of the century when manual finishing flourished and the middle of the century when cotton printing began to dominate, while the price of flour increased three times.

The formation of the proletariat brought in its wake, naturally, the development of a proletarian movement. "Already in the 1870s, and especially in the 1880s of the last century, the working class in Russia started to awaken and began its struggle with the capitalists." [37]

The Industrial Revolution in Russia increased sharply the for-mation of the industrial bourgeoisie. Owners of the capitalist manu-facturing plants, who often were the original owners of small enter-prises, became factory owners and found themselves in the first ranks of the bourgeoisie. If, previously, the first place among the bourgeoisie was occupied by the tax farmer and the merchant, then, the Industrial Revolution brought to the fore the manufacturer, the factory owner, and the railway businessman.

The social importance of the bourgeoisie in Russia increased considerably. But even much later, during the period of imperialism, the bourgeoisie never rose to the same heights in landlords' Russia as it did in England and in France.

Fundamentally, the Industrial Revolution in Russia followed the laws of the development of capitalism common to all countries, but because of the peculiarities of the social development of Russia, this revolution represented a significant departure in the social and economic order compared, for example, with the Industrial Revolution in England.

The basic peculiarity of the social history of Russia compared with Western Europe, and especially with England and France, was the endurance and strength of feudal relations as well as the vestiges of the feudalism which was being superseded by the capitalistic formation. The serfholding landlords represented before and after 1861 these obsolete social forces which exerted a retarding influence on changes in productive relations corresponding to the development of productive forces and at the same time to the tempo and level of development of the most productive forces in the country.

The vestiges of serfdom, retarding the development of the productive forces of Russia after the 1861 reforms, the narrowness of the domestic market, and the reactionary role of the post reform political superstructure did not make it possible for industry to occupy in the national economy of Russia that place which English industry, working for a vast world market, attained. In the social conditions of postreform Russia, the bourgeoisie could not occupy that social position which it acquired in England as a result of the Industrial Revolution.

One must seek in the social conditions of Russia an explanation of those peculiarities in the supply of machines and in the consumption of metal and fuel by Russian industry and transport which have been mentioned above. The trade balance especially, as well as natural conditions, played a considerable role.

The differences in character between the Industrial Revolution in Russia and in the leading countries of continental Europe were less than the differences in this regard between Russia and England. But all the same, these differences were extremely important.

VI

The early accumulation of capital and the pioneering of capitalist commercial and industrial enterprise have been undertaken in many cultures by heterodox religious communities, whose outcast status and cooperative efforts worked to stimulate business activity. So it was with the Old Believers and other outcast religious groups in nineteenth-century Russia. The process as seen in the large communities of Old Believers in Moscow at that time is described by William L. Blackwell, who is Professor of History at New York University and is the author of The Beginnings of Russian Industrialization *(Princeton, N.J., 1968);* The Industrialization of Russia *(New York, 1970); and the editor of this anthology. The article is reprinted with the permission of the publisher,* The Slavic Review, *having first appeared in XXIV (1965), 407–24.*

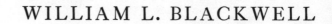

WILLIAM L. BLACKWELL

The Old Believers and the Rise
of Private Industrial Enterprise in
Early Nineteenth-Century Moscow

The origins of modern Moscow can be traced to the early nineteenth century, when smokestacks began to supplement church cupolas on the city's skyline and the forsaken palaces of boyars were being converted into factories or homes of wealthy merchants. Pushkin observed this process with a mixture of romantic nostalgia and patriotic optimism as early as 1834. The old Orthodox and national shrine of Russia was starting its evolution as a major industrial center of the empire. Along with this, however, came a later chapter of Russian religious history. Moscow during this same period also became a center of the Old Believers; Raskolniki, scattered for over a century on the frontiers of Russia, began to flock back to the ancient capital. The two events are linked. Many of the private industrial entrepreneurs in Moscow were Old Believers. The focus of their business activities was the textile industry. Here the peculiar beliefs, way of life, and organization of the larger communities of the schismatics seemed admirably suited to the accumulation of industrial capital, the provision of incentive for master and worker alike, and the mobilization of the lower social strata of Moscow and the surrounding countryside into a factory labor force.

The history of private enterprise in Russia is unique in many ways and generally obscure. While several studies since the pioneering work of Tugan-Baranovsky have emphasized the social origins of the industrial entrepreneur in nineteenth-century Russia,[1] the role of religious sects in this process has remained relatively neglected. Although Orthodoxy did not necessarily inhibit the growth of business among its adherents, we know that the dissident sects and minority religions, ranging from the Old Believers and Skoptsy to the Jews, provided many of Russia's big industrial, commercial, and financial capitalists.[2] In contrast to the European pattern, the Russian capitalist class was recruited as much from outcasts and disadvantaged elements of society—religious minorities, serfs, and foreigners—as from indigenous merchants or townsmen. However, the general picture remains vague, the statistics are spotty and often inaccurate, and the relationship of ideology to entrepreneurship is unclear. The early nineteenth-century industrial history of the Moscow Old Believers, somewhat more fully documented than that of other Russian religious sects and minorities, may thus provide a convenient point of departure for mapping out the general history of religion and private enterprise in Russia.

During this period the Old Believer movement continued and even expanded as a major force in the life of the people of Russia. Perhaps as high as a third and no less than a fifth of the peasants had embraced it. It was a power which the state feared and fought and which even the revolutionary leaders acknowledged to be a vital element of peasant and urban life and a vehicle for the destruction of the old order in Russia.[3] The Old Believer entrepreneurs emerged in Moscow during the reigns of Alexander I and Nicholas I from the two main factional streams which flowed from the schism of the seventeenth century—the Priestists (*Popovtsy*) and the Priestless (*Bezpopovtsy*), or, more specifically, the great communities which became the national centers in Moscow of these two factions, the Rogozhsk and Preobrazhensk communities or "cemeteries" (*kladbishche;* so called because the communities were built around the sites of Old Believer burial places). These communities were established in the late eighteenth century in what at that time were outskirts and village suburbs of Moscow but in the nineteenth century became the city's main industrial districts. According to one of the best-known students of Old Belief of the last century, P. I. Mel'nikov, the Raskolnik segment of the population of Moscow and its suburbs jumped from about 20,000 in 1800 to 186,000 by 1848, about half of the total number of inhabitants. Most of this number worked in factories controlled by Old Believers or at home-work farmed out by the same industrialists. The elders of the communities controlled the factories; for 1838, 138 families of the Rogozhsk Cemetery were registered in the first and second merchant guilds, and many were "Hereditary Honorable Citizens as well as Commercial and Manufacturing Councillors," [4] dignities which designated only the most important and wealthiest mercantile and industrial entrepreneurs at that time in Russia.

It took a century of Old Belief to give birth to these industrialists. The religious history of the first period of the Russian schism —from the Nikonian revolution to the reign of Catherine the Great —is one of persecution, flight, dispersal, and factionalism. There is also an economic history of Old Belief during this same time. The Priestists, the moderate wing of the original schismatics, who continued to accept the notion of a priesthood and of a true church and who were unwilling to go to the extremes of torture, incarceration, or self-inflicted death in the face of government persecution, fanned out to the forests of the west, south, and east, to the Ukraine and Poland, to the Lower Volga, the Don, the Urals, and western Siberia, and even a few to China.[5] By the end of the eighteenth century, hundreds of thousands of Priestists had set up communities in these desolate areas, groups which, although largely self-sufficient, maintained contact with each other and with religious centers that had developed, such as the monastery at Kerzhenets (near Nizhnii Novgorod). In return the religious centers received financial support from such wealthy communities as Ekaterinburg, where Old Believers owned most of the private metallurgical industry and numbered, according to most estimates, some 150,000, or the Lower Volga area, where they came to control the east-west trade, the fairs, and the shipbuilding industry.

Labor, money, and commercial information apparently circulated along with religious teachings in this frontier world of the Old Believers. Not only spiritual but economic cooperation was necessary to survive in the face of a hostile government and a wild frontier environment.[6] It was a recapitulation of the commercial history of many of the world's harried, migrant, and sometimes pioneer religious sects. Yet the tsarist government, rigorous in matters of political submission and ideological conformity, was indulgent with the Old Believers when it came to taxes and other pecuniary obligations. This policy was no doubt influenced by the problems of assessment and collection in the hinterland of Russia, where even the military arms of the tsar could not always stretch. The Old Believers paid only the "double" head tax and were exempt from many of the commercial, military, and labor obligations that burdened the Orthodox peasants and merchants. Catherine the Great expanded these exemptions to a general policy of toleration. Under her policy of "enlightened despotism," they were invited to return from frontier banishment, and measures were taken toward further legalization of their position.[7] With such concessions, the Old Believer communities grew and prospered. But the state could always reverse itself and launch out on new persecutions. The period of toleration inaugurated by Catherine the Great and continued by Alexander I was ended by Nicholas I. Persecution intensified during the last years of his reign, when a police terror was imposed on the Raskolniki. The commercial and industrial fruits of the earlier period, however, endured.

The history of the Priestless faction of the schism during the eighteenth century carries us deeper into the ideological and organizational background of the entrepreneurial activities of the Old Believers. The economic prosperity of the Priestless was encouraged by the same external factors of frontier cooperation and eventual state tolerance that we have seen in the case of the Priestists. The peculiar doctrines and way of life of the Priestless sects were equally decisive in determining their business future. The Priestless fled to the north rather than to the south to escape the troops of the tsar. As Miliukov and Nikol'sky point out, their isolated communities in the wilderness, the lack of government control, the weak influence of Orthodoxy, and the scarcity of priests were conducive to a nonhierarchical type of religion, simple, puritanical religious services, and self-sufficient, hardworking, and austere religious communities.[8] One of the most important of these early communities of the north was the Vyg Commune, the birthplace of the "Shore Dweller" (*Pomortsy*) faction. Vyg established the organizational pattern that would be followed by many of the later Priestless communities. The community was headed by an elected council of elders who controlled its religious and economic life. As time went on, the elders became businessmen and businessmen became elders. Vyg became a federation consisting of a large number of industrial and agricultural communities and subsequently expanded from agriculture and ironmaking until it handled much of the fishing, whaling, and commercial activity of the north. Wherever they traded, the Shore Dwellers set up communities.[9]

Developing at about the same time as the Shore Dwellers, closely akin to them but irreconcilable on certain issues, was the Theodosian faction of the Priestless schismatics, named after its founder, the Novgorod clerk, Theodosii Vasil'ev, who died in prison in 1711. The Theodosians during the eighteenth century were the most puritanical of the main branches of Old Belief. In varying degrees at different times they remained hostile to the state, to private property, to sex and marriage, to rituals, to dealings with people of other beliefs, to priests and church hierarchy, and to tobacco, alcohol, coffee, tea, potatoes, Western dress, and the shaving of beards.[10] In the course of a century and a half of secularization, most of these attitudes were qualified or obliterated. The austere, puritanical outlook, however, endured long enough to create sober, hardworking communities throughout northern Russia, where labor and asceticism quite soon produced large reserves of capital. The prohibitions on sex, marriage, and family life were soon, of necessity, revised or evaded, but the concept of communal property and the prohibition of familial inheritance were not eliminated in practice, as we shall see, until the mid-1800s, allowing for almost a century of accumulation of vast capital in the treasuries of the communities, a fund which usually fell into the hands of the merchant elders of the groups.

Such was the case when the Theodosians founded their wealthiest and most important community, the Preobrazhensk Cemetery, in a suburb of Moscow in 1771. The story is a dramatic one. Moscow was being ravaged at the time by a cholera epidemic. Il'ia Kovylin, a brick merchant and Theodosian, seeing the plague as a visitation of God for man's sinful departure from the true religion, set up a pesthouse, cemetery, and place of refuge and prayer for his cobelievers in Moscow. Catherine the Great, following her policy toward Old Ritualists and seeing the settlement as a useful and "enlightened" social service, legalized the Preobrazhensk community. This was the signal for the return of schismatics to the holy capital of pre-Nikonian days. At almost the same time, the Priestists established their own community at the Old Ritualist cemetery of the suburban village of Rogozhsk. As Old Believers flocked to Moscow and the fame of the communities spread, they expanded their operations. To the refuges for the old and sick were added numerous chapels, shops, and homes. The Moscow organizations were soon recognized as supreme by the other schismatic communities of the empire. Further legal guarantees and privileges were obtained, as in 1808, when Alexander I permitted the expansion of commercial activities by the Preobrazhensk community. By this time the growing wealth of the two schismatic centers was finding new outlets in the textile and other industries. Many of the Moscow cloth manufacturing enterprises of the early nineteenth century were founded by the Old Believers, or, rather, by the industrial entrepreneurs who emerged at this time from among the elders of the local communities or who joined the sect to get hold of capital. Utilizing the unique system of capital and labor which the ideals and organization of the Moscow schismatic groups made possible, a new class of textile industrialists appeared in the city. In the end the second generation deserted the Old Believer communities which had provided their capital but as members of which they could not themselves expand that capital, while the schism itself, under the double shock of this secularization and of renewed state oppression in the last years of the reign of Nicholas I, fell into decline.

Several unique methods were employed by the Theodosian community in Moscow to build up its capital, gather its labor force, and manage its industries. They are a commentary both on the growth of private enterprise and the decay of a religious utopia, as well as an example of the disintegration of the communal principle before the force of materialistic individualism. At the beginning of the nineteenth century the Preobrazhensk community was still largely the embodiment of a social and religious ideal—the national center of a religious cult, a democratic society (which was later to be compared by some to institutions in the United States), and a refuge for the needy and the elderly, supported by contributions of the faithful and the wealthy, given to enable the community to continue its charitable works and to spread the Theodosian teachings.

As a national religious center it had obtained by the turn of the century one vast source of income in the monopoly on the manufacture and distribution of sacred art and religious articles—icons, crosses, incense, holy oil, rare manuscripts, sacred books, candles, and the like. A profitable business developed from the shrewd buying and selling of religious antiques and from the manufacture and sale of imitations, copied in the ateliers of the community and sold in shops at Moscow and at the great fairs. Candles proved an important source of revenue, as they did for the Orthodox Church at that time. Members of the sect were required to use only candles manufactured at Preobrazhensk. Another source of income for the Moscow Theodosian community was the public baths built by the industrialist Grachev and used by the workers of the Old Believer factories and shelters for an admission price of 4 to 5 kopecks.[11]

In addition to this income, money poured into the Preobrazhensk treasury from schismatics in all corners of Russia in the form of gifts and bequests. The Malyshevs, for example, a wealthy merchant family, made an annual donation of 50,000 rubles and added to this a gift of 300 poods of sturgeon.[12] The legacies, however, provided the major funds for an initial capital expansion sufficient to serve as a foundation for ventures into industry. To join the commune and to enjoy the use of its shelter entailed the signing over of one's entire estate. A small amount of the total might be withheld for the personal needs of a member, but on his death even this reverted to the common fund. The Moscow police reports on the schismatic communities for 1845 provide the example of one elderly Semen Fomin, who bequeathed 35,000 rubles to the Theodosians upon entering their home for the aged, reserving the sum of 4,000 for himself. Upon his death, his relatives attempted in vain to secure the balance of this fraction.[13] In other instances we see that the commune understood these legacies to be total, to include every kopeck, every stick and stitch of the member's property: icons, clothing, cash, and particularly precious metals and stones. The gold and silver objects were melted down into ingots and added to the community's treasury. The commune did not hesitate to assert its claims aggressively. In one case, in the middle of the night, immediately upon the death of a merchant obligated to the group, and in an effort to foil his relatives, the Preobrazhensk Cemetery dispatched its own horses and carts to haul away the deceased's property. A coachman was regularly maintained for this purpose.[14]

As the monetary capital of the commune accumulated, it was found expedient to lend to both the rich and the poor, the enterprising and the desperate. Such loans were attractive to borrowers, since they involved little or in many cases no interest. The condition of the loan was conversion to the Theodosian creed and discipline. Larger business loans usually meant the reversion of the borrower's entire estate to the commune upon his death. For serfs the loan of a sum to cover their redemption and recruitment obligation meant employment in a Preobrazhensk factory to pay off their debt. The size of some of these loans indicates the wealth of the Preobrazhensk community by the mid-nineteenth century. In 1847 the Nosov brothers, already owners of a woolen factory, were lent 500,000 rubles by the Moscow Theodosians, with no interest to pay for the first three years and a 4-percent rate thereafter. They received the sum upon their conversion to the sect.[15]

The disposal of the capital of the Preobrazhensk community —estimated to be as much as 12 million rubles at one point—was given to caretakers selected from among its wealthiest supporters. Since the organization was not permitted legal ownership of real and movable property, these men in fact came to use most of the vast capital of the commune as they saw fit, and it was used to expand their own enterprises and holdings. In the case of two of the most prominent leaders, Grigor'ev and Guchkov, this meant the creation of millionaires. Most of the first generation of Old Believer capitalists remained within the discipline and habits of their religion—they observed its rites and planned to turn over their vast fortunes to the commune. However, power over the large amounts of capital they had established could be used in quite a different way by their more materialistic sons and prospective heirs.

The treasure chest which acted as a magnet for businessmen even more powerfully attracted workers to the industries allied to the Preobrazhensk community. In 1846 the police reported the following kind of talk in villages several miles outside of Moscow: "Formerly our village was all Orthodox, but preachers from the Preobrazhensk Cemetery began to visit us and to corrupt the women and children. The men, working in the factories, returned converted to Old Belief. These and others forsook the Church. Our priests [*popy*] hold their tongues about the fact that the conversions were well paid for." [16]

As perhaps a more compelling lure, conversion to Old Belief was a road to freedom for some peasants. It was also, according to the police reports, a release from land hunger and its resultant poverty and want in both private and state villages. Word that someone might readily provide a loan of money which could buy both liberty and security and might also be used to liquidate debts or pay one's way out of military obligations could not long remain obscure. Lists of rich Theodosian industrialists willing to put up a peasant's redemption were posted or circulated in Moscow. [17] The price of these loans was again conversion to Old Belief and employment in the creditor's establishment to work off the debt. This might take a lifetime at low wages. Apparently the workers as well as the industrialists preferred this form of free labor over factory employment as *obrok* serfs. One master was a lesser evil than two for all concerned —or three, since the industrialist in many cases was purchasing not only a redemption from the lord but freedom from the tsar's army.

Other segments of the labor force did not always come knocking willingly at the doors of future employers. Some had to be enticed, and many were pushed by hard necessity. Many girls and children, who made good candidates for the textile industry, were actively recruited in the villages. A number of women left the countryside for summer employment in the Theodosian industries, and some would remain hidden in workshops in Moscow or were smuggled to other cities until they could obtain urban passports. Orphans and impoverished women from the Moscow *lumpenproletariat* were brought into the community in large numbers. Pregnant girls were taken in, their children to be cared for and educated in the teachings of the sect. Free apartments were provided for many of these people, who would work at home or in the factories of the Preobrazhensk industrialists. In one section of the Lefort suburb, the industrial magnate and leader of the Moscow Theodosians, Guchkov, owned a block of thirty such houses. Elsewhere, in the area surrounding the city, the Old Believers went so far as to squat on state land, where they built factories and houses.[18] Furthermore, a schismatic community could become a hideout for lawbreakers. In Leroy-Beaulieu's words, it "offered a safe refuge to sectarians under pursuit, to deserting soldiers, to vagabonds sporting forged papers. In this crowd of outlaws, the wealthy leaders always found workers at half price and blind tools." [19]

The fugitive could be hidden among the ranks of the Theodosian factory proletariat. A new urban identity could be provided in the passport of a deceased townsman (*meschchanin*), or officials could be bribed to turn over the papers of dead soldiers. A few Theodosian craftsmen became expert passport forgers. If the police were hot on someone's trail, he could be smuggled to some distant Theodosian community or refuge, as far away as Poland if necessary.[20] A kind of "underground railroad" operated in the cities of the Russian Empire, most of which contained Theodosian communities in close contact with Moscow centers. The predominance of Old Believers in the coach transport business on Russian roads and highways facilitated communication in this fugitive network. The laborers in the factory of an Old Believer were also placed in a special tax category which released them from certain bothersome municipal obligations levied on ordinary workers (contributions to sick houses, for example).[21]

If all of this made the factories of Preobrazhensk attractive, one should not describe the proletarianization of schismatic Moscow as a process whereby the leaders of the Theodosian community cynically squeezed greedy peasants, starving children, and criminals. The religious element was not absent from the motivations of employer or worker, any more than in the case of many of the businessmen who gave and borrowed from the capital of the community. Master and servant were bound not only through promissory notes, but also by ties of belief and bonds forged by the state persecution they shared. They protected each other. The richer industrialists set up schools and chapels where the teachings of Old Belief could be instilled and perpetuated. For example, preachers were sent into the Guchkov factory after mealtime to spread the true religion to the workers. The habit of reading holy scripture in the mornings and evenings before and after work, or at spare moments in the shops, was cultivated by all age groups. A woman received a special salary from Guchkov to convert his factory girls to Old Belief.[22] The result was a religious training the keenness of which was noticeable to Russians and foreigners alike. Eventually, secularization would dissipate this bond of faith between workers and employers, just as it would erode the religious ethic of the businessman.

Near to the Theodosians, the equally significant Rogozhsk Priestist community, located in an eastern Moscow suburb a few miles away, followed a similar socioeconomic pattern in the building of capital and a labor force through conversions, legacies, concealment, forged passports, and interest-free loans.[23] The Rogozhsk community, even as Mel'nikov described it in decline in the late nineteenth century, remained an impressive example of a highly organized business and charitable organization. In addition to the cemetery and several churches and chapels, the walled compound contained several poorhouses and homes for the aged of both sexes, convents, an orphanage, a school, an insane asylum, and a reception center, many of these equipped with central kitchens and dining halls. These establishments were supported by the community treasury, although some received money from wealthy merchants and industrialists, who also endowed several dozens of families living in small private homes erected in the same area. At the center of the enclosure was a larger two-story structure which served as the administrative center of the Rogozhsk community. This building contained a large meeting room for the forty-odd elders and caretakers of the organization, business offices, a kitchen and dining room, archives, a crypt, and a rich library of rare books and manuscripts.[24] In the 1830s over one thousand people were estimated to have been living within the Rogozhsk enclosure proper. The number that passed through its shelters and settled into a new urban way of life in the factories, ships, homes, and apartments of the surrounding area was much greater; in 1825, the larger congregation numbered perhaps 68,000. In this larger area were located the establishments of at least 74 industrialists who during the same period were connected with the community.[25]

The Theodosian community at nearby Preobrazhensk was even larger and more impressive than the Rogozhsk enclosure. As Baron von Haxthausen saw it in the late 1840s, there were "two enormous fortress-like quadrangles: high walls and towers, large arched gateways above which rose the numerous cupolas of several churches." Behind the massive gates, taken from an abandoned palace of Peter the Great, were shelters for the poor and aged, hospitals, madhouses, stores, kitchens, and stables, as at Rogozhsk. Unlike the family arrangements of the Priestist community, the Theodosian community segregated the sexes, with one quadrangle reserved for the women. Each quadrangle housed at least a thousand inmates. Fifty to sixty persons occupied each dormitory, which was connected to a chapel. No children were to be seen.

The Preobrazhensk community had more than one hundred officers, ranging from the prior, treasurer, and curators at the top to numerous clerks and sevants for the various shelters and chapels. An iconographer was retained. The prior *(nastoiatel')* was the formal head of the community, but the police reports refer to the richest industrialist of the Moscow Theodosians as his "co-ruler." The actual title of the several wealthy businessmen who ruled Preobrazhensk along with the prior was "curator" *(popuchitel')*. The leading businessman controlled the economic life of the community and owned many houses and tracts of land. He ran its industries. The big merchants and industrialists, together with other leaders of the community, formed a council of twenty-six in the 1840s, which met every Friday morning to discuss and conduct the business and government of Preobrazhensk. It should be noted that this organizational pattern with its merchant control was repeated in the communities of other sects of Old Believers in the Moscow suburbs, even the very small ones. A nearby community of only thirty-five "marrying" Shore Dwellers had the merchant Morozov as its chief curator and custodian of a capital of over 80,000 rubles.[26]

By the mid-nineteenth century, the area around the Preobrazhensk community became the most heavily industrialized part of Moscow. Most of the enterprises were small in scale, not much larger than shops. The recent Soviet student of the Moscow Theodosians, Ryndziunsky, considers only thirty-two of more than two hundred establishments located in the bordering Lefort suburb to have been true factories, that is, by his definition, employing more than twenty-five workers. Among these, of course, were included some very large operations for their time, such as the main Guchkov factory, with a force in the 1840s of nearly one thousand, a number which doubled by the end of the reign of Nicholas I. The Alekseev factory, also located in the Lefort district, employed 645, and there were several others which counted a staff of over one hundred.[27]

The walled compounds which housed the chapels and shelter houses of the Preobrazhensk and Rogozhsk communities thus became large-scale operations which served both as the headquarters of nationwide cults and the nerve centers of local industrial complexes. "They became a combination of convent, seminary and chamber of commerce, a consistory and an exchange."[28] Not just shrines for pilgrims from distant parts of the empire, the Moscow communities were convenient as well to Old Believer merchants from provincial Russia as financial centers where business could be transacted and deals made, new ventures launched. From the Moscow suburbs, Theodosian influence spread to an estimated thirty-eight villages or hamlets in the area of the capital, while the Priestists of Rogozhsk fanned out to dominate the important Russian fairs as far as Siberia and Central Asia.[29]

"The firm and stable organization of these rude masses," commented Baron von Haxthausen on his visit to the Preobrazhensk Cemetery at midcentury, "which has already lasted so long, without any definite system, theology, nobles, or priesthood, is something marvellous. The remarkably powerful spirit of association and the unparalleled communal institutions which have sprung from it, alone explain this phenomenon."[30]

This romanticization, with its Slavophile overtones, was written at a time when the Old Believer communities of Moscow actually were undergoing a rapid disintegration, a process which had been in evidence for at least two decades and one which Haxthausen himself elsewhere recognized.[31] The communal solidarity of Preobrazhensk and Rogozhsk was giving way to a spirit of capitalist individualism and private-property consciousness, while the puritanism, piety, and nationalism of the first century of the schism were losing the battle with Westernism, secularism, and materialism.

The general causes and obvious symptoms of this disintegration were in evidence by the 1830s. The growth of large personal fortunes and involved business holdings, as well as simply a general rise in the material situation of many members, particularly of the Theodosian community, caused frustration within the cramping restraints of the old puritanism. Few still held to the injunction of celibacy, but many wished to have conjugal unions and families dignified by formal community recognition. There was a growing reluctance to obliterate private estates that had been built up painfully over the years or to surrender fortunes the fruits of which people had been accustomed to enjoy and which they had jealously come to consider rightful and exclusive inheritances. The result of these growing tensions was the withdrawal of members of the Theodosian creed to join other sects, such as the Shore Dwellers, who recognized marriage. Some withdrew to form new, small splinter groups like the Moninists, whose allowance of marriage invited as early as 1812 the secession of a number of wealthy merchants from the Preobrazhensk Cemetery. Some of the Theodosians of St. Petersburg made an even earlier and far more radical break; they joined the Westernized society of the capital, adopting its fashions in European clothing, abandoning the old prohibitions, and even marrying outside the sect.[32]

This foreshadowed a general tendency among all of the Old Believer industrial communities by the 1840s and 1850s. Like the "fathers" and "sons" Turgenev described among the nobility and intelligentsia during the same period, a new materialistic and Westernizing second generation emerged from amidst the Old Believers. Businessmen rather than religious leaders, they found Westernization far more conducive to their profit-making and their pastimes than the old Russian austerities. Like the Nihilists, they repudiated their heritage. As Leroy-Beaulieu later reflected on a process that continued for some decades:

To the great scandal of good provincial souls, young Old Believers are already seen in Moscow smoking, shaving, dancing, frequenting the theatres. Wealth, which has begun the Raskol's social eman- ciaption, will end by accomplishing its intellectual emancipation also, so that, after having been temporarily a source of strength, money and the conditions it creates will become a cause of weak- ness and undermine the Raskol's doctrines and principles.[33]

In vain the "fathers" of the schismatic suburbs of the old capi- tal, like their Slavophile contemporaries in the salons of the Mos- cow aristocracy, attempted to preserve the past. In 1846 we see Semen Kozmin, one of the Theodosian leaders of the old genera- tion, banishing from the chapels and from among the new arrivals to the community all who were wearing European clothing or who sported Western fashions.[34]

The tsarist state of Nicholas I unwittingly accelerated the secu- larization of the schismatic middle class of Moscow through perse- cution. The Old Believer communities came under increasing police surveillance in the 1840s in the fear that they were hotbeds of her- esy, subversion, and corruption. The fact of cloistered communal living and the existence of conjugal bonds unsanctified by the mar- riage sacrament were compounded by rumors and lurid reports into accusations of sexual immorality and concubinage concealed behind the walls of Preobrazhensk and Rogozhsk. Politically the Theodo- sians had long before compromised themselves in the eyes of the state by the suspicious dealings of certain of the Moscow commu- nity with Napoleon in 1812.[35] It was also believed by many that the Old Believers were engaged in counterfeiting, profiteering, and other criminal activities.

In 1847, after two decades of harassment, the government struck with full vigor. The asylums and homes of Preobrazhensk and Rogozhsk were seized and put under direct state administra- tion. The altars of the churches were padlocked. Some leaders were arrested and banished. Finally, the Theodosians were forced to marry officially, an obligation which many no doubt welcomed.

The reaction to this persecution was no longer resistance, sui- cide, and flight, as had been the case a century earlier, but rather compromise, disavowal, and indifference. In the 1850s, many leaders of the Theodosian community rejoined the Orthodox Church in the *Edinoverie* movement, a kind of halfway house for the Old Believers sponsored by the government to recapture dissenters for the official faith.[36] Others had become secularized and Westernized businessmen for whom religious duties were of little concern and who abandoned the precarious status of Old Believer with ease. A half century of heavy tsarist oppression descended on the Moscow Raskolnik communities, but they managed to survive it, as well as to endure the Revolution and the atheist regime which followed. Over 100,000 Old Believers of the two main sects still inhabit Moscow,[37] and Rogozhsk, with its vast Pokrovsky cathedral and magnificent icons, still stands. The state superintendent of the Old Believers is the descendant of a wealthy Moscow manufacturing family.

The story of another such family—the Guchkovs—during the last century of tsarism epitomizes this entire area of Russian social and economic history. Four generations of Guchkovs illustrate three stages of social evolution: the original accumulation of capital by the religious leader of a dissenting group; the building of an industrial empire by his secularized, capitalist sons and grandsons; and, finally, a fourth generation making a decisive move from business to politics. It is a story that is not unique to Russia, but the Russian overtones are unmistakable.

The founder of what became one of the great industrial fortunes in Moscow was Fedor Alekseevich Guchkov, an *obrok*-paying serf who was permitted by his master to migrate to the city at the end of the eighteenth century to set up a weaving shop. In less than three decades he had developed one of the largest woolen factories in Russia and had put up the small fortune necessary to buy himself and his family out of serfdom. Fedor Guchkov's devotion to business was surpassed by his loyalty to the Preobrazhensk community, which he had joined and of which he remained one of the leaders until his political exile in the repressions of the last years of the reign of Nicholas I. Devout in his belief, he was content to retain his beard and peasant overcoat and an essentially old-Russian religious and personal life. His factories he viewed as congregations of the faithful and as schools as much as business enterprises. In 1825 he transferred to his sons, who had been trained in the business, the control of his factories. The elder Guchkov continued to assume a major responsibility for the business affairs and the exchequer of the Theodosian community. Since his own property and enterprises were bound intimately with the financial affairs of the group, as a way of both conforming with government property restrictions and deceiving the state as to the holdings of the community, Guchkov's sons soon came to assume a major voice in the disposal of the Preobrazhensk purse, although they stood outside the formal religious leadership of the group. Even after 1847, when they became converted to the less restricting Shore Dweller sect to further consolidate the family fortune, they retained this control. By 1853, the main plants of the Guchkovs employed 1850 workers and were mechanized, producing goods to the value of 700,000 rubles yearly. In addition, they were founding new factories and farming out work to hundreds of homes and shops in the Preobrazhensk area.[38]

Ivan and Efim Guchkov were modern businessmen who dressed in Western clothing, had Western education, and had traveled to Europe. They devoted themselves fully to the expansion of their enterprises and fortunes, and when their religious background became an obstacle or a disadvantage, it was sacrificed to the interests of of the business. Their conversion to the Shore Dweller sect was followed in 1853 by their rejoining the Orthodox Church in the *Edinoverie* movement. Efim's son, Ivan, remained in the business but also served in urban government posts and in the imperial administration. The fourth generation was essentially *rentier*—they closed down the family business, invested their money in stocks and bonds, and turned their energy and enthusiasm almost wholly to politics. Nikolai Guchkov was the mayor of Moscow for several years. Aleksander Guchkov—adventurer, public servant, liberal politician of the last years of the tsarist regime, Octobrist leader in the Duma, and minister of war for the Provisional Government—best represents the final variant of the several generations of the Russian schism and of the nineteenth-century Russian middle class. It is interesting to note that one of Guchkov's colleagues in the early leadership of the government of 1917 was the liberal minister of commerce and industry, A. S. Konovalov, heir to another famous textile enterprise, which also had been founded by a serf and Old

Believer in the early nineteenth century.[39] The small Russian industrialist bourgeoisie had attained partial political power, if only briefly.

The business activities of the Old Believers provoked both hostility and sympathy on the part of their contemporary Russians and in the subsequent century produced a variety of interpretations as to the motivations and significance of the Raskolnik entrepreneur. Policemen saw crime at the source of the Old Believer's wealth—counterfeiting, smuggling, profiteering in scarce goods, and the raiding of legacies; "the milch-cow of rascally millionaires," said one.[40] For some observers, the appeal of Old Belief for factory workers and entrepreneurs alike was purely a materialistic one, a new way of getting money and labor rather than a better road to salvation. Other writers, during the Populist period, viewed the business activities of the Raskolniki sympathetically as a democratic expression of the Russian people against the state, a kind of economic struggle following upon the earlier religious and political resistance of the schismatics. The revolutionary intelligentsia of the same era saw potential allies in the Old Believers. In our own century Soviet historians have alternated between praising the Old Believers as a progressive democratic movement in conflict with tsarism and condemning them as capitalistic exploiters operating behind a screen of religion.[41] In the West such distinguished scholars as Leroy-Beaulieu and Max Weber both suggested comparisons of the social status, ethos, and prosperity of the Russian Old Believers and sectarians with European Calvinists, Quakers, and Methodists and such groups as the Copts, Parsees, and Armenians of the Orient.[42]

The investigation of these several interesting theories and interpretations forms a substantial subject in itself, beyond the scope of this article. It should be noted, however, that none of the authors in the West devoted any comprehensive or systematic study to the problems and relationships of Russian business and religious history; they have given us only passing references. What might appear to be a tempting model in the Weberian analysis of the Protestant ethic and the rise of capitalism in Western Europe could easily be misleading when set in the Russian context. At any rate, if his few observations of the Old Believers and sectarians provide food for thought, Weber never attempted an application to Russia of his more general theories of entrepreneurship.

The materials which have been utilized for the present investigation limited to the Moscow Old Believers suggest the following conclusions. Making themselves felt in their surroundings like outcast religious and national minorities in many parts of the world, they played a limited but not insignificant role in initiating the commercial and industrial modernization of the hitherto traditional agrarian society of the Moscow region. Persecuted, relegated to a position of social inferiority, cut off from the normal channels of political, bureaucratic, and agrarian power and privilege, yet consigned to an outcast legal status which opened to them a commercial freedom not permitted the traditional, recognized classes of society, the Moscow Old Believers, as a matter of belief and survival, closed ranks in austere, disciplined, self-sufficient religious communities. These communities came to assume many of the commercial and, at the beginning of the factory age in parts of Russia, industrial functions of the society. Money, as Leroy-Beaulieu observed, became "its *nervus rerum,* the ruble has all along been its great weapon, for self-defense and conversion." [43]

The significance of the Old Believers for the formation of a Muscovite industrial working force in the early nineteenth century is comparable to the role attributed to the enclosure movement in England or to the Irish migration to the United States. For all the differences in tradition and geography, each was an important part of the process of getting peasants off the land and into cities, shops, and factories. To be sure, the extent to which the Theodosian community facilitated this modernizing function is by no means equal to that of the transatlantic Celtic migration or the English enclosures and poor laws, even if we add to the Theodosian community the several tens of thousands of workers in the equally significant Rogozhsk community, as well as the Shore Dweller and other smaller schismatic and sectarian factions in Moscow. Nevertheless, through this process, a substantial segment of the textile enterprises of the city and the surrounding towns could undergo a first stage of industrialization and the formation of a factory working class.

In the case of the Moscow schismatic enterprises, the institutional aspect was more important than the ideological in the accumulation of capital and the organization of production. Not individual capitalists moved by a worldly ascetic "calling" in the accumulation of wealth in business affairs so much as a group capital through legacies, contributions, and a communal way of life and enterprise determined the economic expansion of the Moscow Old Believers. The Russian communal tradition, glorified by the Slavophiles and the *narodniki,* asserted itself, although not for long. Money and commerce brought with it materialistic individualism, property consciousness, and the appearance of a class of secularized, private entrepreneurs.

VII

Although the state and foreign entrepreneurs were important in the industrialization of Russia in the late tsarist period, a native industrial "bourgeoisie" reached maturity at the same time, and by 1914 had come to play a significant economic and political role. This home-grown Russian capitalism was strongest and most characteristic in Moscow. In his analysis of the Muscovite textile capitalist families, Roger Portal *portrays both the significance and the peculiarities of an important segment of the Russian bourgeoisie. Professor Portal teaches at the Sorbonne and is head of the Institut D'Études Slaves. He is author of* L'oural au xviii siecle *(Paris, 1950),* Pierre le Grand *(Paris, 1962), and* The Slavs *(1969). He has written numerous articles on the evolution of the industrial bourgeoisie in tsarist Russia. His article first appeared in* Cahiers du Monde Russe et Sovietique *(1963), IV, 5–40, and is reprinted here with the permission of the publisher, Mouton and Co.*

ROGER PORTAL

Muscovite Industrialists: The Cotton Sector (*1861-1914*)

Nineteenth-century Russia, a big village! And yet from this peasant people a bourgeoisie with very particular traits was born: it appeared late and was small in number, since around 1850 the three guilds which encompassed almost all the people in commerce and industry (among whom, moreover, a great number tended more toward craftsmanship and shopkeeping) added up to only about 178,000 members in a population of 68 million inhabitants. Furthermore, those that we can truly consider bourgeois and who belonged to the first two guilds added up to less than 8,000. Russia's feeble economic development explains this late appearance of the bourgeoisie. Still purely commercial in the eighteenth century, functioning in a framework of traditional commerce where barter continued to play a large role, the Russian bourgeoisie did not reach the category of industrialists until the middle of the nineteenth century. Before this time the nobles fulfilled the industrial role (particularly in metallurgy) which limited the economic importance of the bourgeoisie. What was needed was the industrial thrust of the nineteenth century,[1] and the rapid development of cotton textile mills, in order to bring forth from the peasantry—even more than from small-trade and urban craftsmen—an industrial bourgeoisie. As for the financial bourgeoisie, in a country where banking was more or less nonexistent around 1860, it only began to develop timidly at the end of the nineteenth century.

At the core of this new bourgeoisie, textile manufacturers occupied first place, particularly those of the cotton sector, by virtue of their origin, the geographical placement of their enterprises (situated for the most part in the central region), and by their very Muscovite character. The goal of this essay, which only scratches the surface of this theme, is to recall the general conditions under which the cotton industry developed in Russia after 1861; to follow the destiny of some of these bourgeois families whose economic and social importance grew steadily until the Revolution; to examine to what extent their ranks were increased by new additions born of economic development and the Industrial Revolution; and finally to pose some questions for debate on the character, function, and role of a social class born a hundred years before its fall, in a state which remained right up to the end, in spite of its constitutional appearances, autocratic and authoritarian.

The great reforms under Alexander II mark a turning point in the history of the Russian bourgeoisie. The liberation of the peasant (1861)[2] and the *Zemstva* (1864) were among the major decisions which suddenly widened its field of activity. The application of the statute weighed on the fate of the peasant up till the Revolution of 1905; partition operations lasted way into the 1880s; the payment of redemption indemnities only stopped in 1906, the date when it was purely and simply suppressed. By liberating the serfs, the statute facilitated the recruitment of an industrial manual labor force, while the terms and conditions of the new repartition of lands accelerated the process of social differentiation in the villages. The development of a more comfortable peasantry tended to create a more demanding clientele; the textile industries had not only to respond to a greater demand for fabrics, but also to offer a greater variety of them as well. The moment when the Jacquard craft spread in Russia corresponds precisely to the formation of a clientele which, in the country as well as in the city, desired fabrics of quality and richer design.

However, the increase in purchasing power of a part of the peasantry was also linked to the situation of wheat in the world market, and to the government policy of developing means of transportation. The second half of the nineteenth century was the period of railroad construction which mobilized an abundant labor force and brought about the creation of numerous factories; the industrial thrust of the 1890s was due in great part to the initiative of the state in this domain, especially affecting the metallurgy sector. This industrial surge manifested itself as well in a rapid growth of consumer industries. But the construction of railroads, in this immense country where the major problem was that of distance, served also to free the centers of cereal production which, up until then, had been poorly connected with backward regions and ports of export.[3] The commercialization of agricultural products—particularly of wheat and rye which were bought in large quantities by Western European countries, and represented on the average, from 1870 on, 46 to 50 percent of the total value of exports—rapidly increased the capital market. This market, in the form of investments, distribution of salaries which were converted into consumer goods, and direct purchases, created conditions which were very favorable to the growth of textile industries and to the enrichment of the industrial bourgeoisie. The general movement of the economy was marked not only by the development of the big businesses, but also by a swarm of hand-labor trades, at least in the slowly developing industrial districts. In this respect the cotton industry occupied a special place, since it was already a pioneer in the front lines of progress. The marginal working class, which prosperity harbored in the shadow of large, but, as yet, underdeveloped enterprises, scarcely emerged. If, in the first half of the century, numerous small businessmen had raised themselves up to the level of big industrialists, this was no longer the case after 1861; an important source of recruitment for the upper bourgeoisie was dried up. In the cotton industry, the newcomers, although few in number as we will see, came mainly from a milieu of rich merchants or concessionaires franchised by the state; and, thanks to considerable financial means, they were able to compete with established manufacturers. The consumer market, rapidly expanding in this area, became a kind of *de facto* monopoly.[4]

This monopoly, however, had rather narrow limits: the general standard of living rose very slowly, in fits and starts, provoked by political events, bad harvests, the stoppage and slowing down of railroad construction. The reforms in the 1860s had a regressive effect on those industries which relied upon servile labor. These reforms caused a crisis in the metal and wool industries which were then in the hands of great noble proprietors. The cotton industry, whose manual labor force was hired, suffered little. But it had to reduce its production considerably during the Civil War, which interrupted deliveries of American cotton: cottons from Central Asia before the 1880s still counted for little in supplying factories. Also the growth of textile industries did not resume until around 1865; the increasing demands of the rural market and the military orders, during the Russian-Turkish War, explain why the annual average consumption per person of cotton fabrics had doubled in twenty years, going from 7.5 arshins (5.32 meters) to 15 arshins (10.65 meters) from the years 1856–1860 and 1876–1880, the population having increased, indeed, by some 20 million inhabitants.

After 1880 the textile industries, particularly cotton, which was more sensitive to fluctuations in the peasant market than the wool industry (sustained more by state orders), suffered two major slumps, between 1880–1882 and 1890–1892. The consumer market stagnated; the needs per person for cotton fabric—in a population which rose from 98 million in 1880 to 118 million in 1889—climbed painfully and slowly from 15 arshins (10.65 meters) to 17 (12.07 meters). After the great famine of 1891—during the so-called Witte period—the textile industries grew again, less marked, however, in the consumer market than in that of military equipment. The accumulation of national capital, the call for foreign capital, the great projects undertaken by the state directly profited the metallurgy, construction, and building industries. However, this was also the period when the cotton bourgeoisie consolidated its position, completed the modernization of its materials, developed its production, and increased its profits. The crisis of 1900–1902, a serious one for the metallurgy industry, on the whole scarcely touched the cotton bourgeoisie. The link between the cotton sector and the peasantry, its close dependence vis-à-vis the agricultural sector, protected it from the repercussions of cyclical crises, as long as these did not coincide with a bad harvest. But the harvests of 1899 to 1903 were satisfactory and, on the average, 16 percent superior to former harvests. In this regard, the nature of crises in Russian is complex; it is difficult to place them, at least before 1900, in a valid pattern among the great industrial nations of Western Europe. In any case, and this fact is self-evident, between 1900 and 1913 the textile industries (and, in general, consumer industries) suffered their particular difficulties, but did not seem interdependent on other sectors of production in a country where, in spite of the development of cities and the growth of industry, the market still remained essentially constituted of an enormous peasantry. Although the crisis was prolonged elsewhere, the cotton sector experienced a new vigor from 1902 on, and especially after 1905. The suppression of redemption indemnities in 1906, which represented a sum of 80 million rubles—a rise in salaries which could be evaluated at 15 percent between 1906–1910 [5]—raised the purchasing power of a population which now numbered 160 million inhabitants. But the peasant market expanded also, thanks to the colonization of Siberia, the increase—favored by world agreement —of the price of wheat on the national market (20 percent between 1899–1913), and lastly, and most importantly, a series of good harvests, particularly in 1909, allowing exports to reach a record figure of 847 million poods (13.5 million tons). The cotton industry, therefore, was maintained at a more or less even keel up to the eve of the First World War; [6] it benefited, between 1910–1913, from the general economic thrust, the importance of which is comparable to that of the Witte period. However, this thrust (1910–1913) had a somewhat different basis, since it can be explained more by the development of cities and the rapid growth of the national market than by the initiative of the state.

The Russian bourgeoisie, born of a half-servile,[7] "feudal" society, remained for a long time peasant-like in its mentality, submissive to the authorities, poorly structured though varied. Whether it appeared in the country among the well-to-do peasants, lending themselves to commerce, usury, and hand-labor trades, or in the city among the *posad* people (the *posad* being the tradesmen's quarter), whether it was rural or urban, the bourgeoisie as a class was never in real opposition to power. It never conquered the cities. Although it had participated, in the past, in popular riots, it never acquired its freedom through force. Russian cities were not equipped with a belfry whose bell would assemble the members of a commune, thereby demonstrating the power of the urban bourgeoisie. If the bourgeoisie participated in municipal life in the nineteenth century, it was by virtue of a granted statute which, even on the threshold of the twentieth century, only gave power to a very small bourgeois minority, among which the great textile owners occupied a preponderant place. Moreover, the majority of the bourgeoisie before the suppression of serfdom, mainly merchants and manufacturers (the latter only appearing after 1820), were not exclusively of rustic origin, but more often of servile origin (that is to say, they passed from servitude directly to the bourgeoisie); they carried for a long time the weight of that servitude in their behavior vis-à-vis the nobles and power in general.

A bourgeoisie, in the Western sense of the word, free and playing a political role, scarcely appeared in Russia before 1905. Before, in the period between 1861–1905, in spite of the efforts of certain bourgeois representatives to play a political role, they counted for very little in the government; compared to the bourgeoisie, even the *gosti,* one of the groups among the entourage of Alexis Mihailovich, who held in their hands Russia's main export trade in the seventeenth century, enjoyed a greater audience! The Russian bourgeoisie of the nineteenth century remained confined to municipal administrative tasks, and also to those offered them by the *zemstva*. At the economic level, for example, in matters dealing with tariffs, the bourgeoisie was hardly called upon by the tsar to give its opinion before the years 1880–1890.[8] It is only at this time that the bourgeoisie begins to group together through meetings of manufacturers and merchants, to take cognizance of its existence as a class and to oppose the nobles and criticize power. As V. K. Yatsunsky expressed it,[9] "The dominant figures of the bourgeoisie were more and more the big manufacturers and the representatives of high finance." Among them, the promoters of spinning and weaving cotton, who set themselves up in the central region (of Moscow-

Ivanovo), did their utmost to work side by side with ironmasters of noble status from the Ural region and with Petersburg bankers involved in international finance. They were proud of their Muscovite origins. To be exact, foreigners, in this country where Belgian and French capital was plentiful, where the worth of the Ukraine was largely determined from the outside, furnished a very small contingent to the Russian bourgeoisie, with the exception of Germans of Baltic origin who were rapidly assimilated into Russian culture; these Germans were numerous in the region of St. Petersburg, of Estonia and of Livonia where, moreover, textiles occupied an important if secondary place.[10] Foreign enterprises were in fact usually managed by directors who were themselves only provisionally residing in Russia. In relation to the St. Petersburg region, highly cosmopolitan, and the Ukraine, almost taken over by foreign companies, the Moscow center, in its broadest sense, appeared as the fortress of the true Russian industrial bourgeoisie, cultivating both a patriotism tainted by a sense of regionalism, and feelings of bitterness toward the privileged capital on the banks of the Neva. However, the bourgeoisie remained faithful to the ruling powers, to the regime. On a political level the bourgeoisie was conservative; on a social level, conformist, more even perhaps than in the preceding period, that is, the few decades which preceded the liberation of the serfs.

It can be noted that a good number of the bourgeois manufacturers were Old Believers. Up to 1850, their position in regard to the ruling powers was cautious and reserved; the ruling powers alternated between tolerance and persecution in regard to them.[11] After 1861, a climate of tolerance prevailed, and the Old Believers, now wealthy, had themselves evolved, fitting well into privileged society. They no longer needed to play along with the ruling powers. By a veritable secularization of economic activity, which brought about improved education of children both in Russia and abroad, participation in local administrative life, worldly relations, and reconciliation with Orthodoxy (sometimes even a return to it), the once original character of this relatively closed society disappeared. The Old Believer manufacturers had doubtlessly never been opponents on the political level; they were nonetheless suspect by the government. In the vast current of capitalism which marked the

years between 1880 and 1890, religious differences faded and social behavior became uniform. The Old Believers, like the more
devout orthodox, firmly supported the regime which assured order
in the factories. There could have been, before 1861, a conflict between the interests of the state which defended the feudal system by
seeking out fugitive serfs, and those of the Old Believer manufacturers who were gathering and integrating these serfs into the sect,
while camouflaging them in order to assure for themselves a submissive hand-labor force. By the end of the nineteenth century, the
objectives of the state and the great capitalist bourgeoisie were essentially consolidated. The amount of power gradually gained by
the bourgeoisie before 1905, however, was mainly determined by
immediate economic considerations. It was after 1905 that its role
suddenly grew in the Duma (through the help of the Kadet Party),
in the political and financial press, in industrial contracts which
placed great pressure on the regime—in all these things the Russian bourgeoisie was present and increasingly active; now we encounter some of the great names of cotton sector manufacturers.
The Provisional Government marked the peak of the influence of
the bourgeoisie. The Bolshevik Revolution swept it away in a few
months. Here, then, is the tragic fate of a social class which disappeared, scarcely one hundred years old, before having even won a
place in the state that its economic role merited.

The period of time which extends from the suppression of servitude (1861)—a date which marks, in the "periodization" accepted by Soviet historians, the end of feudalism and the beginnings
of the capitalist period—to the First World War (during which
Russia broke little by little into the circle of great industrial powers) merits a kind of special attention. We would indeed expect to
find the bourgeoisie of the textile industry, born in the precapitalist
period, growing fat on new orders and developing in the core of an
expanding economy, particularly during the so-called Witte period.
But it does not seem that its overall strength really increased. According to Yatsunsky, there would only be a minuscule number of
new textile manufacturers after 1861. Even if a more thorough
study forced us to modify this statement, it is nevertheless true that
among the representatives of the big bourgeoisie who, on the eve of
the war, began to play a political role from 1905 on—furnishing

advice to ministers, dominating the stock exchange committees, and holding in their hands the most important enterprises—newcomers who became rich were rare. Almost all of these bourgeois date back to the first half of the century and some, although exceptions, to the eighteenth century. This isn't surprising, for in a country whose economic development only began to move ahead in the 1890s, whose market is, between 1870–1880, relatively narrow, the goals that were set and the possibilities of achieving them for newcomers, if they didn't have any exceptional financial means, were not very encouraging. Social advancement, so rapid between 1820–1860 (and, moreover, including only a restricted number of manufacturers), stopped. The great names of the cotton sector—Morozov, Prokhorov, Konovalov, Garelin, Khlyudov, Malyutin,[12] to mention only a few—were those from solidly established enterprises, already set up in the 1880s, and these would occupy a dominant place until the Revolution.

It would be impossible to cite equally numerous examples of new manufacturers in the textile industry after 1860. Some manufacturers in the cotton-spinning sector were able to establish themselves in Russia after 1840, at a time when it was possible to buy English machines; however, the majority of spinners, of course, were already textile manufacturers or printers whose businesses had been established for twenty years. The textile industry, therefore, grew, but remained in the same hands; *the industrial bourgeoisie increased only slightly in number.*

It is important to add that a certain number of manufacturers whose businesses were born in the second half of the century were ennobled and detached themselves from the bourgeois class. This is not an unusual situation. A veritable *cursus honorum* elevated the merchants to titled positions and noble privileges. Among those who belonged to the guild, a rather imposing number received the title of "Honorable Citizen" (*pochetnii grazhdanin*), which was a transitional role between the bourgeoisie and the nobility. Also, the number of bourgeois still belonging to the three merchant guilds (especially the first two) at the end of the nineteenth century was very small in proportion to the size of the population. In the Census of 1897 (the only complete census taken before the Revolution), the total force of merchants (and consequently also of manufactur-

ers) was evaluated at some 280,000, to which figure it is necessary
to add nearly 343,000 Honorable Citizens who were at the threshold of nobility (for the title of "Honorable Citizen" could be personal or hereditary) and who constituted, on the whole, an upper
bourgeoisie, their title being linked to their success in business. On
the whole, then, this bourgeoisie numbers a bit less than 625,000
citizens from the three guilds in a population of 128 million inhabitants. The majority of manufacturers who formed an elite merchant class were among the Honorable Citizens. Among the manufacturers the textile bourgeoisie formed dynasties; they were few in
number but rich and powerful on the local and municipal levels.

In other words, industrial development, without having attained the enormity which coincided with Russia's resources . . .
had nonetheless taken monopolistic forms of organizations which
brought on the beginning of a sclerosis not only in the economic
domain, but also in that of society as well. The wealth of Siberia itself, which scarcely extended beyond the stage of commercial and
agricultural activity, enriched only a few merchants and manufacturers who were already established in central Russia. In the recent
histories of Russia and the United States, one could compare the
immensity of Siberia to that of the Far West; but the chances of
succeeding for the American pioneer were singularly greater than
those of a Russian settler. In Russia there is hardly an impression
of a fluid society, not that that society, on the other hand, was totally fused; but again, its mobility could only be judged following
an in-depth study, this time putting to one side the great families in
order to study the mass of well-to-do people on the verge of attaining real wealth; that is, people who were on the threshold of large
commerce and industry.

The great success of cotton enterprises occurred between
1880–1890. These enterprises benefited not only from general conditions having to do with the development of Russia, but also from
special circumstances as well, such as the policy of tariff protection
and the enlargement of the interior market around the Ukraine (undergoing great change) and Siberia (where cottons abounded as a
result of the railroad at the end of the century). It is by geographi-
cally extending their field of action that the manufacturers developed their businesses, and the necessities of selling led them to or-

ganize their trade, which had become, because of this, more fruitful. But especially by modernizing and mechanizing their businesses, they rapidly increased their profits at the same time as they increased their production. Lastly, the great cotton manufacturers often got rich and consolidated their position in the business world—once again we are dealing essentially here with industrialists from the Moscow region—by coupling banking activity with industrial activity.

It is impossible to separate completely the industrial bourgeoisie from the commercial bourgeoisie. The majority of manufacturers sold at least a part of their production in the markets and fairs, and some of them, as late as the middle of the nineteenth century —such as in the case of the Konovalov family[13]—dealt in trading products they didn't even manufacture. The Konovalov family inundated the Ukrainian market with table linen and fabrics which they bought from other government manufacturers in Vladimir, and their personal production represents only a percentage of the total figure of the business.

However, the relationship between textile industry and textile commerce changed during the course of the nineteenth century. Manufacturers had always sought to develop their sales without having to pass through the hands of merchants who, up to the *ukaz* of 1842, had a theoretical monopoly over retail trade. To be exact, the distinction between retail and wholesale trade scarcely existed for the manufacturers, and the *ukaz* of 1842 simply reinforced a *de facto* situation by suppressing every legal hindrance. In the 1840s stores opened up in Moscow, Petersburg, and other cities where the Prokhorovs, Guchkovs, and Soposhnikovs sold their products directly from their factories. The manufacturers also avoided big middlemen by bringing their fabrics to market themselves, and the fabrics were bought by peddlers whose role, by assuring a distribution in small quantities of manufactured products across the country, was immense: in 1846 at the Nizhnii Novgorod Fair, transactions on cotton fabrics reached the sum of 7,734,000 silver rubles; of this figure the peddlers' sales represented 5,600,000 rubles, close to 68 percent.[14]

But in the second half of the nineteenth century the situation changed. The development of railroads and the organization of credit facilitated the formation of a more and more active sales market where the manufacturers found it more advantageous to go through wholesale middlemen in order to dispose of their goods. Wholesale trade was organized then in the capitals and large cities rather than at the fairs where, at Nizhnii Novgorod as well as at Irbit (the second greatest fair in Russia in terms of its important transactions), the peddlers' purchases were reduced, to the advantage of the wholesalers. Department stores were constructed in order to house the more and more valuable masses of merchandise.

A large part of the sale of textiles was in the hands of certain big middlemen, the *skupshchiki,* who, around the 1870s, busied themselves only with commerce. Numbering about fifteen, there was among them the Shchukin family, one of the members of which, Peter Vasilevich, who died in 1912 and was a famous art collector, dominated almost all the wholesale trade of cotton fabrics. The Shchukin family, whose business was made into a company in 1878 (a limited partnership), sold mainly printed cotton fabrics from the Ivanovo-Voznesensk region (products from Derbenev, Polusin, Gandurin, Garelin, etc.). The immensity of the country and the difficulties of communication led, on the other hand, to a geographical specialization of commerce. The Siberian market gave rise to middlemen as well, among whom the richest was certainly Aleksei Federovich Vtorov who, in 1866, opened a wholesale trade in Irkutsk and founded a chain of stores in many Siberian cities. Vtorov sold a little of everything—haberdashery, shoes, and especially fabrics—and he drew on important capital from outside sources, since he wasn't able to dig into his own funds, in order to make a profit from one year to the next: indeed, he needed a month and half to travel to and from Moscow, three to four months to prepare his supplies and goods, which were then sent by wagon to the places where they would be sold. The opening of the Trans-Siberian Railroad did, of course, completely transform the conditions of Siberian commerce. In 1897 Vtorov moved to Moscow where he constructed a huge commercial building. In 1900 he organized his business into a company backed by a capital of 3 million rubles, absorbed another Siberian business—a trading firm—and finally, in order to best assure a large diversity of fabrics, bought up the cotton fabric factory of A. G. Gusev. The company, directed by Vtorov until his

death in 1911, had therefore a mixed character—it was both commercial and industrial.

However, Vtorov's activity contains another interesting aspect.
He was, at the onset of the First World War, the principal organizer of wholesale trade for several industrial companies—in particular three large businesses from the Moscow region, the N. N.
Konshin Company,[15] Danilov Manufacturing,[16] and the Hubner
Company [17]—and he formed from the three of them, on his own initiative, a commercial company of retail stores selling cotton, yarn,
and fabrics in Russia's principal European and Asiatic cities. In
this respect Vtorov's activities are tied up with efforts of Russian
industry to organize commercially which can be observed in a later
period, before the end of the nineteenth century, and which also
point up more striking analogies between the economic activity of
the Russian and Western bourgeoisie.

Another reason for the rapidly growing wealth of the textile
bourgeoisie, from 1880–1890, was the mechanization of business.
Spinning mills equipped with machines spontaneously shot up in
the 1840s. But in the cotton industry, in 1861, manual labor prevailed in weaving, and the industry depended mainly on distribution
warehouses. In 1866 there could be counted only forty-two mechanical looms in this area of production. But in 1879 the number
climbed to ninety-two, and at the same time the amount of laborers
working on mechanical looms in the factory increased from 94,600
to 162,700, while those rural laborers working on hand looms for
factory warehouses decreased in number from 66,200 to 50,200. At
that time domestic weaving (weaving done in the home) already
represented no more than one-fortieth of the total production of
cotton fabrics. It was in the 1880s that domestic and handweaving
of cotton fabrics almost totally disappeared; [18] the factories concentrated their energies on manufacturing activity, and factory labor
organized itself and became more intensive. A certain number of
factories continued to submit to the rhythm of the seasons, and
were thus almost inactive (even in a city like Moscow), during the
summer months, since their workers went off to work in the fields
at this time of the year. However, it was during this era that businesses began to report large profits and that their industrial boom
took place, favored by tariff protection legislation. It was also the

time when the industrial bourgeoisie started to buy land—no longer
only in proportion to what was basically needed to run the factories
(peat bogs, forests which supplied materials for fuel and construction, and plots of land allotted to master workers in order to keep
them), but land which maintained the family and, above all, ennobled its new owner. This transfer of land was rather rare before
1861; up to this time the nobles held a monopoly on landed property. Toward the end of the century, sales of the nobles' lands to
the bourgeoisie multiplied; the bourgeoisie as a class improved its
station and grew strong through this activity of buying land. Lastly,
there was another form of activity which was closely linked to the
textile industry and was also a decisive factor in the increasing
wealth of the bourgeoisie: this was banking. Textile manufacturers
were generally their own bankers at this time; they hadn't yet added
to their industrial activity the banking affairs which would one day
greatly surpass the textile domain. Self-banking was a particular
trait of the textile bourgeoisie from the Moscow region, who never
depended on Petersburg banks, who founded their own banks, with
Russian capital, and without the help of foreigners; in relation to the
Petersburg bourgeoisie, these manufacturers had a very nationalistic
character.

Among the families who solidly established their fortune in
the first half of the nineteenth century, the Morozov family—so
great and important because of the number of its enterprises (which
were dispersed among the Moscow, Tver, and Vladimir regions),
and because of its role in the economic and political life of Russia
at the onset of World War I—merits a special study which will not
be made in this article. We will use as an example the case of the-
Prokhorov family, a typically Muscovite family with regard to its
mentality as well as the special nature of its business activities. The
Prokhorov family [19] who owned in Moscow the great Three Mountains Factory (today opposite the Ukraine Hotel on the west side of
the Moskva River) had its origin in serfdom, but was liberated from
the time of Catherine II and moved up to the merchant class (or
"station") before embarking upon its industrial career. Its businesses, which were concerned mainly with printing calico, were
consolidated into a firm in 1843. In the 1840s it added spinning to
weaving. Its essential acitivity, however, remained printing calico,

and the business grew in 1877 through the purchase of both a dye factory and a nearby printing factory; the Prokhorov factory grew so much that it henceforth occupied an entire quarter along the Moskva. The firm expanded into a company in 1874. A fire destroyed the factory in 1877; it was reconstructed and modernized between 1877–1882; it then kept 700 workers busy.

In the 1880s the head of the family, Ivan Yakovlevich Prokhorov (1833–1881), disappeared at the age of forty-eight, leaving behind six children, two of whom were boys—Sergei and Nikolai. The mother, Anna Aleksandrovna (1840–1909), seemed to play a great role in the development of these two youngsters, whom she wanted to shield from foreign influence; the Prokhorov family was clearly nationalistic, hostile to cosmopolitanism which already marked certain elements of the industrial bourgeoisie, but open-minded enough to recognize that the Moscow milieu was necessary to their becoming great industrialists, who, by necessity, would be in continual contact with the outside. Also, like other boys, Sergei and Nikolai were sent to the Revel (Tallin) Gymnasium where teaching was conducted in German (the usual language of commerce) and discipline was severe. After having graduated from the gymnasium in 1877, Sergei and Nikolai enrolled in the University of Moscow, Sergei at the School of Physics and Mathematics, Nikolai at the Law School. Afterward Sergei took courses at the Mulhouse School of Chemistry where he was initiated into the art of printing; he then interned in several factories in Alsace before returning to Moscow in 1882. His father had died the preceding year. Sergei pursued the modernization of the Three Mountains Factory where he set up a chemical laboratory under the direction of one of the best professors from the university (Oskar Karlovich Miller); in this laboratory remarkable experiments were conducted in the making of artificial colors (in regard to one of the experiments, Russians and Germans vied over who had discovered it first). Sergei devoted himself almost entirely to the technical management of the business, while his brother Nikolai managed the commercial end. Nikolai, equally as active as his brother, was responsible for opening wholesale and retail stores scattered throughout Russia and even parts of Persia.

Sergei and Nikolai represented the fourth generation of the

Prokhorov family. Both had many children—Sergei (who died in 1899) had six children, and Nikolai (who died in 1915) had eight children. These two brothers number among the enlightened manufacturers, concerned with technical progress, devoted to science. Sergei Prokhorov, collaborating with Yesai Ivanovich Baranov (who owned a cotton factory in Karabanovo, in the district of Aleksandrov, Vladimir province), created and directed, a "cooperative company for the perfection and development of the manufacturing industry." The Prokhorov factory was one of the first in Russia to utilize petroleum residues for fuel and electricity for energy. In the spring, when factory activity had slowed down, Sergei went abroad to Paris to see the new fashions in fabrics, to Germany and Mulhouse to learn about the latest progress in industrial chemistry (in particular work which concerned dyes), and to Switzerland and England to discover the latest models of machinery. A great change in the Prokhorov factories took place in the 1880s. This change was linked to the policy of the Ministry of Finance which raised the tariff duty and demanded that this duty be paid in gold from 1877 on. The policy, then, meant a considerable increase in these duties. This change is also linked to excellent harvests at the end of the 1870s, which increased the purchasing power of the peasantry. When Sergei and Nikolai Prokhorov took over the management of the factory in 1881, Russia was undergoing an economic crisis from which the Prokhorovs didn't seem to suffer very much, since the factory's production between 1877–1882 almost doubled in uninterrupted progression.

Up to 1885 the factory mainly produced printed cottons, particularly neckerchiefs made from calico. Until this time mechanical weavers were not really capable of manufacturing the floral-patterned fabrics which were imported from abroad. The Jacquard and the Dobby carriage looms were still a rarity. However, the raising of duties on fine fabrics and threads of medium thickness permitted, and at the same time obliged, manufacturers to produce fine fabrics at higher prices, thus opening up a new avenue for trade in the cities. In 1889 then, the Prokhorov brothers set up a weaving mill next to their printing factory.

In 1895 the company, authorized to increase its endowment capital (from 1.5 to 3 million rubles) and to begin selling stocks and bonds, created a spinning factory equipped with 40,000 spindles and expanded its weaving factory which had, by the end of the century, 1500 power looms. The problem of fuel forced the company to expand a part of its activity (spinning and weaving) outside of Moscow; in 1907 it grabbed up the Yarsev factory in Smolensk province and considerably developed this new addition which included, by 1914, a weaving factory with more than 2000 looms and a spinning factory with more than 140,000 spindles.

All the Prokhorov businesses combined in Moscow, in the year 1914, kept 7500 workers and 500 employees busy (in 1900, 5000 workers and some 300 employees). It should be noted that if the average salary of the worker [20] was raised between 1894 and 1914, that of the employees was lowered—the reason being that highly qualified foreign technicians, who had once been well paid, were progressively replaced during this period by Russians who were former students of technical schools. Thus the proportion of mediocre staff among the total personnel increased.

The Three Mountains Factory had an extensive commercial organization, both wholesale and retail (even at the factory and in Moscow); depots were established in Moscow, Kharkov, Baku (from 1889), Warsaw (from 1892), and sales were extended throughout the empire (Central Asia included) and Persia. It must finally be added that Nikolai Prokhorov, production adviser to the company as was his brother before him, belonged to several banking organizations, and, in 1912, when he received hereditary nobility, the family definitively escaped the bourgeois class forever.

A certain number of businesses, born before 1861 (generally in the 1840s) and concerned mainly with spinning, enjoyed great development in the latter half of the century. Their owners were sometimes, but not too frequently, former employees of large factories who in turn went into business for themselves, and although they acquired their fortunes at a later date, they were still linked to the earlier generation of industrialists. As an example of this, note the Smirnov family [21] whose forefather, a peasant from the village of Likino (Vladimir), worked in a factory owned by Savva Morozov (the first in the famous cotton manufacturers' dynasty), and, after this, set up his own business which, though modest in its beginnings, took on greater breadth with his son, Aleksei. But still, by

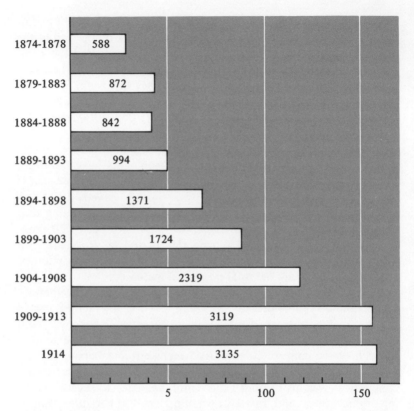

Production of the Prokhorov printed calico cottons in Moscow from 1874–1914.
(Annual average production per every five-year period), scaled in thousands of pieces, each piece being measured at 50 arshins, or 35.50 meters.

1870, the factory hardly produced more than 15,000 to 20,000 pieces, hand-woven and hand-tinted, in the mills' workshops. Between 1870 and 1880 the business really got started. Aleksei installed finishing workshops and, in 1881, a weaving factory with thirty power looms. In 1900 the business consolidated all its operations and hand labor was eliminated. A spinning factory with 80,-000 spindles was constructed; the automatic weaving factory now had 1000 power looms. Smirnov employed some 2400 workers and his production output was valued at 6 million rubles. But it was only in 1911 that the business was transformed into a limited partnership. When Aleksei died, in 1915, his inheritance was valued at 10 million rubles.

It should be noted that on the whole the Smirnov enterprise between 1900 and 1914 didn't develop very extensively: the spinning mill was equipped with 54,000 spindles, the weaving factory less than 1500 power looms, and the number of workers, about 3700. It was a kind of average, solid business which, although assuring its owner a dividend of from 10 to 11 percent, was not able to raise him to the heights of the bourgeois hierarchy.

Among the newcomers, the Gorbunov family [22] represented a transitional type. They accumulated most of their wealth in the second half of the nineteenth century, but the origin of the business goes back to 1826. In that year the forefather of the family, Osip Afanasevich, a peasant from the village of Sirokov (district of Nerekhta, Kostroma province), born in 1780, founded a small workshop which he would soon expand into the neighboring village of Kiselovo while buying threads which he distributed for weaving to the surrounding peasants. O. A. Gorbunov also executed preliminary warp-weave operations in order to prepare the manufactured fabrics. At his death the business was taken over by his two sons, Andrei and Klimenty, and then by the latter alone who died in 1829, leaving behind a modest capital of 35,000 rubles.

The Gorbunov family therefore belonged to that generation of artisans from the first half of the century who began their social ascent through the profits made from manual labor and trade; but different from those artisans of that generation who were already rich by the middle of the century; it was only with Klimenty's heirs, his sons Gregory, Aleksandr, and Maksim, that the business began to flourish in the 1860s.

By 1868 the Gorbunov brothers employed 6000 families on handlooms (these peasants only worked for the Gorbunovs during a part of the year, autumn and winter); and through a store which they set up in Moscow, as well as at the fairs of Nizhnii Novgorod Simbirsk, and Rostov-on-Don, they sold 330,000 rubles worth of diverse fabrics. Apart from calicos, they also furnished the markets of Ivanovo with materials that they had printed in that same region.

At this time the Gorbunov business was still mainly a distribution warehouse. Beginning with 1870 the situation suddenly changed. In 1869 the Gorbunovs installed, at Kiselovo, a mechanized weaving factory with 112 looms on which 150 laborers worked; these looms, which were ordered from England through Knoop,[23] were shipped via the Marya Canal and the Volga. Taking into account work done in the homes (already diminishing), the business, in 1870 produced 70,000 pieces valued at 350,000 rubles. The mechanical weaving factory developed rapidly. In 1872 it employed 500 workers on 392 looms, weaving without interruption in three continuous shifts. The business's assets rose to 600,000 rubles; after 1869 it utilized steam power.

In 1872, the business was formed into the firm of Gregory, Aleksandr, and Maksim Gorbunov Brothers. By 1876 their turnover was valued at 1.25 million rubles. In 1879, the Gorbunovs bought up the mechanical weaving factory owned by the Kuciny brothers who, up to this time, had been living on the premises—a factory situated in the village of Kolobov, Vladimir district (428 looms). In 1882 the firm became a limited partnership with 2 million rubles capital, the shares being divided among the founders' close relatives. At this time the two factories of the company together were equipped with 1464 power looms, manufactured 649,000 pieces of fabric, and employed 2000 workers.

In 1892 the business was equipped with 1650 looms and employed 2900 workers; its turnover reached a value of 3.3 million rubles. It hadn't progressed much since 1882; however, it is necessary to take into account the crises of 1881–1882, and 1891. After 1892, during the Witte period, and also at the onset of the First World War, the business began to flourish, as balance sheets and statistics on profits and returns reveal (Yuksimovich, pp. 81–85). Wishing to make himself independent of other spinners, Gregory Gorbunov and his nephew Vasily (who replaced his father, Aleksandr after 1889) created their own spinning mill in 1892 at Kiselovo (25,000 spindles), equipped with machines that were bought in England through Knoop. Circumstances were favorable then because the price of threads was on the rise. By 1893 the spinning mill already had 60,000 spindles. By 1912 the entire business employed some 8500 workers.

DEVELOPMENT OF THE GORBUNOV ENTERPRISES
(*in round figures*)

	1892– 1893	1896– 1897	1902– 1903	1906– 1907	1911– 1912
Finished Cotton (in poods)	37,000	219,000	300,000	317,000	404,000
Thread Production (in poods)	30,000	179,000	255,000	273,000	346,000
Fabric Production (in pieces) [24]	1,110,000	1,078,000	1,469,000	1,492,000	2,070,000
Number of Workers	2900	4160	6470	7200	8570
Number of Spindles	42,000	73,000	110,000	115,000	130,000
Number of Looms	1650	1655	3000	3450	4486 [25]

Another example of a family who acquired its fortune late was the Bardygin family [26] (in Yegorevsk, province of Ryazan). The founder of the business was the son of a baker who set up a weaving workshop in the 1850s. In reality he didn't limit himself to that activity; he bought cotton threads which he had woven for him in the country and continued to do this throughout the manufacturing process. In 1859, in order to avoid the interruption of work caused by the peasants' abandoning their weaving during the harvest, he set up a weaving factory with forty looms to which he later added a small dye works. This baker's son, a manufacturer who suddenly appeared in the middle of the century, remained, as of yet, unimportant, since, in 1870, the total value of his output did not surpass 137,000 rubles.

Between 1870 and 1880 the Bardygin enterprises grew rapidly, and the family began its social climb. In 1897 the fabrics factory was equipped with 1000 looms, and the number doubled in 1914; by this time the Bardygin family employed 3500 workers and, in addition to their own business, owned half the shares of the Malyutin factory in Ramenskoch. It must be added that the founder of the business, Nikifor Mihailovich Bardygin, who died in 1901, was the first manufacturer who wanted to do without the *skupshschiki,* and thus installed a chain of retail stores to sell his products. The family was proud of having been the precursors of this type of trade organization run by the manufacturers themselves, a process which was generally practiced at the beginning of the twentieth century. The family played an important role in regard to technical progress: Nikifor's son Mikhail created, in 1907, in memory of his father (on the fiftieth anniversary of the founding of the business), a technical school of machinery and electrical power, remarkably equipped and having a pupil enrollment of 400.

From this limited group of new manufacturers, the Ryabushinsky family [27] is certainly the most original in respect to the role it played in banking and industrial activities (and, it must be added, in the political life of the country after 1905).

The origins of the Ryabushinsky family are obscure. The beginnings of its fortune were a symptomatic example of the kind of hazardous fate suffered by merchants during the period of the Napoleonic Wars. On June 18, 1802, a certain Mikhail Yakovlevich Ryabushinsky, who managed a store in the *Gostinnii Dvor,* where the commercial activity of the city was centered, included himself among the circle of Moscow merchants. It is probable that he left Moscow at some time near the invasion, perhaps earlier; [28] in any case, in 1814 he came back from the Tver district, where he was selling shoes, and set up his business again in Moscow; however, he now no longer belonged to the merchant class, associating himself this time with *meshchanstvo.*[29] But this was only a momentary decline for the family, since, ten years later, Mikhail became a member of the third merchant guild (during that ten years very little is known of the family's activities).

In the 1840s the Ryabushinsky family came into its fortune. In 1844 M. Ya. Ryabushinsky bought, in the *Gostinnii Dvor,* a fabric store from the merchant Mikhail Petrovich Sorokanov, whose clerk (*prikazchik*) he had been at one time, and whose incompetent sons had fallen back among the *meshchanstvo.* In 1846 Ryabushinsky set up a mechanized weaving factory in Moscow (in the Golutvinskii Pereulok) which marked the beginning of his industrial activity. The Ryabushinsky family thus belonged to that category of entrepreneurs whose capital was of purely commercial origin.[30] In the first half of the nineteenth century, this type of entrepreneur was rare; the majority of manufacturers were former artisans who had acquired their wealth by both their trades and their commercial or usurious activities. Nevertheless, toward the middle of the century, manufacturers appeared who had accumulated their capital through commerce (or perhaps through the sale of liquor). The appearance of this new industrial category, small in number, bore witness to Russia's economic development and to its more rapid formation of a commercial capitalism which, during the previous era, had only lent limited assistance to industry.

However, if the trade of linens and cotton and wool fabrics was at the source of the Ryabushinsky fortune, the way in which M. Ya. Ryabushinsky progressively set up his manufacturing enterprises was no exception to the general rule. First buying the merchandise from peasants in the country, he then furnished the raw material to these artisans and ordered from them the fabrics which he needed. The mechanical weaving workshop that he set up in Moscow only made up a small part of the business; a large part of the production came from those workshops dispersed among the villages. However, the needs of manufacturing naturally called for consolidation. When the second and third sons of M. Ya. Ryabushinsky, Paul and Vasily, born respectively in 1820 and 1826, began to show commercial capabilities, their father created for them two additional cotton and wool textile factories, one in the Medyn district in Nasonovo, and the other in the Malo-Yaroslavl district in Kurikovo (Kaluga province), probably before 1850. It is thus in the middle of the century that the Ryabushinsky family went from commerce to manufacturing and acquired significant financial means. However, socially they did not undergo the progressive social climbing characteristic of the majority of the textile manufacturers before 1850; the Ryabushinsky family, on the contrary, never escaped their country–working-class background.

Thus, the Ryabushinsky family retained traditional characteristics which could be seen for instance among the manufacturers of serf origin from the Ivanovo region. The father, M. Ya. Ryabushinsky, was an Old Believer who must have converted to the sect around 1818–1820. He was an austere, authoritarian man who raised his sons with great severity. He allowed them, however, through private tutors, an elementary education; but he kept strict watch over the lessons they learned and the time used for leisure.

His son, Paul, played the violin under the instruction of a French emigrant who had remained in Russia after the Napoleonic Wars; one day Ryabushinsky, enraged since he had formally forbidden music instruction in his home, broke the violin over his son's head. A pious man who filled his home with religious portraits and relics, he left, at his death in 1858, a splendid collection of icons which he divided up among his children.

It was common among these manufacturers to have very large families. M. Ya. Ryabushinsky had five children, two daughters and three sons. In 1842 one of his sons, Ivan, married a young woman whom he happened to love—she was, moreover, a rich Moscow proprietress—and, as a result of the union, he and his father severed all relations, leaving Ivan to set up a business on his own. He later made up with his family, after the death of his wife, and married a second time, fathering two daughters. He died in 1876. As for the other two sons of M. Ya. Ryabushinsky, Paul and Vasily, it was they, together with their father, who, in the 1850s made sure that their factories prospered. Both sons became merchants of the first guild. Vasily died a bachelor in 1885. Paul, however, had a large descendency. In 1855, when the Old Believers were being persecuted, Paul was responsible for saving the business. At the time he was thirty-five years old and, because of his youth, was still looked upon as a "merchant's son"; thus, he didn't yet need to enroll officially in a guild. But after January 1, 1855, the Old Believers no longer held the right to belong to the *kupechestvo,* and those among them—mainly tradesmen and manufacturers—who had not adhered to Orthodoxy nor declared their assets (which was exactly the case of Paul Ryabushinsky) were forced to fulfill their military service—a period of twenty-five years. By these means—taking strict measures against the commercial activity of the Old Believers —the government hoped to force them into converting to Orthodoxy.[31] The Ryabushinsky sons did not, however, leave themselves open to the danger of being excluded from the commercial profession. Momentarily falling back into the *meshchanstvo,* they learned of a certain new city, Yezhsk (400 kilometers from Moscow), created in 1848 and located on the Azov Sea, that accepted the Old Believers. This may seem curious, but it should not surprise us in this immense country where often strict measures taken in the capitals and those taken in the country as a whole differed greatly in their severity and in the way they were carried out. Paul went to Yezhsk, where he enrolled his brother, Vasily, his son-in-law, Yevsei Alekseevich Kapustin, and himself as third guild merchants. He returned to Moscow bearing the certificates which permitted the family to pursue their manufacturing and commercial activities. M. Ya. Ryabushinsky was, in regard to the regime, a typical example of the manufacturers' attitudes of that era, especially of those manufacturers who were Old Believers: he had an extreme mistrust of officials and public offices. Until almost the very end of his life he had always refused to participate in the civic activities of the Moscow merchants. When he died, in 1858, the business retained the characteristic of a close-knit, isolated family, and stayed that way until 1862. In the hands of Paul and Vasily Ryabushinsky, the business's total capital could be valued at 2 million rubles (in assignats).[32] The business's progress can be traced from 1835 on (particularly in 1845), thanks to the bookkeeping records that were conserved. Unfortunately, M. Ya. Ryabushinsky's will does not give us any precise indication of his personal and real wealth; beyond the private gifts which are enumerated (for example, gifts to his daughter, Pelagie, and his son, Ivan, who were excluded from the will), the property described was not evaluated in detail.

After 1858 the business expanded extensively. The two brothers, Paul and Vasily, were in fact very different. The first, Paul, who by the way outlived his brother Vasily (Paul died in 1899), was enterprising and artistic. He loved music and literature and, in the 1860s, even brought the artists from the Maly theatre to his home. Paul was part of that group of merchants (small in number even though they appeared well into the middle of the century) who wore German-type styles, were worldly, and participated actively in civic life (in regard to this last activity, the reforms of Alexander II had completely transformed these merchants' way of life in relation to their communities). Already, after 1860, Paul Ryabushinsky was the representative for the Moscow guilds to the City Council, and throughout his life he continued to hold a great many public offices. On the other hand, his brother Vasily, who was reserved, introverted, and timid, occupied himself solely with the business, and especially with financial matters. He lived always in the shadow of his older brother, even to the point where he sacrificed his personal happiness for his brother's sake. Paul, who had already lived through one unhappy marriage, got divorced in 1859 and married (in 1870) the woman whom Vasily was supposed to marry. Originally Paul had arranged the marriage between Vasily and a rich wheat-merchant's daughter through correspondence. In 1870, when Paul went to the capital to arrange the ceremony for Vasily, he fell in love with the beautiful and intelligent woman himself and proceeded to marry her. This incident, however, apparently didn't alter the relationship between the two brothers.

Paul had eight children by his first marriage (two boys who died at the age of one month, and six girls whose ages at the time of the divorce ranged from six to thirteen years old). His second wife gave him sixteen children, nine of which were boys. Their births ranged from 1871 (Paul was then fifty-one years old) to 1893 (Paul died in 1899 at the age of seventy-nine). One of his sons, Dmitri (born in 1882), had a brilliant scientific career as a specialist in aerodynamics; he was the author of several inventions during World War I and went to live in France in 1919, where he resided till his death in 1962. He was a teacher at the Sorbonne as well as a corresponding member of the Academy of Sciences. Dmitri was the last survivor of the family.

The Ryabushinsky family was a particularly large one. However, the majority of these manufacturers fathered families of equal size. Consequently, when their businesses expanded, the companies that they formed were family-like in nature, not only because of the origins of their capital, but also because the members of those companies were all related by blood. Because of this kind of nepotism, then, the legal structure of the companies was subject to the individual will of the family members, since they held the management of the business in their own hands. In 1862, four years after the death of M. Ya. Ryabushinsky, the two brothers, Paul and Vasily, formed a company under the name of "Paul and Vasily Ryabushinsky Brothers." Then, after Vasily's death in 1885, once his will was settled, the business was formed in 1887 into a limited partnership under the name "Paul Mikhailovic Ryabushinsky & Sons Manufacturing Company."

The company, whose assets were valued at 2.5 million rubles, included seven members: Paul Mikhailovich, who held 787 shares and 10 votes on the board of directors; one of his sisters who held 200 shares, and also 10 votes on the board; and finally five associates, whose 13 shares were insignificant in comparison to 987 shares owned by Paul Ryabushinsky and his sister, later relinquished their shares to the family. Two of these five associates (each holding five shares) were technical advisers to the business: one of them, Klimentov, who had formerly been employed by another factory, died in 1899 after forty years of service; the other, a former peasant named Tarakanov, spent his entire career in the Ryabushinsky firm until 1911. The family-like characteristic of these companies in Russia was common, particularly when the companies were made up of Russians and not foreigners.

Aside from their Moscow factory, the company kept for some time two other factories under the Kaluga government—one, in Nasonovo (Meydn district), probably constructed in 1849, and the other, in Churikovo (Malo-Yaroslavl district), constructed after 1850. It is interesting to note that the oldest factory, created in 1846 and situated in Moscow, was started without official authorization, if we can rely on a police report of 1849. In the beginning, then, the business, which numbered among those numerous clandestine enterprises of which the government knew nothing (and thus are not recorded in the statistical census), was in the hands of manufacturers who did not belong to the merchant class but were rather associated with the *meshchanstvo,* that vague and indistinct category which characterized a part of the bourgeoisie which was sometimes wrongly referred to as the "petite bourgeoisie." This first factory of the Ryabushinsky family did not expand; in 1849 it was described as a small business without machines, and with 140 looms manufacturing muslins, linenettes, and some shoddy goods. The Nasonovo factory grouped together 600 looms worked by 650 laborers. As for the factory at Churikovo (probably constructed between 1854–1856), it was equipped with a steam engine and 200 looms bought from Manchester. At the same time the Moscow factory was undergoing transformation and modernization.

However, these factories which had made the early fortune of the Ryabushinsky family didn't survive; the Moscow factory was sold in 1872, the Nasonovo one was closed in 1870, and the Churikovo factory burned down in 1874 and was never rebuilt. Shortly before Paul's second marriage the Ryabushinsky family acquired, in 1869, an important factory (located a few versts from Vyshnii-Volochek, where the Volga-Baltic Canal Junction, constructed under the reign of Peter the Great, had been made into a railroad station, opened in 1855 to accommodate the Nicholas Line between Moscow and St. Petersburg), that of the Shipovs, a spinning mill with 46,000 spindles whose annual production was valued at 286,-000 rubles. The site of this new factory, magnificently situated between the two capitals, near the principal railway of the country and on a canal whose traffic was then still significant,[33] made it little worth their while to keep the other factories in Moscow and Kaluga. From 1870 on, then, the Vyshnii-Volochek factory constituted the main manufacturing activity of the Ryabushinsky family. Factory? It must rather be called a group of factories, for, when the Churikovo factory disappeared in 1874, Paul Ryabushinsky founded a new factory for weaving, dyeing, and bleaching at Zavorovo (located a few versts from Vyshnii-Volochek). The business as a whole called for all sorts of manufacturing activity (spinning, weaving, dyeing, and so forth), as well as social services, a hospital (constructed in 1875), workers' quarters (the region was sparsely populated), and lodging for personnel from neighboring districts. In 1887 the property of the company was made up not only of buildings, machines, and cotton stock, but also of more than 3000 hectares of land worth nearly 35,000 rubles. The modernization of these factories can be traced in some detail, since it corresponded directly to two fires, one in 1880 at the Zavorovo factory and the other in 1893 at the Vyshnii-Volochek factory. Of all the factories, the cotton spinning mill at Vyshnii-Volochek factory was the most important; however, it underwent the effects of the economic crises at the end of the nineteenth century (1880–1885) and again after 1900. On the other hand, it was also influenced by the general economic thrust characteristic of the 1890s. The number of active spindles decreased slightly around 1890, then doubled within a few years, reaching the figure of 70,000 in 1900; following that, the figure decreased, descending to 67,000 in 1905, but it picked up again in 1910, reaching its highest figure—70,000. In the weaving factory, the number of active looms equally varied, but in smaller proportions. The amount of looms was scarcely affected by the crises from 1880–1882, remaining steady at a figure between 710 and 740. The number increased between 1895 and 1900, reaching 1200, decreasing to 960 between 1900 and 1905, and rising once again to 1220 in 1910.

In sum, then, these factories were of average importance, employing in 1900 a thousand workers for spinning, a thousand for weaving, and some several hundred for dyeing and bleaching. The sales on fabrics and threads reached about 1.8 million rubles in 1900, but rose rapidly to an average of more than 4 million rubles between 1903 and 1908, and to more than 6 million between 1908 and 1912.

The activities of the Ryabushinsky family are doubly interesting because they didn't limit themselves solely to manufacturing. Around 1900 the family entered into the domain of big banking. It is well known that the development of banking organizations in Russia was retarded. Until the creation in 1860 of the State Bank, the needs of commerce and industry were largely served by private individuals and religious groups. Institutions were created by the sect of the Old Believers, such as the Preobrazhensk Cemetery in Moscow which lent money, without interest (or with minimal interest), to manufacturers who belonged to the sect. Since many of the manufacturers later remembered the lenders in their wills, the latter often were able to invest large sums of money in manufacturing businesses. After 1860, joint-stock commercial banks appeared, six between 1864–1868, and thirty-three between 1869–1873. By 1875 there existed some 80 mutual credit firms and 235 urban banks. These credit firms then began to increase in number, but were insufficient to fill the growing needs of manufacturers. Thus, private and individual credit continued to play a major role up to the end of the nineteenth century. Certain manufacturers, particularly those in textiles, augmented their regular activities with discount and loan operations. This was true of the Ryabushinsky family [34] before they purchased the Bank of Alekseev in Kharkov, at the end of the century. The bank had had to sell its assets in order to cover its debts, and was consequently liquidated. The great crisis of 1900–1905, striking hardest at the metallurgy industry in the Ukraine, permitted the Ryabushinsky family to consolidate their position as bankers. In 1901, at a time when many businesses in the Ukraine were going bankrupt, the Ryabushinsky family rearranged the management of the Kharkov Bank and, in 1902, transformed it into a company whose direction and management were in the hands of seven family members (all of whom were Paul's sons): Paul Pavlovich (born in 1871), Vladimir Pavlovich (1873), Stefan Pavlovich (1874), Sergei Pavlovich (1872), Mikhail Pavlovich (1880), Dmitri Pavlovich (1882), and Fedor Pavlovich (1885). After 1905, the bank extended numerous branches into the north and west of Russia: in Vyshnii-Volochek (1906), Rzevin (1908), St. Petersburg (1909), Ivanovo (1910), and Smolensk (1910). In January of 1912 the bank formed a joint-stock company under the title, "Bank of Moscow," with a total capital of 20 million rubles. Among the founders, the Ryabushinsky sons worked side by side with groups of important manufacturers who belonged mainly to the textile businesses. Among these manufacturers, the Bardygins, the Konovalovs, the Krestovnikovs, the Morozovs, and the Tretyakovs are of particular importance. At the onset of the war, manufacturing associations that were owned by numerous families were quite common, but for the most part businesses involved mainly in manufacturing continued to retain their one-family character.

The examples cited concern families about whom there exist printed private sources, since this material has mainly to do with brochures or yearbooks reedited at the request of the manufacturers themselves in order to commemorate, through a historical account, their participation in some exposition or the centenniel celebration of the founding of one of their businesses (these centennial celebrations almost all took place at the onset of World War I). The same information can be found in the work of Yuksimovich, concerned mainly with the textile industry, which described the manufacturing operating in 1905, while briefly mentioning factory histories and family genealogies. This abridged work (volume I alone appeared), which scarcely deals with anything beyond the cotton sector, contains balance sheets taken from financial journals and photographs of manufacturers. Compiled upon request, it constitutes a monument raised to the glory of manufacturers whose obscure origins are celebrated. The author emphasizes the social character of their paternal management, their personal relations with the personnel (there is no mention of their relationship to workers, except perhaps to evaluate the manpower). It is nonetheless a basic reference work which, in any case, allows us, if not to know truly the family histories, at least to know the ups and downs of the businesses and to compile an approximate list of the manufacturers and their genealogies.

We say an approximate list, since it would only be valid for the beginnings of the twentieth century.[35] During the course of the preceding century, a certain number of manufacturers disappeared after having founded factories. There is frequent mention of these little-known (or unknown) manufacturers in regard to their businesses being bought up by more fortunate industrialists, after which the former usually disappeared, creating a total mystery as to their origins, careers, and social roles. It is particularly around the middle of the century that the rise in the number of manufacturers who met with success, and the good fortune of several merchants who had invested capital in manufacturing enterprises, spurred not only the creation of new firms, but also the absorption of already existing businesses. It doesn't appear, however, that the world of cotton manufacturing experienced any significant variations of this type. Declines and disappearances were the exception here, and when they did occur, they were doubtlessly caused—though this remains to be verified—by family matters (default of heirs, arguments, bad management, selling of shares) rather than by economic predicaments.[36] Merchants' memoirs [37] allow us to probe rather deeply into the daily and professional lives of a certain number of manufacturers. But generally speaking, in the absence of accessible family archives, and the impossibility of knowing the reality of bourgeois fortunes through wills and notarized deeds, it is necessary to limit ourselves, for the moment, to reconstructing the history of the businesses rather than that of the families. By shifting our study to the economic history of the families, therefore, we can indirectly place some landmarks in the field of the social history of the bourgeoisie. Likewise, the bibliography of studies devoted to the industrial bourgeoisie in Russia is very brief. The work of Berlin [38] presents the world of merchants and manufacturers—their relationship with the government, their municipal role—but deals in generalities; furthermore, this work is already well outdated. The recent work of Buryskin,[39] a Russian emigrant to the United States who belonged to the merchant class, deals primarily with the merchants and manufacturers of Moscow. Although this work is filled with vivid and interesting memories, and presents a great deal of facts, they are unfortunately often uncertain and undated. Therefore this work hardly constitutes a social study. We must also mention the small article by Kovalevsky [40] which throws some light on the manufacturing families of the Old Believers. The importance of an accurate social study did not escape the attention of Soviet historans; nevertheless, the only one who really writes from a social point of view is Ryndzyunsky, and his works deal mainly with the first half of the century.[41] V. K. Yatsunsky [42] and I. F. Gindin [43] are two historians who deal with Russia's economy in the nineteenth century. Yatsunsky treats mainly of the industrial life, while Gindin is concerned with banking and financial activities. As a result of their interests, therefore, they could not help but study the business society—whether indirectly, in its relationship to economic activity, or globally, as a social group engaged in a class struggle. Thus, they concentrated on the external history of the bourgeoisie, not on its internal history.

In review, let us first remark on the geographical distribution of the industrial bourgeoisie. In general, they were concentrated in the two capitals (we have omitted a study of St. Petersburg and its surrounding region), from whence they extended their activities not only to the neighboring areas of Moscow and St. Petersburg, but way beyond, into the "provincial" cities of the south and east; there, they participated in local industrial life, even sometimes in production activities which had no relation to textiles (for example, the Krestovnikov family [44] in Kazan were owners of a stearine factory). It is particularly in these cities (where the bourgeoisie sent many of its children to settle) that they began to play an important social role alongside the local Russian, Ukrainian, and Tatar bourgeoisie.

Secondly, let us remark on the consequences of the geographical distribution of the bourgeoisie. The study of the bourgeoisie must begin with the families, with their internal ties, and with those representatives of the foreign bourgeoisie who had set up businesses in Russia. The importance of foreigners, of course, cannot be measured by their number (Knoop is a good example), since it is necessary to take into account that, firstly, they assimilated rapidly into the national milieu, and, secondly, bourgeois alliances were almost always concluded behind closed doors, at least in the Moscow region where the rather prolific manufacturing and merchant families had strong ties which excluded foreigners.

Thirdly, let us remark on the recruitment of the textile bourgeoisie. We saw how it barely opened its doors to the lower classes, despite the general economic upheaval at the time. By the twentieth century, it was no longer possible for a man to rise from working-class origins to a solidly held, respected position; those few newcomers who did fit into the already established industrial bourgeoisie were persons who had accumulated capital through commerce. Doubtlessly, the improvement of education and particularly of technical education in the twentieth century aided well-to-do families (living almost solely in the cities) to attain the necessary qualifications to meet industrial needs. But the former students of the universities, the engineers and chemists, did not, as a result, suddenly become factory owners. Rising to the ranks of the intellectual bourgeoisie, they generally remained salaried workers. This was not only because the industrial families (almost always fertile and in little need of new blood) could sufficiently provide the men needed for the management of their businesses (men who were at the same time, by their origin, shareholders in the business), but also because Russia's economic evolution was still too slow to allow ample opportunity for one to rise in the social scale. Taking into account the Industrial Revolution at the end of the nineteenth century, and the rapid increase in industrial production after 1905, it must not be forgotten that Russia started off very poorly compared to the industrial powers of the West. The mediocre prospects available to small businessmen and capitalists prevented them from competing with established manufacturers and from attaining the heights of the big textile bourgeoisie. However, the trend of business was already moving toward a lower- and middle-class bourgeoisie composed of newcomers, all of which served to create a factor of social pressure. The importance of this factor, which must not be underestimated on the eve of the fall of tsarism, cannot be fully and justly evaluated except in light of a thoroughly detailed study of the bourgeois class (a study, moreover, which has not yet been undertaken). Doubtless, if such a study were undertaken, it would be of considerable size.[45] Recent studies by Soviet economic historians emphasize the fact that monopolies [46] as well as Malthusianism must have contributed to the economic policy of closed doors and industrial ententes in Russia at the onset of the war in 1914. The profit motive must have hindered expansion—this fact is particularly evident in regard to the metallurgical industries, but is less clear in the textile domain. But the observations made by these historians aim in general to demonstrate that industrial progress after 1910 was greatly inferior to what it should have been, even taking the regime into account.

In any case, it is certain that the textile bourgeoisie was not limited solely to the great families who so readily attract our attention and who, furthermore, had monopolized the greater part of manufacturing activity. Numerous small manufacturers, whose existence is only acknowledged, at present, by searching through factory lists, merit recognition for the significant social roles they played, if they were not economically important. The great families disappeared in 1917. The question should then be raised, to what degree was this industrial bourgeoisie absorbed by the new regime? In view of this, it would be interesting to study industry's mentality at the onset of the war, and also to isolate the role of small and average manufacturers in regard to trade organizations and stock committees. The most prestigious names are not always to be found on these committees where the big manufacturers exercised their influence through middlemen.

In addition to their businesses, the textile manufacturers entered the political arena after 1905. What was their real influence? The big bourgeoisie was more or less openly in favor of the Kadet Party; in fact, declared opponents were rare. The bourgeoisie remained loyalist; their material interests were effectively looked after by a monarchy which was bourgeois on the economic level, aristocratic on the political level, but which, however, did not depend on the bourgeoisie for support. In this respect, the Moscow cotton manufacturers appeared to have been the least silent and most demanding group. The Ryabushinsky family were among the leaders of a liberal bourgeoisie, very hostile to the imperial bureaucracy; they even possessed a newspaper, *Russia's Morning* (*Utro Rossii*) in which one family member, Paul Pavlovich, had a regular column.

The example of the Ryabushinsky family, as well as others, whether they were new or old manufacturers, allows us to characterize only a part of the bourgeoisie, but nonetheless a part which was, without a doubt, the most dynamic and elite of the bourgeois society. This elite had to suffer through crises and political events; their businesses went through ups and downs; nevertheless, they managed to get through half a century (from the time of the suppression of serfdom to the onset of World War I) without an upheaval; the same names in the same families [47] remained unchanged in 1914. Economic development did help some new manufacturers to get started, but they remained small businessmen. Among the textile manufacturers, already established by the middle of the century, a few rare names were added of newcomers who conquered, for all intents and purposes, the few remaining domains still open to their initiative. *The ability to move up and down on the social scale was therefore limited in this area.*

It must be said that the majority of the textile businesses were well managed. Manufacturers' sons, almost always plentiful—a fact which easily counteracted the possibility of any black sheep cropping up in the family—had the chance, in the second half of the century, to receive a good technical education. They went to universities in Russia itself, with some parts of their studies abroad, traveling every year to keep up with the latest inventions and fashions in England, Switzerland, Alsace, and Paris. They generally had open minds and were always ready to expand their businesses or to found new ones. They were interested in art, the theater, painting, and music. The austerity, narrow-mindedness, and mistrust of civic life so characteristic of their fathers disappeared with them. A penchant for diverse interests was not, however, to be found in each and every family member; the case of Paul Ryabushinsky was unusual. But the children were almost always numerous enough to represent a full range of interests and activities. We can be sure that the merchants described here are a far cry from those depicted by Ostrovsky—the 1860s notwithstanding—the latter being types who already belonged to the past and pertained mainly to a middle-class bourgeoisie of merchants and not to the big textile manufacturers.

The division and sharing of labor, as well as the diverse fields of interest, among the members of bourgeois families only made for better family unions which endured until 1914 and were reflected in the managing and administrative boards of the companies. Textile manufacturing businesses rarely took the form of anonymous companies which called for foreign capital and thus involved outsiders to the family. In this respect, the Moscow bourgeoisie is unique at the onset of the war. It distinguished itself from the Petersburg bourgeoisie by scarcely participating in the manufacturing businesses of the Ukraine where the role of foreigners and the amount of anonymous companies are preponderant. Thus, this group, although open to foreign influence and encompassing large horizons, remained very Muscovite and provincial in its interests, as well as its state of mind. Therefore, we can understand why, in Soviet historiography, the Moscow bourgeoisie is treated with a sort of secret tenderness when it is alluded to for any reason other than to illustrate class conflicts—for example, when it is noted for its achievement on the economic level, and especially on the national scale.

VIII

The Russian ministers of finance under the last three tsars, most notably Sergei Witte, developed a viable if precarious and exploitative method of industrialization. It aimed to attract foreign investment, enterprise, and loans through fiscal stability achieved by high levels of grain export which produced favorable trade balances. This "Witte system," however, impoverished the peasantry and exposed state finances to the danger of collapse under the pressures of war and famine. It was a house of cards mined with social dynamite, but it helped to achieve in the 1890s one of the highest industrial growth rates in modern history. The tsarist industrialization system is analyzed by Theodore H. Von Laue, author of Sergei Witte and the Industrialization of Russia *(New York, 1963);* Why Lenin? Why Stalin? *(New York, 1969). Dr. Von Laue is Professor of History at Clark University, Worcester, Massachusetts. His article was published in* The Transformation of Russian Society *(Cambridge,*

Mass., 1960), edited by C. E. Black, and is reprinted with the permission of the author and the Harvard University Press. A short concluding section on Soviet development has been omitted.

THEODORE H. VON LAUE

The State and the Economy

I

The changing relations between state and economy in the de velopment of Russian society since 1861 is a highly complex and voluminous subject. It might therefore be more suitable in this context to select only those aspects which may help to put the entire topic in the proper light and deepen our understanding of "the Russian condition."

These crucial aspects—they will emerge more clearly later—center around a persistent problem: how could the Russian state sustain the role of a great power with the imperfect and limited resources of an underdeveloped country? This essay will deal, at least tangentially, with the Russian state as a member of the European, and, from the 1890s on, of the emerging global state system; it will do so not only in the objective terms of international relations, but also according to the subjective estimate of the Russian public and the government as to what political role Russia should play. As for the objective facts, one reminder may suffice: in the twentieth century the Russian state has twice passed through crises far more extreme than those faced by any other of the present great powers of the West. And as for the evolution of Russian state ambition, there is room only for a very brief but necessary characterization. For a minimum goal it aimed at, it is fair to say, the protection of the boundaries of Russia, the preservation of her native institutions: in short, at sovereignty in the traditional sense. For a maximum goal —coming to the fore at a time when the other great powers either voiced or actively pursued universal aims—it expressed a desire for the expansion, even global expansion, of the Russian way of life, or her system of government.

The fact that Russian state ambition has been a product of Western influence and not of native origin has never received the attention which it deserves. Even the theory of Russia as the Third Rome has its Western antecedents. One need only look at the origins of Spanish or French nationalism in the fifteenth and sixteenth centuries, or of English Protestant imperialism in the seventeenth. Western nationalism became secularized earlier than its Russian counterpart. Yet concerning global universality, what could be more ambitious than the Girondist sense of mission in 1792, German philosophy in the age of Schiller and Fichte, Palmerston's arrogance, or, say, Cecil Rhodes' boast that if he could reach the planets he would annex them too?

Imperial and Soviet state ambition can be interpreted properly only in the European context. Seen in this perspective it will appear that it was by no means extreme, and that it followed, like an echo, the Western trends. For instance, when Lenin said in 1915 that, if he came to power, he would stir up the European proletariat against their governments and the colonial peoples against the imperialists, he merely put into revolutionary and Russian phraseology a sentiment voiced by German national liberals. They proclaimed at the same time that it was Germany's task not only to win a place in the sun for herself, but also for the Egyptians, Persians, Moslems, Boers, Chinese, and others. In other words, Germany too had a world mission, the liberation of human civilization from the yoke of English influence. In the last analysis, of course, both German and Russian imperialists expressed sentiments taught them by the British imperialist example.

If there was an ingredient peculiar to Russian state ambition, it was not the reckless sweep of her global pretensions, but the hypersensitivity concerning all threats to her power, a sensitivity conditioned over the centuries very largely by the tremendous disparity between the material and cultural resources of Russia, on the one hand, and those of her political rivals, on the other. The great powers of the West were, and to this day are, able to support their ambitions from the wealth and achievement created more or less spontaneously by their citizens. Russia, by contrast, was a backward country with an underdeveloped economy for the better part of the period under consideration. How, then, could she sustain her political aims with her greatly limited economic resources? How could she do so in a century in which the material progress of Western civilization was breathtakingly rapid, the gap between the advanced and the backward countries widening, and the price of sovereignty constantly and steeply rising? What, in short, were the unique experiences over the past hundred years of an underdeveloped country which also claimed to be a great power (or a great power which also happened to be an underdeveloped country)? The following sketch, starting with specific problems of economic policy and advancing to a general thesis, will offer an answer to this question.

II

Modern Russian economic policy began, vaguely, when Alexander II and his advisers recognized that the defeat of Russia at Sevastopol called for a far-reaching recasting of Russian society and economy after the Western pattern; from the outset Russian economic policy thus stood under the *Primat der Aussenpolitik*. The emancipation of the serfs was the most spectacular and obvious corollary, yet by no means the first one. The adoption of an extensive program of railroad construction and of a unified budget under the minister of finance, the lowering of tariffs in order to permit a freer influx of Western European goods, the effort to restore the convertibility of the ruble—all preceded emancipation. These innovations were intended to help Russia achieve the advantages of private enterprise which had given her enemies their superiority. Yet it was paradoxical that, in its efforts to increase the economic resources of Russia, the government should adopt a policy of nonintervention in the economic affairs of the country and abdicate—for the time being—its control over Russia's economic development.

Thus for the next decades the roots of modern Russian economic policy cannot be found at the top level, in the decisions of the emperors, but within the more limited responsibilities of the finance ministers. How could the minister of finance find enough funds for all the expenditures it took to become a great power? He had to finance the Russian army and navy, which claimed rarely less than one-quarter and more often around one-third of the budget; and the court, church, civil administration, education, and public works as well. While he never managed to satisfy the military, he had to be even more thrifty in regard to cultural and economic needs. As for revenue, the taxes were harsh and increasing. In the forty years before 1900, indirect taxes were raised four and a half times, direct taxes doubled (while the population increased by only 78 percent and the price level remained fairly constant).[1] Each retiring minister of finance warned his successor about the exhaustion of "the paying powers of the population." Inevitably, the deficits in the budgets rose rapidly.[2] Obviously the Russian government could not make ends meet, even though it taxed its population to the utmost, curtailed its expenditures drastically, and under its policy of free trade shifted the burden of Russian economic development largely to its subjects. But how could they fully assume this responsibility when the government took from them almost every kopeck which they might have invested in economic expansion?

In one respect, indeed, the government had to come quickly to the rescue: the financing of railroad expansion. Immediately after the Crimean War, the government had launched an extensive construction program. Russia needed railroads for defense and, still more, for economic development. While the construction and management were left to private initiative, the expense had to be borne by the state, which guaranteed the railway loans. Yet even so, what with the poverty of the treasury, there were definite limits to the speed of railroad construction and thus to the economic and cultural development of the country as a whole.

Deficits and the overriding need for railroad expansion drove the minister of finance to heavy borrowing at home and abroad and raised the state debt to new heights. By the end of the century it amounted to about 3.5 billion rubles, of which 1 billion was held abroad, the largest foreign debt of any great power.[3] The management of such a large foreign debt imposed upon the minister of finance—and the government as a whole—a tremendous responsibility. The financial sacrifices needed for the prompt service of this debt and for the maintenance of Russian credit abroad were very considerable. For the sake of its foreign credit, the government also was forced to maintain an unusually optimistic if not false interpretation of Russian economic conditions—which was bound to antagonize the public. And inevitably Russian, unlike American, foreign credit became a tool of power politics and a limitation upon Russian sovereignty in general. No other great power found its foreign policy so hampered by its dependence upon foreign credit, and its foreign credit subject to such political pressures.[4]

The urgent need for foreign capital also foisted a number of other obligations upon the minister of finance, some of considerable technical complexity. In order to facilitate the influx of foreign loans into Russia and to promote international trade in general, he had to provide a stable currency—a freely convertible currency based on gold. The experiment of free conversion was made twice after the Crimean War, with disastrous results. No subsequent minister of finance until Witte dared to undertake it again, although all worked hard to prepare for it. Their problem, not unlike that of modern British chancellors of the exchequer, was how to accumulate a sufficient gold reserve in the face of an uncertain balance of trade and a passive balance of payments. Remedies were difficult. The modernization of Russia required heavy imports for the sake of her economic and industrial development and her cultural progress in general. In order to offset these heavy imports, the Ministry of Finance did its utmost to facilitate Russian agricultural exports— the railway network was designed primarily for this purpose. In the late 1880s, a period of falling world prices, it even began forcing the peasants to throw their grains on the market when they were cheapest, thus deliberately depressing the level of domestic consumption and indirectly also drying up its future sources of revenue and again slowing down the modernization of the countryside. These measures slowly took effect. While in half of the years between 1860 and 1880 the balance of trade was negative, it improved thereafter and provided a constant surplus almost to the end of the century.[5]

Yet the surplus was not sufficiently large to create an active balance of payments; the invisible imports were too large. Among them loomed very prominently—and gallingly—the expenses of Russian travelers in Europe. One minister of finance even proposed a prohibitive tax on passports for foreign travel in order to reduce the loss of valuable foreign currency.[6] At any rate, with a constantly adverse balance of payments, convertibility was hopeless. But without convertibility, the supply of foreign capital remained limited and thus also the rate of economic growth. At the most, the minister of finance could hope to build up a sufficient gold reserve through a constant recourse to state-guaranteed or state-owned foreign loans paid in gold, which however only increased the foreign indebtedness of the government and all the evils thereof. Wherever, in short, the Russian minister of finance turned for an escape from the basic poverty of Russia, he ran into a network of interrelated and highly technical dilemmas, each reinforcing the other.

How did the successive Russian ministers of finance try to break out of the vicious circle of poverty breeding further poverty? Reutern, who had reorganized Russian finance after the Crimean War, succeeded fairly well in making ends meet at the three buckles of state finance: the budget, the balance of trade, and the balance of payments. He taxed heavily, limited government expenditures as much as possible, and covered the deficit in the budget and the balance of payments by foreign loans. Then came the Turkish War and its staggering costs, which undid all of his work. The next minister of finance to cope with the fiscal riddles was Bunge. Except for some tariff increases, he concerned himself less with the buckles—they were all left gaping—than with the fabric of the Russian economy. He tried to improve public welfare by winding up the transition period of emancipation, abolishing the capitation tax, establishing a Peasant Land Bank and a Nobles' Land Bank, and assisting Russian industry by a series of excellent labor laws. But when the international crisis over Bulgaria demanded extraordinary expenditures, his deficits were held against him and he gave way to a new man, Vyshnegradsky. Vyshnegradsky devoted his attention again to the official buckling points. He created surpluses both by skillful accounting methods and by curtailing government expenditures, even those for railroad construction; he forced the agricultural exports to the utmost so as to cover both visible and invisible imports. Equally drastically, he curtailed imports by a monster tariff, the tariff of 1891. Fortune played into his hands the sympathies of the French money market, which strengthened Russia's foreign credit. Yet after five seemingly highly successful years, the old misery suddenly reappeared with a vengeance. While the buckles held, the very fabric of the Russian economy went to pieces in the great famine of 1891. The state had taken everything from the peasants, who had no surplus whatever to guard against crop failures. And to add insult to injury: German and Austrian diplomats sneered that Russia was too poor to be a great power; a civilized state did not suffer from disastrous famines.[7]

Russian economic policy thus experienced a profound setback at the very moment when the government, for reasons of state, was contemplating further heavy expenditures in connection with the building of the great Siberian trunk line. The decision to build the Siberian line was the result of the rise of Japanese power in the Far East, the increasing Western penetration of China, and rising imperialism in general. In view of such competition, Russia—given her political ambition—had to build a modern link between the European and Far Eastern boundaries, and had to start building it at a time of economic catastrophe.

III

Thus the famine of 1891 also became a turning point in modern Russian history in the relations between state and economy. In the thirty years since the emancipation, the economic condition of the Russian government and of Russian society had not improved. On the contrary, the countryside showed many signs of deterioration. The government, even while avoiding international complications, was unable to carry out needed state projects like the Siberian railroad. While the high tariff restricted the influx of Western goods, it also slowed down the modernization of Russia—although it gave some encouragement to Russian industry. To make matters worse, the public grew increasingly hostile to the government over its unsuccessful financial policy and the persistent poverty of Russia. The Russian ministers of finance were fully familiar with the special urgency of the accursed Russian question: what was to be done? It was at this point that for the first time in modern Russian history a comprehensive economic policy emerged, linking state and economy under a common necessity. It was the work of Sergei Witte.

In Witte's view—to give a brief summary of the "Witte system" and advance the analysis one step further—economic policy was more than ever an instrument of power politics. "Russia," he said, "needs perhaps more than any other country a proper economic foundation for her national policy and her culture," so that she will be "a great power not only politically and agriculturally, but also economically." [8] And in an age of rapid industrial progress in the West, economic development meant to him above all the most rapid industrialization.

> International competition does not wait. If we do not take energetic and decisive measures so that in the course of the next decades our industry will be able to satisfy the needs of Russia and other Asian countries which are—or should be—under our influence, then the rapidly growing foreign industries . . . will establish themselves in our fatherland. . . . Our economic backwardness may lead to political and cultural backwardness as well.[9]

Thus from the start Witte had a clear recognition of the backwardness of Russia. Repeatedly he spoke of her colonial economy in contrast to that of the Western "metropoles." Occasionally he even dropped hints about "the peculiar conditions of Russia" in general which slowed down her economic development. In education, for instance, he observed that Russia was not only behind Europe but behind some Asian countries as well.[10]

At the same time he adjusted Russian state ambition to the rising tide of imperialism. "Russia is an empire," he always emphasized with a keen sensitivity for the ambitions of the other great powers. She had a great cultural and political task in Asia and Europe. Now she must catch up to what had been missed in the course of two centuries, since Peter the Great. This required great sacrifices, but "a great power cannot wait." [11] All of Witte's work thus was permeated by a sense of extreme urgency and haste. As he once remarked with reference to Nicholas II's indifference: "Was Russian power to increase as it had after 1861, or was it to decline again? . . . He who does not go forward will, for that very reason, fall back compared with the countries that move forward." [12] Hence there arose for the first time the question of the forced tempo of economic development, of "artificial" measures disrupting the organic pattern of a native economy.

Witte thus jettisoned the premises of liberal economics. It was up to the state, he wrote in his first budget report, to order the country's economic life:

> As a result of the special historical conditions of its political structure and development, fiscal policy in our fatherland cannot be contained in the strictly limited framework of the financial needs of the government as they are traditionally understood. In the understanding of the Russian people the conviction prevails that it is within the power of government authority to be concerned with everything touching the welfare and the needs of the people. In all cases of public misery, whenever it assumes considerable proportions, the people turn to the authority of the Tsar with their hopes and their trusts. Considering the weak development of the habits of self-help among the population, the whole burden of the struggle with public misfortune falls inevitably upon the government. [13]

But, furthermore, the government's policy must be comprehensive: "Every measure of the government in regard to trade and industry affects almost the entire economic organism and influences the course of its further development." Hence, Witte continued, Russia required "that this policy be carried out according to a definite plan, with strict system and continuity." [14]

Witte's plan, or "the protective system" as he called it in connection with the tariff of 1891, called for stepped-up government expenditures for the development of Russia's riches.[15] And under his guidance between 1894 and 1902 more than two-thirds of the government's ordinary and extraordinary expenditures were poured into the economic development of the country, the highest proportion of any period between 1861 and 1917.[16] The largest single item, of course, was spent for railroad construction. Witte's emphasis upon railroad construction served a double purpose. It not only improved communications but, even more important, also stimulated industrial expansion. The Witte system was based on a rudimentary theory of economic development. Through extensive railroad construction, the heavy industries and their subsidiaries could be developed, giving Russia a heavy industry of her own. The expansion of the heavy industries in turn would stimulate the growth of the light industries, and eventually agriculture would improve through the increased demand for food and the cheaper supply of better equipment and chemicals. In the end, the government would be amply repaid for its outlay through the increased prosperity of the country and the rising tax yield.

For the time being, unfortunately, the sacrifices of the population were even greater than ever. As Witte admitted himself, in strictest secrecy, the population was paying for industrialization out of current necessity.[17] And what was not paid from tax revenue and the limited domestic capital was financed by foreign loans. Under Witte the foreign indebtedness of Russia mounted drastically, particularly after he introduced the gold standard, and thus prepared the way for the influx of foreign capital under nongovernmental auspices as well. But, as Witte argued, except for foreign capital the population would have to make still further sacrifices.[18] As one of his apologists added: it was difficult enough for Russia not to fall further behind, even with the utmost efforts. The only way to make some progress was through the resort to foreign capital.[19]

There is no need to discuss the results of such "artificial" stimulation. Suffice it here to cite the fact that of all types of industrial enterprises existing in 1900, 40 percent were founded after 1891; and that the smallest ones employing less than fifty workers multiplied most rapidly.[20] The boom reached quite deeply into Russian

society. Concerning fiscal necessities, Witte succeeded not only in
making ends meet in the budget, but also in the balance of payments, so that he accumulated a gold reserve sufficient for convertibility. Thus he made possible a stable currency and all the advantages for Russian credit and foreign trade which followed from it.
Yet in the last analysis he balanced accounts only by borrowing
heavily at home and abroad. He also charged the current expenditures for the economic development of Russia up to the future, and
the question remained whether the development of Russian productivity would ever overtake Russian foreign indebtedness. But how
could her productivity win this race, his critics demanded, considering the misery of the mass of the Russian population to which at
tention was again called by the onset of the depression in 1899?
Someday soon, the pessimists declared, Russia would have to face
the results of having lived beyond her means for so many years.

The depression of 1899 laid bare again the weaknesses of the
Witte system: when the foreign loans stopped, as they did in 1899
and through no fault of the government, the boom also collapsed.
Obviously Russia was not master of her own economic development. Furthermore, the latent discontent with the government's economic policy, muffled by the industrial boom of the nineties, broke
out in a rising crescendo that led to Witte's fall and culminated in
the revolution of 1905. But what else could the government have
done? There was no escape from the dilemma: the Russian people
would remain poor and backward whether the government pursued
a policy of laissez faire, or whether it made a special effort through
a planned protective system. And they were to remain poor and
backward while the peoples of Western Europe and the United
States became noticeably more prosperous. Was the Russian public
to stand for this seemingly perpetual backwardness?

Witte was quite aware that his economic measures were insufficient for the industrial progress of Russia; they were constantly
obstructed by a hostile social and political framework. Thus he was
increasingly driven to recast Russian society in the image of the
capitalist society of the West. His "system" was, one might say, a
huge wager on the Russian capitalists. For its success, however,
Witte needed a legal and institutional setting in which the Russian
capitalists could eventually take over the development of Russia's

resources. He wanted to enhance, not limit, private initiative. But, like Colbert and Peter the Great, he discovered that he and his businessmen did not necessarily agree. He found the Russian *kupechestvo* sluggish and inflexible, reluctant to take advantage of the opportunities which he held out. They in turn complained about the heavy hand of the government. Thus there was a flaw at the very center of his system.

Of greater consequence, however, was the collective order of peasant life. Witte realized that capitalism in industry, in order to stimulate the Russian economy, must be backed by capitalism in agriculture. Thus after 1897 he became a determined foe of the extended peasant family, the peasant commune, strip farming, and the legal separation of the peasantry from the rest of Russian society. He was also a keen protagonist of elementary and, still more, advanced education. Perhaps education was undermining the loyalty of the people, so he told Tsar Nicholas, but even if it did, it was necessary so that Russia could move forward.[21]

There was no stopping point in this line of reasoning. The logic of economic development pushed the minister of finance ever further afield. From his concern over economic institutions he progressed to criticism of the social structure of Russia, and thence to a questioning of the bureaucracy, of foreign policy, and even of the nature of autocracy. In 1898 Witte demanded the overhaul of Russian local administration in order to produce a streamlined, modernized civil service.[22] In 1900, finding himself opposed on all sides by government officials who did not share his ideal of an industrialized Russia, he demanded that all economic policy be concentrated in his hands. The emperor, he pleaded, should make it clear that he considered industrialization of primary importance for the spiritual and political welfare of the country and should enforce compliance for the views of the Ministry of Finance in all branches of the government.[23] Constantly he meddled, in the name of economic necessity, in Russian foreign policy. Industrialization, he knew, demanded peace, stopping the arms race, and avoiding any costly ventures in foreign policy. And even in the Far East, where he became committed to an expansionist policy for the sake of the prosperity of his Siberian railroad, he was constantly restrained by his fear for the financial stability of the government.[24]

But the most significant conclusion which Witte drew from his economic policy was concerned with the nature of autocracy. Russia, he realized, required an autocratic regime, but an autocracy with its ears to the ground and working patiently and with modern efficiency for the welfare of all its subjects. He demanded greater unity of purpose at the center of the government, concentration upon the task of catching up, and a streamlined bureaucracy reaching from the capital to the smallest village and motivated by one will. Extensive public relations creating a close relationship between the ruler and ruled were also essential. He himself set forth in his annual budget reports the reasons for his economic measures and the overriding need for industrialization, and he was in constant consultation with the economic groups whose fortunes were affected by his policies. He was the first to celebrate industrial victories by parading favorable statistics. The government as a whole, he said, must discuss and consult with its subjects, and convince them that all its acts were necessary for their welfare. Only thus, he warned amidst incredible incomprehension, could a revolution be avoided.[25]

The foregoing discussion, I trust, has shown how the political ambition of the Russian state and economic necessity combined to prompt a revision of the very basis of the Russian state and society. Starting from the need for industrialization, Witte was driven step by step to advocate a profound reform of current autocratic practice. What he envisaged was a government capable of carrying out a revolution from above, a revolution which would recast not only the Russian economy, but also her society and administration after the contemporary pattern of Western urban-industrial life. Yet at the same time he was a prophet crying in the wilderness.

How alien his "system" was to public opinion may be seen from the fact that his most famous accomplishment, the introduction of the gold standard, was carried out by an unusually sharp assertion of autocratic prerogative against the determined opposition not only of the public, but also of the bulk of the imperial bureaucracy as voiced by the State Council.[26] The gold standard, like all his other measures, and above all his entire philosophy of rapid industrialization, would have been instantly repudiated by an overwhelming majority, if it had ever been submitted to a popular vote.

At the turn of the century Witte had enlisted against himself the zemstvos, many committees of trade and industry, the overwhelming majority of the intelligentsia, the peasants, the revolutionaries, the bulk of the imperial bureaucracy, and the emperor himself.

The public distaste for Witte's policy was understandable, for its appalling cost in terms of popular welfare were well understood at the time. Few Russians shared Witte's faith in modern industry; the scientist Mendeleev was his only ally among the public. Russian society was still deeply rooted in an agrarian orientation. It despised not only factories and cities, but also the cold rationality, punctuality, and uniformity of modern industry, its adaptability and pride in specialization. On the other hand, there is no evidence that the bulk of the population did not favor the basic political ambitions of the government; on the contrary, too often they wanted more than what the government considered feasible. Incredible as it may seem in retrospect, the public craved the benefits of the European, urban-industrial way of life without being willing to change its own essentially preindustrial habits.

At this point another unjustly neglected phase of the relations between state and economy in a backward country with the ambitions of a great power must be briefly discussed: the element of constant subversion of all governmental authority as a result of the constant comparison with the advanced countries of the West. In Witte's Russia one could always hear the reproach that the other countries, France, Germany, England, the United States, could manage to be powerful and civilized without excessive sacrifices on the part of their populations. Why not Russia? Just as the Russian public was eager to buy foreign goods in unlimited quantities without any recognition of the limits set by their poverty, they also wanted to be powerful without making any undue exertions. In their ignorance of the dilemmas of backwardness, they simply would not accept the fact of Russian poverty, which in itself was an indication of their ambition. The difficulties of government under these circumstances, even of one more efficient than that of Nicholas II, can be imagined. The government, after all, was obviously assuming full charge of economic development. Yet everybody saw how little it could accomplish. Therefore, so the conclusion ran, it was no good. As Stalin put it many years later: you are backward, therefore you are wrong.[27]

There were lesser, yet equally insoluble, problems posed by the Witte system. How would Russian society agree to the government's wager on the Russian capitalists? From Witte's point of view, of all social groups in Russia only the *kupechestvo,* the energetic elements in the *meshchanstvo,* and the kulaks could be expected to make intelligent choices for the productive investment of scarce capital. But would these groups ever be able to win the confidence of the other groups of Russian society as they rose to prominence? All evidence points to the contrary: no segments of Russian society were more despised or hated than these "bourgeois" groups. And how was the government to overcome the elemental antagonism of the emerging industrial working class or of the peasants whom rural starvation and unemployment drew into the factories? Witte was more aware of this second problem than of the first. Yet he never gave it his full attention.

Finally, there was the problem of foreign intervention in Russian affairs resulting from the foreign indebtedness of Russia. As mentioned above, Russian foreign loans had assumed from an early moment an unusually political character. It could hardly have been otherwise considering the power competition in the European system. The Russian government thus always faced the danger that its financial dependence would be exploited as a check on its sovereignty. It could not pursue a foreign policy liable to antagonize its creditors or an internal one that undermined their confidence in the financial stability of the country. Thus it had far less freedom of maneuver than its rivals among the great powers. Whatever it undertook, it had to consider the reactions of the European investing public. The suppression of political disorders or anti-Semitic measures, for instance, tended to reduce Russian creditworthiness and thus, in fact, exerted a restraint. Between 1887 and 1917 Russian policy was tied to French policy, inasmuch as French investments in Russia were controlled, to a large extent, by the French government. The degree of foreign control through financial ties has often been exaggerated, yet there can be no question that it was a very real check bitterly resented not least by the emperor himself.[28] One can well understand the desire for true economic sovereignty stated so often before 1917 in Russian economic literature. Yet here lay another unpalatable paradox of the underdeveloped: they must become more dependent on foreign aid in order to become independent of it—unless, of course, they were willing to "go it alone."

Needless to say, in Witte's time the full consequences of Russian backwardness and conversely of her rapid need for industrialization were barely perceived; his work remained incomplete. After his fall as minister of finance, no further effort was made by the emperor to carry out his vision. Tsarist economic policy never assumed the comprehensive character that Witte had planned to give it. Stolypin carried out only part of Witte's grand design, and that incompletely. This is not to deny that considerable industrial progress occurred before 1914, much again with the help of large state orders.[29] Yet the basic disparity between Russian industrial production and Russian political ambition remained. No matter how much the rate of growth in Russian industry exceeded that of the other great powers, imperial Russia did not command the industrial potential necessary for her station.[30] In 1913—to cite but one example—37 percent of Russia's annual consumption of technical equipment was imported, and more than half of her industrial machinery.[31] When the war came she did not possess industrial equipment sufficient to hold her own and accordingly she suffered brutally.

IX

Six years of war, revolution, and civil strife had left the Soviet economy in ruins. The New Economic Policy (NEP) instituted in 1921 was not a modernization program, but one of recovery, based on the existing tsarist plant. When this had been achieved by the mid-1920s, the NEP became a system perpetuating stagnation, rather than stimulating growth. Soviet leaders and economists differed in their prescriptions for solving the crises of the NEP and embarking on a modernization drive. The Right faction wanted essentially a gradual industrialization to be achieved by stimulating the productivity and purchases of the peasant smallholder. The Left faction opted for a much more radical departure from the NEP, which would give priority to the rapid development of heavy over consumer industry, and would be financed through rigorous taxation of the peasantry. Stalin did not commit himself until very late in the game, when he had consolidated power in his hands. He then *launched his own industrialization drive which combined the more realistic and dynamic aspects of both the Right and Left programs with highly coercive methods that neither had anticipated. The Soviet industrialization debates of the 1920s and the evolution of Stalin's views are traced by Alexander Erlich. Born in Russia, Dr. Erlich is Professor of Economics at the Russian Institute, Columbia University, and the author of* The Soviet Industrialization Debate 1924–1928 *(Cambridge, Mass., 1960). The article here reprinted first appeared in the symposium,* Continuity and Change in Russian and Soviet Thought *(Cambridge, Mass., 1955), E. Simmons, editor, and is presented with the permission of the publisher and author.*

ALEXANDER ERLICH

Stalin's Views on Soviet Economic Development

I

On s'engage, et puis on voit: this phrase borrowed from Napoleon was used by Lenin more than once to describe the position of his party after November 1917.[1] With regard to the issues of economic policy, the interval between getting involved and seeing, or even looking, was rather protracted. During the first few years the pressure of external events was so overwhelming as to leave virtually no room for choice. The spontaneous seizures of factories by the workers in early 1918 and the exigencies of the Civil War forced upon the reluctant Lenin and his collaborators the policy of "War Communism." With similar inevitability the swelling tide of popular unrest climaxed by the Kronstadt revolt and by the peasant uprisings of Central Russia imposed the retreat toward the NEP. And in both cases there was always the great expectation that the

European revolution would link up before long with its Russian bridgehead and assist the Soviet republic with equipment, industrial consumers' goods, and organizing ability. In 1924 the situation was entirely different. Chances of a quick rescue from the West, which had already been declining at the time of the transition to the NEP, had now passed. The discontent of the peasants, moreover, was no longer restrained by the fear of the "White" counterrevolution: they had just forced the regime off the "War Communist" path, and they were grimly awaiting the results of this victory. Under such circumstances the policy could no longer consist of spasmodic responses to catastrophes and of fervent hopes for the future. Only positive action directed toward improvement in the wretched living standards of the population could stabilize the regime; only forceful economic development aimed at enlargement of the productive capacity of the country could provide a durable basis for such action and make the Soviet Union a viable state. But how could this be done, how could these two objectives be reconciled in conditions of a backward, war-ravaged country in the thick of a great egalitarian upheaval? This was a question to which the "old books" provided no answer.[2]

Bukharin, who was at that time the leading economic theorist of the Party, felt that the solution was clearly at hand. It was contained, according to him, in continuing the NEP as conceived by Lenin and as elaborated on in his famous O prodnaloge. The vicious circle of idle industrial capacity in the cities and the supply strikes in the villages was to be broken by lifting restrictive measures which had hitherto inhibited the peasant's willingness to produce a surplus above his bare needs or at any rate to part with it. Transformation of the wholesale requisitioning into a limited "tax in kind"; opening the channels of trade through which the nontaxable part of peasant surplus could be profitably sold; denationalization and encouragement of small-scale industry which would not need, because of the nature of its plant, any protracted reconditioning in order to start producing goods demanded by the peasants— these were the key devices which were expected to unfreeze the productive energies of agriculture and make increased supplies of foodstuffs and raw materials flow into the nearly empty pipelines of the urban economy. The part of this flow which would reach the large-scale industrial sector would set some of its idle wheels turning and make possible a counterflow of manufactured products to the goods-starved village, thus providing the latter with an additional incentive to increase its marketings. A genuine process of cumulative growth would be set in motion hereby. The logic of the reasoning seemed compelling, and even more impressive was the impact of facts: between 1920 and 1924 the output of large-scale industry increased more than threefold.

Could this upward trend be relied upon to start off a process of long-range expansion and set the pattern for it? Lenin was never explicit about it: but his strong emphasis on the need of attracting foreign investment seemed to indicate some doubts whether the policy of "developing trade at all costs" would be sufficient to do the job. Bukharin, writing three years later, betrayed no such qualms. He enthusiastically proceeded to sharpen up Lenin's analysis by praising the high allocative efficiency of the market mechanism, denouncing the tendencies toward "monopolistic parasitism" in the nationalized industry, and sounding solemn warnings against "applied Tuganism" (*prikladnaia Tugan-Baranovshchina*), which postulated the possibility of expansion of productive capacity without proportionate increase in effective demand on the part of the final consumer. This disproportion, in his view, had been ultimately responsible for the downfall of tsarism as well as for the Soviet "scissor crisis" of 1923. In order to prevent this from happening again, a consistent policy of "small profit margins and large turnover" was called for. Nor was this all: Bukharin outlined an elaborate system of institutional arrangements serving the same purpose. Marketing und credit cooperation in agriculture were, in his opinion, the most desirable devices for enlarging the peasant demand for industrial goods. But he had some words of appreciation also for the village kulak whose relentless drive to raise his output and to expand his demand made him, like Goethe's Mephisto, *ein Teil von jener Kraft, die stets das Boese will und stets das Gute schafft*. In the long run, this stratum was expected to be gradually squeezed out under the joint pressure of the proletarian state and the growing cooperative movement among the peasants.

It was the last-mentioned aspect of Bukharin's conception that evoked particularly violent attacks. The conciliatory attitude toward the village rich could not but arouse most deeply the Left Wing of

the Party, which had considered the compromise with the individu-
alist peasantry a bitter, if temporarily unavoidable, sacrifice and
which was pushing toward resumption of the offensive against
propertied classes both on the domestic and on the international
scene. But spokesmen of this group, with Preobrazhenskii as its
leading economist, did not leave things at that; they penetrated to
the core of Bukharin's reasoning and denounced his extrapolation
of past experience into the future as a typical "psychology of the
restoration period." They were explicit, if rather brief, in dealing
with long-range issues like modernization of industry, opening up
areas with untapped natural resources, absorption of agricultural
surplus population, the importance of what we would call today
"social overheads" like transportation and the power system (as
well as of industrial development in general) for the efficiency of
peasant farming, and, last but not least, the requirements of national defense. They were equally specific in emphasizing some of
the basic characteristics of modern productive technology which
made its adoption a costly proposition. But the crux of their argument lay in pointing to definite short-term features of the situation
of the Soviet economy which made it imperative to move toward
these long-range objectives at a high speed in spite of the high cost
involved. According to Preobrazhenskii and his friends, people who
rejoiced in record-breaking rates of increase in industrial growth up
to 1925 lived in a fool's paradise. The expansion at small cost was
easy as long as the large reserves of unutilized capacity existed; but
with every leap forward in industrial output, the time at which future increases would require investment in additional productive facilities was drawing closer. To wait with such investment until that
stage, however, would be dangerous. The replacement of a large
part of equipment actually in service had been due, but not carried
out, in the period of Civil War and in the early years of the NEP.
Yet while such a life extension was possible for a while, each passing year would increase the probability of breakdown of overaged
equipment; and this would imply a shrinkage in the capital stock of
the economy unless the replacement activities were drastically
stepped up. Another powerful source of increased pressure for expansion of capacity lay in the redistribution of income along egalitarian lines which was brought about by the Revolution and which

expressed itself in a steep increase in the share of consumption in income. At the same time the large-scale import of capital which had played an important role in the economic development of pre-revolutionary Russia was now reduced to a trickle.

But the very circumstances which called for rapid expansion created a grave danger for the stability of the economy. The limitations of resources permitted the required increase in investment to develop only by keeping down the levels of current consumption, while the low real income and the egalitarian mode of its distribution made it more than unlikely that this restriction in consumers' spending would take place voluntarily. Such a situation, if left uncontrolled, would mean a "goods famine," more specifically, a shortage of industrial consumers' goods; and since the Russian peasant then enjoyed, in Preobrazhenskii's words, "a much greater freedom [than before the Revolution] in the choice of the time and of the terms at which to dispose of his own surpluses because of the decrease in 'forced sales,' " [3] he would be likely to respond to an unfavorable turn in the terms of trade by cutting down his marketable surplus and thus administering a crippling blow to the industrial economy. The way out of this deadlock was to be sought in compulsory saving, with monopoly of foreign trade and price manipulation at home as its main tools; the first would secure high priority for capital goods in Russian imports, the second was expected to contain the pressure of consumers' demand at home against the existing industrial capacity by keeping the prices of industrial commodities higher than they would be under conditions of a free, unrestricted market. As a result, the capital stock of the society would be permitted to increase up to a level at which the demand for high current output of consumers' goods and requirements of further expansion of productive capacity could be met simultaneously and not to the exclusion of each other. In the planning of this initial increase, moreover, particular care had to be exercised to keep its inflationary potentialities to a minimum: the largest volume of capital outlays would fall into the initial year of the plan, when large reserves of the old capacity could provide a cushion for the unstabilizing effect of newly started construction projects, and then gradually taper off in the following years during which these reserves would approach exhaustion.

This last-mentioned point caused little interest at the time of its enunciation; it was, incidentally, brought up not in the actual debate but in a rather technical proposal of a committee of experts known by its initials as *OSVOK*.[4] But the proposals for compulsory saving (bracketed by Preobrazhenskii under the anxiety-provoking name of "primitive socialist accumulation") did call forth an immediate reaction; indeed, they proved an ideal target for attack. The representatives of the Bukharin group were quick to point out that a policy recommended by the Leftists would in its immediate effects greatly increase the tensions which its long-range consequences were expected to alleviate. The policy of monopolistic price manipulation would make the peasants worse off; they would be certain to resist this deterioration by using all the devices Preobrazhenskii and his friends had so eloquently described; and the possibility of steering through the economic and political trouble caused by such a policy toward the time at which the new investment would smooth the waves by starting to deliver the goods could be asserted merely as an act of faith.[5]

II

The assertion that Stalin's interventions in the "debate of 1924–1928" did not break the impasse would be an understatement. Indeed, his pronouncements on controversial issues of economic policy in these years exhibit such a definite tendency against sin and in favor of eating one's cake and having it too that it appears at first almost hopeless to distill out of them a clear view not only of the nature of the problems, but also of the attitude of the man. But after a closer examination of the record, there can be no doubt that Stalin's statement at the Fourteenth Party Congress: "We are, and we shall be, for Bukharin," [6] provides a substantially correct description of his position at that time. True, in certain respects he sounded a somewhat different note. He showed a strong inclination to indulge, on every propitious occasion, in exalting the glories of the coming industrialization; moreover, the aspect of the future developments which received the fondest attention on his part was the possibility of making Russia a self-contained unit, economically independent of the outside world—"a country which can produce by its own efforts the necessary equipment." [7] He started to emphasize the need for intensive reconstruction of Soviet industry earlier than Bukharin did; and in the same speech in which he dramatically refused to give "Bukharin's blood" to the opposition, he did not hesitate to disassociate himself from the "get rich" slogan.[8] But neither these nor similar instances could alter the fact that on issues which were relevant for actual policy, the agreement was practically complete. When Stalin was applauding the removal of "administrative obstacles preventing the rise in the peasant welfare" as "an operation [which] undoubtedly facilitates any accumulation, private capitalist as well as socialist," [9] or when he denounced on an earlier occasion any attempt to fan the class struggle in the village as "empty chatter," while praising peasant cooperation as a road toward socialist transformation of agriculture,[10] he was talking like a Bukharinite pure and simple; his wailings about "get rich" sounded, in view of this, very much like the famous admonition given to Eduard Bernstein, the father of German "revisionism," by one of his senior friends: "Such things should be done but not said." The identity of position on the larger issue of relationships between industry and agriculture was equally evident. Although Stalin did not invoke the ghost of Tugan-Baranovskii (he was at that time somewhat chary of incursions into the field of theory), he believed firmly that "our industry, which provides the foundation of socialism and of our power, is based on the internal, on the peasant market." [11]

The last point, to be sure, did not jibe very well with his other declared objectives: if industry had to be oriented primarily toward the satisfaction of peasant needs, it would be impossible to spare an adequate amount of resources for a large-scale effort toward reconstruction of industry, particularly if this should be done with a view to future self-sufficiency in the sphere of capital-goods production. But to proclaim long-term goals was one thing, and to rush toward them at a high speed was another. Stalin in these days showed no inclination toward the latter. In the same speech in which he extolled the virtues of economic independence, he readily admitted that large-scale imports of foreign machinery were, at least for the time being, indispensable for the development of the Soviet economy; and in his polemics against Trotsky at a somewhat later date, he went to considerable lengths in order to emphasize that the Soviet Union would not endanger her economic sovereignty by trading extensively with the capitalist world—first of all because the dependence involved would be a two-way affair and, secondly, because nationalization of large-scale industry and banking as well as state monopoly of foreign trade would provide powerful safeguards against any attempt at foreign encroachments.[12] His attitude toward the problem of the rate of industrial development was characterized by similar circumspection. At one point he would attempt to sidetrack the issue by injecting a larger one and by insisting that a reconstruction of fixed capital in industry would not solve the problem of building socialism in Russia as long as agriculture had not been transformed along collectivist lines.[13] On another occasion, he praised glowingly the rapid increase in output of the Soviet metal industry as proof that "the proletariat . . . can construct with its own efforts a new industry and a new society," [14] without mentioning the obvious fact that this increase had been so rapid precisely because it had been based on increased utilization of the old industrial capacity and *not* on the creation of the new. But when he actually came to grips with the problem in his report to the Fourteenth Congress, he left no doubts as to his real attitude:

> In order to switch from maximal utilization of everything we had in industry to the policy of constructing a new industry on a new technological basis, on the basis of the construction of new plants, large capital outlays are needed. But since we are suffering from a considerable capital shortage, the further development of our industry will proceed, in all probability, not at such a fast rate as it has until now. The situation with regard to agriculture is different. It cannot be said that all the potentialities of agriculture are already exhausted. Agriculture, in distinction from industry, can move for some time at a fast rate also on its present technological basis. Even the simple rise in cultural level of the peasant, even such a simple thing as cleaning the seeds could raise the gross output of agriculture by 10 to 15 per cent . . . That's why the further development of agriculture does not yet face the technological obstacles our industry has to face . . .[15]

Stalin could not be more frank in formulating the basic problem which was, as we have seen, at the core of the whole discussion: the very same factors—limited productive capacity and low levels of income—that called for expansion in Soviet industry were putting obstacles in its way. In the paragraph quoted, the emphasis was clearly on the obstacles. Still, when the arch-moderate Shanin applauded heartily, he must have done so with a twinkle in his eye: in fact the Fourteenth Party Congress did signalize the transition from "filling-in" to reconstruction—but reconstruction on a limited scale and in a cautious mood. Although the volume of capital outlays increased substantially in the years 1926 and 1927, the Leftists led by Preobrazhenskii and Trotsky immediately opened fire. The new investment program, they claimed, was neither here nor there; it was too limited to secure an increase in capacity large enough to stabilize the situation in a not-too-distant future, too ambitious not to cause inflationary disturbances now in view of the absence of drastic taxation measures.

In the face of these attacks, and of actual difficulties which did not fail to materialize, something more than a sober and judicious description of the two horns of the dilemma was called for. A characteristic division of labor developed at this point. Bukharin and Rykov, who were the guiding spirits of the new line, were wrestling with large, clear-cut issues—the relation between heavy and light industry, the limits for investment in time-consuming projects, the possibility of absorbing the surplus labor in production lines with low capital requirements—in a desperate search for solutions which would make the adopted policy work. Stalin followed a different procedure. He visibly tried to avoid sharply delineated problems; instead, he let his argument seesaw from bold statements of principles to sobering but comfortably loose observations on present-day realities, and he switched from obtuse mystique to gruff common sense. Rapid industrialization? Yes, indeed! More than that: it should be kept in mind that "not every development of industry constitutes industrialization" and that "the focal point of industrialization, its basis, consists of development of heavy industry (fuel, metals, etc.) and of eventual development of production of the means of production, development of domestic machine-building." [16] But right on the heels of such proclamations there would come a caustic remark about those who "sometimes forget that it is impossible to make plans either for industry as a whole or for some 'large and all-embracing' enterprise without a certain minimum of means, without a certain minimum of reserves," [17] and a warning that "an industry which breaks itself away from the national economy as a whole and loses its connection with it cannot be the guiding force of the national economy." [18] Could the Soviet economy in its present shape afford a rate of economic development which would exceed that of the capitalist countries? Of course! The capitalist countries had based their expansion on exploitation of colonies, military conquest, or foreign loans. But the Soviet Union expropriated the capitalists and the landlords, nationalized strategic areas of the economy, and repudiated the tsarist foreign debts. This circumstance enabled her to provide a sufficient volume of accumulation without having recourse to any of these devices.[19] Furthermore, it permitted this accumulation to unfold alongside of "a steady improvement in the material conditions of the working masses, including the bulk of the peasantry . . . as contrasted with the capitalist methods of industrialization based on the growing misery of millions of working people." [20] No specific reasons for any of these assertions were given. However, the most elaborate of such attempts at solution by definition concluded by admitting that the socialist principles along which the Soviet economy was organized offered merely a *possibility* of achieving the appropriate level of accumulation, but no more than that; and the concrete proposals for policy which followed were in their sum total excruciatingly modest not only in comparison with the grandiloquent claims that preceded them, but also, and more significantly, with regard to the size of the investment programs they were supposed to sustain.[21]

All this looked very much like trying to buy a secondhand Ford for the price of a discarded piece of junk while pretending that a brand-new Packard was being obtained. True, there was another line of defense: to play down the importance of recurrent spells of "goods famine" and to present them as transient phenomena. Although Stalin tried this device occasionally, it was obviously a tenuous argument to use, particularly since the assertion that "quick development of our industry is the surest way to eliminate the goods famine" [22] sounded too much like conceding a point to the Left opposition. It was therefore only logical for him to shift the battleground to the territory of the adversaries, to concentrate on the crucial weak spot in their position and to pound relentlessly upon it:

> The oppositionist bloc assumed a conflict between industry and agriculture and is headed toward breaking industry away from agriculture. It does not realize and it does not admit that it is impossible to develop industry while neglecting the interests of agriculture and hurting these interests in a rude fashion. It does not understand that if industry is the guiding force of the national economy, the agricultural economy represents in turn the basis on which our industry is able to develop . . .
>
> . . . The Party cannot and will not tolerate [a situation in which] the opposition continues to undermine the basis of the alliance of workers and peasants by spreading the idea of an increase in wholesale prices and in the burden of taxation upon the peasantry, by attempting to "construe" the relationships between proletariat and peasantry not as relationships of economic *coöperation* but as relationships of exploitation of the peasantry by the proletarian state. The Party cannot and will not tolerate this [23]

At the Fifteenth Party Congress, which carried out this solemn vow by expelling the Left-wingers, Stalin was surveying the field once more. He displayed again the full array of the familiar arguments: praise for the growth of the Soviet industrial output at a rate which, while declining continuously since 1924–1925, was still showing "a record percentage which no large capitalist country in the world has ever shown"; [24] reaffirmation of faith in the superiority which the Soviet system possessed with regard to capitalism in its ability to accumulate and which should make it possible to increase the industrial output by roughly 75 percent during the coming five years in spite of the exhaustion of the capacity reserves; strong emphasis on the possibility of developing "in an atmosphere of constant *rapprochement* between city and village, between proletariat and peasantry," [25] as one of the greatest advantages of Soviet industry. His backhanded remarks about what he termed the "shadowy aspects" of the Soviet economy ("elements" of goods famine, lack of reserves, etc.) contained no specific proposals for remedy but carried a clear implication that if people on the spot would apply themselves to their tasks with more energy, all would be well. There was, however, no complacency in his remarks on agriculture, and here indeed something new was added: in view of the slowness of agricultural development, Stalin declared, the task of the Party would now consist in bringing about "a gradual transition of pulverized peasant farms to the level of combined large-scale holdings, to the social collective cultivation of land on the basis of the intensification and mechanization of agriculture." [26] He was careful not to give any hint as to the anticipated speed of this movement, and, in an enunciation antedating by a few weeks his report to the Fifteenth Congress, he was explicit in emphasizing that it would take a long time to collectivize the bulk of the peasantry because such an undertaking would require "huge finances" which the Soviet state did not yet have.[27] Still, his statement was surprising: but events which were even then fast advancing were to provide *ex post* a clue to it.

III

The beginning of 1928 saw large consignments of the Leftist "super-industrializers" move toward places of exile in Siberia and Central Asia. But at the same time their dire predictions were coming true. For the first time since the "scissors crisis" of 1923, the peasant bolted the regime. By January 1928 the amount of collected grain fell by roughly one-third as compared with the same period of the preceding year. During the following few months, it rose again only to drop in the spring; and the emergency methods by which the temporary increase was enforced stirred up once more the feelings of bitterness and resistance which had been dormant in the villages during the seven years of the NEP. The crisis of the system was there—the first crisis Stalin had to cope with as the undisputed leader of the Party and of the state. During the eighteen months that followed, Stalin was no longer arguing, as before, against opponents who had been isolated and outmaneuvered before they began to fight; he was reappraising a policy which had promoted his rise to power and which seemed now to explode in his face. It is therefore not surprising that his pronouncements of that period differ significantly from those of the earlier years. They certainly contain their due share of crudeness, obfuscation, and outright distortion; but at the same time they show flashes of astonishing frankness and incisiveness clearly due to realization that everything was at stake and that the time of muddling through was over.

The prime task consisted understandably enough, in providing the explanation of the agricultural debacle. One can clearly distinguish several parallel lines of attack in Stalin's statements on the subject. The first of them was already indicated in his report to the Fifteenth Congress when he mentioned the low productivity of small-scale peasant agriculture and its low marketable surplus as a serious obstacle for the rapid industrial development of the country. This proposition was in itself neither new nor controversial, provided that the "obstacle" was taken to be a retarding factor rather than an insuperable barrier. It was a breathtaking jump to conclusions, however, when Stalin went on to claim that "there is no other way out" except for collectivization. In the audience to which he was addressing himself there were, to be sure, no doubts as to the superiority of the large-size units in agricultural economy. But it was generally understood that there was still a wide range of opportunities for increases in the productivity of peasant farming which would not call for large-scale mechanized equipment and for drastic expansion in the size of the productive unit; and it was agreed that the extensive application of the latter category of improvements should be postponed, in view of the high capital requirements involved, until after the capital-goods industry had been sufficiently expanded. Consequently, while the idea of collectivization of agriculture as a long-range objective held a place of honor in the Party program of 1919 and was repeatedly invoked after that, particularly in the pronouncements of the Left, no one had thus far suggested putting it into effect on a large scale within the next few years in order to solve difficulties facing the Soviet economy at the end of the "restoration period." In fact, Stalin himself seemed to take quite an edge off his argument and to hark back to

his earlier views when he admitted the existence of considerable reserves for improvement within the framework of the small-scale
economy,[28] and as late as April 1929 he still kept insisting that
"the individual farming of poor and middle peasants plays and will
play the predominant role in supplying industry with food and raw
material in the immediate future." [29] But, and most important, the
whole point seemed to have no direct bearing on the concrete issue
under consideration. By the end of 1927 and at the beginning of
1928, the Russian peasants had not less but more grain at their disposal than in the preceding years; still, they were willing to sell less
of it than in the years of bad harvest. The reference to the low productivity of small-scale farming, even if reduced to sensible proportions, was definitely too "long run" to provide an explanation for
this phenomenon.

The second line of argument was succinctly summed up in the
phrase "as long as the kulak exists, the sabotage of grain collections
will exist too." [30] This point, made in Stalin's speech in January
1928 and repeated by him with increasing vehemence ever after,
was certainly straightforward enough; still it raised more questions
than it answered. The fact of formidable kulak resistance did not fit
very well, to begin with, into the rosy picture of the Soviet village
Stalin had been unfolding before his listeners only slightly more
than a year earlier when he proudly referred to the steadily increasing proportion of middle peasants in the agricultural population and
asserted, with a long quotation from Lenin on hand to bear him
out, that nobody but panic-striken people could see a danger in the
growth of "small private capital" in the villages because this growth
"is being compensated and overcompensated by such decisive facts
as the development of our industry, which strengthens the positions
of the proletariat and of the socialist forms of the economy." [31]
True, in this case also there were, at first, important qualifications
which softened the impact of the shock: stern warning against any
talk about "dekulakization" as "counterrevolutionary chatter," con-
demnation of the excessive zeal in applying reprisals, and announcement of moderate increases in prices of agricultural products.[32] But after all this had been said and done, it was still to be
explained why the kulak was so successful in his criminal endeavor
—more particularly, why he was able, as Stalin reluctantly ac-

knowledged, to carry along with him the "middle peasants" who were supplying the bulk of the marketable surplus at that time.[33]

Stalin had a clear answer to this as well as to all other questions the previous explanations had left unanswered; between the "low-productivity" argument and the cloak-and-dagger theory of the kulaks' plot he had a third line of reasoning which hit the nail straight on the head. It was less publicized than the former two and for good reasons: it amounted to a clear and unqualified admission of a complete impasse. Stalin no longer tried to play down the impact of the goods famine; he stressed instead that the shortage of industrial goods on the peasant market, aggravated by an increase in peasant earnings in the preceding period, had hit not merely the kulaks, but also the peasants as a whole and had made them strike back by cutting the grain deliveries.[34] He spelled out more fully than ever before the connection between the goods famine and the discontinuous increase in the volume of investment:

> Industrial reconstruction means the transfer of resources from the field of production of articles of consumption to the field of production of means of production . . . But what does it mean? It means that money is being invested in the construction of new enterprises, that the number of new towns and new consumers is increasing while, on the other hand, the new enterprises will begin to turn out additional masses of commodities only in three or four years' time. It is obvious that this does not help to overcome the goods famine.[35]

He rounded out the picture when he dropped his usual double talk and shocked his colleagues of the Central Committee by revealing his views on the true sources of accumulation in the Soviet economy:

> The peasantry pays to the state not only the normal taxes, direct and indirect, but it *overpays*, first of all, on the relatively high prices of industrial goods, and is being more or less *underpaid* on the relatively low prices of agricultural products . . . This is something like a "tribute" [*nechto vrode "dani"*], something like a supertax we are temporarily compelled to impose in order to main-

tain and to develop further the present tempo of development of industry, to secure the industry for the whole country, to raise the well-being of the village still further, and to abolish entirely this supertax, these "scissors" between the city and the village.[36]

All this sounded very much like a somewhat awkward rephrasing of Preobrazhenskii's "law of primitive socialist accumulation." The crucial task at that time of the day, however, was not to restate an old diagnosis but to construe a "tribute"-collecting device that would work: and this was exactly what Stalin did. The collective farm, in which decisions about size and disposal of the marketable surplus were made not by individual farmers but by management carrying out the orders of the state, was to serve as a high-powered tool for enforcing the necessary rate of saving in the most literal sense of the standard Marxian definition: it could make the peasants "sell without purchasing" to a much greater extent than they would have done if left to themselves. Here was the decisive point. Still, Stalin was undoubtedly right in not being too ostentatious about it and in holding on firmly to the two other arguments referred to above in spite of their inadequacy. To proclaim in so many words that collectivization was needed in order to squeeze out the peasants in a most effective way would clearly be a poor tactic; it was much smarter to present the collective farm as an indispensable vehicle for modernizing Soviet agriculture and for drastically increasing its productivity. In view of everything Stalin had to say about the impact of the "goods famine" on the peasantry as a whole and about the inevitability of the "supertax," the diatribes against kulak sabotage could not be taken very seriously. They could, nevertheless, be of appreciable help in whipping up emotions against an alternative solution which was advanced at that time by Stalin's former comrades-in-arms. The representatives of the Bukharin-Rykov group did not propose to revise the investment plans below the fairly impressive levels set by the Party leadership at the end of 1927. They believed, however, that in order to carry out these plans it was not necessary to abandon support for individual peasant farming and to renounce the policy of no interference with the growth of large-scale kulak farms while curbing the nonproductive and exploitative activities of their owners. On the contrary, although by that time the controversy had already been quite muffled, and it was difficult to ascertain what exactly the leaders of the Right Wing were prepared to do, the general tenor of their pronouncements, as well as occasional statements of second-string representatives and "fellow travelers" of this group, indicated a willingness to go to greater lengths than ever before toward placating the peasants in general and the kulaks in particular, in order to provide them with incentives for increasing the marketable surplus and the volume of voluntary saving in an effort to contain the mounting inflationary pressures.

Stalin never earnestly tried to assail the economic logic of this position. He never attempted to prove that it was impossible for socialized industry and kulak farming to operate smoothly within one economic system, although he made a few obiter dicta to that effect. Neither did he care to show (which would be a more serious point) that an investment policy, sustained to a considerable extent by the peasants' free decision to restrict their consumption, would tend to be rather narrow in scope and susceptible to rude shocks as a result of such uncontrollable events as drought or changes in international terms of trade. Instead, he asked: "What is meant by not hindering kulak farming? It means setting the kulak free. And what is meant by setting the kulak free? It means giving him power." [37] Taken literally, this seemed to be one of the dubious syllogisms Stalin was notoriously fond of whenever a weak case was to be defended. It is quite conceivable, however, that in this particular instance he believed every word he said; and, what is vastly more important, there can be no doubt that the consistent application of the Rightist recipe would be fraught with gravest political dangers. The efforts to enlist voluntary support of the peasantry for the industrialization developing at considerable speed would require a veritable tightrope performance on the part of the Soviet rulers. In order to maintain the precarious balance and to steer clear of trouble at every sharper turning of the road, the regime would have to combine compulsory control measures with additional concessions; and since there was little room for compromise in the economic sphere, it could become well-nigh indispensable to explore a new line of approach and to attempt to earn the goodwill of the upper strata of the peasantry by opening up for them avenues of political influence even if confined, at first, to the level of local government. There was nothing either in the logic of things or, for that matter, in the tenets of the accepted doctrine to warrant the conclusion that such a situation, if permitted to endure, would inevitably result in "giving power to the kulaks" and in restoring capitalism. But it is quite probable that under the impact of initial concessions and of further maneuvering, the system of authoritarian dictatorship would have become increasingly permeated by elements of political pluralism and of quasi-democratic give-and-take. The vacillating and conciliatory attitude which, judging by Stalin's own testimony,[38] was shown by the lower echelons of the Party hierarchy and governmental apparatus, during the critical months of 1928, underlined the gravity of the situation. The choice was clear: either a deep retreat and the gradual erosion of the dictatorial system or an all-out attack aimed at total destruction of the adversary's capability to resist.

Stalin's pronouncements since early 1928 showed beyond possibility of doubt that he had decided in favor of the second alternative. The transition from theory to action, however, was all but a masterminded advance toward a well-defined goal. Stalin evidently planned at first to move in the agricultural field by stages; his repeated declarations about the predominant role of individual farming for many years to come, as well as his condemnations of "dekulakization" and readiness to meet the restive peasantry part of the way by granting price increases, can be taken as a clear indication of this. And the impression of caution and groping for solution is still further reinforced when the position on issues of agricultural policy is viewed in a broader context. There was, undoubtedly, a perceptible change of emphasis in Stalin's declarations on questions of industrialization policy after January 1928. He no longer spoke about Soviet industry as "the most large scale and most concentrated in the world," as he had at the Fifteenth Party Congress.[39] Instead, he denounced its "terrible backwardness" and sounded a call for catching up with the West as a condition for survival: the old aim of "economic independence" was now transformed into "superiority" and further dramatized by the stress upon the element of tempo at which the catching up was to take place. And while all this talk was still couched in most general terms, the language of the drafts of the First Five-Year Plan, which were at that time being prepared by the official governmental agencies and which reflected in their successive versions the changes of the official policy, was much more outspoken: during the whole period between the Fifteenth Party Congress and adoption of the final draft of the First Five-Year Plan in the spring of 1929, there was a clear upward trend in all the crucial indicators of the "tempo"—rate of growth in industrial output, volume of investment and its increase over time, share of heavy industry in the total capital outlays. But at the same time there was strong evidence that the momentous implications of the new policy were not yet fully grasped. Stalin was, no doubt, most persistent in stressing that industry and agriculture were interdependent, the first constituting a "leading link," and the second being a "basis." Still, whenever he went beyond these generalities, he pointed out that industry would have to expand and to reequip itself in order to start reequipping agriculture; in fact this was, in his view, one of the strongest forces pushing for speedy industrialization.[40] The implication was clear: the bulk of the reorganization of agriculture was to take place *after* the completion of a cycle of intensive industrial expansion and not *simultaneously* with it. Moreover, although Stalin kept extolling the superiority of *"smytchka through metal"* over *"smytchka through textile,"* he could not refrain from remarking wistfully that it would be very fine indeed "to shower the village with all kinds of goods in order to extract from the village the maximum amount of agricultural products" and from leaving at least a strong implication that the attainment of such a happy state of affairs was one of the major objectives of the industrialization drive.[41] Stalin was merely hinting at these diverse points, but they were spelled out fully in the targets of the First Five-Year Plan: more than doubling of the fixed capital of the whole nonagricultural sector over the quinquennium, increase in output of industrial consumers' goods by 40 percent, and no more than an 18-percent share of the collective farms in the marketable output of agriculture.

No doubt, if the planned sizes of the first two items of the blueprint had been mutually consistent, the comparatively moderate targets for the third would be appropriate. But they were not; moreover, in view of Stalin's own statements about the causes of the "goods famine," the high target for consumers' goods could be to him only a pious wish, if not plain eyewash. As a result, there was an awkward dilemma. From the standpoint of reducing the pressures on the facilities of the capital-goods industry, a postponement of full-dress collectivization seemed wise. But the function of collective farms consisted, first and foremost, in providing the technique for imposing the required volume of compulsory saving, and since the astronomic rate of planned expansion in fixed capital would inevitably entail, at the very least in the first years of the plan, a drastic cut in consumption levels, such a technique was desperately needed from the very beginning of the process. How could the conflict be resolved? The answer was not slow in coming. Before the plan was two months old the moderate targets in the agricultural field mentioned above went overboard, because Stalin had reversed himself; in response to the repeated and more dismal failure of the grain collections, all-out collectivization was sweeping the country.

Up to this point the whole development looked like some sort of cumulative process gone mad. To begin with, there was a "goods famine" generated by expanding industry and throwing agriculture into a crisis, with an incipient collectivization drive as a result. Then, there was the perspective of an extremely rapid transformation of agriculture imparting additional impetus to plans of industrial expansion and pushing them to lengths which would disbalance agriculture more than ever, and, finally, the sudden burst of all-out collectivization spread disruption in the social fabric of the countryside and left in its wake the wholesale slaughter of livestock by rebellious peasants. But after reaching what seemed to be the stage of explosion, the fluctuations began to subside as the new device went to work. Collective farming pulled the plan over the hump because it did what an agriculture based on individual ownership would never have done, even if confronted with an equally formidable display of terror and repression: amidst mass starvation, in the face of contracting agricultural output and an appalling shortage in industrial consumers' goods, the new setup secured an iron ration of food sufficient to keep alive the workers of rapidly growing industry, and provided an export surplus big enough to finance record-breaking importations of foreign machinery. The feat was achieved to a large extent on the basis of old, decrepit equipment;

the capital-goods industry was permitted to make huge forward strides in its own expansion before being called upon to supply the collective farms with technology which would correspond to their size. The moral of the story was clear: if a half-completed structure of collective farming and a capital-goods industry still in the throes of acute growing pains succeeded in making possible economic expansion at an unparalleled rate, there was every reason to maintain this pattern of development after these two key elements had been firmly established and to continue using up at a high rate the opportunities for investment in enlarged productive potential and increased power, with the satisfaction of consumers' needs firmly relegated to the rear.

Such was, in fact, the conclusion Stalin had drawn. But while the practical consequences of this decision were momentous, little would be gained by discussing his running comments on them in any detail. There is no doubt that after 1929 Stalin was more assertive than ever before in proclaiming his long-range goals and in exhorting to further efforts. All his earlier pronouncements on the need of catching up with the West look pallid in comparison with his famous "we-do-not-want-to-be-beaten" speech.[42] Although the successes of the five-year plans failed to improve the quality of their architect's theorizing, it was only natural that in the process of directing Soviet industrialization he sharpened some of his earlier notions of its distinctive features and made a few new observations: his remarks on short-term profit considerations as an inadequate guide for developing new areas of economy, and on Russia's advantage in not being weighted down in her attempts to adapt new technology by the massive stock of old-type equipment already in existence are cases in point.[43] And he displayed to the full his uncanny ability to change tactics and recast arguments in the face of unexpected difficulties.[44] For all these new touches and variations, however, there was no longer any real change either in the structure of the system or in the views of its builder. He summed up his ideas once more shortly after the war when he contrasted the "capitalist" pattern of industrialization, putting the development of consumers'-goods output first, and the "socialist" pattern starting with the expansion of heavy industries.[45] And he restated the same position in a more generalized way a few years later when he answered one of his last self-addressed questions: "What does it mean to give up the preponderance of the production of the means of production [over production of consumers' goods]? This means to destroy the possibility of the uninterrupted growth of the national economy." [46] Bukharin would have called it *prikladnaia Tugan-Baranovshchina*. Indeed, this it was: "applied Tuganism" harnessed to the service of a totalitarian state.

X

The Russian Revolution of 1917 in Petrograd and other cities was accompanied by a peasant revolution in the countryside of massive proportions in which the land tenure of Russia was atomized into over twenty-four million small holdings. Such an agrarian system ran contrary to the professed political aim of the Bolsheviks, frustrated any comprehensive industrialization, confronted the cities with food shortages, and threatened the stability of the regime itself. Collectivization as a system of production and taxation was one way out of this dilemma. The decision to collectivize, which came in 1929, and which brought an economic and social cataclysm to the countryside in its wake, was thus one of the major turning points in modern Russian history. Beyond the Russian borders, in Eastern Asia and Eastern Europe, collectivization became a dogma for Communist governments. For a long time, the Soviet argument that collectivization, in the way that it was implemented, was eco-

nomically, politically, and ideologically necessary, was widely accepted. Recently, scholars (and some Communist political leaders) have questioned this argument. Herbert Ellison summarizes and criticizes the official and other interpretations of collectivization in his essay, which first appeared in the American Slavic and East European Review, *XX (1961), 189–202. Dr. Ellison is Professor of History at the University of Washington and the author of* History of Russia *(New York, 1964). The article is reprinted with the permission of the publisher, now called the* Slavic Review.

HERBERT J. ELLISON

The Decision to Collectivize Agriculture

Few major decisions of Soviet history can be ranked in importance
with the decision of the Fifteenth Party Congress of December
1927 to collectivize agriculture. Not only did it have tremendous
consequences for the Soviet peasantry (and ultimately the peasantry
of other Communist states), forcing them to leave individual for
collective farming in a struggle that cost millions of lives, but it also
created a form of agricultural organization which has become an
unchallengeable element of Communist organizational orthodoxy.
Only Yugoslavia among Communist states has dared to reject this
orthodoxy, though there is abundant evidence that most of the peasants of Communist countries would reject it if they could.

   In view of the immense importance of the decision to collectivize, it is indeed surprising that so little critical examination of its
background has been undertaken by non-Soviet scholars, and that
the Stalinist rationalization of the decision, doubtful though its valid-

ity is, is widely employed in Western scholarly studies. Elements of
this rationalization have long been evident in Western historical, political, and economic studies of the Soviet Union, and very recently
the economic elements of the rationalization have been used to
erect one of the "models" of economic development employed by
students of the problems of underdeveloped areas. The accuracy of
the Stalinist explanation of the decision to collectivize is therefore a
matter of real significance to scholars in many fields.

The official explanation of the decision to collectivize agriculture can be briefly summarized. An attempt was made to achieve
collectivist agriculture during War Communism, but it was premature and had to be followed by the New Economic Policy (NEP)
concessions to peasant individualism necessary to restore agricultural production. Under NEP both industry and agriculture had
generally regained prewar levels of production, but the further advance of industry was hindered by a constant shortage of grain for
the cities and for export. The Party wished and history willed a
rapid development of industry and the socialization of agriculture.
But industrialization required that the farms produce cheap grain
and industrial raw materials for domestic consumption and for export. And meanwhile both the inefficiency of small-scale peasant
agriculture and the hostility of the kulaks, who had grown in number as a process of class differentiation took place among the peasantry, stood as obstacles to progress. Only by taking stern measures
against the kulaks could the Party mobilize the middle and poor
peasants against the kulaks in a drive for collectivization. Collectivization then solved the grain crisis and provided the agricultural
products for the cities and for export, since large-scale socialist agriculture is more productive than individual peasant agriculture.
The Right Wing of the party, led intellectually by Bukharin, opposed collectivization and supported the interests of the kulaks, but
its resistance was broken.

The official Soviet explanation has not changed basically since
it was first elaborated by Stalin. There have, however, been some
significant changes in emphasis over the years. In the Stalinist Party
history published at the end of the purges, the emphasis was on
class struggle and political deviation. Thus the "agitation" of both

Left- and Right-Wing political leaders was said to "stiffen the kulaks' spirit of resistance against the policy of the Soviet government. They refused en masse to sell to the Soviet state their grain surpluses, of which they had considerable hoards." [1] Thus did the Party realize "that until the resistance of the kulaks was broken . . . the working class and the Red Army would suffer from a food shortage and the movement for collectivization among the peasants could not assume a mass character." [2] The effect of the measures taken against the kulak was to create precisely the class alliances that Leninist agrarian theory had predicted: "the poor and middle peasants joined in the resolute fight against the kulaks; the kulaks were isolated, and the resistance of the kulaks . . . was broken." [3] The Right Wing of the Party which raised objections to Stalin's agrarian policy simply acted as the ideologists of the kulak. "The kulak soul of the Bukharin-Rykov group got the better of them, and they began to come out openly in defense of the kulaks." [4]

In Professor A. M. Pankratova's textbook history of the USSR (1946), the official explanation of the decision to collectivize was extended far beyond the largely political discussion of the Party history to include economic arguments. Indeed, the economic arguments precede the class struggle analysis. After reciting "the achievements of ten years of proletarian dictatorship," Pankratova comments that "agriculture, and particularly grain production, still lagged badly." [5] Noting the inadequacy of the grain supply reaching the market, she turns first for explanation not to the hoarding of kulaks but to what she considers the inevitably low productivity of small-scale peasant farming: "peasant farming could not reach a high level of productivity. It did not have the means to apply machines, fertilization, and the attainments of science and technology." [6] Moreover, the *pomeshchik* estates, which had once provided a large part of the marketed grain, were gone, while the lands had been rapidly divided into ever smaller peasant holdings. Thus the words of Stalin to the Fifteenth Congress: "The solution lies in the transition from small, divided peasant farms to large, united farms based on the social exploitation of the land, in the transition to the collective exploitation of the land on the basis of a new, higher technology. *There is no other solution.*" [7]

Pankratova's analysis in no way departs from the earlier official explanation. The Bukharin "deviation" is stigmatized in the same terms, and the effects of the measures undertaken to stimulate the class struggle in the village and encourage a "popular" movement toward collectivization are treated as before. The difference is in the elaboration of an economic justification of the decision. One can observe this tendency developed still further, and in a much more sophisticated fashion, in the recently published (1958) history of the USSR intended for use in higher educational institutions.[8] Here the economic problems of industrialization are developed much more fully, and are extended to include even the failings of industrial management as a cause of the problem. Then attention is turned to the problem of grain supplies for the cities and for export, and it looks for a moment as if the problem is to be analyzed in strictly economic terms: "The basic causes of the grain procurement difficulties were the splintering (*razdroblennost'*) and the low level of commercialization of agriculture." [9] In the next paragraph, however, the transition is neatly if obliquely made to a class-struggle analysis: "But the grain difficulties also possessed a class basis, and it was specifically because of this that they were transformed into the grain procurement crisis of 1928." [10] The tendency in Soviet interpretation seems to be toward an ever more elaborate structure of economic rationalization whose political foundation obtrudes as little as possible.

Western scholars have produced a variety of interpretations of the Soviet decision to collectivize agriculture, and these interpretations are sufficiently distinct that one cannot place them in a few neat categories without misrepresenting the intentions of individual analysts. But it is possible to make comparisons between interpretations in terms of the presentation of the reasons for collectivization on the one hand, and the alternative possibilities on the other.

There are, first of all, some who present the Soviet rationalization of the collectivization decision—the inevitability of agrarian socialism, the class struggle and economic analysis—in more or less full form. This is true of such prominent interpreters of Soviet economic development as Alexander Baykov and Maurice Dobb.[11] It is also true of E. H. Carr, at least so far as he has developed the subject chronologically in his masterful analysis of the Bolshevik Revolution.[12] These works—especially Carr's—are generally more literate and thorough than the Soviet studies, and lack the polemical tone so often characteristic of the latter. On the major points of interpreting this question, however, there is implicit agreement.

Most Western analysts, however, appear to reject the materialistic determinism on which the Soviet interpretation is founded. Indeed, they switch the argument decisively to emphasize the causative role of the Communists' desire for socialist agriculture so that Communist ideology is seen as a vital force in the transformation of reality, not a simple reflection of it. With such an approach, the political, or ideological, inspiration for collectivization can be placed alongside a description of the economic developments which also helped effect the decision. In most studies the economic and political "factors" are simply listed without any explicit rating of the importance of either,[13] though occasionally one finds a cryptic judgment, such as Michael Karpovich's statement that "one might even say that politics predominated over economics in the motives for its adoption." [14] There are, however, implicit differences of interpretation evident in the relative emphasis given to ideological and economic influences.

One school of thought emphasizes the economic reasons for the decision to collectivize, sometimes giving them an almost independently decisive role. Thus one writer emphasizes the economic developments which brought the Soviet government to the conclusion "that its only way out of the ever more menacing grain crisis was the collectivization of the great bulk of Soviet agriculture and the wiping out of the independent kulaks." [15] Another, having listed the economic problems of agriculture in the late 1920s, concludes: "Hence the decision to launch the collectivization program . . . and thereby to make possible the agricultural surplus necessary for an industrialized country." [16] Other scholars plainly see political commitment as the more important influence in the making of the decision and therefore give primary attention to the political debates and to the power struggle between groups offering rival interpretations of party doctrine.[17] The assumption in such cases seems to be that ideology is the decisive factor, setting the goal of full socialism (industrial and agricultural), and that economic developments are important as they influence the course of the debate and help to precipitate a decision.

It is striking to discover how commonly some or all of the elements of the Soviet rationalization of the decision to collectivize are incorporated in Western studies. One such element is the conceptual structure of Leninist agrarian theory, the idea of a rural class struggle, parallel to the urban, and based on the three classes of peasants—poor, middle, and well-to-do (kulaks). These concepts are widely employed in Western historical and economic studies of Soviet developments.[18] However, they have been the object of trenchant critical analysis which demonstrates not only the doubtful Marxist legitimacy of the "class" divisions, but also notes the lack of evidence of an authentic class struggle.[19] And since much of this criticism is very recent, it is hardly necessary to reexamine the issues here. The remaining elements of the official economic interpretation are almost universally and uncritically repeated. And though many of these have been critically examined by Western scholars in the past, their inaccuracies and their roots in party doctrine are much less obvious. The criticisms have been largely ignored, or at least have failed to find their way into most of the major studies of Soviet history and economic development. They deserve reexamination. But before examining critically the Soviet economic analysis of the background of collectivization, it is necessary to summarize briefly the analysis itself.

Both the official Soviet rationalization and many Western studies paint a picture of Soviet economic life in the late 1920s which suggests that there was no feasible alternative to the collectivization of agriculture. In the official analysis this is the key point, the economic demonstration, as it were, of the will of history made manifest. The analysis insists, first of all, that by 1927 it was plain that industrial development was being retarded by agriculture. Industrialization depended on funds from agriculture, for such means as the government had at its disposal for this purpose came largely from the agricultural tax and from surcharges on industrial commodities. But the peasant wished to eat more and get his industrial goods more cheaply, aspirations at odds with the government's industrialization objectives. A special villain of the Soviet (and many Western) versions is the kulak, for he wished to exploit his neighbor's labor and coveted his land. He also produced most of the surplus grain and hoarded it in order to charge the state an inflated price.

The policy of the government for this situation was to use all available means of "alienating" whatever surplus product the peasant possessed so as to assure a steady growth of industry without at the same time causing the peasant to balk and refuse to sell his produce (or even curtail production) because of a high grain tax or unfavorable terms of trade for industrial products. This policy served its purpose for the first three years of NEP, helping to achieve economic recovery through the maintenance of an alliance between workers and peasants. It seemed at the time that it might be possible to achieve agricultural socialism gradually through the extension of the cooperative organizations, and that enough funds could be drawn from agriculture to maintain a satisfactory program of industrialization.

By 1925, however, it was plain that agricultural production and agricultural deliveries to government procurement agencies and to urban markets were too small. After cautiously trying a policy of concessions to the peasants from 1925 to 1927, the government was forced to recognize that the policy had failed. The annual grain collection crises remained, socialist agriculture was more remote than before because of the strengthening of the kulaks through the concessions on leasing land and hiring labor, and industrialization was proceeding at a snail's pace. According to the official analysis, therefore, collectivization was the only means of improving agricultural efficiency and of getting more grain for the cities and for export.

Criticism of the economic rationalization of the collectivization decision can be pursued initially simply in terms of the accuracy of the picture of economic conditions on which it is based. Then can one question whether it was true that there was no alternative to collectivization.

The Soviet leaders were not empirical economists. Their theoretical commitments led them to distort economic realities and to overlook or misunderstand the effects of their own measures. An

example of outright distortion—and one very widely repeated in
Western works—is the claim that the peasants hoarded a grain surplus. Grain production had not regained prewar levels even in
1925–1927, and "there was not the slightest reason to expect marketings of farm products to reach pre-war magnitudes." [20] The production of grain—the mainstay of the diet—was still below the
prewar level, while the population had grown, and the problem was
not hoarding but low production.[21] However, when low production
was discussed at all, it was explained as deriving from the inevitable inefficiency of small-scale peasant farming (an assumption contradicted by West European experience) and remediable by the
transition to large-scale socialist farms which would be more efficient (an assumption contradicted by the experience with the sovkhozes).

It was indeed true that Soviet peasant agriculture was backward. Land tenure rights were vague, and with the persistence of
communal tenure and the strip system over most of Great Russia,
the individual holder had no security of tenure. Efficient farming
was frustrated by the constant division of households and multipli-
cation of ever smaller holdings. Nearly half of the households
lacked draft animals; technique was generally at an exceedingly low
level, and poverty was more the rule than the exception.

It is also true that most of these conditions were inherited
from the prerevolutionary era. The point is, however, that before
World War I there was a wide range of programs in effect aimed at
rationalization and modernization of agriculture: the land tenure reforms for the provision of security of tenure, consolidation of landholdings, and abolition of communal land controls; arrangements to
facilitate the leasing and selling of land so that owners of exces-
sively small holdings might migrate to free land areas or resettle in
the cities; improvement of technique through demonstration stations; growth of credit societies to provide cheaper short- and long-
term loans; encouragement of the cooperative movement for the development of the profitable sale of agricultural commodities and
economical purchase of industrial goods, and so forth. These were
programs which called forth the energy and leadership of the most
vigorous and able elements in the villages and brought a steady in-

crease in agricultural production and peasant prosperity in the years before the war.

But the firm sense of direction in agricultural policy—so long in developing—was negated by the contrary purpose of the Soviet government in the era of War Communism—the erection of a socialist agricultural system. With the frustration of this purpose by peasant opposition, Soviet agricultural policy reached an impasse. According to the code of 1922, the agrarian commune was neither encouraged nor discouraged. There was no consolidation of landholdings; instead, peasants were encouraged to split up their landholdings into ever more uneconomic holdings because of the official persecution of kulaks. The agrarian resettlement scheme never regained its prewar vigor, and opportunities in the cities were at a minimum with unemployment always at a high level.[22] The cooperatives, having been converted into a brittle, centralized bureaucratic apparatus during War Communism, never managed to regain their independence or the peasant's confidence.[23] The peasant's taxes, direct and (more importantly) indirect, were higher than before the war, and their level was always uncertain. The terms of trade for industrial goods were less favorable than they had been since the 1890s, and agricultural implements were both scarce and expensive. If a peasant managed to overcome this impressive array of obstacles and achieve a modest prosperity, he was open to the danger of being branded a kulak and relieved of his gains. As one well-informed observer of Soviet agriculture in the 1920s put the question simply, "How can he be expected to do productive work under such conditions?"[24]

Thus, not only did Soviet agricultural discussions tend to ignore or misrepresent the problem of production, but Soviet agricultural policy tended gravely to aggravate it, contributing handsomely to the creation of a situation where it was a miracle that agricultural production was as high as it was.[25] Meanwhile, the long-suffering peasant was expected to bear greater burdens than ever before. For political reasons the government had effectively renounced the use of foreign capital for industrial development (or for agricultural development), and yet it wished to maintain a high level of industrial growth, the cost being paid largely from the earnings of agriculture. The neglected goose must reward her owners with a golden egg.

Seen from this perspective, collectivization cannot be described "as the only solution to the riddle of how to industrialize on the basis of NEP . . . the only release from that closed circle of interdependent limiting factors." [26] On the one hand, many of the economic circumstances which purportedly compose the "closed circle" were either created or in one way or another affected by politically inspired policies. And on the other, collectivization was by no means an obvious or exclusive solution to these problems, unless one was already committed to agrarian socialism. Political doctrine, then, played the vital role in making the decision. One is obliged to conclude that the primary force behind the decision was not impersonal economic "forces" but rather preconceived political objectives and economic experience politically interpreted.

This, then, puts the question in an altogether different form. It is not "What were the economically viable alternatives to collectivization?" Of these there were many. It is rather "What were the politically viable alternatives?" For the limitation of alternatives was primarily (though obviously not exclusively) a political matter.

Stalin's assertion that "there is no other solution" followed a chain of arguments which were largely economic. But non-Soviet interpreters, even those like Dobb sympathetic to Stalin's reasoning, have qualified the assertion that this was the only solution with the alternative of reversion "to the pre-war Stolypin road." [27] Indeed, the existence of this alternative was implied by Stalin himself in his charges that Bukharin and other Right-Wing leaders sought a "kulak program," for Stalin treated "kulak" and "Stolypin" as veritable synonyms.

This, then, would suggest that, given Communist ideology, one was bound to have eventually either full-fledged collectivization or a full-fledged "capitalist" (that is, Stolypin) agricultural policy. And one has, of course, the evidence that in the period of vacillation Bukharin did suggest a policy of encouraging the abler elements of the village to "Enrich yourselves!" and that he sought to remove some of the stigma attached, irrationally he felt, to the term "kulak." [28] It is important, however, not to mistake the meaning of

Bukharin's recommendations. And it is misleading to write, as one author has, that "For a while the Bolsheviks toyed with the idea of a solution similar to Stolypin's." [29] Bukharin remained a Communist in his agrarian theory, and it is as wrong to suggest that he had departed from his commitments as it would be to say that Lenin had done so in 1921. For these commitments prevented him, as they prevented other leaders of his Party, from formulating a coherent alternative to the objective of agrarian socialism. Even Stalin, who was seldom overscrupulous about the charges he hurled at his opponents, spoke of the Rightist "deviation" in agricultural policy in 1928 as "unformulated and . . . still unconscious." [30] To have formulated the kind of alternative to collectivization with which he is frequently and mistakenly credited, Bukharin would have had to undertake a major revision of Party agrarian theory. But if he had done this, it would certainly have come out—as it does not—in his last major commentary on the agrarian question, the *Notes of an Economist*.

What Bukharin and his allies stood for in the discussions that followed the Fifteenth Congress was not an alternative to the collectivization the congress had resolved upon, but rather an interpretation of how the decision should be applied that Stalin opposed. They thought at the time of the congress that Stalin—their erstwhile ally in the struggle against the Leftists—held the same views as they, that he would support a gradual collectivization policy, a policy which, as the Five-Year Plan adopted late in 1928 indicated, would provide for collectivization of no more than 20 percent of the farms by 1933 and envisaged a long-term retention of a substantial proportion of individual peasant farming. Bukharin's position as opposed to Stalin's was fully elaborated in his *Notes* of September 1928, after the "emergency measures" against the peasant sanctioned by Stalin had already made plain the differences of intention and method between Stalin and the Right-Wing leaders in agrarian policy.

It is revealing of Stalin's tactics to examine the charges he leveled against the still unnamed parties responsible for the "rightist menace" on which he addressed the Moscow Committee in mid-October 1928, and to compare these charges with Bukharin's statement of his position in the same month. Stalin charged, first of all, that the Rightists were opposed to the "perspectives of development" laid down by the Fifteenth Congress. Beyond this the main specific charges were that the Rightists denied "the necessity of repressing the capitalist elements of the village," and that they "demand the shriveling up of our industry." [31] The entire speech was pervaded with ominous references to the danger of renascent capitalism, a danger described as implicit in the small-peasant character of Russian society: "while we live in a small-peasant country . . . capitalism has a firmer economic basis than communism." [32] The point, then, was that the Rightists would do nothing effective about changing the predominantly small-peasant social structure or about developing industry and thus their "proclivity towards bourgeois ideology."

None of Stalin's charges can bear up under critical examination. The men he was later to name as the key figures in the "Rightist conspiracy"—Bukharin, Rykov, and Tomsky—had given unstinting support to the decision on collectivization at the Fifteenth Congress, and continued to support that policy. They had approved the industrialization policies of the Fourteenth Congress and had been in the van of the movement to hasten the pace of industrialization. The difference was not, as Stalin suggested, concerned with ends, but rather with means. And in this context the matter of agricultural collectivization was particularly vital.

Stalin's means of achieving collectivization, as described in the same speech, differed not at all from the means approved by the "Rightists" at the Fifteenth Congress: "the gradual unification of individual peasant farms into general, collective farms, the development of sovkhozes, the limitation . . . of the capitalist elements . . . of the village." [33] However, the speech also contains an ominous passage which indicates an attitude toward the means for achieving collectivization diametrically opposed to that of Bukharin and his colleagues. Talking of the small peasant as the basis of the danger of renascent capitalism, Stalin inquired rhetorically: "Do we have, in our Soviet land, the means and the power needed to destroy, to liquidate the *possibility* of the restoration of capitalism? Yes, we have." [34] For Stalin, in other words, the means were the instruments of power at the Party's disposal. And these means were available, so no delay could be justified. This, then, raises the question of what were the means suggested by Bukharin. These were set forth in some detail in his *Notes,* published in *Pravda* in September 1928, in reaction to the signs of Stalin's intentions as they appeared in the "emergency measures" of the spring of 1928 and after.

In writing about the planning of the development of the economy, for Bukharin the key word was "balance." Just as Rykov emphasized the need for a sensible balance between light and heavy industry, so Bukharin wrote of the need for balanced growth of industry and agriculture.[35] Referring admiringly to the way in which a vigorous growth of agriculture had accompanied and stimulated American industrialization, Bukharin insisted that this course, in a socialist context, was the best course for Russia, not the course earlier proposed by the Trotskyites. "The Trotskyites, when they put the problem of the *greatest possible* pumping of resources out of the village . . . wanted to put the USSR *in the same line with old Russia,* at a time when what is needed is to put us *in line with the United States of America."* [36] He would reject the policy of maximum exploitation of agriculture for the benefit of industry because "if any branch of production . . . fails to receive in return for its products the costs of production, plus a certain addition corresponding to a *part* of the surplus labor which can serve as a source of expanding reproduction, then that branch of industry either stagnates or *retrogresses."* [37] On the other hand, one cannot refrain from taking from agriculture for the development of industry. The problem is to keep both agriculture and industry growing simultaneously. "The industrialization of the country is for us a *law.* . . . Socialist industrialization, however, is not a parasitic process in its relations with the village." [38]

Regarding the current situation, Bukharin rejected the "fairy tales" about grain hoarding, noting that the real problem was low production. In this situation "a Trotskyist 'solution' [such as Stalin later applied] would lead straight to a real, and not an imaginary collapse." [39] In his specific recommendations on agricultural policy, the crux of Bukharin's position—and its uniqueness—is that he faced honestly (as he had on several occasions previously) the failures in agricultural production and the Party's responsibility for many of the failures. He even spoke of the necessity of dealing with the backwardness of agriculture from what he called the "pure pro-

duction standpoint" as well as from the standpoint of "class transformation." One had to be sure of a steady increase in agricultural
technique and production at the same time as one worked toward
"the gradual replacement of the capitalist elements in agriculture by
. . . large scale and socialized agricultural production." [40] And
while one built socialist agriculture, "limiting the kulak sector," one
should avoid "neglect of the individual farms of the working peasantry" and rather seek "improvement of the individual farms."
Bukharin's summary of the policies appropriate to the decision to
collectivize was probably the ablest possible synthesis within the
limitations of Communist agrarian theory of the views of Lenin in
his last years and the experience which had followed in the years
since Lenin's death:

> It is a matter of making large capital investments in agriculture.
> . . . A rise in the individual peasant sector, especially that devoted
> to grain, a limiting of the kulak sector, the construction of the sov-
> khozes and kolkhozes, in combination with a correct price policy,
> and along with a development of co-operatives embracing the mass
> of the peasantry . . .[41]

What Stalin stigmatized as the "Right-Wing deviation" was,
then, so far as agriculture was concerned, not a departure from the
objective of agrarian socialism but a gradualist approach which
aimed at a simultaneous technical and productive rise in Soviet
farming.[42] This core of the difference Stalin never chose to deal
with, partly because of his own appalling ignorance in economic
questions and partly because his struggle for personal power led
him to favor the technique of discrediting his rivals rather than the
forthright debate of national issues.

There is a real need, then, for a more critical historical and
economic analysis of the background of collectivization, and there
has too often been a facile acceptance of the Soviet rationalization
of this decision by Western scholars. However widely they may reject the historical determinism on which the rationalization is
based, Western writers tend nonetheless to echo the Soviet economic arguments and to accept uncritically Stalin's presentation of

his opponents' policy alternatives. The economic arguments that purport to show the economic "necessity" of collectivization in order to achieve a rise in agricultural production and hasten industrial growth will not stand. Examination of these arguments only proves that the objective of agrarian socialism was settled in advance, politically, and subsequently rationalized economically, often with striking distortions of economic reality. A causal analysis of the decision to collectivize should therefore be focused on the political doctrine of the Party leaders.

Here one must, however, take note of the varied interpretations of doctrine. As long as it retained a voice in Party debates, the Left Wing continued to insist on a maximum draining of agriculture for the benefit of industry, holding off on collectivization until the revolution should spread abroad (permanent revolution).[43] The dominant group in the Party rejected this proposal in favor of simultaneous development of agriculture and industry and a very gradual advance on agrarian socialism. What Stalin brought forth in 1928–1929 was essentially a refurbished Left-Wing program, including the traditional Left-Wing emphasis on rapid industrialization at the expense of agriculture and adding rapid agrarian collectivization without waiting on European revolution. It was Stalin, then, who challenged the hitherto accepted Party line. The general decision in favor of collectivization at the Fifteenth Congress was simply a reaffirmation of established Party doctrine. What followed in 1928–1929 was the supplanting of the interpretation of that decision made by Bukharin, Tomsky, Rykov, and other Party leaders by the interpretation sponsored by Stalin. And the victory of Stalin's "line" was in turn the result of his conquest of the Party apparatus, a conquest which meant not only the firm victory of a policy, but also the enthronement of a dogma which has meant unspeakable hardship for hundreds of millions of peasants in Communist countries from that day to this.

XI

The Stalinist industrialization drive required a new fiscal system geared to an autarchic economy which was rigidly restricting consumption through sharp curtailment of consumer industry and rapid expansion of the urban wage earning force, and which at the same time needed vast amounts of domestic capital to finance the development of heavy industry. This was done shortly after the beginning of crash collectivization mainly through the instruments of the turnover tax and the grain levy, the heaviest incidence of which fell on the peasants and urban consumers. The turnover tax and other aspects of Soviet taxation as these relate to financing economic development in the Stalin era are discussed by Professor Franklyn D. Holzman. Dr. Holzman is Professor of Economics at the Fletcher School of Diplomacy, Tufts University, and is author of Soviet Taxation: Fiscal and Monetary Problems of a Planned Economy *(1955). The text part of the article is reprinted with the permission of the author and the publisher, the National Bureau of Economic Research.*

F. D. HOLZMAN

Financing Soviet Economic Development

The purpose of this paper is threefold: to explain Soviet choice among sources of finance, to present and analyze the relevant data, and to evaluate the fiscal and monetary policies pursued. It should be stated at the outset that the sum of amounts collected from the various sources of finance always substantially exceeds the value of gross national investment. This is because from the same pools of funds the Soviet Government finances not only investment in fixed and working capital, but government stockpiles of strategic materials, expenditures of the Ministry of Armed Forces for defense, administrative activities of the various departments of the government, expenditures on health and education, transfer payments, subsidies

Part of the research for this paper was accomplished while I was attached to the Russian Research Center, Harvard University. The financial assistance of that organization is gratefully acknowledged, as are the critical comments of Mathilda Holzman and Gregory Grossman.

to state enterprises which sell their output at below-cost prices, and gross expenditures of the machine tractor station complex.[1] Since budgetary receipts, the largest single source of funds, are not earmarked for specific expenditures, there is no way of determining how the one category of expenditures which is directly relevant to economic development, namely gross investment, was financed. We are limited to discussing the sources of finance of the whole of the "nonconsumption" activities of the Soviet state, loosely defining "nonconsumption" as the sum of goods and services purchased by the state plus transfer payments to the household. Because of our interest in how the state planned its economic expansion, investment from private profits and private depreciation funds will not be considered; private investment expenditures were, however, insignificant in all but the first year or two of the period under review. Discussion will center around the first three Five-Year Plan periods, that is, from 1928–1929, when the first plan went into operation, until 1940, the third and last completed year of the Third Plan (which was truncated by World War II). This period is adequate to illustrate the problems faced and policies adopted by Soviet planners.

Before turning to the sources of finance, a few words will be devoted to a consideration of the significance of money and finance for the functioning of the Soviet economy. Those unfamiliar with the Soviet economy may be misled by the emphasis on the words "planning" and "controls" into thinking that money is not important in the Soviet economy. While the Soviets rely more on direct economic controls than any other nation in the world today, and while such controls, where they are used, substitute for money and the market mechanism as the allocator of scarce resources, money has not been replaced by direct controls. There are no direct controls in large sectors of the Soviet economy. Consumer goods, for example, are distributed at present by the market mechanism; the amount of consumer goods which any household can purchase is determined by its current and accumulated earnings. The labor market, though less free than it was in the 1930s, still depends primarily on differential wage payments for the allocation of labor. Other markets (raw materials and producer goods), though on the whole more subject to direct controls, do nevertheless contain sub-

stantial areas in which free market forces are still allowed to operate. Even where allocation is accomplished directly, to the extent
that prices provide the planners with a basis for allocation, money
functions as a standard of value, if not as a medium of exchange.[2]
Failure by the Soviets to keep their financial house in order will
have a deleterious effect on the economy (through reduced incentives, misallocation of resources, and so forth) so long as markets
and prices are used by them to perform economic functions.

1. CHOICE AMONG SOURCES
OF FINANCE

A listing of the major Soviet sources of finance has a conventional ring: direct taxation of the population, sales taxes, profits
taxes, sales of government bonds to the population and to state institutions, retained profits of enterprises, depreciation reserves,
bank credit, household savings. While there are many real similarities between the above categories and their Western counterparts,
closer examination reveals substantial differences both of an institutional nature and in their relative importance. A cursory glance at
Table 1 reveals that the financial path followed by the Soviet Union
differs in several significant respects from the paths followed by
many Western nations.

TABLE 1
SOURCES OF SOVIET FINANCE AS PERCENTAGES
OF ADJUSTED TOTAL, 1937

Major indirect or commodity taxes	71.9
Direct taxes	3.8
Sales of government bonds to population	4.1
Miscellaneous budgetary receipts	7.3
Retained profits of state enterprises	4.6
Indivisible fund of collective farms	1.7
Depreciation reserves	5.4
Voluntary household savings	1.0
Increase of currency in circulation	1.4

Foreign Borrowing

Outstanding for its absence from Table 1 is foreign borrowing. I do not think it would be possible to single out over the past 150 years many nations which have industrialized, especially in the early stages, without some foreign aid. The Soviets industrialized without any significant foreign aid, not because they wanted to— they did not—but because the Western world was hostile to them [3] and they, in turn, were hostile to and distrustful of Western nations. This was not a climate in which international capital was likely to flow freely and abundantly. With some minor exceptions, the Soviets paid in gold, commodities, and in imperial crown jewels for all goods purchased from other nations in the interwar period. In recent years the situation has changed somewhat. During the war, of course, the Russians received considerable help from the United States in the form of lend-lease shipments; and since the war reparations have contributed, in some years, respectable sums to budget receipts.[4] Finally, there may be considerable capital flow between the Soviet Union and the countries within its political orbit, but on this there is very little reliable information as to either amount or direction.

Voluntary Savings

The Soviets have always encouraged voluntary saving by the population. A large network of banks in both urban and rural areas has been developed to foster the saving habit; the 5-percent interest on time deposits (six months or more) is the highest obtainable in the Soviet Union;[5] the Currency Reform of December 1947 applied a much more favorable conversion rate to savings deposits than to either cash or government bonds. Nevertheless, understandably enough, savings have never amounted to much in the Soviet Union. The annual increment to savings deposits is only a fraction of 1 percent of total household money income.[6] The average Soviet citizen is in much too great need of current goods and services to put aside large sums of money to meet future needs. And those future needs which induce the greatest amount of saving in Western nations (for example, provision against sickness, accidents, old age, unemployment, and so forth) are relatively well provided for in the Soviet Union by a comprehensive social security system. Furthermore, the incentive to save must certainly have been vitiated by twenty years of rapidly rising prices in the consumer-goods markets, not ending until the currency reform of 1947.[7] Finally, of course, the state imposes upon the population such a high rate of compulsory saving that little is left to individual initiative.[8]

Commodity Taxes

Most of the compulsory savings of the economy are collected by the state in the form of taxes and are reflected in the budget accounts;[9] and indirect or commodity taxes are responsible for from two-thirds to three-fourths of budgetary receipts. The three principal commodity taxes are the turnover tax, deductions from the profits of state enterprises (profits tax), and the social insurance markup. The turnover tax is essentially a sales tax levied, at present, exclusively on consumer goods—except for petroleum and petroleum products, where the tax substitutes for explicit rent payments. Before 1949 it was levied on producer goods as well, but for fiscal control of the tax-paying enterprises rather than for revenue. The rates on consumer goods are highly differentiated, varying from 1 percent of the *selling price* on some commodities to as much as 90 percent on others.[10]

The deduction from profits is correctly not called a tax on enterprise [11] by the Soviets because it applies to nationalized industries. The state does not tax the profits of its own industries; it simply transfers money from one state account to another. From a fiscal point of view the deduction from profits, as part of profits, adds to the price paid by the consumer; in this respect it does not differ from the turnover tax and can properly be considered a commodity tax on the household. Every enterprise pays a minimum 10-percent tax on profits for purposes of fiscal control. The remaining profits are used as needed to finance investment planned for the enterprise and to make payments into the Directors' Fund.[12] Any surplus above these needs is *deducted* into the budget.

The social insurance markup is a form of payroll tax, and for our purposes can be looked upon as adding to the price of commodities bought by the household, just like the turnover and profits taxes. The receipts from this tax are derived as additions to the wage funds of enterprises, the percentage varying from 3.7 to 10.7, depending on conditions of employment and other factors in the separate branches of the economy. It is claimed that part of the receipts from this tax are earmarked for sickness and old age insurance.[13]

Why is commodity taxation the dominant method of extracting savings from the population in the Soviet Union? Conversely, why is little reliance placed upon income (direct) taxation, the form of levy preferred in the United States and in many other Western nations? [14] Soviet preference for commodity taxation is certainly not to be explained on ideological grounds. In fact, the predominance of the turnover tax among Soviet taxes has proved embarrassing to Soviet economists. Marxist writers consistently attacked indirect taxes as socially inequitable and regressive; bad associations also stem from the reliance of the tsars on highly regressive excise taxes (especially on alcoholic beverages) for the bulk of their revenue. That the Soviets rely on commodity taxation in spite of their "ideological" bias attests to its superiority for their purposes.[15]

Soviet preference for commodity taxation appears to rest primarily on three considerations. First, there is the "money illusion," which has it that workers are more conscious of the impact on their economic position of changes in wages than of the impact produced by changes in prices. A corollary to this is the hypothesis that workers are more sensitive to changes in direct taxes (and thus in take-home pay) than to changes in indirect taxes (reflected in commodity prices). The money illusion, therefore, would cause commodity and income taxes of equal size to have different impacts on work incentives. This is particularly important in the Soviet Union, where almost all income is earned income. Analytically, it is possible to separate the impact of taxes on incentives into at least two categories: the effect on the work-leisure ratio and the effect on differential wages as a factor in choosing between jobs. Most writers dealing with this subject concentrate on the work-leisure ratio, arguing that high taxes, and particularly high marginal rates of tax, reduce the incentive to work, and that indirect taxes, as a consequence of the illusion, minimize the disincentive effects of taxes. This line of reasoning ignores the income effect of taxation,[16] or at least assumes that the substitution effect between work and leisure is more important than the income effect. There is no empirical evidence, to my knowledge, to support this assumption, and, in fact, the income effect may actually be strong enough to induce Soviet workers to greater effort. If this were the case, it could not be argued that the Soviet choice of commodity taxation preserves work incentives.

It can be argued, without equivocation, that the Soviets took advantage of the money illusion effects of commodity taxation to preserve the effectiveness of their differential wage structure as an incentive mechanism for allocating labor. In order to attract workers, Soviet policy has been to pay higher wages to persons in jobs requiring greater skills, in expanding industries, and in jobs or areas where work conditions are undesirable. Up until the late 1920s or early 1930s this policy had not been implemented successfully, hampered to a considerable extent as it was by the hangovers of an earlier "equalitarian" philosophy regarding wage differentials.[17] An attempt was made to improve the situation; in 1931 Stalin intervened and, in a speech calling for greater wage differentials, set the new policy. He said: "In a number of our factories, wage scales are drawn up in such a way as to practically wipe out the difference between skilled labor and unskilled labor, between heavy work and light work. The consequence of wage equalization is that the unskilled worker lacks the incentive to become a skilled worker and is thus deprived of the prospect of advancement; . . . in order to get skilled workers we must give the unskilled worker a stimulus and prospect of advancement, of rising to a higher position. . . ."[18] Bergson's wage study indicates that wage differentials in the Soviet Union in 1934 were about as great as those in the United States at a comparable stage (1904) of economic development.[19]

In the late 1920s and early 1930s, at the same time that Soviet wage differentials were being increased for incentive reasons, taxes were also being increased. The average rate of taxation about doubled from 1926 to 1936, increasing by substantial amounts almost every year of the period;[20] by 1930 it amounted to about 50 percent of household income.[21] Clearly, Soviet differential wage policy was in danger of being weakened by Soviet tax policy. Reliance upon income taxation under these circumstances would have had a much more adverse impact on the incentive-wage system than commodity taxation for at least two reasons. First, under the Soviet pay-as-you-earn system of income taxation, workers are as likely to base job decisions on differential take-home pay as on gross wage differentials. On the other hand, if no income tax were levied, gross wage differentials would probably retain much of their incentive effect, even with high levels of commodity taxation. Second, for political reasons, income taxation would almost necessarily have to be progressive, or at least proportional, thereby reducing wage differentials relatively as well as absolutely; this would not necessarily be so for sales taxation, especially when the tax is hidden, and when it has a highly differentiated rate structure, as is the case in the Soviet Union.[22] This facet of the money illusion is undoubtedly an important reason for Soviet use of commodity taxation.

A second factor explaining Soviet reliance on commodity taxation is administrative in nature. The turnover tax, particularly in the early stages of its development, was levied on and collected from state industrial enterprises (procurement agencies in agriculture) and wholesale organizations. This provided the cheapest and least evadable method of collecting money taxes from the population since the number of industrial enterprises and wholesale organizations was not large and they maintained relatively good money accounts; it also provided a continuous source of funds—the larger enterprises made daily payments to the budget. These considerations were quite crucial in the late 1920s and the early 1930s, before the administrative apparatus of the state had achieved anything like its present-day efficiency. Reliance upon income taxation would have meant levying and collecting taxes from 30 to 40 million householders, many of whom were still illiterate. Furthermore, at that time a large segment of the peasant population still had not been herded into collective farms, where it could be reached without excessive costs by tax collectors.

A third consideration, and one which is stressed by Soviet economists, is the use of the turnover tax to facilitate price planning. The Soviets have attempted to maintain a market for consumer goods in which free choice prevails. Prices are not set freely by decentralized agents as is usually the case in Western nations; rather, prices are centrally administered and the state is responsible for adjusting relative prices. Maintenance of appropriate price flexibility is, for obvious reasons, facilitated by the existence of a large element of tax in the cost-price structure. In fact, without either a commodity tax or a subsidy (which can be considered a negative commodity tax in this case), it would not be possible to alter relative prices much faster than relative changes in productivity would permit [23] (that is, prices would approximate long-run cost).

Income Taxation

In spite of the advantages and magnitude of Soviet commodity taxation, the population is also required to pay an income tax. The only significant function which this tax seems to serve is to discourage private practice by professionals [24] (for example, doctors and lawyers) and other "nonworker" elements in the urban population. These groups pay a discriminatorily high tax, which reaches 55 and 65 percent, respectively, on incomes in excess of 70,000 rubles; workers and salaried employees, who comprise 90 percent or more of the nonagricultural labor force, pay according to a schedule which reaches a maximum rate of 13 percent on all income over 12,000 rubles annually. While the "class policy" feature of the income tax may have been important twenty years ago, before the private sector of the economy had been thoroughly squelched, it can hardly be considered so anymore. Moreover, the tax certainly has little fiscal importance.[25] It is difficult to understand why the Soviets continue to use direct levies on income when they could be replaced very easily by a small increase in commodity taxation. Perhaps they are continued through inertia, or because the Soviets wish to maintain intact the direct tax apparatus for possible future use.

Sales of Government Bonds

Sales of government bonds constitute, in effect, another form of direct levy on the Soviet population. Similarity of these bond sales to taxation rests on the following characteristics: considerable social pressure is brought to bear upon the population to subscribe from two to four weeks' wages a year; these amounts are deducted from workers' wages every month just as direct taxes are; most bonds are not redeemable until the full term has expired; [26] a series of conversions (1930, 1936, 1938) and the 1947 Currency Reform have together resulted in extended maturities, reduced interest rates, and a reduction by two-thirds, in 1947, of the value of all outstanding obligations; rapidly rising prices have steadily reduced the real value of these highly illiquid assets. The disadvantages of direct taxes, in general, seem to apply to sales of bonds also, although bond sales in the late 1920s may have been more "voluntary" in nature. To the extent that they were (are) voluntary, disincentive effects would, of course, have been (be) reduced.

Since the Currency Reform of 1947, consumer-goods prices have declined steadily. If this trend should be continued, the usefulness of bonds as a form of taxation will have been substantially reduced. On the one hand, falling price levels will cause the real rate of interest on the bonds to exceed the nominal rate so that, in time, repayment may become a real burden on the current Soviet budget. Before 1947 the real rate of interest was undoubtedly negative due to continuous inflation—the burden of repayment was insignificant.[27] On the other hand, it seems doubtful that price levels will fall rapidly enough to increase voluntary savings, especially in the form of illiquid bonds, to the amount of the annual issue of bonds. Thus, as prices fall, the disadvantage of larger "real" repayments would seem to more than offset the advantage of smaller disincentive effects as the bonds become a slightly less unattractive form of investment.

Retained Profits

Funds for investment are also available in the form of retained profits accumulated by both state enterprises and collective farms.[28] The annual plans usually call for a substantial part of the investment in the fixed and working capital of established state enterprises to come out of the retained profits of these enterprises. State enterprises also receive grants from the budget for the same purpose. It is difficult to understand what difference, if any, there is between these two methods of finance, and why the Soviets do not concentrate on either one or the other. It is frequently contended that managerial incentives are sharpened if managers are allowed to finance investment from retained profits rather than by budget subsidy. There is the implication in the case of retained profits that, if the manager is more (less) efficient, he may have more (less) funds to invest because profits will be larger (smaller). This implication does not square with the usual conception of an enterprise's fulfilling its investment plan from retained profits and then automatically transferring the remainder, after deductions into the Directors' Fund, into the budget.[29] Part of the Directors' Fund is, of course, used for extra-plan investment; but the incentive to increase profits by reducing costs and increasing output exists regardless of whether the enterprise has its own profits to begin with or receives a budget subsidy.[30] Soviet preference for budget-financed investment probably lies in the greater administrative flexibility which this method *may* confer; it is, undoubtedly, simpler to alter investment plans in the short run if funds are doled out from the budget than if they are accumulated by enterprises in which the investment is planned.

The collective farms (and other cooperatives) not nationalized and the property of the state (though under strict state control, of course) must meet the bulk of their investment requirements from their own resources. The farms are required by law to withhold from 12 to 20 percent of their total net money income (after meeting costs of production, excluding payments to labor) in a so-called "indivisible fund" which is to be used for capital investment.[31] Most of the current money income of the collectives is, of course, distributed among the collective farmers in payment for their labor. Investment by the collective farms (except in kind) has never amounted to much because most of their machinery requirements (tractors, combines, and so forth) are met, for a price, by the state-owned machine tractor stations (MTS). The MTS have been since 1938 included in the budget on a gross basis; all of their expenditures, including new investment, are financed by budget subsidy.

Collective farms with insufficient funds to finance their investment requirements can borrow small sums from the Agricultural Bank.

Fund for Amortization

Most economic organizations which use capital equipment are required to consider depreciation a cost of production and to maintain depreciation reserves. Western economists generally consider that these reserves understate depreciation in view of the extensive Soviet cost inflation, because of the fact that original rather than replacement cost is used in computing depreciation, and because inexpert handling of equipment appears to be widespread and may have had the effect of reducing the physical life of much equipment. Originally, the reserves were devoted exclusively to replacing old, and constructing new, equipment. Since 1938, part of these funds have been made available for capital repair.

Minor Sources of Budget Receipts

The more important sources of budget revenue have already been noted: turnover tax, deductions from profits of state enterprises, the social insurance markup, direct taxes on the population, and sales of government bonds. The budget derives revenue from many other sources. Customs are, perhaps, the most important of these. In the prewar period they amounted to as much as 2 percent of total budget receipts in some years. During the war, receipts from tariffs on regular imports were strongly supplemented by local currency resulting from lend-lease sales; since the war, regular receipts have been supplemented by reparations. Other sources are an inheritance tax which at present is simply a fee for the processing of legal documents, fees for commercial forestry and fishing, fines, licenses, the *gross* receipts of the machine tractor stations, and taxes on the profits of the collective farms and other cooperatives. Taken individually, these items do not generally provide much revenue; in the aggregate; however, their contribution is not insubstantial.

The State Bank: Changes in
Currency in Circulation

A substantial share of the working capital requirements of the economy are financed by the State Bank (Gosbank) in the form of short-term loans. In the early 1930s, when the basis of the present Soviet banking system was established, the bank was given authority to extend short-term credit to finance goods in transit, seasonal production processes and expenses, and other temporary working capital needs connected with the production and turnover of goods.[32] Permanent working capital was to be furnished to new enterprises needing it by the budget in the form of interest-free grants; additions to permanent working capital were to be financed either by the budget or out of the retained profits of the enterprises. If the working capital needs of enterprises had been seasonally stable, there would have been no necessity, in the original Soviet scheme of things, for the short-term credit operations of the State Bank. "The function of short-term credit in the Soviet economy . . . [was], broadly speaking, to level out fluctuation in the flow of materials and goods." [33] The functions of the State Bank were extended in the mid-1930s, however, when it was authorized to finance a large percentage of the *permanent* working capital requirements of trade organizations; and again in 1939 when it was assigned the task of regularly financing part of the *permanent* working capital needs of heavy industry. This deviation from the original principle which guided the granting of short-term credit was introduced with the purpose of giving the State Bank control over the activities of enterprises in these sectors.[34] Apparently, these enterprises "experienced little variation in working capital requirements, and thus were able to escape the control and supervisory functions of the Gosbank." [35] This is the situation at present; it should be noted, however, that during the war the bank was authorized to advance large credits for the reconstruction of enterprises in liberated areas, to make payments to military personnel under certain special conditions, to facilitate the evacuation of industries eastward during the German advance, and to meet other extraordinary needs. Presumably, credit is no longer granted for these special purposes.

It is important to note that the State Bank is, in normal times, the *only* source of currency issue in the USSR. With the exception of the years 1941–1943—years of great internal disruption, when the budget ran deficits which were financed by currency issue— short-term loans to finance the above-noted working capital needs of enterprise have been the sole source of new currency in circulation. The extension of new short-term loans does not always, or usually, lead to a currency increment, however. New currency is issued to finance short-term loans only if no currency is returned by the population from other sources. Other sources of funds are excesses of budget receipts over budget expenditures, of retained profits over investment financed from retained profits, of depreciation reserves over expenditures from depreciation reserves, and so forth. These funds and others mentioned above are all reflected in the accounts of the State Bank either by direct deposit or indirectly through the deposit in the State Bank of the reserves of the special banks for long-term investment (see below). To the extent that currency receipts in the State Bank are greater than expenditures (including long-term loans) from these receipts, new short-term credit can be extended without the issuance of currency; in fact, if there should be a surplus of deposits over expenditures, including short-term loans, currency will be withdrawn from circulation. If, on the other hand, expenditures, including short-term loans, exceed receipts, new currency is circulated. If, therefore, we were interested in measuring the amount of Soviet nonconsumption expenditures (as we are below) from sources of finance, we would not include gross changes in the amount of short-term credit outstanding; this would involve a double count, because bank loans are an expenditure item in the national financial accounts. We simply add (subtract) increases (decreases) in currency in circulation. To clarify this point, an estimate of Soviet financial accounts for 1936 is presented in Table 2.

It would hardly be necessary to discuss the special banks for long-term investment had they not been misnamed banks. Their primary function is to disburse and supervise the use of funds previously collected rather than to create new credit. The bulk of these funds are budgetary grants to enterprises in the national economy for investment in plant and equipment and working capital. Other funds held and disbursed by these banks are retained profits of state

TABLE 2

ESTIMATE OF SOVIET NATIONAL FINANCIAL ACCOUNTS, 1936

(*billions of rubles*)

Receipts		Expenditures	
1. Budget receipts (including bonds)	94.4	1. Budget expenditures	92.5 [1]
2. Retained profits		2. Investment and other expenditures financed outside budget	
a. State enterprises	8.9		
b. Collective farms	1.5		
c. Others	?	a. From retained profits	
1. Depreciation reserves	4.9	i. State enterprises	8.9 [2]
		ii. Others	2.6 [3]
		b. Depreciation	?
		c. Net increase in short-term credit (State Bank)	8.1
		d. Long-term loans to collective farms and farmers	1.5 [4]
Subtotal	109.7		
1. Currency issue	1.6	Subtotal	113.6
2. Discrepancy	2.3	3. Currency withdrawal	0
Total	113.6	Total	113.6

Figures for which sources are not cited were taken from tables later in this chapter (*but not included here—Ed.*).

[1] Same source as budget receipts.

[2] Planned investment in fixed capital from S. N. Prokopovich, *Biulleten'*, March 1936, no. 127, p. 30. Planned investment in working capital from G. F. Grinko, *Financial Program of the USSR for 1936* (Moscow: Foreign Languages Publishing House, 1936), p. 15.

[3] At least 2.6 billion rubles of other investment from profits can be estimated from A. Smilga, *"Finansy sotsialisticheskogo gosudarstvo"* [Finances of socialist state], *Problemy ekonomiki* [Problems of economics], 1937, no. 2, p. 115.

[4] K. Plotnikov, *Biudzhet sotsialisticheskogo gosudarstva* [Budget of the socialist states] (Moscow), p. 140.

enterprises, the indivisible fund, retained profits of other cooperatives, and that part of the reserves for depreciation used to finance new investment.[36] Apparently, the special banks "lend" to both individuals and enterprises, but the amounts involved are not significant and will be ignored here except for long-term loans by the Agriculture Bank to collective farms. The special banks keep their excess funds on deposit with the State Bank; thus the State Bank is seen to be the custodian of excess investment funds for virtually the whole Soviet economy. Long-term loans of the special banks, like short-term loans, are expenditure, not receipt, items in Soviet financial accounts; they are reflected in "sources of finance" only insofar as they affect the amount of currency which has to be circulated by the State Bank to finance its short-term credit operations.

Taxation in Kind

No mention has been made so far of taxation in kind of agriculture because it does not *directly* provide the state with monetary reserves for financing nonconsumption expenditures; indirectly, however, it does. The tax in kind takes the form of compulsory deliveries of agricultural products by collective farms and peasant farmers to state and cooperative procurement agencies. While the farms and peasants are not uncompensated for their deliveries, the price paid by the state (called procurement price) is usually far from sufficient to cover costs of production; and, of course, it is only a fraction of the retail price (minus processing and distribution costs) at which the state resells these items to the population. The high retail price is achieved by superimposing a turnover tax on procurement price plus costs of processing and distribution. The portion of the turnover tax collected by virtue of the below-cost procurement price is the monetary equivalent of the tax in kind on that part of the compulsory deliveries sold to the household.[37] Delivered produce not sold back to the household (for example, stockpiled or used in the production of final products not sold to the household) is not reflected in the budget and may be classified as "investment in kind" by the state.

This classification holds in all circumstances in which producing agents are directly paid less than cost of production or less than the value of their product (or not at all). A major case in point is, of course, that of unfree labor in the Soviet Union. The evidence indicates that workers in this category are remunerated at less than the free market wage for comparable performance.[38] To the extent that the products of unfree labor are sold to the population at high prices and add to the receipts of the turnover tax, the tax in kind on unfree labor (in the form of below-market wage payments) is reflected in budgetary receipts. To the extent that the services of these laborers are directed into nonconsumption activities such as gold mining, construction, irrigation projects, and the building of dams and roads (and these are the sorts of activities typically handled by the MVD), they may be classed as investment in kind by the state.

It should be noted that there is still another important source of investment in kind in the Soviet Union. We refer to that part of the income in kind of the agricultural sector of the economy which is neither taxed away by the state nor consumed by peasant households, but which is devoted to the following years' production (for example, seed, feed, stockpiles, increasing livestock herds). Needless to say, none of the above categories of investment in kind are readily susceptible to measurement; nor can we, for that matter, even say what part of the turnover tax is a tax on the consumer and what part is a tax on the agricultural producer.[39]

How is Soviet preference for taxation in kind of agriculture to be explained? Basically, the difference between taxation of industrial income and taxation of agricultural income stems from the fact that industry and the output of industry are almost 100 percent state-owned, while agriculture consists primarily of collective farms, which are not owned by the state, and of individual peasant farmers.[40] This form of organization of agriculture, rather than state-owned farms with the farmers receiving wages, creates two serious problems for the state. First, the state must secure by some means a substantial share of the output of the agricultural sector to be transferred to the city for personal and industrial consumption and for export. Taxation of the money incomes of agricultural producers would not necessarily secure this result: if the amount of the tax were calculated on the basis of actual money income, the peasants could reduce their money income, hence tax payments, by cutting down sales of agricultural output; even if taxable income were based on production, the peasants could, by cutting back on their consumption of industrial consumer goods, still avoid the necessity of having to sell as much agricultural output as the state needed to meet its requirements. These are not idle possibilities in a country where adequately feeding the population has been—and will continue to be, barring unforeseen developments—a very serious economic problem. By means of money taxation, alone, it might prove impossible to reduce the food consumption of the peasants below a level consistent with the needs of the nation as a whole for food. Second, as we have seen, for incentive and other reasons the state collects most of its budget receipts in the form of indirect taxes. Since the bulk of the turnover tax, the major indirect tax, is collected in the form of a markup on agricultural products (because food is the principal item of personal consumption in the Soviet Union), the incidence of the turnover tax on the agricultural population considered as consumers is relatively small because a large part of its income takes the form of consumption of home-produced food. Another form of tax on the peasantry must be substituted for indirect money taxation if a high rate of saving for the economy as a whole is to be maintained. The tax in kind solves these two problems at once for the state: it ensures state procurement of the required amount of agricultural produce, and it forces a high level of savings upon the agricultural population.

XII

Forced labor was a long-standing institution in old Russia and in many other societies, but the extent to which it was employed in the Stalin era has few parallels in human history. Although it was not necessitated by the industrialization drive of the 1930s, neither can it be seen as an accidental by-product of the psychological and political aberrations of the great purges. Such a gigantic operation, which came to involve several million slaves and an army of guards, inevitably became linked with the Stalinist economic system in a number of important ways. So argues Stanislaw Swianiewicz, who attempts an economic analysis of the function of slave labor in Soviet economic development. An economist, and a former prisoner himself in Stalin's camps, he now lives and works in England. He is author of Lenin jako ekonomista [*Lenin as an economist*] (*Wilno, 1930*), *and* Forced Labor and Economic Development (*London, 1965*). *The selection here is part of the latter book, and is reprinted with the permission of the publisher, Oxford University Press.*

STANISLAW SWIANIEWICZ

The Main Features of Soviet
Forced Labor

The history of Soviet forced labor raises the problem of the role of coercion in economic development in general. Classical education in cconomics, bascd on thc assumption of a libcral socicty, has not paid much attention to this problem. In Marxian doctrine, coercion appears in two aspects: (1) as a phenomenon connected with most forms of class rule; (2) as an inescapable element of any revolution. Georges Sorel considered that violence and coercion were connected with most achievements in economic, social, and political history; and he expected the future collectivist society, whose nucleus he saw in the workers' unions (*syndicats*) also to be based on violence. The idea of violence and coercion is implicit in Lenin's program for the dictatorship of the proletariat. In the immediate post-Leninist years, the theoretical arguments for coercion in development policy were provided mainly by the members of the Trotskyist opposition, and notably by E. A. Preobrazhenskii. The

Stalinist policy of industrialization also expressed a certain spontaneous disposition toward coercive measures among the new Soviet elite brought by the Revolution to the top of the social pyramid.

The consideration of the role of coercion in economic development also involves the problem of bringing about economic growth in those countries where, because of structural deficiencies, tendencies to stagnation prevail. So far as one can venture an assessment of the historical importance of contemporary events, the stimulating role of the Russian Revolution appears to have consisted not in building up a new social system, the advantages of which are, indeed, very doubtful, but in opening up a new era in economic history. Stalinist industrialization has, in fact, opened up a new era of forced economic growth among the peoples still overwhelmed by poverty—the majority of the human race. This growth would probably have come about in any case because of population pressure, but the Russian Revolution acted as a catalyst.

The Soviet Union has also set up a model for this growth based on coercion and entailing indescribable human suffering, to be compared only with the grim pictures of capitalist industrialization provided by the socialist historians. In the countries of the Soviet bloc, the Party program, with its mirage of a millennium, is a typical "ideological superstructure" facilitating the maintenance of obedience and order among the working masses, who are asked to increase their efficiency while restricting their consumption. The Party ideology is a social myth, the present role of which, however, is not to stimulate revolutionary forces but to suppress any attempt at a revolt of the masses, who bear the hardships of the system. A study of the development (and subsequent decline) of the methods of coercion in the Soviet economy is, therefore, important for an understanding of the social role of an official ideology in an underdeveloped country in which the Communist Party comes to power.

Is it inevitable that rapid economic progess should be connected with an explosion of violence and hate and with a growth of social inequality? Or are these "diseases of growth" avoidable? Violence and coercion are probably no more necessary concomitants of rapid economic growth in underdeveloped countries than is the spread of tuberculosis. In the same way as biologists and bacteriologists may help in devising means to extinguish tuberculosis, a social scientist investigating the social anatomy of violence may help to devise means for avoiding this evil.

The question is how to make the underdeveloped countries move on the way to economic reconstruction with a rapidity equal to that of the Soviet Union, but without the injustice and violence connected with Soviet industrialization. If this study should make even a small contribution toward providing the answer, this would be the best tribute I could pay to the memory of the thousands of my comrades-in-arms and my comrades in the servitude of Soviet forced labor whose graves are dispersed over the great plain of Russia.

THE ORIGIN AND GROWTH OF FORCED LABOR

In the Soviet Union the system of forced-labor camps originated at the time of the Civil War which followed the October Revolution of 1918. During the first decade after the Revolution, this system did not assume an economic role of any significance. The camps were considered as places of isolation for political enemies. The theory of the reeducation through hard labor of criminal and political offenders was developed later.[1] By the end of the 1920s, the total number of inmates, though impressive by Western standards, hardly exceeded 200,000, a little more than 2 in 1000 of the population of the Soviet Union.[2]

At the beginning of the First Five-Year Plan, that is to say, by 1930, this situation changed. The population of forced-labor camps started to swell rapidly; and the camps acquired great importance in the carrying out of investment plans, particularly in the field of construction, and in the exploitation of natural resources in the remote regions of that enormous country. A demand for a compulsory labor force seems to have become a contributory factor in the number of arrests and deportations carried out by the security police (called at that time the OGPU and from 1934 the NKVD), though this motive has never been recognized officially and has probably not even been clearly appreciated by the Communist leaders themselves.

Kravchenko, in his well-known book, has described how during the war, when he was Head of the Department of War Engineering Armaments in the Sovnarkom of the RSFSR, he asked one of the top administrators of the forced-labor camps to send some hundreds of prisoners to some rush assignment. The official answered with some irritation:

> But Comrade Kravchenko, be reasonable. After all, your Sovnarkom is not the only one howling for workers. The State Defense Committee needs them, Comrade Mikoyan makes life miserable for us, Malenkov and Voznessensky need workers, Voroshilov is calling for road builders. Naturally everyone thinks his own job is the most important. What are we to do? The fact is *we haven't as yet fulfilled our plans for imprisonment.* Demand is greater than supply.[3]

During my stay in Soviet prisons and camps in 1939–1942, I heard several times of yearly plans for providing by imprisonment the manpower required for NKVD enterprises, though I never, myself, saw documentary proof of their existence. The idea of such a plan seems to be, however, perfectly consistent with the Soviet economic structure at that time and with the principles of dialectics in economic policy.

During the 1930s the NKVD became not only a security police with its own army (including artillery and air-force units), but also a huge industrial and constructional concern which organized production under its own administration. Moreover, the NKVD was a big contractor supplying labor force to enterprises in the administration of the other commissariats. Its activities in the fields of economy and security became interrelated, and growing production targets involved the search for new sources of manpower. The reign of terror which was a characteristic of the Stalinist period was to a certain extent a result of the atmosphere created by this extension of the NKVD's economic sector.

A great outburst of mass arrests in 1937, associated with the name of Commissar of the NKVD Yezhov, coincided with the exhaustion of the sources of supply of compulsory labor in the villages. In 1937 the NKVD was searching for new sources. This search does not provide a full explanation of *Yezhovshchina,* but it is an important element for the understanding of that period in the history of the USSR.

The bottleneck in labor supply which, in the 1930s, appeared frequently in various sections of the national economy produced two contradictory phenomena: a rise in wages above the planned ceiling in enterprises employing free labor and a growth of the army of slave laborers, who received practically no remuneration except prisoners' food and accommodation and who were not protected by social-security legislation.

LIFE IN THE CAMPS

Much has been written in the West on the conditions of life in the Soviet camps.[4] This literature consists mainly of the memoirs of former inmates. Some of those memoirs are not without literary merit, for instance *A World Apart* by Herling.[5] The short description given below is mainly based on my own experience in the late 1930s and early 1940s.

Conditions of life in the camps were gloomy. Forced laborers were treated as prisoners and deprived of elementary personal liberties, even during that part of the day when they were free from work. Their right of postal communication with their families was limited and in many cases cut off completely and forever. They did not enjoy the benefits of social legislation; their working day lasted about twelve hours and very often longer. In principle, prisoners were paid for their work; there was, however, no definite rule to define how this principle should be carried out. In my experience they received only a token remuneration, the monthly wage seldom surpassing the price of a few pounds of bread in the camp's inner black market. I did hear, however, of some camps, particularly those connected with mining, where pay had some real meaning.

The most important factor determining the standard of life of the prisoners was a ration which they received from the camp kitchen. This varied according to time, place, and the percentage of the "norm" executed by a given prisoner. In certain cases the ration was at starvation level, even for those who executed the full norm, and this led to a very high death rate. Sometimes, however, the ration was sufficient to keep one alive and even to maintain physical strength. The policy of camp authorities was to keep most prisoners in a state of semistarvation and to give them an incentive for more efficient work by promising a higher food ration to those who over-fulfilled their norm. If, however, exhaustion became so great that it seriously affected the output of the camp, a special commission was usually appointed to investigate the causes of the fall in productiv-ity. This usually brought some improvement in living conditions, which, however, deteriorated again after a time. In the prewar years these fluctuations in living conditions occurred periodically.

Food conditions in the camps also depended on the harvest and on the political situation. The downfall of the head of the secu-rity police, and his replacement by some new personality, usually found its reflection in altered conditions for the prisoners, since the camps were under the management of the security police (known in different periods under different names: Cheka, GPU, OGPU, NKVD, NKGB, MGB, MVD, KGB). The food situation was toler-able when Yagoda was commissar of security in the middle of the 1930s, appalling under Yezhov in 1937. It improved with the ac-cession of Beria in 1938, deteriorated greatly during the war, and apparently improved again considerably at the beginning of the 1950s. Changes in policy were also reflected in fluctuations of the mortality rate among prisoners. Professor Wiles came to the conclu-sion, on the basis of Soviet censuses of population and on the evi-dence of former prisoners, that in the period 1927–1938 in the USSR, the excess of deaths due to forced-labor camps and forced settlements amounted to about 2.3 million. In 1933 the mortality rate in camps was about 10 percent; in 1938 under Yezhov it rose to about 20 percent.[6] In the winter of 1941–1942 in the Soviet Far North, I witnessed several cases of prisoners dying in the night after a day of work in the forest, or collapsing and dying during the march from the place of work to the camp.

I heard stories of exhausted prisoners being driven from their bunks to go to work by specially trained dogs, but I never saw this myself. In my experience I never noticed any deliberate cruelty on the part of camp authorities of the kind described in the accounts of former Nazi prisoners. The camp authorities were pressed from above to increase their output, while they could not control the supply of food and clothing allocated to their camps; thus their opportunities to improve the lot of their prisoners were very limited. In my experience the people in the medical department of the camps were always willing to help prisoners, but in practice they could do very little, because for one thing they were themselves under constant supervision, and, for another, there were hardly any medical supplies in those camps where I was imprisoned. The source of the evil was in the system which forced people into inhuman behavior.

REEDUCATION THROUGH WORK

From the legal point of view, the prisoners were regarded as offenders who were to be reformed by hard work and the educational influence of the camp. Only a small minority received sentence after a trial before a court. The great majority were committed to camps, on the decision of the security police, as "socially dangerous" or "socially harmful" elements. Instances of the release of political prisoners after the expiration of the term of their sentence were rarely to be heard of. For the most part those who survived the period of their sentence received a communication to the effect that, by a decision of the Special Committee of the security police, their stay in the forced-labor camp was extended for another three or five years. Thus, in practice, the length of the sentence did not make any real difference: forced labor was, in fact, for life.

The idea of correction and reeducation through work may seem plausible if considered from a purely doctrinal point of view. At the beginning of the 1930s in the upper strata of the Party, there were, apparently, people who sincerely believed in this program of reeducation to citizenship in a new Communist society. Even Maxim Gorki appeared to be under this illusion for some time. In practice this idea has turned out to be a kind of grisly joke. In our camp we were visited sometimes by a "tutor" (*vospitatel*), a half-literate youth of eighteen, with the pale face and dull eyes of a born idiot. He read aloud to us articles from a regional newspaper, stuttering heavily in spelling out the more difficult words. It was obvious that he was given this job becuse he was not capable of any useful work in production or administration. Each camp had a Cultural and Educational Department (KVC) which distributed newspapers, lent books, organized, though very seldom, films and concerts, and dealt with the censorship of prisoners' letters. Sometimes they tried to raise the spirit of hungry and exhausted men by playing a lively march tune for them on their departure to work. The influence of the KVC on the life of the camp was negligible; its existence, however, was evidence that, at the inception of forced-labor camps in the Soviet Union, the aim had not been the annihilation of the enemies of the regime, as in Nazi Germany, but their conversion to the new religion. There was not much difference between the situation of the inmates of the Soviet and of the Nazi camps, but a very great difference existed between the subjective moral attitudes of the founders of these institutions in Russia and in Germany.

During my three years' stay in the Soviet Union, it became obvious to me that correction was only a cover for the real task of the forced-labor camps, which was the redistribution of labor resources in connection with the reconstruction of the national economy and with the provision of cheap labor for capital investment projects. The idea of correction may have some real meaning in respect of labor colonies (ITK) where people condemned for minor offenses (such as the infringement of labor discipline) were directed, but here I am dealing only with forced-labor camps. I am not maintaining that all Soviet leaders were hypocrites who fully realized the economic basis of the forced-labor camps, while pretending not to see it. Some of them, apparently, even if they did not believe in correction (because the absurdity of this concept must have been obvious to everybody in the Soviet Union), nevertheless still considered that the main function of the camps was to protect the regime against counterrevolution. The psychosis of fear and suspicion was characteristic of the upper strata of Soviet society. But even this psychosis could not explain the tremendous extent to which various kinds of unfree labor had developed in the Soviet Union. The actors in great historic dramas often do not see the forces by which they are pushed and which determine their decisions and direct their steps. The analysis of those forces is a task for the social scientist.

THE UNITED NATIONS AD HOC COMMITTEE

In 1951–1953 the problem of forced labor in the Soviet Union was investigated within the framework of the general study of systems of forced and corrective labor throughout the world undertaken by a special ad hoc committee of the United Nations. This committee was appointed on the basis of resolutions of the United Nations Economic and Social Council and of the Governing Body of the International Labor Office. It consisted of three members: Sir Ramaswami Mudaliar, an Indian lawyer (chairman), Paal Berg, former president of the Supreme Court of Norway, and Enrique García Sayán, former minister for foreign affairs of Peru. In 1953, after two years' study, they submitted a voluminous report. Its conclusions leave no doubt as to the economic importance of forced labor in the Soviet system. In paragraphs 413 and 414 the following statement occurs: [7]

413. It is evident from several Soviet sources that, since about 1930, the work of both political and other prisoners has been used in the Soviet Union for large-scale public works (e.g., canals, railways and roads), for the development of vast areas with abundant and hitherto unexploited resources of raw materials, and for the economic development of previously uncultivated regions. Several Soviet authors have also stressed the great importance for the national economy of the work done by the corrective labor camps and colonies. This information from Soviet sources actually relates to conditions existing before the Second World War, but nothing either in the statements made in the Economic and Social Council by the representatives of the U.S.S.R., the Byelorussian S.S.R. and Poland on the work of prisoners or in other information which the Committee has been able to obtain would seem to indicate that the situation is different today. It is also clear from the most recent testimonies examined by the Committee that during the war and even after those sentenced to corrective labor were still used on large-scale projects or in big industrial or farming undertakings.

414. In the Committee's view it would therefore seem to be established that the work of prisoners, particularly in corrective labor camps and colonies, is used in the Soviet Union for essential tasks in the interests of the national economy, and that the part it plays is of considerable significance.

In the appendices to the report, abundant factual material has been published substantiating the committee's conclusions, and clearly establishing that though in various colonial territories and some Latin-American countries legislation still exists which may provide a basis for the development of forced labor, the main field of its actual application is in the Soviet Union and some other countries of the Soviet bloc in Europe. The committee did not investigate the problem of forced labor in China.

FORCED LABOR AND SLAVERY

Soviet forced labor is sometimes referred to as slave labor. One of the most penetrating accounts given by the former inmates of the camps bears the title *Katorga: An Aspect of Modern Slavery*.[8] It is therefore pertinent to consider the differences between these two social phenomena.

First, the legal position: slavery involves the permanent social status of a man, while forced labor is only for some limited time, though in the practice of the Stalinist Soviet Union release occurred very seldom.[9] The most spectacular exception to this general rule was the mass release of Poles in 1941–1942 under the pressure of political circumstances after German aggression against the Soviet Union. This was afterward followed by the transfer to the Soviet army of certain categories of younger prisoners.

Secondly, in the Soviet Union a forced laborer cannot be the object of private ownership as in the ancient world; this corresponds to the general principle that private ownership of the means of mass production has been abolished in the Soviet Union. Some analogy, however, may be traced between Soviet forced laborers in the Stalinist era and the slave strata which played a part in the history of Athens and Rome.

The third difference is that, while in the ancient world slavery was inherited, the children of the inmates of the Soviet forced-labor camps were nominally free men, though in practice they were subjected to various restrictions. In the Stalinist Soviet Union great importance was attached to so-called "social origin," and children whose parents were in forced labor for political reasons had very great difficuly in obtaining admission to the universities or a better-paid job. Thus, in the Stalinist Soviet Union, a new social stratum was in process of formation, the hereditary position of which was approaching that of the "untouchable" in India.

The fourth difference is psychological: slavery has not been accepted by the social conscience of Soviet society as it was accepted in ancient communities. This has probably been an important reason why the bar of secrecy has been set against all information connected with the development of forced labor in the Soviet Union. It is also probable that, in part at least, the concepts of the reeducation, the isolation, of socially dangerous elements, the punishment of "enemies of the people," and so forth were propounded in order to appease the conscience of the Communist rank and file, if not of the leadership itself. These concepts, considered in the terms of Marxist sociology, may be taken as examples of "ideological superstructures" built up by governing groups in order to create a psychological atmosphere favorable to the exploitation of the labor force of subjugated social strata.

In the historical perspective Soviet forced labor could be considered as a stage on the way to a new social stratification which might have involved slavery, though this trend was interrupted and even reversed by subsequent events. The attitude of nonacceptance of slavery by the social conscience of Russian society was gradually being overcome. By the beginning of the 1940s the administrative staff in the camps treated the prisoners as inferior creatures, any contact with whom on a footing of equality was insulting to the dignity of a free man. It was considered inadmissible for a citizen of the Soviet Union to eat with a forced laborer, to sleep under the same roof, or to have any kind of friendly relations with him, though it was permissible to work under his direction if he possessed some particular qualifications. In some camps in the Far North the rule was observed that even the dirty clothes of a free man could not be put together with prisoners' garments for delousing in a disinfecting chamber.[10]

This education of at least some section of Soviet society for slavery was interrupted by the events of the war, which brought in their train a feeling of the instability of all existing institutions, though during the war forced labor played a very great role in the Soviet economy. Since Stalin's death the trend toward slavery has been reversed; there is much evidence that objective conditions are pushing the Soviet Union toward some liberalization of political control and toward some decline of the role of physical coercion.

THE FOUR PHASES OF THE SYSTEM

Four periods may be distinguished in the development of forced labor as a phenomenon of recent Soviet economic history: (1) from the beginning of forced collectivization until the mid-1930s; (2) from the mid-1930s until the outbreak of the Soviet-German war in 1941; (3) the war, and the postwar rehabilitation period, the end of which roughly coincided with Stalin's death; and (4) from the death of Stalin onward.

In the first period, the growth of forced labor was closely connected with the absorption of the surplus of agricultural labor by constructional and manufacturing industry. Prisoners taken from the villages predominated among the inmates of camps. The characteristics of the model for an economic interpretation of this period are: a closed economy, agricultural underemployment, and the policy of large-scale public investment carried out by a despotic government.

The distinctive feature of the second period lay in various bottlenecks and particularly that of labor supply. The security police (the NKVD) became a contractor supplying labor force to certain enterprises. By the end of this period the Ribbentrop-Molotov agreement opened the way to military conquest and provided the conditions for offsetting the shortage of labor by introducing manpower deported from the newly occupied territories. The deportations from Eastern Poland in 1939–1941 were followed by those from northeastern Rumania (Bessarabia) and the Baltic countries.

In the third period, which comprised the war effort and post-war rehabilitation, the shortage of manpower was partly offset by the employment of German, Italian, and Japanese prisoners of war, and the deportation to forced labor of whole populations of some non-Russian minorities (Volga Germans, Crimean Tatars, Checheno-Ingushs, Kalmyks, Karachai), and the direction to forced-labor camps of Soviet prisoners of war and civilian deportees returning from Germany.

In the fourth period, a decline in the economic importance of the forced-labor system becomes visible. This had already started before the death of Stalin, but the political and psychological shock produced by his death acted as a catalyst which facilitiated the process. Considerable numbers of prisoners were released, the food supply was improved, and the regime became milder.

The salient characteristics of this last period are technical progress and an increasing standard of living. At the present time Soviet Union production is growing not only through a current addition to the labor force, but also primarily through an increase in its efficiency.[11] In these conditions, the application of brutal compulsion becomes impracticable, and the primary reason for forced-labor camps is once more punishment and political repression, as in the 1920s.

XIII

The achievements of the Stalinist industrialization program have frequently been described; its costs have rarely been estimated. The growth rates and rationality of the Soviet planning system have been recognized; the ups and downs of the economy and the mistakes of planners in the Stalin era have, more often than not, been overlooked. Naum Jasny, born and trained in Russia and for some years a Soviet planner himself, was the first to illuminate this darkened area of economic growth. He was, until his recent death, for decades the dean of economic studies of the USSR in Europe and America, and a particular authority on Soviet agriculture and statistics. Among his numerous books and monographs, perhaps the best known and most definitive are The Socialized Agriculture of the USSR *(1949), and* Soviet Industrialization 1928–1952 *(1961). The selection included here is from the latter work, with the permission of Chicago University Press and the author's heirs.*

293

NAUM JASNY

The Great Industrialization Drive

The quarter of a century covered in this essay was one of truly great events, including a full-scale revolution. It was a great event that a backward agricultural country was converted into an industrial nation in so short a time and in spite of immense handicaps. Another great event was that an indifferently armed country became one of the best-armed countries in the world. The most striking event of all was that industrialization was accomplished without its normal concomitant—the improvement of the living standards of the population.

The Bolsheviks came on the scene as fighters for socialism and against exploitation, for a great improvement in the well-being of everybody. What they achieved was a great increase in the rate of exploitation, reducing the people's share of the national income to an extent nobody had believed possible. This strangulation of consumption put such large funds in the hands of the state as to permit extensive industrialization and even greater militarization, despite loss and waste of every kind caused by wars, internal strife, mismanagement, and so on.

If one looks for figures as evidence of this revolution, there are probably no better ones than these: While the total personal income (calculated at constant prices) of the expanded population increased by about one-third from 1928 to 1952, the real value of the funds in the hands of the state for investment, military and other expenses, grew almost eightfold. This transformation must be considered a financial, economic, and social revolution. Whether one would agree that it is a transformation into a socialist state is another matter (Chart 1).

CHART 1
Growth of Soviet National Income and Its Components, 1928–1952*
(1928=100)

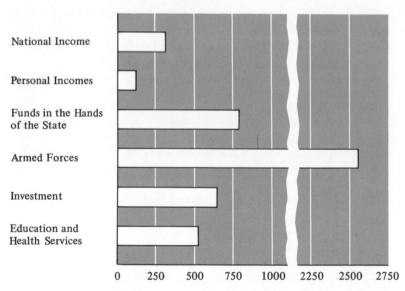

* At real 1926–1927 prices. Only the index for total national income is presumably strongly affected by the selection of the weights.

THE AIMS

By about 1927 the economy of the USSR had recovered from the devastation of wars fought with internal and external enemies, and from Lenin's experiment in introducing communism based on grain confiscated from the peasants. Without any further delays, the Party embarked on a drive aiming at quickly converting Russia from an agrarian into an industrial country. Moreover, the whole economy was to become socialized simultaneously. This new policy meant the end of the NEP (New Economic Policy) which, starting in 1921, had produced the economic recovery, largely with the help of independent and, to a considerable extent, self-sufficient peasants. The inauguration of the post-NEP policies was proclaimed at the Fifteenth Party Congress in December of 1927, which was officially baptized the Congress of Industrialization. The period since this congress may be properly designated the Great Industrialization Drive.[1]

The aim of the Great Industrialization Drive was formulated by Stalin with the greatest clarity in summing up the results of the operation of the first FYP: "The basic task of the FYP's was to create such an industry in our country as to be able to rearm and reorganize not only industry as a whole, but also transportation and agriculture—on the basis of socialism." [2]

The super-rapid industrialization, which was made the basic aim, was obviously equivalent to a rate of expansion of industry considerably more rapid than that of the economy as a whole. Within industry, the production of producers' goods, or of "industries A," as they are called in Russia, was to expand at a more rapid, indeed much more rapid, rate than the production of consumers' goods ("industries B"). Such a large rate of industrial expansion necessarily called for a correspondingly rapid growth of investment. Consequently, investment was to expand at a greater rate than national income, while private consumption was to rise more slowly than the latter.

For years, indeed for the whole period covered in this monograph, almost the whole economy was geared to produce ever more

steel for the construction of ever more steel and other heavy-indus-
try factories, as well as for the output of ever more armaments.
While Joseph Dzhugashvili probably picked his Party name ("Stalin" comes from *stal'*, the Russian word for "steel") for other reasons, it fitted him extremely well in this sense. The obstacle, obviously deplored by Stalin, was that expanding production of steel
and construction of steel factories could not proceed without enlarging the output of building materials and transportation facilities.
Nor could much expansion take place without producing at least
some consumers' goods and housing for those operating and constructing the steel factories, and these were the least desired items.
The principle that the share of investment in national income grows
more rapidly than national income itself became so characteristic of
the Soviet economy that the years and periods when this was not
achieved were definitely marked down as unfavorable, indeed, as
times of great disturbance.

The disproportionately rapid expansion of heavy industry remained the basic principle of the Soviet economy, one of its basic
"laws," until the death of Stalin. In his comments on Stalin's *Economic Problems of Socialism in the USSR,* the last work by Stalin,
E. Lokshin, an official interpreter, wrote:

> Of decisive importance for insuring the expanding reproduc-
> tion is the establishment of correct relationships between the out-
> put of means of production and the output of consumers' goods.
> The principal peculiarity of these proportions, determined by the
> needs of expanding reproduction, is the greater growth of output
> of the means of production.[3]

The idea of priority for heavy industry was temporarily abandoned under Malenkov. Even this occurred only in actions, not pronouncements.[4] Khrushchev at once restored the "law" to its full
rights. The new Seven-Year Plan for 1959–1965 is based on it. In
actual practice, for several years beginning about 1949, heavy industry was hardly expanding more rapidly than light industry. In
general this was brought about by the fact that the share of heavy
industry in the total industrial output had become so large by that

time that the Bolsheviks were satisfied to let light industry retain the small share to which it had been reduced. But specifically in 1956 and 1957 efforts to expand heavy industry more rapidly than light industry were frustrated by poor planning resulting in failure to complete investment projects, heavy industry having been primarily affected by this failure.

Industrialization was not simply the principal initial aim of the drive; it was the only aim. Contrary to official and semiofficial assertions, "defense" was not a problem at the birth of the Great Industrialization Drive. Defense came up only after several years, in 1934 to be exact, but then it grew ever larger in importance, until at a later stage of the drive defense may have assumed more significance than industrialization itself.

Strangulation of the production of consumers' goods may first have been a necessity. Without this the Industrialization Drive could not have got under way at the great rate desired. As industrialization gained more prominence and as limitless defense requirements came to the fore, the Soviets acquired a real taste for keeping down personal consumption. One might say that this had become almost an aim per se.

After 1949, the output of industrial consumers' goods expanded at the same, or almost the same, large rate as producers' goods, but the initial point having been very low, the output of consumers' goods remained small for years. Only recently have the large rates of growth of these goods started to represent respectable amounts. Also, a larger proportion of the building materials classed as producers' goods have recently begun going into housing, a durable consumer good. But all this is so recent (indeed almost all of it is in the future) that it cannot be covered here.

OVERALL RESULTS

The aim of full socialization was attained, if we class as socialism the state ownership of means of production of every kind, including the collective farm (*kolkhoz*), maintained by sheer force. For that matter, Soviet "socialism" in nonfarm pursuits, realized to an even greater extent than in farming, has also been based, not on the economic superiority of socialist enterprise, but on prohibitions [5] and severe taxation. [6]

Industrialization was achieved, but the price in lowered living conditions was great. The rates of industrialization attained did not satisfy those in power, however, and they did not have any intention of disclosing the price paid. Large-scale falsification of statistics was resorted to in order to make the rates of growth seem much bigger than they really were and especially to conceal the fact that instead of rising greatly, as promised and claimed, the level of personal consumption had declined.

The immense rates of growth of industry and national income claimed by official Soviet statistics have been fully discredited. The efforts of pro-Soviet forces to propagandize these rates, which exist only on paper, are only empty gestures and not worthy of much attention. For we have a fair idea of the rates of growth actually attained in the USSR. Indeed, all estimates of the rates of growth of national income, and specifically of industrial output, made outside Russia that are worthy of attention are reasonably close to each other, particularly when compared with the officially claimed fantastic percentage rises. In some cases, there is even full agreement among the estimates of independent analysts. As compared with them, the official calculations of real incomes sound ludicrous.

All estimates presented below are of course only crude. They seem, however, to be sufficiently reliable to permit broad appraisals of the significance for the Russian people of "the second revolution" (as the all-out collectivization drive was called by the Bolsheviks themselves) and other developments of the period.

National income by origin. Gross industrial output appears to have expanded from 1928 to 1950 almost 4 times in size at United States prices and about 4.7 times at Soviet 1926–1927 prices. But the Soviets were not after industrialization as such; they were after expansion of the output of producers' goods and this was enlarged about 8.8 times during 1928–1950. Output of consumers' goods by industry was just about doubled during this period.

Construction increased about fivefold from 1928 to 1950. [7] The much smaller decline in the growth of construction—and, for that matter, net investment—than of output of producers' goods was due to the much greater growth in expenditures on the armed forces as well as to the great shrinkage of imports of machinery, which had been large in 1928.

Contrary to the high rates of growth of industry and construction, farm output appears to have practically stagnated over the same period. The increases in farm output from 1928 to 1950 (or 1953), within the territorial boundaries of the respective years (that is, the figures were not adjusted to pertain to the same territory), was indeed no larger than the growth of the population, in spite of greatly increased needs. Furthermore, it is important to note that the output of cotton, which is the principal nonfood farm product, was expanded greatly. Hence the production of food items makes an even poorer showing than the total farm output.

Recomputed to 1955, the following approximate indices are obtained, at 1926–1927 prices (1928 equals 100):

> Industry. 775
> Construction [a] 782
> Agriculture . . . . 150 or somewhat less
>
> [a] The index was calculated for net investment.

Since agriculture played a very large part in the material production of 1928, the total increase in material production and national income was closer to that shown by agriculture than by industry. Measured at 1926–1927 prices—which means that the results are considerably biased in favor of those goods whose output was expanding rapidly during the Great Industrialization Drive, national income at factor cost appears to have grown 3.7 times in 1928–1955.* Estimates in dollar prices by Colin Clark [8] (retail

---

* Late in 1959, after the above was written, *Economy of the USSR in 1958*, the official statistical yearbook, brought fully revamped official estimates of farm production. For the period from 1928 to 1950 it implies a decline in per capita farm production of about 5 percent, and for the same item in 1928–1955 an increase of 5 percent (ibid., p. 350). The small differences between this writer's and the new official estimates may be partly due to the difference in the concept used. But also, when one tries hard not to picture the situation as gloomier than it actually was, one lands a little bit too high. Finally, it would be inadvisable to accept the new official indices as 100 percent correct.

prices) and by Grossman and Shimkin [9] (factor cost) indicate a doubling of it in 1928–1952 and 1928–1950, respectively.[10]

National income by allocation. Great as was the discrepancy between the expansion of industry, construction, and for that matter transportation, on the one hand, and the creeping growth of agriculture, on the other hand, the discrepancies among the various allocation components of national income were even greater. The almost exclusive attention, common in the West, to the growth of Soviet national income as a whole (this showed quite a large increase, even in per capita terms, during the Industrialization Drive) is likely to mislead. The divergent trends of the major components of national income are at least as important.

As Chart 1 shows, personal incomes increased by only about one-third from 1928 to 1952—a period of immense changes, including a trebling of the urban population. The funds which the state could appropriate for investment and the armed forces increased almost nine times, funds earmarked for expenditures on the armed forces alone about twenty-six times.

The fact that the real value of the funds in the hands of the state grew almost eightfold, while private incomes increased by only one-third cannot be overemphasized. It may be assumed with confidence that this phenomenon is entirely unique; simple comparisons of the growth in Soviet national income with those in other countries thus become rather meaningless.

Net investment increased more than sixfold in 1928–1952, at the same time that national income was growing only a little more than threefold. This would be very important in itself in ensuring great rates of economic growth. However, there were also shifts in the distribution of net investment that operated in the same direction. Investment in heavy industry increased at least twelvefold during the Industrialization Drive.

Accompanying these means of expanding plant capacity at high rates were measures taken to assure a plentiful supply of labor. Peasant women were forced into gainful employment by law; practically all other women also held jobs, because of the low income of the family or strong pressures, moral and otherwise. Sacrificed to the Moloch of industrialization were all interests of the wage earners, not only their incomes, but also the right to choose an occupation, to have a family, and the like. The fact that it would mean leaving her family was not considered an adequate excuse for a married woman to refuse a job.[11] Everything, especially planning, was adapted to the main goal of expansion. The targets of the plans were set, not simply to be fulfilled, but also to be exceeded. Risks of disproportions were taken into the bargain. To the great benefit of industry, markets tend strongly to be sellers' markets in the USSR.

So far as growth in expenditures is concerned, military might seems to have had, at least until quite recently, an even greater claim than investment in heavy industry. Funds *earmarked* for military use increased, in real terms, about twenty-six fold, in 1928–1952, about twice as much as investment in heavy industry. (This expansion continued after World War II on a grand scale, although nothing threatened the Soviet Union except the consequences of her own aggression.) In 1952, the last Stalin year, the funds *earmarked* for military expenditures were more than 60 percent of net investment at 1926–1927 rubles. Total military expenditures [12] may have been not very much smaller than the total net investment in that year.[13]

Against those immense rises in investment and in military expenditures was the increase in personal incomes by only one-third in real terms. Actually the situation was even worse than this overall figure indicates. As in other poor agricultural countries, national income per capita of the nonfarm population was much larger than that of the farm population in the USSR before the Great Industrialization Drive. According to official estimates, the former was 2.7 times as large as the latter in 1927–1928.[14] The nonfarm population in 1955 showed a growth to about 3.6 times its 1928 size, raising its share from about 25 percent to substantially more than half of the total population. Under such conditions, an income of the total population in 1952 only moderately below that in 1928, if calculated per capita on the basis of the whole population, implied a large decline in per capita consumption of both the farm and the nonfarm population. The increase of total personal incomes by about one-third from 1928 to 1952, actually represented a decline of about 25 percent in real per capita income for the wage-earning population and a decline of about 40 percent in real per capita income for the rural population. My calculations, which, it is hoped, are fairly reliable, indicate that even a level of real per capita income equal to 75 percent of that in 1928 was exceeded only after 1951 (1952–1958) for the nonfarm population and only in about five years for the farm population (1937 and 1955–1958).[15] In some nonwar years, real per capita income, calculated separately for the rural and the urban population, may have been less than half that of 1928.

A development may not have been fully considered in those figures. During the period analyzed, a great shift occurred from an economy largely based on consumption of home-produced goods to one based much more on purchases. In 1927–1928, the income in kind [16] of the farm population was about 58 percent of its total income and close to one-third of the income of the whole population. By 1938 income in kind was only about 30 percent and less than 10 percent, respectively. Operations of the transportation system and trade, as well as the national income, were boosted by this shift in the economy, without any effect on actual consumption. The transfer of much processing from homes, where it is not registered statistically, to industry, where it is so registered, is in itself an advantage to the consumer, but the volume of consumption is not necessarily affected by it; and where, as in the USSR, the transfer of processing is largely forced on the consumer, the value to him of the advantage may be only a fraction of its cost.[17]

Even in a dictatorship as strong as that of Stalin, it was not easy to hold private consumption at the described low level. The task may have become impossible after Stalin's death. If at the same time the state desired to maintain the growth rates of the rest of the economy, there may not have been any other choice for Stalin's heirs but to reduce or at least stabilize military expenditures. The recent sudden interest of the Soviet government in "peace" may be due to a certain or large extent to this necessity.

Rate of exploitation. The immense shift in the distribution of national income during the Great Industrialization Drive may also be arrived at in another way. Output per man in industry increased presumably by more than 100 percent over the period 1928–1955. Since labor productivity in construction was particularly low in

1928, the increase in it may have been larger than that in industry. Labor productivity in railway transportation just about quadrupled in this period. It increased by at least 35 percent even in agriculture. Yet real wages in 1952 were less than three-quarters of those in 1928 and per capita peasant incomes were equal to only three-fifths of the respective level.

The rate of exploitation, or, as Marx called it, the surplus product, was small in 1928. But the subsequent rise in exploitation was huge. The surplus value became much greater than the original share of the worker in the total newly produced value.

The figures quoted indicate a worsening of the incomes of the peasants relative to those of wage and salary earners, although they were already particularly low before the start of the Great Industrialization Drive. Small as the total personal incomes were, there was an immense stratification among wage and salary earners and, to a smaller extent, among peasants. The lower strata of the working people, very broad strata at that, were reduced to the position of paupers. Again, if this was socialism, it was a very peculiar form of socialism.

Appraisals. The Soviets and the pro-Soviet forces consider the results of the Great Industrialization Drive amazing—in the form, of course, in which these results appear in the falsified Soviet indices. Looking at the correct figures, one can only be amazed at the strength of the dictatorship, which persisted in holding down personal consumption to such astoundingly low levels. This done, the rest appears modest. The real value of the funds in the hands of the state having been increased almost eightfold through 1952 and all the concerted effort made toward industrialization considered, there is no wonder that industrial output, originally small, could have expanded almost six times in 1928–1952. With full justification, one could say that the actual attainment was much smaller than it looks at first glance.

At least a partial answer to the question of why an economy which per se is heavily geared to expansion shows only a relatively small *overall* growth is found by a more careful consideration of the stages through which the Great Industrialization Drive passed after its initiation late in 1927.

MAJOR STAGES OF THE GREAT
INDUSTRIALIZATION DRIVE

The ascertainment of the rates of growth during the Great Industrialization Drive as a whole, while of considerable importance, is not all that is needed. The Soviets continually proclaim that their socialist economy is developing smoothly and proportionately according to plan (there is even said to be a law of such development). That there is a huge disproportion between the farm and nonfarm sectors of the economy was shown above in the discussion of national income by origin. There are many other important areas where smoothness of "socialist" economic development exists only in the Soviet imagination. The drive actually consisted of stages with quite different rates of growth. These stages lose at least some of their characteristics when combined into the rates for the period as a whole. This remains true even if World War II and the recovery from this war are excluded from the period considered.

The great differences in the rates of growth during the various stages of the Great Industrialization Drive have thus far not been given enough attention by analysts. This lack has prevented a full realization of what has happened in the USSR in the past and, even more important, of what may happen there in the future.

The insufficient attention paid to the various stages has been due partly to the state of the evidence with which the analyst has had to deal and—to a much smaller degree—still has to deal. Five dates stand out in the research on the Soviet economy thus far done, that is, 1927–1928 [18] or 1928 (these dates differ only by three months), 1937, 1940, 1950, and 1955. The initial date of practically all research is 1927–1928 or 1928. The periods covered are mainly 1929–1937, 1938–1940, 1940–1950, and 1951–1955 —or combinations of these periods. These dates and periods were selected not because they had some specific meaning but simply because statistical data for them were accessible.

This great accessibility was to a large extent due to the fact that the dates and periods were those connected with the operation of the FYPs. The period 1928–1929 to 1937 was that of the operation of the first two FYPs, while the period 1938–1940 was the time in which the Third FYP operated (the Third FYP discontinued operating after World War II had started). The Fourth FYP was in force in 1946–1950, but except where it was advantageous to depart from this principle, the official comparisons for this FYP period were based on the period from 1940 to 1950. The period 1951–1955 is that of the so-called Fifth FYP. The period most thoroughly analyzed thus far is 1928–37, and again not because of some features which would stamp it as of particular significance but because the data are more plentiful, or were until recently the only plentiful data.

The Soviets are very proud of their planning. It is supposed to be an inseparable part of the "socialist" economy and applicable nowhere else. The planning takes the form of quarterly, annual, and five-year plans.[19] The importance assigned to each type of plan in official pronouncements increases directly with the length of the plan.

The successive FYPs make very convenient stages of development for the official Soviet economic history. Deliberately—to force on the student the FYP periods as the major stages of the Soviet economic development—or not deliberately, statistical data are most ample for the periods of the FYP. Practically no data, for example, existed until recently for 1939, but there was a certain amount of data for 1940.

My examination, to be printed as an essay, "Perspective Planning," leads to the conclusion that the FYPs are largely facade, not playing the role in the economy ascribed to them, but serving principally as propaganda. A specific advantage of the use of the FYPs as major stages of economic development is that, if the Soviets did not subdivide their economic history since 1928–1929 into FYP periods, they would have to subdivide it into other periods which might permit an undesirably closer insight into Soviet reality than that permitted by the FYP periods.

As soon as one realizes that the FYP periods are not really significant periods of Soviet economic history and are largely facades, the situation becomes clear, and the subdivision of Soviet economic history into really relevant periods forces itself directly on the analyst. The only difficulties arise from the fact that the effects of certain policies continued to operate for some time after the policies themselves had been discarded, and one is, therefore, uncertain whether to consider a certain period as starting with the inauguration of the respective policies or with the time when they had begun to show their effects. Furthermore, in order not to complicate the statistical analysis more than is absolutely necessary, one wishes to limit oneself to whole years (actually calendar years), but neither the discontinuation of certain policies nor the start of the operation of new policies necessarily occurs on January 1 of a given year.

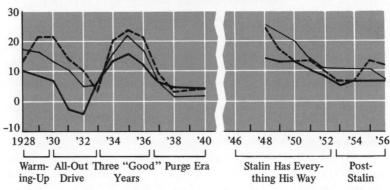

CHART 2
Major Stages: Three Principal Indicators,* 1928–1956
(Year-to-year rises, in percent)

————National Income———— Industrial Output ———— Freight Traffic

* Indices of national income and industrial output as calculated by this writer at 1926–1927 prices. The figure for national income shown under 1928 pertains to 1927–1928. Data for freight traffic in ton-kilometers are official but are here mostly taken from the material of Dr. Holland Hunter.

The Soviet economy passed two stages, the War Communism and the New Economic Policy (NEP), before it embarked on the Great Industrialization Drive. The era here analyzed begins with a short period of less than two years, designated the *Warming-Up* period (Chart 2). The period was characterized primarily by the maturing of ideology, which permitted the Great Industrialization Drive to get into full stride, an ideology fundamentally different from that of the NEP. Actions along these lines, departing more and more from those appropriate under the NEP, were secondary. Farm output stagnated as the result of the fight against the *kulaki* (larger peasant farms), already in progress, while private retail trade was rapidly shrinking for similar reasons. As stated above, the Party Congress of December 1927 is taken as the starting point of the whole era. It is also the starting point of the *Warming-Up* period.[20]

The *Warming-Up* period ends and a new period begins with the start of the All-Out Collectivization Drive in the autumn of 1929. The publication of Stalin's famous "The Year of the Great Turn" in *Pravda* of November 7, 1929, is taken as the specific date when the period started. It was characterized not only by the All-Out Collectivization Drive itself, but also by a similar drive to industrialize almost overnight, which was associated with immense appropriations for investment, and, last but not least, with wildly unrealistic planning. These additional features justify the more general designation of the period as *All-Out Drive,* rather than the narrower All-Out or Full-Scale Collectivization Drive.

Declining farm production; declining rates of growth in industry and transportation, which finally ended in complete stagnation and possibly even in a decline; immense declines in consumption levels; and, at the end, decline also in real national income—these are the features of the *All-Out Drive.* Ideologically the period ended with the acceptance of the 1933 annual plan early in January of 1933. But the catastrophe brought about by the *All-Out Drive* lasted all through the winter of 1932–1933. In our statistical presentation, the period ends with the expiration of the calendar year 1932.

While the first half of 1933 was disastrous, the second half of the year showed recovery features. Hence, the whole of 1933 lacks any definite face and is left outside of the subdivision suggested here.

The Soviets enjoyed a period of rapid expansion, which is assumed to have started at the beginning of 1934 and to have lasted until the end of 1936—the *Three "Good" Years.* (Quotation marks are used here to qualify "good" because the rapidity of the recovery was to a considerable extent assured by keeping consumption levels very low for two years and only relaxing the pressure moderately in the third year.)

The four years 1937–1940 constitute the *Purge Era*. While the purges were over by the middle of 1938, their paralyzing effect on the economy lasted until the end of 1940. The insistence of the government that an upturn had started in the second half of 1940 seems not to be in accordance with facts.

An appropriate name for the postwar period until Stalin's death seems to be "Stalin Has Everything His Heart Wanted" or *Stalin Has Everything His Way*. The characterization of the Great Industrialization Drive as the striving for steel and almost nothing but steel pertains with particular force to this period. The path to be followed was already set early in 1946, but the crop failure of 1946 prevented Stalin's wishes from moving into high gear before the second half of 1947. Thus the features of the period are fully apparent only in the developments of its last five years, if we operate only with full years.

The period *Stalin Has Everything His Way* was characterized by the rapid, indeed super-rapid, growth of industry, construction, transportation, and national income, in spite of the unfavorable effects of the Korean War and, what is even more important, in spite of the slow growth in farm output, which in the last two Stalin years stagnated, or possibly declined.

The rates of economic growth during *Stalin Has Everything His Way,* which would be large anyway, were considerably accelerated by the fact that it was a recovery period, as well as by some other factors. At first glance, it would seem that the recovery period should be counted only until the time the level of the 1940 output was reached, an event which occurred in 1948 for the nonfarm economy. But it seems more accurate to regard as the end of the recovery period the time when the economy achieved the *productive capacity* that had been reached by 1940 (and even later) but was not fully utilized in that year because of the effect of the purges. Until this level was reached, rates of growth could well be substantially larger than in normal years. For some sectors of the economy this point in the recovery was not reached before 1951.

It is of immense importance, considering the present state of the world, that *Stalin Has Everything His Way,* a period favorable for the Soviets, was not followed by a period unfavorable for them as was the case before World War II.[21] The year of Stalin's death (1953) caused some temporary retardation in the rate of economic growth, but the subsequent years until 1956 were on the whole quite favorable. Moreover, they were healthier than the years of *Stalin Has Everything His Way,* because after 1954 expansion had extended, although not in a very satisfactory way, to agriculture as well.

A certain slowdown in the economic growth took place in 1956 and became considerably stronger in 1957. Strange as this may seem, the factors leading to the slowdown probably started to operate as far back as the period *Stalin Has Everything His Way.* For some reasons not clear to this writer (possibly the moral disintegration of the dictatorship), new construction projects were started in numbers far exceeding the ability to complete them. Unfinished construction gradually reached such huge proportions and new capacities entering production became so few that a substantial retardation in the rate of economic growth ensued. A large part of this mismanagement may have originated in 1951 and 1952, the years of the Korean War. The five Great Stalin Constructions of Communism, inaugurated in the second half of 1950, may have been the starting point. Nothing was done in the first *Post-Stalin* years to bring the situation under control.

It is sufficient to say that the rates of growth of industry and investment in the *Three "Good" Years* and during the periods of *Stalin Has Everything His Way* and *Post-Stalin* were very large. The effects of the very considerable share of investment in national income and of the dominating role of heavy industry in the large total investment reveal themselves with the greatest force in these periods. The slowdown in 1952 shown by the statistics of industrial output and investment was due not only to the fact that the recovery was already a matter of the past, but also to the rapid expansion of military expenditures. Taking into consideration these factors and the stagnation in agricultural production, the rate of overall growth in this year still appears very large.

On the other hand, more than half of the thirteen-year period from 1928 to 1940, namely, about three years of the *All-Out Drive* and four years of the *Purge Era,* was extremely bad. The average rates of growth of industry and transportation in these periods were several times lower than during the *Three "Good" Years* and *Stalin Has Everything His Way.* There is no trace of the effect of the large share of investment, especially in heavy industry, in total national income on the overall growth during these periods. Part of these investments simply went to waste. Otherwise the expanding capacities served to offset the declining utilization of capacities previously accumulated. Real national income was actually declining for the greater part of the *All-Out Drive.*

The *All-Out Drive* and the *Purge Era* obviously contributed greatly to the fact that the rates of growth during the whole Industrialization Drive, especially during its prewar period, turned out so much lower than during the periods favorable to the Soviets. The unworkable *kolkhoz* system, the great amount of overall irrationality and inefficiency, the squandering of immense resources on propaganda, and Stalin's plans for changing the climate of Russia, specifically forest-belt plantings on millions of hectares—all these were factors tending to reduce further the overall results. But it may be argued that the Soviet system has advantages over the capitalist system, which may have largely offset the effect of these additional disadvantages.

The disasters of the *All-Out Drive* and the *Purge Era* followed upon the more or less favorable periods. The moment there was some improvement, the Soviets came up with something tremendously wasteful. The restoration of the pre-World War I level in agriculture by about 1926, for example, led to increased pressure on the kulaks and soon thereafter to the "second revolution," with "annihilation of the kulaks as a class" as its battle cry. The restoration of the industrial output to pre-World War I capacity brought about the *All-Out Drive.*

The three favorable years, 1934–1936, were immediately followed by the immense wastefulness of the *Purge Era.* In agriculture the recovery by 1937 to the production levels which had prevailed before the All-Out Collectivization Drive brought an attack on the peasants consisting in encroachment on the small concessions made to them, in the form of plots of private garden land and permission for limited livestock holdings. These were the very concessions which had made possible the *Three "Good" Years*. The attack on the private economy of the *kolkhoz* peasants, which began in 1938, has never ceased. It was only relaxed somewhat during World War II.

After World War II, recovery to prewar levels was followed by the Korean War, associated with great military expenses, Khrushchev-shchina (amalgamation of the *kolkhozy*, agro-cities, etc.), and ultimately by the wasteful practice of starting too many investment projects. Whatever gains there were, the Soviets seemed to be unable to avoid wasting part of them. But the negative effects of all these practices on the rest of the economy in the postwar years were very much smaller than during the *All-Out Drive* and the *Purge Era*.

The stages illustrated. Chart 2 shows the rates of growth in three important indicators (national income, industrial output, and transportation). Chart 3 adds the rate of growth of steel, as representative of the output of heavy industry; cotton fabrics, as representative of the output of consumers' goods; and farm output. Chart 4 shows how the stages of the Great Industrialization Drive were reflected even in the development of production techniques.

Farm output has already been discussed. Steel output reflects clearly the relevant steps of economic growth; rapid growth in the *Warming-Up* period, including 1930, stagnation during the *All-Out Drive* (not including 1930), rapid growth during the *Three "Good" Years,* and renewed stagnation during the *Purge Era. Stalin Has Everything His Way* and *Post-Stalin* show an uninterrupted strong rise in steel output until 1956. Stalin's death did cause a small slowdown of the rate of steel output. More important was the slowdown in 1956 and 1957.

The doubling in the output of cotton fabrics in 1928–1956, as against an almost elevenfold increase in steel output, characterizes the Great Industrialization Drive perfectly. It is also very relevant that the output of cotton fabrics was smaller in 1935 than in 1928, in spite of the great increase in urban population, with its much larger per capita consumption in value terms.

The helplessness of those in power under the conditions of the *Purge Era* is clearly reflected in the fact that the slowdown in the

CHART 3

Major Stages: Specified Indicators, 1928–1956*

(Steel in millions of tons; cotton goods in billions of meters;
farm output in billions of rubles)

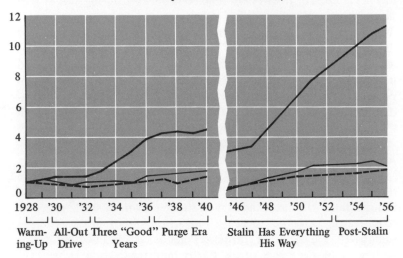

———— Steel ———— Cotton Fabrics — — — — Farm Output

* Data for steel and cotton fabrics from **Industry of the USSR,** 1957, pp.
106, 329; and **Economy of the USSR in 1956,** pp. 69, 90. Data on farm output (volume available for sale and consumption in the farm home) in
pre–World War II years from **Soc. Agri.,** p. 676, with small adjustments; the
1940 figure pertains to pre-1939 territory; the estimates for postwar years
also were made by this writer.

rate of growth in output of cotton fabrics was not as large as that of
the badly needed and badly wanted steel.

It is of great interest that the stages of the Great Industrialization Drive are reflected with great force even in such technical
factors as steel output per square meter of open hearths. While steel
output increased 10.5 times in size from 1928 to 1955, the number
of open hearths was little more than doubled. The latter increased
from 222 in October of 1928 to 489 on January 1, 1956. This
drastic misproportion was made possible by the fact that the surface
of the hearths was enlarged on the average by 63 percent and the

output of steel per square meter of the open hearths rose 3.2 times during the period.[22] But these great enlargements and improvements did not occur at anything like a uniform rate (Chart 4).

The average output of steel per square meter in a twenty-four-hour period increased by 21 percent from 1928 to 1930, but was back almost at the 1928 level in 1932. Then came a jump of 74 percent in the *Three "Good" Years* to a level by 1936 almost double that in 1928. There was a small increase also in 1937, but the 1940 level was below that of 1937. The decline during World War II was equal only to 11 percent. No advance to speak of in utilization of open hearths could have been made in 1946 and 1947.

The great reserve of capacity to enlarge utilization of the surface of the open hearths, accumulated during the decade comprised of the *Purge Era,* World War II, and the first two postwar years, permitted this utilization to jump 38 percent in only three years (1947 to 1950). This rapid rate of increase could not have been

CHART 4

Major Stages: Utilization of Steel Capacities*

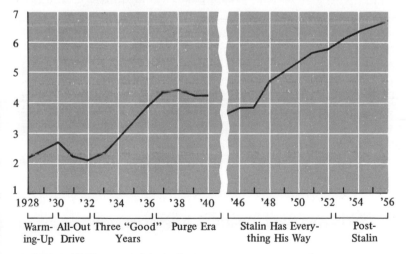

* Steel output per square meter of capacity of open hearths in tons in 24 hours. See **Economy of the USSR in 1956,** p. 68.

maintained, but the steel output per square meter in a twenty-four-hour period still increased by 22 percent in 1950–1955.

The percentage increase in the utilization of open hearths in 1950–1955 turned out somewhat smaller than in 1940–1950. The possibility of utilizing the reserves accumulated during the *Purge Era* and in the war years in this and similar ways helps to explain why the industrial growth of 1940–1950 makes in some respects a considerably more favorable picture than that of the subsequent five years.

The situation concerning the techniques of production of pig iron was similar to that of steel. Here, too, the period 1940–1950 turned out to be more favorable than could have been expected, owing to such a phenomenon as considerable unused capacities in 1940. The output of pig iron was enlarged by 29 percent in 1940–1950. The number of blast furnaces, however, went down from 99 to 92, while the cubic volume of all of them remained unchanged.[23] Thus the total increase in the output of pig iron in 1940–1950 was attained by a more intensive utilization of the volume of the blast furnaces.

Data such as those for open hearths and blast furnaces could be multiplied greatly. All of them reflect the major stages of Soviet economic development during the Great Industrialization Drive with about as great a force as the data for output. Any departures had special reasons. For example, labor productivity on railways continued to stagnate through 1934 (a growth of 3 percent per year in 1932–1934), but then it increased by 45 percent in three years (1934–1937). The behavior of labor productivity on railways in 1933 and 1934 merely reflected the lagging recovery of all rail transportation from the *All-Out Drive*. After a rapid growth in 1935–1937, the rise in labor productivity on railways was again equivalent only to exactly 3.3 percent during the last three years of the *Purge Era*.[24]

OVERALL RESULTS REEXAMINED

With the greatly divergent rates of growth during the various stages of the Great Industrialization Drive established, one can return to the question of why all the great sacrifices had produced relatively little.

To begin with, one has to deduct from the total period of the Great Industrialization Drive about seven years for World War II and the postwar recovery of output. Even less time would have been needed for this recovery than was actually spent if the Soviets had demobilized properly after the end of World War II. Actually, they continued to expend tremendous amounts on the armed forces all through the period *Stalin Has Everything His Way.* In spite of the handicap of large military expenses, recovery was rapid and the annual rates of growth remained very large until 1951. During the whole prewar period of thirteen years, from 1928 to 1940, we find only about five years, of which three were made up of the *Three "Good" Years,* really favorable from the Soviets' point of view. For agriculture, the *Three "Good" Years* were merely part of the recovery from former losses. Agricultural output stagnated in the remaining two of the five years.

But this also stands out clearly: In those periods when the Soviet machine operated with a reasonable smoothness, when major disturbances were absent, or when the Soviets succeeded in reducing the harmful effects of those disturbances, the large sector of the economy consisting of heavy industry, investment, and transportation made big strides ahead. It could not be otherwise in an economy powerfully geared to expansion by the large share of net investment in national income, the distribution of investment so as to foster particularly rapid expansion of the economic potential, and in view of all the other factors operating toward expansion. In these favorable periods even real national income as a whole expanded greatly, in spite of the lagging of farming and, consequently, of personal incomes.

XIV

One of the main concerns of the economic analysis of the Soviet system since the Second World War has been the accurate measurement of Soviet economic growth. This was particularly difficult to do for the dynamic changes of the Stalin era, for which the sources were scarce and misleading. Sophisticated methodologies for the interpretation of these sources were developed, particularly in the United States, and on this basis much more realistic assessments of Soviet development were made. These corrected the highly inflated official image of economic achievements from 1929 to 1953 that had resulted not only from the demands of propagandists, but also because of tendencies to distort and exaggerate that existed within the Soviet industrial administration. Dr. Stanley H. Cohn, Professor of Economics at the State University of New York, Binghamton campus, brings these measurements up to date in his article, and sets them within a historical as well as a comparative context. Pro-

fessor Cohn's article first appeared in The Development of the Soviet Economy *(New York, Praeger, 1968), a collection of studies published for the Institute for the Study of the USSR, and edited by Vladimir G. Treml. The article is here reprinted with permission from the institute and the author.*

STANLEY H. COHN

The Soviet Economy: Performance and Growth

The aim of this study is to evaluate quantitatively the performance of the Soviet economy during its first half century. Soviet economic development and the particular growth formula selected for it will be compared with the approaches and performances of the other major industrial powers, both concurrently and during stages of their development analogous to those of the USSR from 1928 to the present. The technical medium is national accounts analysis, both in terms of GNP (gross national product) and its main elements. In addition, the behavior of the production function of GNP will be comparatively analyzed as an indicator of economic efficiency. In order to provide historical perspective on Soviet performance, the legacies of the tsarist and reconstruction periods will be evaluated. Within the years of centralized planning, growth analysis will be differentiated by appropriate intervals that reflect significant changes in developmental policies. Though it is worthy of extensive separate treatment, the economic experience of World War II will not be evaluated as a distinct phenomenon, but will be looked at only as a phase in the long-term trend of the economy.

This examination of fifty years of Soviet growth and efficiency in economic performance is intended to complement John Hardt's evaluation of economic policy and organization. The theme common to both studies is that the path of Stalinist economic development diverged from the classical Western model by forcing the pace of industrialization at the expense of consumer welfare. As pointed out in Hardt's study, tsarist and reconstruction period (1921–1928) policies provided a basis from which a developmental "takeoff" could be launched, but did not limit the path of development to the one preferred by Stalin. Though the Stalinist solution yielded very rapid growth and ultimately proved itself by successfully providing economic support in time of war, it did so at the cost of inefficient use of resources and by means of postponing essential consumer and infrastructure investments. As long as growth could be sustained by massive infusion of manpower and capital, and as long as resources could be used in ways that did not contribute directly to national power objectives, this atypical path of development could be followed, and the economic institutions directing the effort could remain unaltered. However, toward the mid-fifties, as the pool of resources no longer appeared to be inexhaustible, the effect of their inefficient utilization on the growth process became more acute. This supply constraint was compounded by a proliferation of priority demands as the leadership became more aware of the identification of national power with consumer welfare objectives. The resulting need of belatedly directing resources toward consumer-oriented objectives has meant that the pattern of Soviet development has had to veer toward more traditional market economy paths and suggests that it is likely to do so to a greater degree in future years. At the same time, the leadership has been obliged to reconsider the suitability of the Stalinist organizational structure.

In terms of the general theme of promise and fulfillment, the record of the Soviet economy during its first half century has been one of empty promises in respect of the welfare of the Soviet citizen, but one of fulfillment, at high cost, in respect of the aims of expansion of national power. Through the stresses and strains of war, reconstruction, and intensive industrialization it was possible for a time, to absorb consumer dissatisfaction with pie-in-the-sky promises of rewards tomorrow for sacrifices today. Within the past decade, however, the regime has come to realize that considerably larger regard for consumer welfare is essential if traditional national power aims are to be realized. Much of the present ferment in the Soviet system is to be explained by the realization of the regime that a thoroughgoing reassessment of resource priorities and economic institutions is vital to the effectiveness of the Soviet economy.

THE TSARIST LEGACY

An appraisal of economic performance over the half century of Soviet hegemony would be incomplete without reference to the state of the economy in the tsarist period. In his book, *Economic Backwardness in Historical Perspective,* Professor A. Gerschenkron systematically demonstrates numerous parallels in the techniques and conditions of industrialization under both the tsars and the Soviets: stress on heavy industrial development to support military capabilities, extraction of surplus from agriculture through rigid controls, high rates of forced saving through consumption taxes, and alternations of periods of intensive development with periods of economic recuperation. Though Soviet leaders, by their ruthless command over resources, were able to generate growth much more rapidly and steadily than the tsars, this was a difference of degree rather than of basic orientation.

What were the accomplishments of the tsarist regime and what was the level of economic development in 1913? Gross national product increased at an average annual rate of about 2.5 percent between 1860 and 1913. Though respectable compared with the growth rates of the major industrial economies, this was, nonetheless, somewhat lower than the rate for Germany and considerably lower than that of Japan and the United States (see Table 1). In per capita terms, Russian growth averaged only 1 percent, a rate lower than that of any major power except Italy. As was true later in the Soviet era, growth was very uneven among economic sectors. Industrial output increased by about 5 percent annually,[1] or about double the GNP growth rate, whereas agricultural output advanced by only 2 percent, suggesting a per capita increase of no more than 0.5 percent.[2] Since exports rose rapidly, per capita domestic availabilities probably declined. Thus, large imports of foreign capital for industrialization, were, in part, financed by channeling food crops from domestic consumers for export.

TABLE 1

COMPARATIVE GNP GROWTH RATES PRIOR TO 1913
(average annual rates)

	Aggregate	Per Capita
Russia	2.5	1.0
United Kingdom	2.2	1.3
France	1.6	1.4
Germany	2.9	1.8
Italy	1.4	0.7
Japan	4.8	3.8
United States	4.3	2.2

Sources: Raymond Goldsmith, "The Economic Growth of Tsarist Russia, 1860–1913," *Economic Development and Cultural Change,* Chicago, April 1961, pp. 472–73; Angus Maddison, *Economic Growth in the West* (New York: Twentieth Century Fund, 1964), pp. 28 and 30; and *Historic Statistics of the Japanese Economy,* (Tokyo: Bank of Japan, 1962).

Note: Data relate to 1860–1913 for Russia, 1878 for Japan, and 1870–1913 for other countries.

As a result of this uneven development, the industrial position of Russia at the outbreak of World War I was higher than its general economic status warranted by historical analogy with other major economies. About 75 percent of the labor force was still in agriculture, and per capita income was perhaps no more than a fifth or sixth of that in the United States and a third of that in Western Europe.[3] Yet, according to official Soviet estimates, which, it seems, would be prone to minimize tsarist accomplishments, Russia ranked as the world's fifth industrial producer in 1913,[4] behind the United

States, Germany, the United Kingdom, and France. On a per capita basis, its position would have been less auspicious, placing it behind such small industrial powers as Belgium, Sweden, and Canada. Much of Russian industrial plant was foreign-owned and foreign-staffed, but the economy did possess the human and physical nucleus for an industrial civilization. Progress in agriculture had been slow, but there was the luxury of an agricultural surplus from which to extract savings required for development. Though considerably behind Western Europe in most respects, the Russian educational system did have almost three-quarters of the ratio of university students per capita as in the major West European countries (see Table 14). The illiteracy rate was, nevertheless, much higher than in the leading countries of the West. In the European part of the country, there existed an extensive rail network. Though the Russia of 1913 was backward by advanced market economy standards, it still possessed many of the essentials for a developmental "takeoff," and, in this respect, was far ahead of most of the underdeveloped Asian, African, and Latin-American countries of today.

PERIOD OF CONSOLIDATION OF THE REVOLUTION

In terms of the economy, the years between the Bolshevik seizure of power in 1917 and the inauguration of intensive planning in 1928 were characterized by disruptions of the Civil War period and efforts to restore the levels of output that prevailed before the onset of war and revolution. Inclusion of these years within the spectrum of the performance of the Soviet economic system is based on the thesis that seizure and consolidation of power are as much elements of the system's performance as of its ability to generate growth.

As a result of long years of economic chaos and recovery, the world position of the Soviet Union slipped behind the fifth place it had held in 1913.[5] It held sixth rank in production of iron ore and steel, seventh in production of coal, and eighth in production of electric power, cement, paper, and sulfuric acid. Had the growth rates that prevailed between 1900 and 1914 continued through 1928, the level of GNP would have been higher by 35 percent, of industrial output by 200 percent, and of agricultural output by 15 percent. Therefore, the cost of World War I, the Revolution, and the ensuing Civil War, by 1928, may be estimated at roughly fifteen years of growth.

However, on the eve of its explosive growth phase, the Soviet economy had progressed in two important respects. Industrial output had advanced little since 1913, but output per man-hour had risen by 37 percent, or over 2 percent as an annual average.[6] That this increase in productivity was largely compressed within the four or five years immediately preceding 1928 suggests that the system was capable of rapid assimilation of Western technology. A beginning had been made in the mass educational effort that distinguished Soviet policy in later years. During the 1920s, there was a widespread program of adult education to reduce illiteracy and to train a preindustrial population in modern technological skills. By 1928, enrollment in elementary and secondary schools had increased by more than 70 percent over the prewar level (pre-1939 boundaries).[7] The ratio of university students per 1000 of population was higher by half than in 1914 and equaled or exceeded comparable ratios in Western Europe (see Table 14).

On the eve of the Stalinist era, the Soviet economy had changed little in terms of development from 1913. Per capita income levels (based on 1964 prices) ranged between $200 and $350, or between a seventh and a fifth of the level of the United States (see App. I, Table I-1, this study), or a fifth and a third of that of the major West European economies. Almost 71 percent of the labor force was in agriculture (see Table 13), a proportion similar to that in present-day India, Korea, and Mainland China,[8] and to that of the United States and the principal countries of Continental Europe in the early years of the nineteenth century.[9]

Thus, in terms of factor availabilities and motivation on the part of the regime, the thesis that the Russian economy was ready for a takeoff is even more applicable to the Soviet economy of 1928 than of 1913. For, whereas the tsarist economic ministers had broken the path of pioneer industrialization and infrastructure investment, their Soviet successors possessed, in addition, advantages of growth motivation, intensive educational efforts, and an updated backlog of advanced Western technology.

STALINIST AND POST-STALINIST PERIODS

General growth performance. When the Stalinist program of intensive industrialization was introduced in 1928, the USSR had a national product approximately equal to that of the principal West European economies and about a fifth the size of that of the United States (see App. I, Table I–2, this study). Since its product was heavily agricultural in origin, its economic power position was relatively lower, as its industrial ranking illustrates.[10] In terms of GNP per capita, the USSR stood seventh among the major powers, at perhaps a seventh of the United States and a fourth of the West European level (see App. I, Table I–1, this study). In the fiftieth year of Soviet power, the USSR has become the world's second economy, some half the size of the United States and equal to the combined GNP of West Germany, France, and Italy. In per capita terms, the USSR has moved up to fifth position, reaching two-fifths the level of the United States and two-thirds that of Western Europe. Industrially, the Soviet economy is in second position, with about half the output of the United States and double that of the major West European powers.[11]

This achievement in growth has varied markedly from one period to another since 1928 (see Table 2). The rate between 1928 and 1937, during the most intensive, frenetic years of industrialization, averaged from 4.8 to 11.9 percent annually, depending on the weights selected (see Note to Table 2). Though these rates are high by international standards, and though they are certainly much above those of Western powers caught in the throes of depression (see Table 3), they are not historically unique. At similar or lower per capita levels, the United States approached the lower limit from 1870–1890,[12] and Japan equaled the lower limit from 1890–1900, surpassing it between 1920 and 1930.[13] After 1937, the rising specter of Hitler forced the Soviet leadership to shift resources into armaments on a massive scale. As a result, the growth rate fell drastically, to 3.6 percent per year between 1937 and 1940. The destructive effects of World War II on the economy meant, in effect, that there was no net increase in GNP between 1941 and

TABLE 2

GROWTH RATES OF SOVIET GROSS NATIONAL PRODUCT

(*Selected periods. average annual rates*)

	GNP		GNP per Employed Person		
	Aggregate	Per Capita	Man-Year	Man-Hour	GNP per Capital Unit
1860–1883	2.25	0.75	—	—	—
1883–1900	2.75	1.25	—	—	—
1900–1913	2.20	1.10	—	—	—
1913–1928	0.50	−0.10	—	—	—
1928–1937 [1]	4.8–11.9	3.8–10.8	1.7–7.9	1.8–8.0	−0.1–6.1
1937–1940	3.60	0.70	0.8	−0.4	−4.5
1940–1950 [2]	1.8–2.2	2.6–3.2	1.0–1.3	1.3–2.4	1.3–2.4
1950–1958	7.10	5.20	5.3	5.8	−1.2
1958–1964	5.30	3.50	3.3	4.7	−3.7

Sources: Raymond Goldsmith, "The Economic Growth of Tsarist Russia, 1860–1913," *Economic Development and Cultural Change,* April 1961, pp. 470–73; Simon S. Kuznets, *Economic Development and Cultural Change,* October 1956, p. 81; Frank Lorimer, *The Population of the Soviet Union* (New York: League of Nations, 1946), p. 135; Abram Bergson, *The Real National Income of Soviet Russia Since 1928* (Cambridge, Mass.: Harvard University Press, 1961), pp. 210, 217, 226, and 232; Stanley H. Cohn, "Soviet Growth Retardation: Trends in Resource Availability and Efficiency," *New Directions in the Soviet Economy,* U.S. Congress, Joint Economic Committee, Government Printing Office, Washington, D.C., 1966, pp. 105 and 115; Abram Bergson, "National Income," *Economic Trends in the Soviet Union,* ed. Abram Bergson and Simon Kuznets (Cambridge, Mass.: Harvard University Press, 1963), p. 4; and *Narodnoe khozyaistvo SSSR v 1964 godu* [The economy of the USSR in 1964], (Moscow, 1965), p. 68.

Note: The dilemma of selecting an appropriate base period in which to measure economic trends constantly bedevils the analyst in the use of time series. This is the familiar index-number problem in which there must be a choice between equally appropriate sets of relative prices or outputs over the period being measured, the former variable in the case of GNP indexes. The more rapidly the structure of an economy is evolving, or the longer the period under consideration, the greater will be the divergence between the results obtained from early and late period weights. Since there is a tendency in a progressive economy for relative price trends to vary inversely with output trends, early year price weights will yield a

1948.[14] In the postwar years, national product increased at an average annual rate of 7.1 percent between 1950 and 1958, but declined to a rate of 5.3 percent between 1958 and 1964. Growth during these years was not uniquely high among large, developed economies: most market economies have experienced growth surges

---

faster growth rate than later year weights, as the products which show the most rapid growth trends carry higher prices in earlier years. The Soviet economy was industrializing very rapidly from 1928 to 1937, so the choice of price weights markedly influences the GNP indexes. Since neither set of weights is conceptually superior to the other, the rate of growth of output has been expressed as a range, with the limits representing later and early (1937 and 1928) weights, respectively. The same observations apply to the period 1940–1950, in which both 1937 and 1950 price weights have been used. In the postwar period, structural changes have been more gradual, so only a single set of price weights (1959) have been used.

The problems of intertemporal comparisons are further complicated by those of an interspatial nature in the expression of aggregate and per capita GNP time series in common dollar terms (see App. I, Tables I-1 and I-2, this study). If the GNP of any economy is revalued in terms of the relative prices prevailing in any other economy, its relative national product will be overstated, i.e., if the GNP of country A is valued in prices of country B, the magnitude of country A's GNP relative to that of country B will be inflated. This phenomenon is produced by the inverse relations which exist between prices and output. In the hypothetical example, sectors with high output in country A would be valued at high country B prices rather than lower A prices, and sectors of relatively low output would be valued at low B prices rather than higher A prices.

The degree of divergence in relative price patterns and output structures is the greater, the wider the difference in stages of development of the two economies. The choice of an appropriate conversion ratio between the prices of a relatively advanced and a relatively backward economy is analagous to that in a GNP index between prices of an early and a late period. For purposes of simplification, the conversion ratios selected between foreign and dollar prices are single values—the geometric means of foreign and dollar prices. While not inherently preferable to some other conversion ratios, the geometric means do have the advantage of consistency. They reflect more accurately the relative purchasing power of a country's currency than do official rates of exchange.

[1] Lower limit based on valuation of ruble factor cost in 1937 prices; upper limit on valuation in 1928 prices.

[2] Lower limit based on valuation of ruble factor cost in 1950 prices; upper limit on valuation in 1937 prices.

TABLE 3

COMPARATIVE TRENDS IN GROSS NATIONAL PRODUCT

(average annual rates)

	Aggregate			
	1913–1964	*1928–1964*	*1950–1958*	*1958–1964*
USSR	2.1	4.4–6.3	7.1	5.3
France	1.9	2.1	4.4	5.4
West Germany	2.8	3.7	7.6	5.8
Italy	2.6	2.8	5.6	6.1
United Kingdom	2.1	2.3	2.4	3.9
Japan	3.6	4.3	6.1	12.0
United States	3.2	3.4	2.9	4.4
	Per Capita			
USSR	1.1	3.3–5.4	5.2	3.5
France	1.6	1.8	3.5	4.0
West Germany	1.8	2.6	6.4	4.6
Italy	1.9	2.2	5.0	5.4
United Kingdom	1.6	1.8	1.9	3.1
Japan	3.1 [1]	2.6 [2]	4.8	11.0
United States	1.4	1.4	1.2	2.7
	Per Man-Hour			
USSR	—	2.8–4.4	5.8	4.7
France	1.6	1.9–2.1	3.9	4.4
West Germany	0.9	2.8–2.9	5.9	5.4
Italy	1.9	2.8–3.2	3.9	5.5
United Kingdom	1.7	1.9–2.0	2.0	3.5
Japan	—	2.5 [2]	3.2	11.0
United States	2.4	2.2–2.4	2.4	2.2

Sources: Raymond Goldsmith, "The Economic Growth of Tsarist Russia, 1860–1913," *Economic Development and Cultural Change,* Chicago, April 1961, pp. 470–73; Simon S. Kuznets, *Economic Development and Cultural Change,* October 1956, p. 81; Frank Lorimer, *The Population of the Soviet Union* (New York: League of Nations, 1946), p. 135; Abram Bergson, *The Real National Income of Soviet Russia Since 1928* (Cambridge, Mass.: Harvard University Press, 1961), pp. 210, 217, 226, and 232; Stanley H. Cohn, "Soviet Growth Retardation: Trends in Resource Availability and

since 1950. In the earlier postwar period, Soviet growth was less than that of West Germany, a country with a considerably higher per capita income; in the latter period, less than both West Germany and France, economies with higher per capita incomes. In the latter period, it also fell behind Italy, a country with a slightly lower per capita income, and far behind Japan, a country with 80 percent of the Soviet per capita income level. This slowdown in growth has been a major concern of the leadership as the golden anniversary of the revolution has approached.

Efficiency of growth performance. If the criterion of performance is taken to be some measure of efficiency in the use of resources, such as productivity of labor or capital, the record of the Soviet economy since 1928 is considerably less noteworthy. Output per man-hour in the period 1928–1937 rose at an average annual rate of 1.8 to 8 percent and declined in the period 1937–1940 by 0.4 percent. Within the perspective of international experience, all the major Continental European economies as well as that of the United States considerably exceeded the lower limit of man-hour productivity advancement during the decades of the nineteenth century in which their per capita income equaled that of the Soviet Union between 1928 and 1937 (see Table 4). This relatively poor productivity record is explained by the prodigious infusion of manpower into urban occupations during the Stalinist years. Employment rose by 3.7 percent annually from 1928 to 1937 and by 3 percent annually from 1937 to 1940 (see Table 5). No other economy

Efficiency," *New Directions in the Soviet Economy,* U.S. Congress, Joint Economic Committee, Government Printing Office, Washington, D.C., 1966, pp. 105 and 115; Abram Bergson, "National Income," *Economic Trends in the Soviet Union,* ed. Abram Bergson and Simon Kuznets (Cambridge, Mass.: Harvard University Press), 1963, p. 4; Central Statistical Administration, *Narodnoe khozyaistovo SSSR v 1964 godu,* (Moscow, 1965), p. 68; Angus Maddison, *Economic Growth in the West* (New York: Twentieth Century Fund, 1964), pp. 28, 232–33; Michael Kaser, "Education and Economic Progress," *The Economics of Education,* ed. E. A. G. Robinson and J. E. Vaizey (New York: St. Martin's Press, 1966), p. 169; and *Historical Statistics of the Japanese Economy,* Tokyo: Bank of Japan, 1962).

[1] Initial year: 1910.

[2] Initial year: 1930.

TABLE 4
COMPARATIVE HISTORICAL TRENDS IN GROWTH OF
GNP PER MAN-HOUR
(*average annual rates*)

	Period	Rate
USSR	1928–1937	1.3–3.0
	1937–1940	− 0.4
France	1880–1890	2.5
	1890–1900	2.2
Germany	1871–1880	2.5
	1880–1890	2.4
	1890–1900	1.9
United Kingdom	1880–1890	3.8
	1890–1900	1.2
United States	1871–1890	2.7
	1890–1900	2.2
Italy	1900–1913	2.6

Sources: Raymond Goldsmith, "The Economic Growth of Tsarist Russia, 1860–1913," *Economic Development and Cultural Change,* Chicago, April 1961, pp. 470–73; Simon S. Kuznets, *Economic Development and Cultural Change,* October 1956, p. 81; Frank Lorimer, *The Population of the Soviet Union* (New York: League of Nations, 1946), p. 135; Abram Bergson, *The Real National Income of Soviet Russia Since 1928* (Cambridge, Mass.: Harvard University Press, 1961), pp. 210, 217, 226, and 232; Stanley H. Cohn, "Soviet Growth Retardation: Trends in Resource Availability and Efficiency," *New Directions in the Soviet Economy,* U.S. Congress, Joint Economic Committee, Government Printing Office, Washington, D.C., 1966, pp. 105 and 115; Abram Bergson, "National Income," *Economic Trends in the Soviet Union,* ed. Abram Bergson and Simon Kuznets (Cambridge, Mass.: Harvard University Press, 1963), p. 4; Central Statistical Administration, *Narodnoe khozyaistvo SSSR v 1964 godu* (Moscow, 1965), p. 68; and Angus Maddison, *Economic Growth in the West* (New York: Twentieth Century Fund, 1964), p. 232.

Note: For derivation of historical analogues see app. I, this study.

TABLE 5

COMPARATIVE HISTORICAL RATES OF INCREASE IN LABOR FORCE
(*average annual rates*)

	Period	Rate
USSR	1928–1937	3.7
	1937–1940	3.0
United Kingdom	1821–1831 to 1851–1861	0.9
	1851–1861 to 1871–1881	0.7
Germany	1851–1855 to 1871–1875	0.7
	1871 to 1886–1895	1.4
	1886–1895 to 1907	1.7
United States	1874–1889	2.8
	1889–1914	2.4
Japan	1883–1887 to 1903–1907	1.0
	1893–1897 to 1913–1917	0.6
	1918–1922 to 1938–1942	0.9
Italy	1861–1881	0.2
	1881–1901	0.2
	1901–1921	0.3
	1921–1936	0.3

Source: Simon S. Kuznets, *Economic Development and Cultural Change,* Chicago, July 1961, pt. II, pp. 34, 35.

has even remotely matched the Soviet rate of labor influx at comparable periods of development.

Such a rapid increase in employment without a proportional increase in population was achieved through a rapid jump in the participation ratio—that is, the labor force as a percent of the work-age population (15 to 64). This went from 56.8 percent in 1928 to 70.1 percent in 1937 (see Table 6). Within the periods for which statistics have been compiled, no other economy has experienced so rapid a rise in the participation ratio. In fact, since 1913, the ratio has fallen in most West European countries.[15] The increase in the ratio between 1928 and 1940 is mainly a function of the shift from underemployed agriculture to fully employed urban occupations, whereas in the postwar years, it is a function of the rising proportion of females in the labor force.[16] In other words, the rapid rise in employment, in full-time labor equivalents, was a function of the unusually rapid transfer of manpower out of agriculture, a phenomenon to be analyzed at a later point in the discussion.

TABLE 6

TRENDS IN THE LABOR PARTICIPATION RATIO IN THE USSR

	Work-Age Population	Employed Population	Participation Ratio
1928	87,000,000	49,400,000	56.8%
1937	98,000,000	68,700,000	70.1%
1950	115,100,000	82,500,000	71.7%
1958	133,900,000	94,800,000	70.8%
1964	140,100,000	106,600,000	76.1%

Sources: Abram Bergson, *The Real National Income of Soviet Russia since 1928* (Cambridge, Mass.: Harvard University Press, 1961), pp. 442, 443; James Brackett (working paper), "Estimated Population of the USSR by Single Years and Sex," Model 3, Foreign Manpower Division, Bureau of Census, Washington, D.C.; and Murray Feshbach, "Manpower in the USSR," U.S. Congress, Joint Economic Committee, *New Directions in the Soviet Economy,* (Washington, D.C., Government Printing Office, 1966), p. 746.

After the powerful upsurge of the thirties, until 1958, the participation ratio, excluding the war years, remained on a plateau. The delayed impact of low wartime and early postwar birth rates on the rate of entry of youth into employment became evident in the late fifties. As an offset to this constraint, the regime accelerated the flow of youth into employment by cessation of the trend toward universal secondary education and by inducing an even greater ratio of remunerative employment for women. By 1964, the Soviet participation ratio was the highest among the major industrial powers, and probably it cannot be increased further.[17]

During the postwar years, the Soviet economy exhibited considerably greater efficiency in use of manpower resources. Its rise in man-hour productivity compared favorably with the performances in other major economies, though slipping in both rate and rank after 1958 (see Table 3). This great improvement in labor productivity is to be explained, at least in part, by a much slower rate of increase in employment, 1.7 percent annually from 1950 to 1958, and 2 percent annually between 1958 and 1964 (see Table 7). If the sharp reduction in the length of the work week after 1958 is taken into account, the manpower input increased at a rate of only 0.6 percent. The impact of demographic losses in the wartime period on the rate at which school graduates entered the labor force was felt during these years. In order to sustain growth, it was necessary to substitute other productive factors for the depleted labor reservoir. Necessity, of course, does not guarantee success, but through a combination of maintaining a high rate of capital input (see Table 7) and reaping the return on a more highly educated labor force as well as on the intangible improvements to efficiency that must have accrued from the more relaxed atmosphere following Stalin's death, the economy managed to improve its labor-productivity performance greatly (see Table 2), with some deceleration after 1958.

Whereas the Soviet economy was wasteful of labor resources during the 1930s, it has been wasteful of physical capital throughout the entire period since 1928. With the exception of the atypical war and recovery decade of 1940–1950, the rate of change in inputs of fixed capital per unit of output has been negative—that is, the marginal capital output ratio has been rising (see Table 2). Historical estimates for the United States and postwar estimates for Western Europe indicate that such a persistent negative trend is probably unique.[18] The expectation of a decline, or at least a relatively constant marginal capital output ratio, would appear to be particularly applicable in an economy like the Soviet one, with extensive technological borrowing possibilities and the presence of a large corps of trained engineers, scientists, and managers to assimilate the technology. Postwar experience in Western Europe, where, unlike in the USSR, capital output ratios have tended to remain low, below historical trends, supports this generalization.[19]

This persistent inefficiency in utilization of fixed capital may be explained by the rapid rate of increase in capital stock (see Table 7). Except during the disrupted decade of the 1940s, incre-

TABLE 7

GROWTH RATES OF EMPLOYMENT, FIXED CAPITAL, AND
EDUCATIONAL STOCK IN THE USSR
(*Average annual rates*)

	Employment		Fixed Capital	Educational Stock
	Man-Years	Man-Hours		
1928–1937	3.7	3.6	10.4–12.0	11.2–11.8 *
1937–1940	3.0	3.8	8.1	
1940–1950	0.3	0.6	− 0.2–0.5	4.8–5.0
1950–1958	1.7	1.2	8.3	7.1
1958–1964	2.0	0.6	9.4	4.7

Sources: See App. II, this study.
* These figures are for 1926–1939.

ments to capital stock, exclusive of retirements, have not been less than at an annual rate of 8 percent. During the middle nineteenth century, the comparable rate for the United States ranged between 4.5 and 4.8 percent.[20] According to conventional economic theory, any tendency toward diminishing returns ought to have been offset by the technological advance embodied in new capital invested. However, in the Soviet case, this expectation may have been undercut by the very high rate of increments to capital stock, as evidenced by high capital-labor ratios (see Table 8). Substitution of capital for labor was especially prominent after 1958. Incremental fixed capital-labor ratios in the United States in the nineteenth century were far lower than any experienced by the Soviets, except during the atypical war and recovery decade.[21]

Undoubtedly, the peculiar nature of the Soviet system of pricing played a role in the disproportionate infusions of capital through the absence of an interest charge. In a market economy, with the imposition of interest charges, diminishing returns to, or marginal productivity of, capital investment would become evident long before attaining the rate of investment reached by the Soviet economy. This condition would have been particularly relevant for the 1930s, a period in which scarcity of capital would have led to very high implicit rates. Bent as it was on fostering rapid industrial-

TABLE 8

INCREMENTAL CAPITAL-LABOR RATIOS:

AVERAGE ANNUAL RATES

(*increase in fixed capital, net of retirements,*
divided by increases in man-hours)

USSR		United States	
1929–1937	2.9–3.3	1879–1889	1.5
1937–1940	2.1	1889–1899	2.2
1940–1950	0.3–0.7	1899–1909	1.7
1950–1958	6.9	1909–1919	2.1
1958–1964	15.7	1919–1929	2.9

Sources: See Table 7, this study, for respective rates of growth for the USSR. Simon S. Kuznets, *Capital in the American Economy,* National Bureau of Economic Research (Princeton, N.J.: Princeton University Press, 1961), p. 64; and John W. Kendrick, *Productivity Trends in the United States,* National Bureau of Economic Research (Princeton, N.J.: Princeton University Press, 1961), pp. 308–10, 328–31.

ization, the regime may have ignored the rising cost of a high rate of investment, but at least it would have possessed an adequate criterion for determining an appropriate investment ratio and for making choices among investment alternatives.

Total factor productivity. The efficiency of the economy is best measured by including the maximum number of productive factors in the estimating equation. In this way, unknown influences on growth are minimized. The multifactor model used in this study combines manpower (man-hours), fixed capital (net of retirements, gross of depreciation), agricultural land, and productive livestock. For the postwar period, educational stock has been added to the other four factors (see Table 9).

The performance of the economy between 1928 and 1937 is obscured by the widely varying results that alternative price weights yield. If 1937 weights are employed, there is little increase in productivity; with 1929 weights, the rate of increase is 7.9 percent. In the armament years, from 1937 to 1940, output per unit of combined inputs was slightly negative. In the early fifties, combined fac-

TABLE 9

SOVIET GROSS NATIONAL PRODUCT PER UNIT OF COMBINED INPUTS
(*Average annual rates*)

	Four-Factor Model	*Five-Factor Model*
1928–1937	1.0–7.9	—
1937–1940	− 0.2	—
1940–1950	1.2–1.6	—
1950–1958	3.9	3.4
1958–1964	2.3	2.0

Sources: See App. II, this study.

tor productivity sharply increased for reasons previously noted in the discussion of labor productivity. Since 1958, the rate of growth in combined factor productivity has decelerated, with stagnation in agriculture and falling productivity in industry.

What has been the relative importance of the increases in factor inputs and of the productivity of these inputs for Soviet growth? Some perspective may be gained on this question by comparing the historical growth experience of the Soviet Union and the United States (see Table 10). With the exception of the period 1950–1958, which was influenced by the liberalizing effects of de-Stalinization, Soviet growth has depended more on inputs of factors than on the increased efficiency of their utilization. In the twentieth century, in the United States, factor productivity has been considerably more important than increases in volume of factors, though the Soviet-type pattern was prevalent in the last three decades of the nineteenth century. The significance of parallel experience during years of comparable levels of per capita income must be left for further investigation.

It would appear that any margin of growth that the Soviet economy has achieved over the United States can be entirely explained in terms of factor inputs rather than factor productivity.[22] Such a comparison casts doubt on the efficiency of Soviet planning, as distinguished from its ability to command productive resources.

Resource allocation trends and policies. Having reviewed trends in Soviet growth and the efficiency of the growth process, let

TABLE 10

GROWTH CONTRIBUTIONS OF FACTOR INPUTS AND
COMBINED FACTOR PRODUCTIVITY
(*average annual rates*)

	Inputs	Productivity
USSR		
1928–1937	3.7	1.0–7.9
1937–1940	3.8	− 0.2
1940–1950	0.6	1.2–1.6
1950–1958	3.2	3.9
1958–1964	2.9	2.3
United States		
1869–1878 to 1899–1908	3.0	1.5
1899–1908 to 1929	1.5	1.8
1929–1948	0.4	2.2
1950–1957	1.2	2.4
1957–1963	0.8	2.4

Sources: See App. II, this study.

Note: Figures for inputs represent weighted values for man-hours, fixed capital, farmland, and productive livestock. Productivity equals index of GNP divided by index of inputs.

us now turn to an analysis of the resource policies that facilitated this performance. In general terms, rapid growth occurred because the regime could channel a large share of national product into investment. This policy, of course, meant that a relatively small share of national product could be used to satisfy consumer needs, a share that was further reduced as defense claims burgeoned after 1937 (see Table 11).

Even in 1928, before the progressive squeezing of the consumer, aimed at directing resources into growth, and later, additionally, into defense, the share of GNP allocated for purposes of private consumption was low by the historical standards set in other major economies at similar levels of per capita GNP. Abram Bergson's estimate of 64.7 percent compares with 83.0 percent for the

TABLE 11
TRENDS IN ALLOCATION OF SOVIET GNP AT FACTOR COST
(percent of total)

	1928	1937	1940	1950	1955	1964
Private Consumption	64.7	52.5	51.0	51.0	50.6	46.5
Communal Consumption [1]	5.1	10.5	9.9	8.0	8.2	9.4
Investment [2]	25.0	25.9	19.2	23.0	25.3	30.5
Defense [3]	2.5	7.9	16.1	13.3	13.0	11.3
Other [4]	2.7	3.2	3.8	4.7	2.9	2.3

Sources: Abram Bergson, *The Real National Income of Soviet Russia since 1928* (Cambridge, Mass.: Harvard University Press, 1961), p. 237; Stanley H. Cohn, "Soviet Growth Retardation: Trends in Resource Availability and Efficiency," *New Directions in the Soviet Economy,* U.S. Congress, Joint Economic Committee, Government Printing Office, Washington, D.C., pp. 129, 132.

Note: The prewar and postwar proportions of GNP should not be directly compared with one another, except as general orders of magnitude, because of methodological differences. The first difference concerns adjustment of market prices to factor cost. The prewar Bergson estimates, after deduction of turnover taxes from the prices of farm products and consumer goods, do not include an allowance for agricultural rent; whereas the postwar estimates, based on the 1955 national accounts constructed by Morris Bornstein, include an estimate of land rent. The Bergson estimates value farm income in kind at average realized farm prices, while the original Bornstein estimates use the higher valuation of weighted state retail and collective farm market prices. Lastly, the Bergson estimates compute investment as a residual between calculated total incomes and expenditures, while the Bornstein estimates compute investment directly from official estimates and assumptions as to unspecified state budgetary expenditures of an investment nature. The net effect of these methodological differences is to give private consumption a lower proportion and the other end uses, particularly investment, higher proportions in the Bergson than in the Bornstein calculations. For further analysis of differences in methodology, see Abram Bergson's source noted below; Morris Bornstein and Associates, *Soviet National Accounts for 1955,* Center for Russian Studies (Ann Arbor, Mich.: University of Michigan, 1961); and Stanley H. Cohn, "Comment on 2½ Percent and All That," *Soviet Studies,* Glasgow, Scotland, January 1965.

[1] Outlays for public education, health, and science.

[2] Fixed investment and inventories.

[3] Budgetary category of defense, 1928–1940; budgetary plus estimates of defense expenditures under other portions of state budget, 1950–1964.

[4] Largely composed of governmental administrative expenditures.

United Kingdom in 1860–1869, 82.6 percent for Germany in 1851–1860, 79.7 percent for the United States in 1867–1878, 84.1 percent for Italy in 1891–1900, and 82.0 percent for Japan in 1931–1940.[23] Equally without historical precedent is the rapidity with which the proportionate claim of private consumption on GNP declined, reaching a share of 52.5 percent in 1937. No other major economy approached this low proportion in peacetime until Japan did in the late 1950s.

The initial diversion of GNP from private consumption went into investment. Beyond this initial surge of investment, there was little further increase in the GNP share allocated to investment through 1937, and a considerable drop thereafter, as defense requirements loomed ever larger. Instead, through 1937, there was considerable emphasis on communal, at the expense of private, consumption, with a subsequent leveling off in the communal share until the outbreak of war. This trend reflected in particular the massive educational effort, and can be quite properly evaluated as an ingredient of growth policy: large-scale physical investment could not yield returns without concomitant investment in human capital.

Consumption trends. The process of economic development is normally accompanied by a decline in the share of private consumption. The rate at which this decline takes place and whether this decline is absolute or relative on a per capita basis reflect the changes in consumer welfare during the development period. The 12-percent reduction in the share of private consumption in GNP required only 9 years in the USSR. In Germany, it took 40 years; in the United Kingdom and Italy, 50; in the United States, 30; and it was not attained in Japan until the 1950s.[24]

Another way of gaining perspective on Soviet consumption policy is to compare rates of change in per capita private consumption levels in other major economies during periods when they had similiar levels of per capita income (see Table 12). Depending on the base-year prices used, Soviet per capita private consumption either declined steadily from 1928 through 1941, and very drastically during the war, or showed a moderate increase between 1928 and 1937, and declined during the following three years. If there was an increase, it was more nominal than real, as much of it would reflect the cost of urbanization, that is, the commercial purchase of ser-

TABLE 12

COMPARATIVE TRENDS IN PER CAPITA PRIVATE CONSUMPTION
(*average annual rates*)

	Period	Rate
USSR	1928–1937	− 1.0–2.6
	1937–1940	− 1.0
	1940–1944	− 8.1– − 8.9
	1944–1950	9.5
	1950–1958	5.3
	1958–1964	2.2
United Kingdom	1880–1889 to 1890–1899	1.7
	1890–1899 to 1900–1909	0.6
	1950–1958	1.6
	1958–1964	2.8
Germany	1851–1860 to 1861–1870	1.9
	1861–1870 to 1871–1880	1.4
	1871–1880 to 1881–1890	0.8
	1881–1890 to 1891–1900	1.8
	1950–1958	6.2
	1958–1964	4.2
Italy	1861–1870 to 1871–1880	0.1
	1871–1880 to 1881–1890	—
	1881–1890 to 1891–1900	1.2
	1950–1958	3.5
	1958–1964	5.7
United States	1869–1879	4.2
	1879–1889	2.0
	1889–1898 to 1899–1908	2.9
	1950–1958	1.1
	1958–1964	2.6

Sources: Abram Bergson, *The Real National Income of Soviet Russia Since 1928* (Cambridge, Mass.: Harvard University Press, 1961), p. 236; Stanley H. Cohn, "Soviet Growth Retardation: Trends in Resource Availability and Efficiency," *New Directions in the Soviet Economy,* U.S. Congress, Joint Economic Committee, Government Printing Office, Washington, D.C., 1966, p. 107; and Simon S. Kuznets, "The Share and Structure of Consumption," *Economic Development and Cultural Change,* Chicago, July 1961, pp. 80, 82, 86.

vices and commodities formerly supplied by the consumer himself in a rural environment. In no case did consumption decline in other economies at a similar stage, nor were increases so largely reflective of urbanization costs, because shifts out of agriculture were more gradual.

In contrast, the rate of increase in communally supplied consumption was very large, averaging around 15 percent annually in this period. Defense claims after 1937 halted further progress in this sphere until after the war.

The postwar period, particularly the years following Stalin's death, was the only time in Soviet history in which the consumer enjoyed a continued, rapid advance in his living standards. Between 1950 and 1958 the Soviet economy distinguished itself among major economies in growth of per capita consumption. A primary factor was the upsurge in agricultural output. The year 1958 marked the end of this trend, with the onset of agricultural stagnation. Since 1958, per capita increases in private consumption have been less in the USSR than in any other major industrial nation.

Investment policy. Ultimately, the rapid rate of industrialization in the USSR after 1928 was a function of the high rate of investment. As the ratio of private consumption to GNP was unusually low in terms of the historical experience of more advanced economies, so the ratio of investment was unusually high. Customarily, low income economies cannot invest a large portion of their national product, as consumption cannot be easily diverted from a population living close to the margin of subsistence. Through its close control over resources, especially in agriculture, the state was able to sequester the savings that enabled the economy to enjoy a high rate of investment.

No other major economy—in historical periods in which per capita income was similar to that of the Soviet Union in 1928–1937—has been able to invest anything like the quarter of GNP that the USSR did in these years. In the middle of the nineteenth century, the British economy was able to divert only about an eighth of GNP for this purpose; the German economy, only about a seventh. By the end of the nineteenth century, the German economy was able to contribute as much as a fifth of GNP for investment; the Italian economy, early in the twentieth century, a seventh; the Japanese economy, in the 1920s and 1930s, only as much as a sixth; and the United States, in the 1870s and 1880s, with a higher level of per capita income than the USSR in 1928, a fifth.[25] It was only in the 1950s that some large market economies began to approach the high Soviet investment ratios, and none of these has a relative defense burden comparable to that of the USSR.

The ability of the Soviet economy to devote so large a share of national product to investment at low per capita income levels appears all the more unique if it is realized that the entire burden of saving occurred within national boundaries. In contrast, other economies at the stage of development of the USSR in 1928–1940 were able to draw on capital inflows from more highly developed nations. The United States was partially dependent upon foreign sources of financing until the 1890s. Foreign sources provided about 11 percent of its net capital formation in the 1870s and probably considerably more earlier.[26] Japan was heavily dependent on foreign investment until World War I and Italy for most of the period under review. Such dependence was particularly important for countries like Canada, Australia, and Argentina.[27]

Another distinguishing characteristic of Soviet investment has been its concentration in growth-supporting sectors. The most graphic illustration of this propensity has been the unusually small portion of fixed investment devoted to housing. Between 1928 and 1940 the proportion was only 15.5 percent,[28] compared with around 25 percent for the United States in the 1870s and 1880s, a third for Germany from 1851–1890, a quarter to a third for Italy from 1861 to 1915, and a quarter for Japan from 1887 to 1906.[29] The small Soviet proportion is even more significant, given the rapid rate of urbanization in these years. The combination of circumstances led to a drastic decline in housing standards, with per capita availabilities falling from 5.8 square meters in 1928 to 4.6 in 1937 [30] and only increasing to 6.4 in 1964.[31]

During the period of relaxation following Stalin's death, the share of housing in fixed investment increased to around 21 percent, just under the proportions for the United Kingdom, Germany, and Italy.[32] However, in the investment productivity constraint that developed after 1958, the regime chose to sacrifice housing in favor of an accelerated rate of productive investment. As a result, the housing share fell to less than 20 percent, considerably below the proportions for all major economies other than the United Kingdom. In fact, there was an absolute decline in the annual volume of housing investment from 1959 to 1964.[33]

Lack of available data precludes historical comparison of distribution of fixed investment on a more disaggregated basis, other than bilaterally between the United States and the Soviet Union. Using the same historical time analogues, Norman Kaplan has demonstrated the Soviet investment in the period 1928–1940 was much more heavily oriented toward industry and agriculture and correspondingly less toward trade and services than in the United States in the middle of the nineteenth century.[34] He also indicates that Soviet industrial investment was much more directed toward the metallurgical and machinery sectors.[35] In the postwar period, Soviet investment orientation toward industry and agriculture has been conspicuously high among the leading economies, with relative neglect for the service sectors and transportation.[36]

Structural transformation. The rapid industrialization of the Soviet economy after 1928 was accomplished, as noted earlier, by heavy infusions of manpower and capital into productive enterprises. This process was accompanied by a rapid transformation in the structure of the system. In terms of the proportion of the labor force employed in agriculture, the Soviet economy of 1928 was far less industrialized than other major market economies at comparable levels of per capita income (see Table 13). The forced transfer of labor from farm to urban occupations, through collectivization and organized recruitment, reduced the proportion of the labor force employed in agriculture by 20 percentage points.

The shift was far more rapid than in the large market economies, with shifts of comparable proportions requiring 60 years in France, 65 in Italy, 40 in the United States, and 30 to 35 in Japan (see Table 13). Yet, because of the huge size of the farm population in the Soviet Union initially and the rapid increase in population as a whole, agricultural employment actually increased by 2.4 million between 1928 and 1937 and by another 4 million between 1937 and 1940. The latter increase is largely explained by the territorial acquisitions of the Soviet Union in 1939–1940.

The unbalanced nature of Soviet growth between 1928 and 1940 is reflected in divergent sectoral productivity trends. In terms

TABLE 13

AGRICULTURAL EMPLOYMENT AS PROPORTION OF TOTAL EMPLOYMENT

	Year	*Proportion*		*Year*	*Proportion*
USSR	1928	71	Japan	1897–1902	70
	1937	54		1907–1912	63
	1940	51		1920	54
	1950	46		1940	42
	1958	41	Germany	1882	42
	1964	34		1895	36
France	1788	75		1907	34
	1845	62		1925	30
	1866	52		1939	27
	1886	48	England and	1841	23
	1906	43	Wales	1861	19
	1926	39		1881	12
Italy	1861	62		1901	9
	1881	57	United States	1870	50
	1901	59		1890	42
	1921	56		1900	37
	1936	48		1920	27
Japan	1877–1882	83		1940	17
	1887–1892	76			

Sources: Abram Bergson, *The Real National Income of Soviet Russia since 1928* (Cambridge, Mass.: Harvard University Press, 1961), p. 443; Murray Feshbach, "Manpower in the USSR," and Stanley H. Cohn, "Soviet Growth Retardation: Trends in Resource Availability and Efficiency," *New Directions in the Soviet Economy,* U.S. Congress, Joint Economic Committee, Government Printing Office, Washington, D.C., pp. 112 and 786; and Simon S. Kuznets, "Industrial Distribution of National Product and Labor Force," *Economic Development and Cultural Change,* Chicago, July 1957, pp. 84, 85, 88, 89, 91, 93.

of man-hours, industrial labor productivity increased within an average annual rate range of 3.1–10.4 from 1928 to 1937 and at an average annual rate of 2.7 from 1937 to 1940.[37] In contrast, in agriculture, the rise in employment was coupled with a decline in production,[38] implying, of course, a fall in productivity. Historically, especially since World War I, in market economies the transfer of labor out of agriculture has been accompanied by rising labor productivity trends at rates not too different from those of industry.[39] In no instance has agricultural productivity declined. Though the rapid reduction in the share of employment in agriculture in the Soviet Union and the apparent decline in production were not functionally related, they both stemmed from the drastic collectivization campaign, with its emasculation of incentives and wholesale destruction of working and productive livestock.

The lack of balance between industrial and agricultural development is a corollary of the policy of suppression of consumption in favor of investment. Within the aggregate of industrial production, output of industrial raw materials and producer durables rose much more rapidly than that of consumer goods, inclusive of home-processed food and clothing. Within the broad category of services, production- and investment-oriented services increased far more swiftly than did consumer services. This dichotomy makes generalizations about output and productivity trends in the services sector as a whole meaningless as a guide to developmental policy.

In the postwar years, following Stalin's death, the former pattern of unbalanced sectoral growth was considerably rectified, with rapid progress in agriculture through 1958. Since the rapid increase in output was extensive in nature, being partially based on an 18-percent increase in cultivated acreage,[40] as well as on greater incentives for production on private plots, farm employment actually increased by a million from 1950 to 1958.[41] Though the proportion of manpower of the farm continued to fall, the relative decline was far slower than the breakneck pace of the period from 1928 to 1940.

These were years of rapid growth and technological progress throughout the Western world in all spheres of economic activity. In most market economies, productivity in agriculture since 1950 has risen more rapidly than overall productivity.[42] In contrast, in the USSR, the average annual increase in man-hour productivity in agriculture was 5.5 percent from 1950 to 1958 and 3 percent between 1958 and 1964.[43] For the economy as a whole, the rates were, respectively, 5.8 and 4.7 percent.[44] As a result, the proportionate decline in the share of total employment in agriculture was less in the Soviet Union than in any other major economy.[45] It would appear, therefore, that unusually rapid structural transformation in the early years of planning, with its unfavourable impact on consumption, has led to an unusually slow transformation in the postwar years as higher priority has been accorded to consumer interests.

Prospective changes in the structure of the economy will reflect the belated necessity to pay the full costs of industrialization. By suppressing consumer interests, it has previously been possible to economize on investment in such areas as housing, agriculture, and consumer services. Solution of the critical agricultural problem through mechanization, greater use of fertilizers and insecticides, and some degree of decentralization of decision-making is capital intensive in all respects and should lead to reduced labor requirements, thus enabling the economy to reduce substantially the present high proportion of the labor force in agriculture. Much of this reduction would take the form of a reduction in female participation rather than in a transfer of manpower from the countryside to the city. The need to expand the labor-intensive, consumer-services sectors, including retail trade, will result in a higher proportion of employment in the services. The historical, atypical structure of the Soviet economy thus reflects a resource allocation policy of forced industrialization, and as the economy is compelled to invest belatedly in infrastructure and consumer needs, its structure will begin to resemble the normal developmental pattern.

Educational development and policy.   Just as the pattern of Soviet economic development has featured unusually high allocation of resources to investment in plant and equipment, so has it been distinguished by heavy emphasis on investment in human resources. Without a concomitant effort in educational development, the great commitment in physical investment would not have yielded the resulting high growth of accomplishments. In the prewar years, the main objective of educational policy was mass literacy through universal elementary education and an extensive program of adult education. Since the war, the emphasis has been on universal secondary education and rapid expansion of higher and technical education.

The most meaningful indicator of educational effort would be enrollment ratios giving the proportion of a particular age group enrolled in school; however, lack of data precludes use of this measure for international comparisons in all but the most recent years. As a substitute, the comparison made here is in terms of the ratio of university students per thousand of population. Such a ratio may be affected by the age distribution of the population, but not in a large enough magnitude to distort the comparison. The Soviet ratio of 1.2 per thousand in 1928 was far higher than that of other countries, except Japan, at comparable historical levels of per capita. This ratio was not attained by the United Kingdom until the 1930s, by Germany until just prior to World War I, by France and Italy until the 1920s, and by the United States until the 1880s (see Table 14).

Though the increase in the ratio for most other market economies was slow until after World War II, the Soviet ratio rose steadily during the years of comprehensive planning, reaching 3.3 by 1937, 4.7 by 1950, and 6.7 by 1964. Since 1932, the Soviet university enrollment ratio has been second only to that of the United States, with the exception, since 1958, of Japan, even though the relative per capita income level of the Soviet Union warrants a much lower ranking. The parallel between the USSR and Japan in this respect is striking, as it is in terms of other comparative developmental features.

The effect of educational policy on economic growth can be measured by estimates of rates of increase in educational stock. This magnitude is defined as the capitalized value of the varying levels of educational attainment among the employed population on the bench-mark dates of the historical trend.[46] Until 1958, the stock of human capital was rising at about as rapid a rate as the stock of physical capital and considerably more rapidly than that of employment, whether measured either in man-years or man-hours (see Table 7). A similar relationship has been measured in the United States in recent years. According to Theodore Schultz, educational stock in the United States increased at an average annual rate of 4.1 percent from 1929 to 1957,[47] while fixed capital increased at less than half this rate (1.5 percent from 1929 to 1955 and 1.9 percent from 1939 to 1955).[48] Employment increased at a much lower rate,

TABLE 14
COMPARATIVE UNIVERSITY ENROLLMENTS PER
THOUSAND OF POPULATION

	Year	Ratio		Year	Ratio
United Kingdom	1901	0.9	Japan	1950	2.9
	1911	1.1		1958	7.1
	1921	0.9	USSR	1914	0.8
	1931	1.1		1928	1.2
	1937	1.1		1932	3.2
	1951	1.9		1937	3.3
	1958	2.2		1940	3.0
Germany	1901	0.9		1950	4.7
	1911	1.1		1958	6.4
	1922	1.8		1964	6.7
	1932	1.9	United States	1870	1.3
	1937	1.1		1890	2.5
	1951	2.5		1910	3.8
	1959	3.7		1920	5.6
France	1921	1.1		1930	8.9
	1931	1.5		1940	11.3
	1954	3.3		1950	17.6
	1959	3.7		1960	20.0
Japan	1890	0.3	Italy	1881	0.4
	1910	0.9		1901	0.8
	1920	1.3		1921	1.3
	1930	2.5		1941	3.2
	1940	3.2		1951	3.1
				1958	3.4

Sources: Nicholas DeWitt, *Educational and Professional Employment in the USSR* (Washington, D.C.: National Science Foundation, 1964); Central Statistical Administration, *Narodnoe khozyaistvo SSSR v 1964 godu* [The national economy of the USSR in 1964] (Moscow, 1965), pp. 667, 678; and Michael C. Kaser, "Education and Economic Progress," *The Economics of Education,* edited by E. A. G. Robinson and J. E. Vaizey, New York, St. Martins Press, 1966, pp. 99–105, 165–173.

1.2 percent.[49] Earlier experience in the United States is less clear, but Edward Denison estimates the rate of increase in average educational attainment among the labor force from 1909 to 1929 at only a little more than half the rate from 1929 to 1957, while the growth rate for fixed capital was some two-thirds higher in the earlier period.[50] These rough approximations would imply that the growth rate for physical capital exceeded that for the human variety prior to 1929. If this observation for the United States is generalized for the other major market economies, with their much lower enrollment ratios, the Soviet stress on human capital investment appears unique.

The decision in 1958 to suspend progress toward universal secondary education and expanded higher education in order to satisfy short-term manpower needs reduced the annual rate of increase in human capital to half that of physical capital. Continuation of this growth discrepancy would eventually restrict rapid expansion through a deficiency of a sufficient inflow of technically qualified man power. The new Five-Year Plan reinstates the former policy of attainment of universal secondary education. Of course, the huge rates of growth in educational stock realized prior to 1958 cannot be expected to continue once universal secondary education is a fact, and further expansion must occur on the higher level. Moreover, this prospect does not imply lessened investment expenditure, since per student costs in higher education are two to three times above those on the secondary level. However, since the USSR has not hesitated to support an even relatively greater educational burden in the past, it can be expected not to hesitate to support this one in the future.

Appendix

APPENDIX 1

*Historical Trends in Per Capita and
Aggregate Gross National Product*

Per capita GNP has been selected as the most convenient index of stage of economic development (see Table I-1 of this appendix). Since most analogues in major market economies to Soviet per capita income levels before World War II are to be found in the early or mid-nineteenth century, historical time series have been derived. For the United States and the United Kingdom, estimates are not available for early enough periods to match 1928 Soviet levels, but the approximations for the earliest dates are close enough to the Soviet levels to be relevant.

Most of the time series for the market economies have been

obtained from Michael C. Kaser, "Education and Economic Progress: Experience in Industrialized Market Economies," *The Economics of Education,* edited by E. A. G. Robinson and J. E. Vaizey. They have been supplemented and checked by estimates of Angus Maddison, *Economic Growth in the West.* Both Kaser and Maddison base their estimates on postwar official data adjusted to a common conceptual framework that takes historical estimates of private scholars and official statistical agencies into consideration.

Estimates are in terms of 1964 dollars. Methodology and source of derivation are described in Table 7 of my article in *New Directions in the Soviet Economy,* p. 108. The 1964 estimates are moved either to 1950 or to 1958 by the growth rates noted in Table 2 of the article. Pre-1950 Soviet levels are based on the growth rates noted in Table 1 of this study. Kaser's and Maddison's indices have been used for pre-1950 or 1958 series for the market economies.

The estimates are subject to two limitations in interpretation. The validity of much of the early data is questionable by current standards. National income accounting is largely an art developed within the last thirty years. As a result, many earlier statistics are based on limited indicators. However, the directions, as distinguished from the degree, of the indicated trends are probably not seriously distorted.

The other important limitation is that of the index-number problem (see Note to Table 2), which is greatly magnified over a time span as wide as a century. Though most of the scholarly estimates are noted in secondary sources as being in constant prices, they are actually in linked series, the validity of which cannot be tested without close perusal of the original sources. Time limitations have precluded this investigation. It is improbable, however, that any systematic bias would arise from the selection of base period weights or methods of linkage. The same methodological remarks and source citations govern the derivation of the aggregate GNP trends in Table I-2 of this appendix. In their derivation, the principal source for estimates prior to 1950 is Maddison, with confirmation from Kaser.

TABLE I-1

HISTORICAL LEVELS OF PER CAPITA GROSS NATIONAL PRODUCT
(*1964 dollars*)

	Year	Level		Year	Level
USSR	1913	207–374	Japan	1940	554
	1928	204–368		1950	382
	1937	500–531		1958	556
	1940	510–542		1964	1,040
	1950	699	France	1851	293
	1958	1,049		1872	369
	1964	1,289		1881	445
United States	1870	452		1891	525
	1880	725		1901	667
	1890	868		1921	690
	1900	1,049		1931	1,017
	1920	1,417		1950	1,172
	1940	1,886		1958	1,544
	1950	2,536		1964	1,953
	1958	2,790	Germany	1860	338
	1964	3,273		1870	423
United Kingdom	1861	557		1880	381
	1871	699		1900	780
	1881	742		1911	938
	1891	960		1925	827
	1901	1,073		1937	1,101
	1921	1,032		1950	1,001
	1937	1,234		1958	1,644
	1951	1,393		1964	2,154
	1958	1,592	Italy	1881	339
	1964	1,910		1901	399
Japan	1880	97		1921	488
	1890	128		1941	580
	1900	184		1951	626
	1920	252		1958	866
	1930	442		1964	1,187

TABLE I-2
COMPARATIVE HISTORICAL AGGREGATE LEVELS OF GNP
(*billions of 1964 dollars*)

	1913	1928	1937	1950	1958	1964
USSR	30–58	32–62	90–93	124	215	293
United Kingdom	36	45	56	68	83	104
France	38	46	42	50	70	96
Germany	32	34	43	50	90	126
Italy	17	23	27	28	43	61
Japan	11	28	37	32	51	101
United States	132	203	228	387	487	629

APPENDIX II

Derivation of Combined Factor
Inputs and Productivity

Indexes of factor productivity are based on the conventional Cobb-Douglas production function in which trends in GNP are explained by trends in explicit factors of production, weighted according to their marginal productivities, and by trends in unmeasured productive factors. This last term can be alternatively considered as the combined productivity of the explicit production factors. In its simplest version: $P = aL^{\alpha}K^{1-\alpha}Z$ where P = percentage change in GNP; a = autonomous variable; L = employment (man-hours); α = proportion of GNP accruing to labor; K = capital stock; $1 - a$ = proportion of GNP accruing to capital; and Z = combined factor productivity or contribution of unmeasured productive factors.

The production function, as used in this study, has been expanded to include land and livestock in addition to employment and physical capital in the prewar period for the USSR and a fifth factor of educational stock in the postwar period. The first four factors are used throughout the historical comparison for the United States. Man power is measured in terms of man-hours.

Soviet factor productivity weights. The prewar weights are those of Bergson. The "B" alternative comes from his article in *Economic Trends in the Soviet Union,* p. 19. The "B" alternative has been selected because it assumes the same return of 8 percent on fixed capital as assumed in the postwar weights. My estimate for the postwar weights begins with proportions for three factors: 69.7 for manpower, 26.6 for capital, and 3.7 for land.[1] The weight for land is determined by the estimate for land rent. The weight for capital is the sum of interest return on fixed and working capital and depreciation charges. The weight for manpower is the sum of wages and supplements and incomes in kind. The weight for livestock is taken from Douglas Diamond's estimate for capital in this form and for agricultural capital as a whole.[2] Diamond provides an estimate in 1955 rubles for the value of productive livestock in 1959. As in the case of other forms of capital, an 8 percent annual rate of return is assumed to prevail for this productive factor. The land weight of 3.7 and the livestock weight of 0.8 are subtracted from the previously computed weight for capital. This breakdown comprises the four-factor model. For the five-factor model, the weight for educational capital stock is based on Nicholas DeWitt's estimate for 1959.[3] The return on educational stock is assumed to be 8 percent—that is, the assumed return on physical capital.[4] The resulting weight of 9.6 is subtracted from the previously computed manpower weight. The weights are presented in Table II-1.

TABLE II-1
SOVIET FACTOR PRODUCTIVITY WEIGHTS
(*percentages*)

| | | Postwar | |
	Prewar	*Four-Factor Model*	*Five-Factor Model*
Manpower	80.5	69.7	60.1
Capital	8.3	25.8	25.8
Land	10.0	3.7	3.7
Livestock	7.0	0.8	0.8
Education	—	—	9.6

Soviet factor input indices.   Indices for 1928 through 1950 are estimates of Bergson, p. 4. Post-1950 indexes are derived from several sources: those for manpower and educational stock, from Stanley H. Cohn, "Soviet Growth Retardation," *New Directions in the Soviet Economy,* p. 131; those for capital stock, from *Narodnoe khozyaistvo SSSR v 1964 godu,* p. 68; and those for land and livestock, from Diamond, p. 373.

United States weights and indices.   Factor inputs and weights and indices for the United States through 1948 are those of Bergson, p. 25. Manpower indices are based on unpublished estimates of the U.S. Bureau of Labor Statistics. The capital stock index is based on estimates of George Jaszi, Robert Wasson, and Lawrence Grosse, "Expansion of Fixed Business Capital in the United States," *Survey of Current Business* (Washington, D.C., November 1962), and unpublished estimates of the Office of Business Economics. The Bulletin F depreciation alternative is used. Land (cropped acreage) and livestock indices are U.S. Department of Agriculture estimates obtained from the Council of Economic Advisors, *Economic Report of the President* (Washington, D.C., 1966), p. 296.

Notes

Introduction

1. The theory of traditional Russian despotism was first fully elaborated by George Plekhanov in the book-length introduction to his *Istoriya Russkoi obshchestvennoi mysli* [History of Russian Social Thought] (Moscow, 1914), vol. 1. More recently, this interpretation has been given further treatment by Karl Wittfogel, *Oriental Despotism* (New Haven, Conn.: Yale, 1957), and by George Vernadsky, *The Mongols and Russia* (New Haven, Conn.: Yale, 1953). An earlier, partial version of the theory was suggested by Marx and Engels. See the articles included in Bert Hoselitz, ed., Karl Marx, *The Russian Menace to Europe* (Glencoe, Ill., 1952). This part of the Marxist corpus was disavowed by both the Russian and Chinese Communist parties in the late 1920s.

2. P. N. Milyukov and V. O. Klyuchevsky, whose views are summarized by Arcadius Kahan in the article included here.

3. The socialist motivation of the policies of "War Communism" has recently been reemphasized by Paul Craig Roberts, " 'War Communism': A Re-examination," *Slavic Review,* 29 (1970), 238–61.

4. Alec Nove, Leopold Labedz, and other English scholars debated the collectivization among others of Stalin's policies in 1962, in *Encounter,* "Was Stalin Really Necessary?" beginning in the April issue, 86–92. M. Lewin's extensive treatment of the subject appears in his *Russian Peasants and Soviet Power: A Study of Collectivization* (London, 1968).

5. For the numerous estimates of Soviet economic growth, see section 9 of the Bibliography here.

I The Economic Development of Russia

1. See detailed data: P. A. Khromov, *Ekonomicheskoe razvitie Rossii,* vols. XIX–XX vekakh (Moscow, 1950), pp. 79, 434–38, 452–54; P. I. Lyashchenko, *Istoriya narodnogo khozyaistva S.S.S.R.* (Moscow, 1947), vol. 1, *Dokapitalisticheskie formatsii,* p. 485.

2. See S. S. Balzak, V. F. Vasyutin, and Ya. G. Feigin, *Economic Geography of the U.S.S.R.* (New York, 1949), pp. 188–89; J. H. Clapham, *An Economic History of Modern Britain, The Early Railway Age, 1820–1850* (Cambridge, 1950), pp. 53–54.

3. See Khromov, op. cit., p. 423; Lyashchenko, op. cit., p. 537.

4. See data: Khromov, op. cit., pp. 30–34.

5. See data: Lyashchenko, op. cit., pp. 484–86, 601–602.

6. The danger of the destruction of crops by frost limited the choice of crops possible for cultivation. The longer coverage of the fields by snow and the shorter periods for spring and autumn fieldwork (due to spring floods and excessive autumn precipitation) imposed requirements different from those of West European countries as regards the seasonal use of labor. The necessity of keeping livestock for longer periods indoors and the consequent higher expenses of fodder and of building imposed additional difficulties in comparison with West European countries.

7. See interesting material on early history of development of Russian iron industry: S. G. Strumilin, *Chernaya Metallurgia v Rossii i v S.S.S.R.* (Moscow, 1935).

8. See data: Strumilin, op. cit., p. 231; T. S. Ashton, *Iron and Steel in the Industrial Revolution in England* (Manchester, 1924); E. A. Pratt, *A History of Inland Transport and Communications* (London, 1912); T. S. Ashton and J. Sykes, *The Coal Industry in the Eighteenth Century* (Manchester, 1929); J. H. Clapham, op. cit., pp. 430–32.

9. See very informative material on the development of Ural industries: B. B. Kafengauz, *Istoriya khozyaistva Demidovykh v XVIII–XIX vekakh* (Moscow, 1949); Roger Portal, *L'Oural au XVIIIe siècle* (Paris, 1950); Roger Portal, *L'Industrie metallurgique de l'Oural* (Paris, 1950); Pierre Pascal, "La durée des voyages en Russie au XVIIe. siècle," *Revue des études slaves*, XXVII (Paris, 1951).

10. See Khromov, op. cit., pp. 456–57, 462; P. I. Lyashchenko, *Istoriya narodnogo khozyaistva S.S.S.R.* vol. II, *Kapitalizm*, p. 131.

11. See Khromov, op. cit., p. 198.

12. See data: Khromov, op. cit., pp. 468–71; Alexander Baykov, *Soviet Foreign Trade* (Princeton, N.J., 1946), pp. 1–6; Harold G. Moulton and Leo Pasvolsky, *World War Debt Settlements* (New York, 1926), p. 60.

13. For example, the average number of cattle was: 1801–1820, 23.5 million head; 1891–1896, 25.5; 1897–1901, 31.1; 1902–1906, 31.5; 1907–1911, 30.4. See detailed data on harvests of grain and on livestock: Khromov, op. cit., pp. 452–54, 466–67.

14. See material in A. Gerschenkron, "The Rate of Industrial Growth in Russia since 1885," *Journal of Economic History*, Suppl. VII, 1947, and vol. XII, no. 2, 1952; Alexander Baykov, *The Development of the Soviet Economic System* (Cambridge, 1946).

15. The United Kingdom already in 1836 produced more coal (30.5 million metric tons) than Russia in 1913 (29.1 million metric tons), whereas in 1950 Kuzbass (36 million metric tons) and Karaganda (17 million metric tons) produced together more than double the total coal production of Donbass in 1913 (25.3 million metric tons) and in 1953 total coal production of the USSR amounted to 320 million metric tons and of Great Britain 227.8 million metric tons.

16. For example, the linking of Kuznetsk coal with Magnitogorsk iron ore, the use of peat for production of electricity, the utilization of hydraulic energy of the Dnieper and the Volga, became possible only by the application of the most modern techniques.

17. The magnitude of this problem can be realized if we remember that in the next twenty years the net increase of the population of the USSR might amount to some 60 millions (see Frank Lorimer, *The Population of the Soviet Union: History and Prospects* [1946], pp. 183–202), nearly the total population of Germany in 1914 and 1939; and the Russian industrial potential at present is already substantially greater than that of Germany—will Russia also look for *"Lebensraum"* in the development of her economy and in the solution of her population problem?

18. See data: *Bolshaya sovetskaya entsiklopediya, Soyuz Sovetskyhk Sotsialisticheskykh Respublik* (Moscow), pp. 243–72; Balzak, op. cit., pp. 210–11, 219, 242–55; Demitri B. Shimkin, *Minerals, a Key to Soviet Power* (Cambridge, Mass., 1953); Heinrich Hassmann, trans. from German by Alfred M. Leeston, *Oil in the Soviet Union* (Princeton, N.J., 1953).

19. See detailed data: *Soviet Economic Growth, Conditions and Perspectives,* Abram Bergson, ed. (New York, 1953), pp. 136–39.

20. Ibid., p. 166.

21. See reference to these estimates: Ibid., p. 253. See also, Khromov, op. cit., p. 237.

22. See *Pravda,* March 28, 1954.

23. See informative material in S. Prokopovicz, *Krestyanskoe khozyaistvo* (Berlin, 1924); see also *Soviet Economic Growth,* pp. 296–97.

24. See a description of these projects in *Bulletins on Soviet Economic Development,* Alexander Baykov, ed., nos. 2 and 8.

II The Economic Policy of Peter the Great

1. Cf. Strumilin, *Ocherki ekonomicheskoi istorii Rossii* [Essays on the economic history of Russia], p. 288: "Peter's epoch represents,

without any doubt, one of the most important turns in the development of our economy."

2. Cf. Strumilin, op. cit., chap. XV, p. 313, "Peter's economy." See also Pavlenko, *Razvitie metallurgicheskoi promyshlennosti Rossii v pervoi polovine XVIII veka* [Development of Russian metallurgy in the first half of the eighteenth century] (Moscow). Introduction with a critical bibliography, pp. 13–20.

3. For the period prior to Peter's reign, let us quote the introductory chapters of Mme. Spiridonova, *Ekonomiceskaya politika i ekonomiceskie vzglyady Petra I* [Economic policies and view of Peter I], pp. 3–25; of Pavlenko, op. cit., pp. 3–28; and of Strumilin, op. cit., chap. V, "Essays on the Factory Age," pp. 260 sq. Finally let us quote monographs which allow us to study concretely the development of a money economy and its social consequences. Cf. A. C. Merzon and Tikhonov, "The Markets in Ustyug Velikii in the Seventeenth Century," review appearing in *Revue d'histoire moderne et contemporaine*.

4. For the *initially* privileged situation of the noble contractor, see B. Gille, *The Social and Economic History of Russia* (Paris), p. 123, and for foreign manufactures in the eighteenth century, pp. 123–24.

5. For small enterprise in the seventeenth century, ancestor of eighteenth-century manufactures, cf. Kafengauz (*History of the Demidov Firm in the Eighteenth and Nineteenth Centuries*) which talks about the "genetic" links which unite the incipient industry of the Urals to the industrialized central sectors.

6. See the important work by Kafengauz devoted to the formation of the Russian domestic market in the eighteenth century, *Ocherki ynutrennogo rynka Rossii v Perovoi polovine XVIII v.* [Essays on the domestic Russian market in the first half of the eighteenth century].

7. Somov, in his review of Zaozerskaya's book (*The Manufacturing Enterprises under Peter*), quotes examples of very high investments, and insists on the massive proportion of private enterprises. In the magazine, *Voprosy Istorii*, 1950, p. 311.

8. With the reservation that those peasants from the Urals, who were too well-to-do to accept working in the factories willingly, were affected by constraint. Cf. Kafengauz, op. cit., on the Demidovs, p. 118.

9. The procedure is described by Strumilin, op. cit., pp. 269 and 291.

10. For this procedure of social cleavage, cf. Spiridonova, op. cit., pp. 38 sq., and for the history of the Demidovs, Kafengauz, op. cit., pp. 82 sq.

11. It is to this stage of the history of the Russian factory which Pavlenko directs his attention, by focusing upon the progressive subjugation of manual labor in the second quarter of the eighteenth century.

12. This conflict is treated by Baburin, *Ocherki po istorii Manufaktur-Kollegii* [Essay on the history of the College of Manufactures], pp. 70 sq. The college protected the merchants' interests rather than those of the small businessmen. Cf. ibid., p. 270.

13. Cf. E. F. Vilenskaya, "Characteristics of Russian Possessional Factories," *Voprosy Istorii,* 1954, no. II, p. 92.

14. Cf. Pavlenko, op. cit., p. 80, and Strumilin, op. cit., pp. 340–341.

15. *Pierre le Grand et son Oeuvre* (Payot, 1953), p. 148.

16. Spiridonova, op. cit., pp. 56 and 142.

17. Pavlenko, op. cit., pp. 272–75, shows the importance of exports of "state" iron and concludes: "One cannot take seriously the arguments supporting the military aims of state enterprise." Cf. also Baburin, op. cit., p. 43. A Russian supporter of mercantilism, D. Voronov, observed that foreigners "could not survive without Russian products"; as a result, he advises that prices be raised.

18. S. M. Soloyov, *Publichnie chteniya o Petre Velikom* [Public lectures on Peter the Great], SPB, 1903, p. 39.

19. See the Introduction to the "Regulations of the College of Manufactures," *PSZ,* no. 4., p. 378, published in the appendix by Baburin, op. cit.

20. See Klyuchevsky, p. 137.

21. For the relations between the state and the Demidovs, see the already mentioned work of Kafengauz. For the transfer of the Nevyanskii factory, see pp. 99 sq.

22. Pavlenko, p. 330.

23. For the origins, the creation, and the operation of these institutions, as well as for the "Regulations" and the "Privileges," the two main works (which go far beyond Peter the Great's reign) are those by Baburin and Pavlenko; one of them studies the College of Manufactures, and the other studies the Berg-Collegium.

24. For the overlapping of powers, see Pavlenko, op. cit., pp. 89 sq. The stories of the Demidovs' quarrels and those of the *voivodas* from Siberia are mentioned in Kafengauz, op. cit., pp. 138. sq.

25. Pavlenko, op. cit., p. 98.

26. There is a very detailed study of these local administrations in Pavlenko, op. cit., pp. 133 sq. They were at their highest development in the period following Peter's reign.

27. Baburin accurately describes this process of differentiation between the "approved" and those "not approved." It results from the state's action and not from economic phenomena. See pp. 91–94.

28. Baburin, op. cit., pp. 200 sq.

29. Pavlenko, op. cit., p. 105.

30. Strumilin, op. cit., "Factories Under the Tsar in the Seventeenth Century," pp. 249 sq.

31. Pavlenko, op. cit., pp. 172–77 and p. 333.

32. Op. cit., p. 145.

33. Pavlenko published V. N. Tatishchev's *Education at the Sikhtmeistern,* and commented on it in *Istoricheskii Arkhiv,* 1951, no. 6, pp. 198–244

34. Baburin, op. cit., pp. 293–300.

35. Zaozerskaya, op. cit., p. 77.

36. Pavlenko describes this reduction of obligatory deliveries on pp. 420–433. For the deliveries of copper, see pp. 446–452.

37. These are the two antagonistic views of Strumilin and Pavlenko.

38. Pavlenko, op. cit., p. 104.

39. A study on the origins of free labor in Zaozerskaya, op. cit., p. 125.

40. The ukase of 1722 which Pavlenko mentions, p. 353, was the most advantageous for manufacturers. On the other hand, the one of 1724 demanded the payment of indemnities to the *pomeshchiki.*

41. About apprentices (*ucheniki*), see Zaozerskaya, op. cit., p. 121.

42. This conclusion is borrowed from Pavlenko whose aim is to show that the "free" worker was reinstated at the entrepreneur's and the state's wish—in the rigid framework of fiscal laws and compulsory work. See op. cit., pp. 321 sq.

43. See Baburin, op. cit., p. 74.

44. Such is the text of the ukase in Baburin, op. cit., p. 67; *PSZ,* no. 3, p. 711.

45. See Pavlenko, op. cit., pp. 387, 394, and 398.

46. See Pavlenko, op. cit., pp. 388 and 401.

47. See for example B. Gille's book, *The Origins of Heavy Metallurgical Industry in France* (Paris, 1947), chap. II, pp. 53 and 54, which treats Colbertism. It is astounding to realize the similarity existing between the problems which Colbert's France and Peter's Russia were facing, and the analogous solutions taken by both (mine laws, p. 36; appeal to strangers, mainly to Swedes, p. 45; control of the state, p. 50, etc.). See also Kulischer's article, a comparative study: "Heavy Industry in the Seventeenth and Eighteenth Centuries: France, Germany and Russia," *Annales d'histoire economique et sociale,* 1931, pp. 11 and 46.

III   Continuity in Economic Activity and Policy During the Post-Petrine Period in Russia

1. The most widely known members of the liberal school were V. O. Klyuchevsky and P. Milyukov, of the etatist school, M. N. Pokrovsky.

2. *"Die russische Manufaktur und Fabrik ist nicht organisch aus der Hausindustrie und nicht unter dem Einfluss des gesteigerten inneren Bedürfnisses der Bevölkerung herausgewachsen."* Paul Milyukov, *Skizzen Russischer Kulturgeschichte* [Essays in Russian cultural history] (Leipzig, 1898), p. 67.

3. *"Sie wurde vielmehr ziemlich spät von der Regierung ins Leben Gerufen, die dabei einerseits ihre eigenen praktischen Bedürfnisse (Z. B. Tuchlieferungen für die Armee) im Auge hatte, anderseits aber auch die Unentbehrlichkeit einer nationalen Industrie erkannte."* Ibid.

4. *"Wie gering die Früchte der ersten Bermühungen waren, auf dem Wege des Schutzzollsystems eine nationale Industrie zu schaffen, kann man aus den Ergebnissen der amtlichen Fabrikbesichtigungen etwa um 1730 sehen."* Ibid., p. 68.

5. Ibid., pp. 68–69.

6. V. O. Klyuchevsky, *Sochinenia* [Collected works], IV (Moscow: Sotsekgiz, 1958), 335, "Industry after Peter did not make any noticeable progress; foreign trade remained, as it was, in the hands of foreigners."

The error in Klyuchevsky's judgment becomes obvious as soon as one compares the available data for the two major industries: iron and textiles. From 1725 to 1760, the number of enterprises engaged in wool, linen, and silk manufacturing increased from 39 to 145; the number of machines from 2070 to 11,666; and the number of workers from about 10,000 to 33,687. The output of pig iron increased from 13,350 tons in 1725 to 60,050 tons in 1760. The number of private iron and copper works increased from 28 to 138 in 1760, of which ironworks rose from 22 to 95. See E. I. Zaozerskaya, *Rabochaia Sila i Klassovaia Bor'ba na Tekstilnykh Manufakturakh v 20–60 gg. XVIII v.* [Labor force and class struggle in the textile manufactories] (Moscow: Akademia Nauk SSSR, 1960), pp. 48, 72, 73. S. G. Strumilin, *Istoria Chernoi Metallurgii v SSSR* [The history of ferrous metallurgy in the USSR] (Moscow: Akademia Nauk SSSR, 1954), I, 197, 204. We would therefore have to reject Klyuchevsky's thesis as lacking any substantive support from the economic data.

7. The number of peasant serfs drafted during the years 1699–1701 for work in the Voronezh wharves was about 20,000 yearly; for 1703–1705, the number is not available. See Milyukov, *Gosudarstevennoe Khoziaistovo Rossii v Pervoi Chetverti XVIII Stoletia* [The state economy of Russia in the first quarter of the eighteenth century] (St. Petersburg, 1892), p. 269.

8. The number of peasant serfs and skilled workers employed in the construction of the Taganrog harbor was reported as follows: 1701—8886; 1702—5449; 1703—2844; 1704—5920. Ibid.

9. For the employment of forced labor in Azov and Troitsk, we have two estimates—one for the officially drafted, the other for those actually employed. The estimates are the following:

EMPLOYMENT OF FORCED LABOR IN AZOV AND TROITSK

Year	Officially Drafted	Actually Employed
1704	30,370	16,696
1705	32,288	16,466
1706	37,208	7272
1707	26,266	8215
1708	1500	1350
1709	18,100	405

Source: Ibid.

10. The list would probably be incomplete, even if it included the very inefficient (and ineffective) use of resources in the work on the La-doga canal prior to Münnich's appointment as construction head.

11. The approximate number of the mobilized serfs employed in the construction of St. Petersburg can be inferred from the following data for the years for which figures are available. The numbers exclude the labor employed in the massive contruction works conducted by the Admiralty and in the erection of such objects as the neighboring Kron-stadt, Schlüsselburg fortress, etc. The numbers also exclude the employ-ment of prisoners of war and criminals.

DRAFT QUOTA AND ACTUAL NUMBER OF LANDLORD SERFS
EMPLOYED IN THE CONSTRUCTION WORKS IN
ST. PETERSBURG, FOR SELECTED YEARS

Year	Draft Quota	Actually Employed
1706	40,000	20,000
1709	40,000	10,374
1710	43,928	n.a.
1711	30,448	24,381
1712	28,800	18,532
1713	33,779	n.a.
1714	32,253	20,322
1715	32,253	n.a.
1719	n.a.	6232
1720	n.a.	4853

Source: S. P. Luppov, *Istoria Stroitel'stva Peterburga v Pervoi Chetverti XVIII veka* [The history of construction of St. Petersburg in the first quarter of the eighteenth century] (Moscow-Leningrad: Akademia Nauk SSSR, 1957), pp. 80–81.

12. The yearly expenditures out of taxes for civilian construction in St. Petersburg (excluding the Admiralty) were fixed until 1717 at 242,700 rubles; between 1717 and 1721 at 266,700 rubles; and from 1721, when a tax was substituted for labor services of the peasants, at 300,000 rubles. However the actual expenditures from the budget were usually higher. The total expenditures from the budget in 1720 were 316,484 rubles, and during subsequent years the government was called upon to assign an additional 80,000 to 100,000 rubles over and above the tax receipts earmarked for the St. Petersburg construction work. Ibid., pp. 168, 170, 171.

13.

YEARLY NUMBER OF DRAFTEES IN THE ARMY AND NAVY

Year	Number	Year	Number	Year	Number
1701	33,234	1713–14	16,342	1724	20,550
1705	44,539	1714	500	1726	22,795
1706	19,579	1715	10,895	1727	17,795
1707	12,450	1717	2500	1729	15,662
1708	11,289	1718	15,389	1730	16,000
1709	15,072	1719	14,112	1732	18,654
1710	17,127	1720	4000	1733	50,569
1712	51,912	1721	19,755	1734	35,100
1713	20,416	1722	25,483	1735	45,167

Source: L. G. Beskrovnyi, *Russkaia Armia i Flot v. XVIII veka* [The Russian army and navy in the eighteenth century] (Moscow: Voennoe Izadatel'stvo Ministerstva Oborony Soiuza SSSR, 1958), pp. 23–29, 33–34.

14. The available data on manufactories in Prussia and Saxony support the general impression that the "life expectancy" of industrial firms during the eighteenth century was short. See Horst Krüger, *Zur Geschichte der Manufakturen und der Manufakturarbeiter in Preussen* [On the history of manufactories and the manufactory labor in Prussia] (Berlin: Rütten and Loening, 1958), pp. 306–357.

Rudolf Forberger, *Die Manufaktur in Sachsen vom Ende des 16. bis zum Anfang des 19. Jahrhunderts* [The manufactories in Saxony from the end of the sixteenth until the beginning of the nineteenth century] (Berlin: Akademie-Verlag, 1958), pp. 306–357.

15. The inventory of one of the largest private enterprises in Russia, that of the ironworks of Akinfii Demidov (1747), reveals that, while the value of plant and equipment was about 400,000 rubles, the value of the serf peasants employed in his iron and copper works was between 400,000 and 420,000 rubles. Among the various manufactories existing in the eighteenth century, ironworks were the most capital intensive. See B. B. Kafengauz, *Istoria Khoziaistva Demidovykh v. XVIII–v. v.* [The history of the Demidov firm in the eighteenth and nineteenth centuries] (Moscow-Leningrad: Akademia Nauk SSSR, 1949), I, 224–30.

16. In some branches of manufacturing in the eighteenth century, the nature of the technological processes and the type of equipment made it easier to subdivide enterprises than is the case in modern industry, and each part of a divided enterprise could still exist as an economically viable unit. The state-owned linen factory in Moscow (Polotniany Zavod) was divided among five entrepreneurs in the 1720s. The large silk manufactory (of Apraksin, Tolstoi, and Shafirov) was soon taken over and divided into three parts by groups of merchant entrepreneurs. Zaozerskaya, *Razvitie Legkoi Promyshlennosti v Moskve v pervoi Chetverti XVIII v.* [The development of light industry in Moscow in the first quarter of the eighteenth century] (Moscow: Akademia Nauk SSSR, 1953), pp. 213–42, 308–11.

17. This was generally the case in the early silk manufactories and leather factories. The expenditures to import foreign specialists and to train the indigenous labor force exceeded the costs of even imported equipment. Ibid., pp. 297–300.

18. An examination of the activities of 41 merchants engaged in industrial entrepreneurship during 1710–1770 indicates that 36 continued their activities in domestic or foreign trade, in tax farming, in alcohol supply contracts, etc. Thus their involvement in manufacturing depended upon the various alternative opportunities to earn a return on their capital. Under such circumstances, their participation in manufactories depended upon the state of their total business activity. This would explain many transfers of their holdings in manufacturing to relatives and partners and the sales to other entrepreneurs. For sources describing the behavior of various entrepreneurial groups, see ibid.; also, Zaozerskaya, "Labor Force and Class Struggle" (cited in n. 6); N. I. Pavlenko, *Istoria Metallurgii v Rossii XVIII veka* [The history of metallurgy in Russia in the eighteenth century] (Moscow: Akademia Nauk SSSR, 1962); I. V. Meshalin, *Tekstilnaia Promyshlennost Krestlan Moskovskoi Gubernii* [The textile industry of the peasants in Moscow Gubernia] (Moscow-Leningrad: Akademia Nauk SSSR, 1950); and Arcadius Kahan, "Entrepreneurship in the Early Development of Iron Manufacturing in Russia," *Economic Development and Cultural Change*, X, no. 4 (July 1962).

19. The major relocation was connected with the government's conservation policies of 1754, when most of the ironworks, glass facto-

ries, and distilleries within about a 130-mile radius of Moscow were closed. Miliukov's calculation included in the total the enterprises liquidated by the government decree of 1754.

20. Pavlenko, p. 462. The survival rate and life-span of ironworks in Russia were remarkably great in comparison with other countries whose ironworks were also based upon charcoal fuel. This phenomenon of the Russian ironworks can be explained principally by the greater supply of timber in the proximity of the ironworks.

21. Available data for the textile industry (linen, wool, and silk) indicate that out of 39 manufactories existing in 1725 (the year of Peter's death), 28 enterprises were still functioning in 1745. The number of basic machines in those enterprises had increased from about 2070 to 3073. The number of workers had increased in the "old" wool-cloth manufactories by about 8 percent and the value of output by about 50 percent. In the silk manufactories, the output had increased by about 40 percent. Zaozerskaya, "Labor Force and Class Struggle," pp. 34, 46, 48, 50, 52, 53.

22. In 1745, the "old" textile manufactories (established during the Petrine period) constituted 39 percent of the total number of textile manufactories and represented 66 percent of the basic equipment, 68 percent of the labor force, and 70 percent of the output. Ibid., pp. 48, 50–51.

23. For the disappearance of manufactories established during the 1740s and 1750s, see Dmitrii Baburin, *Ocherki po Istorii Manufaktur-Kollegii* [Essays on the history of the Manufacturers College] (Moscow: Glavnoe Arkhivnoe Upravlenie NKVD SSSR, 1939), pp. 189, 296–98. For the later periods, see Pavlenko, pp. 458–68, and K. A. Pazhitnov, *Ocherki Tekstilnoi Promyshlennosti* [Essays on the textile industry of prerevolutionary Russia] (Moscow: Akademia Nauk SSSR, 1958), pp. 168–73, 308–13.

24. The following series, recorded in English sources, represent the pattern of Russian-English trade.

TRADE OF RUSSIA WITH GREAT BRITAIN
(*in £*)

Year	Russian Exports	Russian Imports	Excess of Exports
1715	241,876	105,153	136,723
1716	197,270	113,154	84,116
1717	209,898	105,835	104,064
1718	284,485	79,626	204,869
1719	140,550	55,295	85,255
1720	169,932	92,229	77,704
1721	156,258	95,179	61,079
1722	112,467	54,733	57,734
1723	151,769	56,697	95,072
1724	212,230	35,564	176,666
1725	250,315	24,848	225,468
1726	235,869	29,512	206,357
1727	144,451	21,883	122,568
1728	232,703	25,868	206,835
1729	156,381	35,092	121,289
1730	258,802	46,275	212,527
1731	174,013	44,464	129,549
1732	291,898	49,657	242,241
1733	314,134	42,356	271,778
1734	298,970	36,532	262,438
1735	252,068	54,336	197,732

Source: Sir Charles Whitworth, *State of the Trade of Great Britain in Its Imports and Exports, Progressively from the Year 1697* (London, 1776), pt. II, p. 29.

25. A. Semenov, *Izuchenie Istoricheskikh Svednii o Rossiiskoi Vneshniei Torgovle i Promyshlennosti* [Study of historical information on Russian foreign trade and industry] (St. Petersburg, 1859), pt. 3, pp. 23–25.

26. S. A. Pokrovskii, *Vneshniaia Torgovlia i Vneshniaia Torgovaia Politika Rossi* [Foreign trade and foreign trade policy of Russia] (Moscow: Mezhdunarodnaia Kniga, 1947), p. 89.

27. Semenov, pt. 3, pp. 23–25.

28. The break in Russian-English diplomatic relations, coupled with the deterioration of the quality of Yorkshire coarse wool cloth, made the Prussian woolens competitive in the Russian market. As a result, the following quantities of Prussian cloth were ordered by the Russian Government.

Year	Quantity (in arshins)	Value (Reichsthalers)	Year	Quantity (in arshins)	Value (Reichsthalers)
1725	233,375	119,000	1728	9878	5500
1726	316,792	170,000	1729	211,140	n.a.
1727	365,474	196,000	1730	59,026	33,000

Between 1725 and 1727, cloth for 485,000 thalers was delivered, for which one-third was paid in specie. W. O. Henderson, "The Rise of the Metal and Armament Industries in Berlin and Brandenburg, 1712–1795," *Business History,* III (June 1961), 65–66. Douglas K. Reading, *The Anglo-Russian Commercial Treaty of 1734* (New Haven, Conn: Yale University Press, 1938), p. 380.

29.

INTERNAL TAXES AND CUSTOM-DUTY PAYMENTS COLLECTED
ON THE MAKARIEVSKA TRADE FAIR, 1718–1728
(*in rubles*)

Year	Internal Custom Duties	Total Taxes Collected
1718	15,374	32,579
1719	14,074	30,957
1720	13,719	29,742
1721	13,735	26,845
1722	13,651	28,416
1723	16,525	28,619
1724	14,704	27,441
1725	15,121	27,340
1726	14,457	23,656
1727	15,803	24,278
1728	10,784	21,982

Source: B. B. Kafengauz, *Ocherki Vnutrennogo Rynka Pervoi Poloviny XVIII* v. [Essays on the internal market of Russia in the first half of the eighteenth century] (Moscow: Akademia Nauk SSSR, 1958), p. 119. The figures for the year 1728, being for a terminal year, are not reliable. In addition, they show a very substantial decrease in the custom-duties collection concurrent with a fifteen-fold increase in the salt-tax collection and therefore must be regarded as inconclusive.

30.

OUTPUT OF PIG IRON, 1718–1735
(*in metric tons*)

Year	State	Private	Total
1718	3636	5635	9271
1719	3622	5518	9140
1720	2539	7435	9992
1721	2752	7453	10,205
1722	3125	9831	12,957
1723	2233	8316	10,549
1724	5012	7699	12,711
1725	4717	8633	13,350
1726	3586	8634	12,220
1727	3472	7912	11,384
1728	5025	9390	14,415
1729	6185	8485	14,670
1730	5307	10,369	15,676
1731	6323	13,039	19,362
1732	6387	10,780	17,167
1733	5962	11,483	17,445
1734	6421	13,530	19,953
1735	7198	15,758	22,950

Source: Strumilin, pp. 180, 193, 197.

31. During 1726, the furnaces of the large Kamenskii and Ala-paievskii and, in 1726–1727, of the Uktuskii ironworks were out of order. Serious unrest was reported among the peasant serfs employed in the state ironworks during 1726 and 1727. Ibid., p. 194.

32. The increase in the number of forge hammers, in view of an unchanged number of furnaces, indicates the shift toward harder types of iron products. The number of forge hammers increased from 110 in 1725 to 139 in 1727, while the number of active furnaces remained the same. The shift toward a different product mix of ironworks is substantiated by the data on the output of flat bar-iron, which show an uninterrupted rise.

OUTPUT OF FLAT BAR-IRON, 1725–1730
(*in metric tons*)

Year	State	Private	Total
1725	1704	4455	6159
1726	2604	4570	7174
1727	3325	4144	7469
1728	3096	5242	8338
1729	3486	4930	8616
1730	3440	5618	9058

Ibid., pp. 181, 197.

33. During 1726 and 1727, four new ironworks were completed (Sivinskii, Nizhne-Siniachynskii, Verkhne-Isetskii, and Shaitanskii). Since another three ironworks were completed during 1728–1729, this shows that the investment flow into iron manufacturing did not cease.

34.

COPPER OUTPUT, 1725–1735
(*in tons*)

Year	State	Private	Total
1725	n.a.	n.a.	90.6
1726	155.2	3.2	158.4
1727	164.6	3.0	167.6
1728	150.7	15.8	166.5
1729	176.6	27.9	204.5
1730	166.3	51.2	217.5
1731	168.7	84.0	252.7
1732	143.9	68.8	212.7
1733	134.3	74.7	209.0
1734	179.8	100.3	280.1
1735	145.0	114.2	259.2

Source: N. I. Pavlenko, *Razvitie Metallurgicheskoi Promyshlennosti Rossii v Pervoi Polovine XVIII veka* [The development of metallurgy in Russia in the first half of the eighteenth century] (Moscow: Akademia Nauk SSSR, 1953), pp. 56, 78.

35. The two main uses of copper were the military and the monetary. The expansion of copper output might have been a result of the increase in demand for money, which would contradict the notion of a general slump.

36. While Peter the Great imported most of the wool cloth needed for army uniforms, the lining (*karazeia*) was almost entirely produced domestically. Government prices also made it more profitable to manufacture the lining than the cloth.

37. We have records about one wool-cloth plant (later divided into four enterprises) and two silk factories that were established during those years. See Zaozerskaya, "Labor Force and Class Struggle," pp. 50–51.

38. Incomplete data on yearly government expenditures in the area of manufacturing are available for a number of years, but they include operating expenditures and those connected with the importation of foreign specialists, an item that was declining over time. Hence capital expenditures are difficult to extract from those data.

39. Strumilin, pp. 459–61. N. N. Rubtsov, *Istoria Liteinogo Proizvodstva v Rossii* [The history of castings production in Russia] (Moscow-Leningrad: Akademia Nauk SSSR, 1947), pp. 69–70, gives the following figures for the establishment of ironworks in the Urals:

Peter (1699–1725): 14 (0.5 yearly)
Catherine I (1726–1727): 4 (2 yearly)
Peter II (1729–1730): 4 (2 yearly)
Anna (1731–1741): 25 (2.5 yearly)
Elizabeth (1742–1761): 57 (3 yearly)

40. The data on internal factory consumption of iron (which constituted a sizable share of the gross investment outlays for replacement of equipment and construction of new capacity) by the state-owned Ural ironworks point to the following quantities used (in tons):

| 1722–1725 | 1875 | 1730–1733 | 1261 |
| 1726–1729 | 2105 | 1734–1737 | 2121 |

If we assume the costs of production at 14.64 rubles per ton (24 kopecks per pood), the average yearly investment outlays from this source alone would amount to:

| 1722–1725 | 6860 rubles | 1730–1734 | 4615 rubles |
| 1726–1729 | 7704 rubles | 1734–1737 | 7763 rubles |

The above data do not indicate a slackening in this area of investment outlays for the state ironworks during the immediate post-Petrine period. See Pavlenko, "Development of Metallurgy," table 16, p. 272.

41. *Polnoe Sobranie Zakonov Rossiiskoi Imperii (PSZ)* [Complete collection of the laws of the Russian Empire] (St. Petersburg, 1830), vol. VIII, no. 5821.

42. There are two ways of supporting the assertion about a decrease in the volume of smuggling. One is to cite the diminishing number of official reports, complaints, etc. The other is to investigate the volume of imports to the ports of the Baltic provinces (excepting St. Petersburg) and the volume of overland trade through the customs from the provinces into Russia, making an allowance for the volume of goods consumed in the Baltic provinces. On both accounts the data for the 1740s and early 1750s, when compared with the 1720s, appear to support the above assertion. For the trade to the Baltic ports, see N. E. Bang, *Tabeller over Skibsfart og Varetransport gennem Oresund 1661–1783* [Tables on shipping and merchandise transportation passing through the sund, 1661–1783], vol. II (Copenhagen: Gyldendalske Boghandel Nordisk Forlag, 1930).

43. An interesting case in point was the duty differential established between the ports of St. Petersburg and Archangel, which resulted in almost completely diverting trade toward St. Petersburg. The 1731 tariff equalized the tariffs for both ports and revived Archangel and its vast hinterland. The decrease of some tariff rates led to the abolishment of a number of trade monopolies, thus enabling other producers and merchants to enter the field on a more competitive basis. See Pokrovskii (cited in n. 26), pp. 94–97.

44. The relative profitability of the private manufactories as compared with those owned by the state was pointed out in the report of the Monetary Committee (Monetarnaia Komissia) to the Senate in 1732, in the "Senate Reports" of 1733–1734, etc.

45. The above policy directives are spelled out in detail in the "Berg-Reglament" of 1739. *PSZ*, vol. X, no. 7766, and in the analysis of the conditions of transfer of state enterprises to private individuals. See Pavlenko, pp. 131–33.

46. The last case of summary expropriation of private property (not involving punishment of any particular individual) is the decree of January 6, 1704. The Berg-Collegium Privilege of December 10, 1719, was a major attempt to provide assurance of property rights in the area of mining and iron-producing. During the post-Petrine period, the property rights of industrial entrepreneurs were widened, safeguarding for them not only physical property (plant and equipment) but also serfs. *PSZ*, vol. VII, no. 6255; vol. IX, no. 6858; vol. X, no. 7766.

47. See Dmitrii Baburin, *Ocherki po Istorii Manufaktur-Kollegii* (Moscow: Glavnoe Arkhivnoe Upravlenie NKVD SSSR, 1939), pp. 194–99. Baburin presents the basic features of government economic policy prior to the decree of 1775.

48. As an illustration, the following data pertaining to the iron and copper works could be cited.

ENTRANCE OF NEW ENTREPRENEURS IN IRON AND COPPER WORKS,
1701–1760

Years	*Total*	*Merchants*	*Gentry*
1701–1710	1	1	—
1711–1720	7	7	—
1721–1730	12	11	1
1731–1740	17	17	—
1741–1750	35	32	3
1751–1760	32	16	16
Total 1701–1760	104	84	20

Source: Pavlenko, p. 463.

49. The conclusions about the relative positions of the manufacturers and the government officials are based upon an analysis of documents published in the following sources: N. I. Pavlenko, "Nakaz Shikhtmeisteru V. N. Tatishcheva" [V. N. Tatishchev's instructions to the charge master], in Akademia Nauk SSSR, *Istoricheskii Arkhiv,* vol. VI (Moscow-Leningrad: author, 1951). M. A. Gorlovskii and N. I. Pavlenko, "Materialy Soveshchania Uralskikh Promyshlennikov, 1734–1736 gg." [The proceedings of the meetings of Ural industrialists, 1734–1736], in ibid., vol. IX (1953).

50. V. N. Tatishchev in 1734 got an instruction from Anna that regulated for the private ironmasters the number of peasant serf families per ironwork, depending upon the volume and type of equipment. Anna's decree of 1736, which permitted the enserfment of free skilled workers, nonetheless forbade the nongentry from purchasing whole villages ("only few households at a time"), although one wonders whether this particular clause was operative or followed in practice.

The Elizabethan decree of July 27, 1744, permitted nongentry to purchase whole villages and cited the 1742 precedent of the merchant Grebenshchikov's purchase of 50 households. A decree of the Senate of January 17, 1752, established norms of serf purchases for textile manufactures and was implemented by an instruction of October 5, 1753, which permitted the purchase of serfs without land.

51. For 1743–1762, we have 38,480 "souls" (males of all ages) and 2440 households with land, and 3034 "souls" and 50 households without land.

For ironworks and mining, the figures are 36,860 prior to 1752 and 8683 afterward—together, 45,543 souls.

The Manufacturers College reported purchases of serfs by manufacture owners of 10,328 prior to 1752 and 6532 after 1752—together, actual purchases of 16,860 serfs (males).

The Soviet historian Zaozerskaya estimated the total number of serfs acquired by all types of private-manufacture owners as being about 22,000 during 1720–1743 and about 85,000 during 1743–1750, while Semevskii gives the total for 1700–1760 as about 60,000. See E. Zaozerskaya, "Begstvo i Otkhod Krestian v Pervoi Polovine XVIII v" [Flight and seasonal leave of peasants during the first half of the eighteenth century] in *O Pervonachl'nom Nakoplenni v Rossii XVII–XVIII v.* [About the primary accumulation in Russia of the seventeenth to eighteenth centuries] (Moscow: Akademia Nauk SSSR, 1958), pp. 156–57.

IV Geography of the Iron Market in Prereform Russia

1. Reported at the meeting of the Department of History of Geographical Knowledge and of Historical Geography on April 12, 1954.

2. Concerning this endeavor, see *History of a Half Century of*

the Russian Imperial Geographical Society, pt. I, p. 133 (St. Petersburg, 1890), by P. P. Semenov.

3. Only separate articles were published by D. A. Voronovsky on the iron trade in Odessa, by P. A. Valuev on the iron trade in Riga, and by N. Kh. Bunge on the iron trade in Kiev. *Herald of the Russian Geographical Society,* 1852, pt. VI, bk. 102.

4. Both are kept in the Central State Historical Archive in Leningrad (hereafter abbreviated Ts.G.I.A.L.).

5. Kept at Ts.G.I.A.L. The material of the said investigation by the Geographical society is a part of this fund.

6. Kept in the Central State Archive of Ancient Acts in Moscow (abbreviated below Ts.G.D.A.).

7. Kept at the same place.

8. Kept at the State Historical Museum in Moscow (abbreviated G.I.M.). My thanks are due to V. F. Zakharina and S. V. Tutukin.

9. In 1846, iron from one of the Moscow mining districts was imported by the Shepelevs in the amount of only 40,000 poods, Ts.G.I.A.L., Folio 37.

10. Ts.G.I.A.L., Folio 46, of the Commission on the Question of the Development of the Iron Industry in Russia, Register 1, pp. 82, 82 (back).

11. Calculated by men from the data on exports published in the *Collected Information on the History and Statistics of Russia's Foreign Trade,* ed. V. I. Pokrovsky; and the production data published by P. A. Koeppen in *Material on the History and Statistics of Iron Production in Russia* (St. Petersburg, 1896).

12. The plant owners who exported iron had offices in St. Petersburg. On these offices see below.

13. Ts.G.I.A.L., Folio 46, Register 1, File 6, p. 109 (back); see also File 8, p. 81 (back).

14. Ts.G.I.A.L., Folio 46, Register 1, File 6, p. 109 (back).

15. Ts.G.I.A.L., Folio 46, Register 1, File 5, p. 381.

16. Ts.G.I.A.L., Folio 37, Register 5, File 379, p. 205; Folio 46, Register 1, File 10, p. 164.

17. Ts.G.I.A.L., Folio 46, Register 1, File 2, pp. 74–75, 82–88.

18. The role of the meterological factor in the production of pig iron and iron is stressed by the plant owners in their answers to the questions put to them by the commission. Ts.G.I.A.L., Folio 46, Register 1, File 5, pp. 29 (back), 172 (back), 237 (back); File 6, p. 30.

19. The role the crop played in the increase of demand for iron is stressed both by the plant owners and by the merchant. Ts.G.I.A.L., Folio 46, Register 1, File 5, p. 148; File 6, p. 28; File 8, pp. 107–10.

20. In his reply to the commission Pastukhov said that iron purchases amounted to 850,000 to 900,000 poods. Ts.G.I.A.L., Folio 46, Register 1, File 2, p. 78 (back).

21. G.I.M., Folio 14: the Golitsins, File 992, pp. 1–2.

22. Ts.G.I.A.L., Folio 46, Register 1, File 8, pp. 78–88.

23. Ts.G.I.A.L., Folio 46, Register 1, File 10, p. 129.

24. Ibid., pp. 31–146; see also File 2, p. 92 (back).

25. Ibid., File 7, pp. 134–36.

26. Ibid., p. 152.

27. Ts.G.I.A.L., Folio 46, Register 1, File 8, pp. 107–10.

28. Ts.G.I.A.L., Folio 46, Register 1, File 7, pp. 147–149.

29. B. B. Kafengauz, *The Demidov Economy* (Moscow, 1949), I, 281–90.

30. Ts.G.D.A., Demidov Folio, Register 4, Files 231, 232, 234, 263.

31. Ibid.

32. In the inventory of the branch offices of the Demidov administration in the 1850s, these offices are not mentioned. Ts.G.I.A.L., Folio 46, Register 1, File 6, p. 110 (back).

33. Ibid.

34. As we know, Nakhichevan was situated next to Rostov-on-Don. Today, it is part of Rostov.

35. Ts.G.I.A.L., Folio 46, Register 1, File 5, p. 233 (back).

36. Ts.G.I.A.L., Folio 46, Register 1, File 6, p. 110 (back).

37. Ibid.

38. Ibid.

39. Ibid.

40. Ts.G.I.A.L., Folio 46, Register 1, File 6, p. 110 (back).

41. F. Nosygin, *Ore and its Metal Production* (St. Petersburg, 1858), p. 16.

42. G.I.M., the Golitsin Folio, File 986, pp. 51, 60, 63, 63 (back), 88–98, File 1025, pp. 2, 38–46 (back).

43. Ts.G.I.A.L., Folio 46, Register 1, File 6, p. 106 (back).

44. According to government statistics in 1851, the Urals private plants forged 7.8 million poods. See my article, "Report on a Historical Review of All Government and Private Plants in the Urals," *Historical Archive* (1953), vol. X.

45. Thus a government official, Loginoff, determined the volume of iron imports to the fair. Ts.G.I.A.L., Folio, Register 1, File 2, p. 88 (back). According to other data of the Department of Mining, from the Ural state plants in 1847–1852, the average yearly sale was about 126,000 poods, while 21,000 remained unsold. It results in almost the same amount. Ts.G.I.A.L., Folio 46, Register 1, File 15, p. 171.

46. Ts.G.I.A.L., Folio 46, Register 1, File 5, p. 355 (back).

47. Ts.G.I.A.L., Folio 46, Register 1, File 8, p. 178; File 10, p. 23.

48. Ts.G.I.A.L., Folio 37, Register 5, File 508, p. 157 (back).

49. Ts.G.I.A.L., Folio 46, Register 1, File 10, pp. 128–50.

50. Ibid., File 8, pt. 2, p. 22.

51. Ts.G.I.A.L., Folio 37, Register 5, File 508, pp. 163, 163 (back).

52. Ts.G.I.A.L., Folio 37, Register 5, File 508, p. 158.

53. Ts.G.I.A.L., Folio 46, Register 1, File 97, pt. 1, pp. 129, 130.

54. Ts.G.I.A.L., Folio 37, Register 5, File 508, p. 162 (back).

55. Ts.G.I.A.L., Folio 46, Register 1, File 6, p. 96.

56. Ts.G.I.A.L., Folio 46, Register 1, File 6, p. 96 (back).

57. If we recognize that, out of 100 poods of pig iron, they got about 70 poods of iron. According to data from the Nizhnii Tagil min-

ing district, 1,345 poods of pig iron were consumed in the forging of 1,000 poods of iron, that is, 74 poods of iron were obtained from 100 poods of pig iron. Ts.G.I.A.L., Folio 46, Register 1, File 6, p. 88.

58. Thus, they received, if the forging of pig iron in the Kizelovsk plant amounted to not what was shown in the table, but the normal output, about 225,000 poods per year.

59. Pig iron for processing, as a rule, was obtained from the plants of the same owner; for example, the state Votkinsk plant received pig iron from the state Goroblagodatsk (Mushvinsk and others) plants. The Dobyansk and Ochersk plants of the Stroganovs from their own Bilim-baevsky plants, etc.

60. Ts.G.I.A.L., Folio 37, Register 3, File 203, p. 32.

61. Ts.G.I.A.L., Demidov Folio, Register 8, File 1444, pp. 8, 10, 15, 16. The averages are mine.

62. Iron, sent for export to Central Asia, was transported by land.

63. Ts.G.I.A.L., Folio 46, Register 1, File 6, p. 97.

64. Ts.G.I.A.L., Folio 37, Register 5, File 379, p. 164.

65. Ts.G.I.A.L., Folio 37 of the Mining Department, Register 2, File 203. Reports of the director of the Mining Department on the con-sequences of his inspection of the government mining plants in 1863, 1864, 1865, p. 28.

66. *Historical Archive,* vol. IX (Moscow, 1953). The publication named above.

67. Ts.G.I.A.L., Folio 37, Register 5, File 379, p. 152.

68. Ts.G.I.A.L., Folio 46, Register 1, File 5, p. 363 (back).

69. Ibid., p. 364.

70. The plants situated to the east of the watershed of the Ural range, which shipped iron down the Chusovaya, sent part of their pig iron for processing to the forging plants situated in the vicinity of the Chusovaya to the west of the watershed. This was the case in the Go-roblagodatsk and the Nizhnii Tagil districts situated on both sides of the Ural range.

71. Ts.G.I.A.L., Folio 37, Register 5, File 448, p. 133.

72. Ibid., p. 144.

73. Ibid., p. 23.

74. Ibid., p. 111.

75. Ts.G.I.A.L., Folio 46, Register 1, File 6, p. 98.

76. Ts.G.I.A.L., Folio 337, Register 5, File 448, p. 23.

77. Ts.G.I.A.L., Folio 46, Register 1, p. 97 (back).

78. Ts.G.I.A.L., Folio 37, Register 5, File 379, p. 170 (back). The pilots were hired on the free labor market also for the caravans of this district.

79. See the description of sailing down the Chusovaya in 1849 in the article by Rogov, *Journal of the Ministry of the Interior Affairs* (1852), pt. 37, nos. 1–3.

80. Ts.G.D.A., Demidov Folio, Register 8, File 1792, pp. 60 (back), 61, and 66.

81. Ts.G.D.A., Folio 46, Register 1, File 6, pp. 101, 101 (back).

82. Ts.G.D.A., Demidov Folio, Register 8, File 1792, pp. 68–69.

83. Ts.G.I.A.L., Folio 46, Register 1, File 6, p. 101 (back).

84. Ts.G.D.A., Demidov Folio, Register 8, File 1792, pp. 22, 24 (back).

85. Ts.G.I.A.L., Folio 37, Register 5, File 379, p. 126 (back).

86. Ibid., p. 152.

87. Ibid., p. 163.

88. Ts.G.I.A.L., Folio 46, Register 1, File 6, p. 99.

89. *The Geographical-Statistical Dictionary of the Russian Empire,* ed. P. P. Semenov-Tyan-Shansky, (St. Petersburg), 5, 902.

90. Ts.G.I.A.L., Folio 37, Register 5, File 379, p. 140.

91. Ibid., File 448, p. 160.

92. Ibid., p. 161 (back).

93. Ibid., p. 145.

94. Ibid., p. 133.

95. Ibid., p. 77 (back).

96. On the "horse-powered machines," see *Volga* by Shubin (Moscow, 1927).

97. This is indicated by the majority of the plant owners in their reports to the Geographical Society.

98. To the report of the Nizhnii Novgorod office of the Stroganov plants on the delay of the caravan at The Calf Ford, the owner replied: "If such fools as the caravan leader Nikolai Kreshnikov are sent to control important operations, I shall not be surprised at the poor progress of our business. Kreshnikov, seeing the way the waterway inspector at the Calf Shoal dealt with another boat, instead of preventing the inspector from similarly dealing with our boats by giving him a few dozen rubles for each barge, decided to act most foolishly. . . ." Ts.G.D.A., Stroganov Folio, Register 10, pt. II, File 2517, p. 281.

99. Ts.G.I.A.L., Folio 37, Register 5, File 379, p. 127. See also, Ya. Rogov, "Notes on Sailing on the River Chusovaya," *Journal of the Ministry of Internal Affairs*, 1852, pt. 37, nos. 1–3. Eighty hours out of eight days were used for sailing; the rest of the time was spent on various stops.

100. As also in the eighteenth century, the caravan leaders kept journals and sent from the way reports to the owner concerning the progress the caravan was making. This is how going up the Volga in one of the iron caravans of the Golitsins is depicted in the following extracts from the caravan journal:

"June 11. From morning until nightfall in quiet and clear weather tugged by barge haulers up to 5 versts without accidents.

"June 20. From morning until noon in quiet and clear weather, and in the afternoon until the evening in continuous rain and with a contrary wind, with delays, and with a swift current continued, tugged by barge haulers and with poles about 6 versts without accidents.

"June 21. In windy weather and with a swift current were tugged by barge haulers only about one verst and stopped in caravan formation because of the continuous contrary wind.

"July 15. From the morning until the evening, with a favorable wind sailed under the sail power of the first nine barges approximately up to 40 versts without accidents. S.H.M." The Golitsin Fund, File 987, pp. 74–78 (back).

Records of favorable winds are met with much more rarely than records of contrary winds. The journal is dated 1811. But also in the 1850s traffic had about the same tempo.

101. Ts.G.I.A.L., Folio 46, Register 1, File 6, p. 102 (back).

102. Ts.G.I.A.L., Folio 46, Register 1, File 2, p. 76.

103. Ts.G.I.A.L., Folio 46, Register 1, File 9, p. 148 (back).

104. Ts.G.I.A.L., Folio 37, Register 5, File 448, p. 97.

105. Ts.G.I.A.L., Folio 46, Register 1, File 6, p. 102 (back).

106. Ts.G.I.A.L., Folio 46, Register 1, File 7, pp. 229–30.

107. The three cited regions were: (a) The Cherepovsk, the Belozersk, and Ustyozhsk districts of Novgorod province, the Vesegonsky of Tver province, certain localities adjoining them, a part of Yaroslavl province; (b) the Gorbatovsk and the Semenovsk districts of Nizhnii Novgorod region, situated on the Oka, together with the settlements Pavlova and Vorsma; (c) Tula and its region.

108. Ts.G.I.A.L., Folio 6, Register 1, File 7, p. 234 (back).

109. Ibid., p. 238.

110. Ts.G.I.A.L., Folio 46, Register 1, File 6, p. 96 (back), p. 104 (back), p. 105 (back).

111. Ts.G.I.A.L., Folio 37, Register 5, File 379, p. 249.

112. Ibid., p. 117.

113. Ibid., File 448, p. 51 (back).

114. Ts.G.I.A.L., Folio 46, Register 1, File 6, p. 105 (back).

115. B. B. Kafengauz, *The History of the Demidov Economy in the Eighteenth and Nineteenth Centuries,* vol. I (Moscow, 1949).

116. Ts.G.I.A.L., Folio 46, Register 1, File 6, p. 105 (back).

117. Ts.G.I.A.L., Folio 37, Register 5, File 379, pp. 246 (back), 248 (back).

118. Ts.G.I.A.L., Folio 46, Register 1, File 6, p. 103 (back).

119. Ibid., File 7, pp. 129, 251–55.

120. Ts.G.I.A.L., Folio 46, Register 1, File 7, pp. 103 (back), 104.

121. Ts.G.I.A.L., Folio 46, Register 1, File 7, pp. 103 (back), 104; Barkoch, a merchant, evaluated these expenses at 9 to 12 kopecks per pood. Ts.G.I.A.L., Folio 46, Register 1, File 10, p. 128.

122. Ts.G.I.A.L., Folio 46, Register 1, File 10, p. 128.

123. Ibid.

124. Ts.G.I.A.L., Folio 46, Register 1, File 2, p. 92 (back).

125. Ts.G.I.A.L., Folio 46, Register 1, File 6, p. 104 (back).

126. Ts.G.I.A.L., Folio 46, Register 1, File 10, p. 123.

127. Ibid.

128. Ts.G.I.A.L., Folio 46, Register 1, File 7, pp. 129, 251–55.

129. Ts.G.I.A.L., Folio 36, Register 5, File 379, pp. 56, 61, 66, 72.

130. Ts.G.I.A.L., Folio 46, Register 1, File 8, pp. 214–20.

131. Inclusive of the cost of transportation the whole way, i.e., to Kaluga by water, from Kaluga to Bryansk on sleighs, and from Bryansk to Kiev by water. Ts.G.I.A.L., Folio 46, Register 1, File 6, pp. 104, 104 (back).

132. Ts.G.I.A.L., Folio 46, Register 1, File 7, pp. 57–58.

133. Ts.G.I.A.L., Folio 46, Register 1, File 8, p. 147; see also Folio 36, Register 5, File 508, p. 158.

134. Ts.G.I.A.L., Folio 46, Register 1, File 10, p. 151.

135. Ibid.

136. Ts.G.I.A.L., Folio 36, Register 5, File 508, p. 169.

137. Ts.G.I.A.L., Folio 46, Register 1, File 6, p. 103.

138. Ts.G.I.A.L., Folio 37, Register 5, File 508, p. 163.

139. Ibid.

140. Ts.G.I.A.L., Folio 36, Register 5, File 508, p. 160 (back).

141. Ibid.

142. Ts.G.I.A.L., Folio 37, Register 5, File 508, p. 158.

143. Ibid., p. 165, and Folio 46, Register 1, File 9, p. 267.

144. Ts.G.I.A.L., Folio 37, Register 408, pp. 158, 158 (back).

145. Ts.G.I.A.L., Folio 36, Register 5, File 508, pp. 158, 158 (back).

146. Ts.G.I.A.L., Folio 46, Register 1, File 9, p. 267.

147. Ts.G.I.A.L., Folio 36, Register 5, File 508, and Folio 46, Register 1, File 6, pp. 103, 103 (back).

148. Ts.G.I.A.L., Folio 37, Register 5, File 508, pp. 159, 165.

149. Ibid., p. 165 (back).

150. Ts.G.I.A.L., Folio 46, Register 1, File 8, p. 73.

151. Ibid.

152. Ts.G.I.A.L., Folio 46, Register 1, File 6, p. 111 (back).

153. Ts.G.I.A.L., Folio 36, Register 5, File 508, p. 165 (back).

154. Ts.G.I.A.L., Folio 46, Register 1, File 9, p. 13 and what follows.

155. Ts.G.I.A.L., S.C.H.A. Folio 46, Register 1, File 9, pp. 18 (back), 19.

156. Ibid., p. 199.

157. Ibid., p. 205.

158. Ts.G.I.A.L., Folio 46, Register 1, File 9, pp. 167–70.

159. Ts.G.I.A.L., Folio 46, Register 1, File 8, p. 206.

160. Ts.G.I.A.L., Folio 46, Register 1, File 7, pp. 129–30.

161. Ts.G.I.A.L., Folio 46, Register 1, File 8, p. 204.

162. Ts.G.I.A.L., Folio 46, Register 1, File 10, p. 115.

163. Ts.G.I.A.L., Folio 46, Register 1, File 8, p. 187.

164. Ts.G.I.A.L., Folio 46, Register 1, File 9, p. 142.

165. Ts.G.I.A.L., Folio 46, Register 1, File 9, p. 68.

166. Ts.G.I.A.L., Folio 46, Register 1, File 10, p. 224.

167. Ibid., Folio 46, Register 1, File 10, p. 72.

168. According to the statistics of the administration of the Nizhnii Tagil mining district, 500,000 poods were exported to Siberia via the Irbit Fair and to Ekaterinburg, while according to the statistics of the Ekaterinburg mining officials, Ekaterinburg's share was 150,000 poods.

169. Ts.G.I.A.L., Folio 46, Register 1, File 10, p. 232 (back).

170. Ts.G.I.A.L., Folio 46, Register 1, File 1, pp. 224–33.

171. Ts.G.I.A.L., Folio 46, Register 1, File 6, p. 124.

172. Ts.G.I.A.L., Folio 46, Register 1, File 1, pp. 224–33.

173. Ts.G.I.A.L., Folio 46, Register 1, File 7, pp. 167–67.

174. Ts.G.I.A.L., Folio 46, Register 1, File 6, p. 106 (back).

175. Ts.G.I.A.L., Folio 46, Register 1, File 7, pp. 165–67.

176. It is the average price which differed considerably from the lowest that is meant here. At the Nizhnii Novgorod Fair, the low price went down as far as 80 kopecks.

177. Ts.G.I.A.L., Folio 46, Register 1, File 10, p. 231.

178. Ts.G.I.A.L., Folio 46, Register 1, File 6, p. 97.

179. I have not found any directions from the administration of the plants. It is true that for Moscow there is some data provided by the Department of Mining regarding the prices for iron from the Tagil plants (1 ruble, 50 kopecks), but, apparently, they have been given too high.

180. The explanation of what caused a great increase in the costs of transportation to Nizhnii Novgorod and Kazan requires comparison with the costs of transportation to Moscow and St. Petersburg in a special study. Additional source material is necessary for this purpose.

181. Ts.G.I.A.L., Folio 46, Register 1, File 10, p. 37.

182. Ts.G.I.A.L., Folio 46, Register 1, File 9, p. 256.

183. Ts.G.I.A.L., Folio 46, Register 1, File 10, p. 65.

184. Ts.G.I.A.L., Folio 46, Register 1, File 10, p. 10.

185. Ibid., p. 241.

186. Ibid., p. 231.

V The Industrial Revolution in Russia

1. Zlotnikov wrote this article in the summer of 1941. It was printed in numbers 11 and 12 of the journal *Questions of History* (1946), a few years after the author's death during the siege of Leningrad.

2. S. G. Strumilin, *The Industrial Revolution in Russia* (Moscow: 1944), p. 21.

3. Ibid.

4. *Questions of History*, no. I, 1945.

5. Strumilin, op. cit., p. 5.

6. See the journal *Questions of History,* no. 5 (1952); articles by L. A. Loone, "The History of the Industrial Revolution in Estonia," and by K. A. Pazhitnov, "The Question of the Industrial Revolution in Russia." In the latter article, study is made of the technological aspects of the Industrial Revolution in the wool industry. This aspect of the problem applied to the sugar industry is investigated by the author in "Sugar Plants on the Estates in Russia During the First Half of the Nineteenth Century," *To the Academician Boris Dmitrievitch Grekov on his Seventieth Anniversary, Collected Articles* (Moscow: 1952).

7. Cotton spinning by hand was practiced, on a small scale, in Astrakhan, i.e., beyond the borders of the Moscow-Ivanovo industrial region and St. Petersburg, and it did not develop into a large industry.

8. Central State Historical Archive in Leningrad (Ts.G.I.A.L.), Folio 758, Register 24, File 87, p. 31.

9. Ts.G.I.A.L., Folio 758, File 1795, pp. 8–9.

10. Leningrad District Archive, Folio 1196, Register I, File 5, pp. 4–5.

11. Ts.G.I.A.L., Folio 18, Register 2, File 2204, p. 1.

12. Ibid., Register 7, File 1846, pp. 1, 6, and 16.

13. *Bulletins de la société industrielle de Mulhouse,* (1840), p. 468.

14. Ts.G.I.A.L., Folio 18, Register 2, File 5855, pp. 84–85.

15. I have derived this data from an unpublished dissertation of a historian of Ivanovo, A. V. Shipulina.

16. Ya. P. Garelin, *The City Ivanovo-Voznesensk* (Shuya, 1885), pt. 2, pp. 59–60.

17. E. M. Dementiev, *The Factory: What It Gives the Population and What It Takes from It* (Moscow: 1897), pp. 54–55.

18. It must be taken into consideration that these figures show only the degree of the personal participation of a laborer in agricultural work. Many workers who did not go away to do agricultural work in the fields had their families run the farms for them. These figures must not, therefore, be taken as a criterion of the links between the worker and the village. Even much later, on the eve of the Great October Socialist Revolution, more than one-fifth of the workers possessed land

and farmed with the assistance of their families (according to the data of the professional registration in 1918 when information was collected for the years before the Revolution as well).

19. K. G. Vobly, *An Introduction to the History of the Beet-Sugar Industry in the USSR* (Moscow, 1928).

20. Ts.G.I.A.L., Folio 571, Register 9, File 828, p. 15 (back).

21. *Survey of the Various Branches of the Manufacturing Industry in Russia* (St. Petersburg: 1862), I, 22. When I was disputing in 1945 with S. G. Strumilin, I did not have at my disposal these data (see *Questions of History,* 1945, no. I). In the given case, I must now introduce into my remarks of that time a small correction in favor of Strumilin.

22. Ts.G.I.A.L., Folio 44, Register 2, File 567.

23. Ts.G.I.A.L., Folio 46, Register 1, File 2, pp. 318–37.

24. There is no data for this in the 1870s.

25. There is no data for this in the 1870s.

26. I. A. Shubin, *The Volga and Volga Shipping* (Moscow: 1927).

27. On textile-machine construction in the Alexandrovsk plant, see my article, "The Role Our Machinery Construction Played in Supplying Looms and Other Cotton-Spinning Equipment to Russian Cotton-Spinning Factories During the First Half of the 19th Century," *Historical Notes,* vol. 42.

28. From the group of the Vyksunsk plants of the Prioksk mining district.

29. Ts.G.I.A.L., Folio 37, Register 10, Files 26, 27, and 28.

30. The old St. Petersburg plant nevertheless continued its works on a small scale. Later on, the well-known Putilov plant was established on its foundations.

31. See V. I. Lenin, *Sochineniia,* vol. 13, p. 250.

32. That part which stayed to work at the enterprises.

33. P. A. Peskov, *Factories in the City of Moscow Engaged in Processing Fiber* (Proceedings of the Commission appointed by the Governor General of Moscow, Prince V. A. Dolgoruky, for the Inspection of Factories and Plants in Moscow), no. I, pp. 133–41, 882.

34. E. M. Dementiev, op. cit., p. 47.

35. Ya. P. Garelin, *The City Ivanovo-Voznesensk* (Shuya, 1885), pt. 2, pp. 100–102.

36. Ibid. See also the table he gives in "The Commission by Imperial Command Appointed to Investigate the Present Position of Agriculture and of Agricultural Production in Russia," *Report of the Commission* (St. Petersburg, 1873), app. I, Sec. 2, p. 226.

37. *History of the All-Union Communist Party [of Bolsheviks], Short Course,* p. 8.

VI The Old Believers and the Rise of Private Industrial Enterprise in Early Nineteenth-Century Moscow

1. Most of the bibliography on the subject has been noted in Roger Portal, "Origines d'une bourgeoisie industrielle en Russie," *Revue d'histoire moderne et contemporaine,* VIII (1961), 35–60. Portal focuses on the social origins, as does H. Rosovsky, "The Serf Entrepreneur in Russia," *Explorations in Entrepreneurial History,* VI (1953), 207–29.

2. Little has been written about the commercial and industrial activities of these groups in Russia. For recent short accounts and bibliographies, see the excellent analyses in Salo Baron, *The Russian Jew Under Tsars and Soviets* (New York, 1964), pp. 101–13, 367–68; and (on the Skoptsky) N. M. Nikolsky, *Istoriya Russkoi tserkvi* [History of the Russian Church] (Moscow and Leningrad, 1931), pp. 298–307. The best short Soviet account we have of the Moscow Theodosians is P. G. Ryndzyundsky, *"Starobryadscheskaya organizatsiya v usloviyakh razvitiya promyshlennogo kapitalizma"* [Old Believer organization during conditions of industrial capitalist development], *Voprosy istorii religii atheiszma* [Problems of the history of religion and atheism], I (1950), 188–248. The question of Protestant enterprise is bound up with that of the foreigner in Russia. See E. Amburger, *"Der fremde Unternehmer in Russland bis zur Oktoberrevolution im jahre* 1917," *Tradition,* 1957, 337–55.

3. See Anatole Leroy-Beaulieu, *The Empire of the Tsars and the Russians* (New York, 1896), III, 358–59. Leroy-Beaulieu's perceptive

study of the Russian schismatics is still very usable. On the numbers of Old Believers in the nineteenth century, see Serge Zenkovsky, "The Ideological World of the Denisov Brothers," *Harvard Slavic Studies,* III (1957), 64; and John Curtiss, *Church and State in Russia 1900–1917* (New York, 1940), p. 138. A conservative estimate of the dissenting population of Russia about 1850 would be 9 million. The official figure was less than a million, a bureaucratic attempt to hide the fact of major religious disunity.

4. Melnikov, *Polnol sobranie sochinenii* [Complete collection of works], 2nd ed. (St. Petersburg, 1909), VII, 204–206. Melnikov was better known under the pseudonym of Andrei Pechersky. In addition to his numerous studies of the Old Believers, he wrote a fictional trilogy about them.

5. F. C. Coneybeare, *Russian Dissenters* (Cambridge, Mass., 1921), pp. 101–105; P. Milyukov, *Outlines of Russian Culture* (Philadelphia, 1942), I, 61; V. V. Andreev, *Raskol i yeyo znachenie v Russkoi narodnoi istorii* [The Schism and its significance in the history of the Russian people] (St. Petersburg, 1870), p. 149.

6. Nikolsky, pp. 218–21, 275.

7. Ibid. Andreev, p. 155.

8. Milyukov, pp. 61–63; Nikolsky, p. 234.

9. On the Vyg Commune, see Zenkovsky, 52–64; and P. G. Lyubomirov, *Vygovskoe obshehezhitelstvo* [The Vyg commune] (Moscow and Saratov, 1924).

10. Nikolsky, pp. 236–37; Andreev, p. 157; Ryndzyundsky, 189–90. Although I cannot agree with some of his interpretations, Ryndzyundsky has had access to the archives and has provided many new facts on the economic activity and the ideology of the Moscow Theodosian community; his article ranks with more general work by Nikolsky. An earlier study of the Theodosian community by O. Rustik, *"Starobryadcheskoe Preobrozhenskoe kladbishche (kak nakoplyalis kapitaly v Moskvye)"* [The Preobrazhensk Old Believer cemetery (how capital was accumulated in Moscow)], *Borba klassov* [Class struggle], no. 7–8 (1934), 70–79, is of less value. Pierre Kovalevsky, in *"Le Raskol et son rôle dans le développement industriel de la Russie,"* *Archives de sociologie des religions,* III (1957), 37–56; and Valentine Bill, in

The Forgotten Class: The Russian Bourgeoisie from the Earliest Beginnings to 1900 (New York, 1959), are the first scholars in the West to have raised the question of the business significance of the Old Believers, but in their general surveys, neither has explored the Moscow communities in any depth or detail.

11. A. A. Titov, ed., *"Dnevnyya dozornyya zapisi o Moskovskikh Raskolnikokh"* [Daily patrol reports on the Moscow Schismatics], June 10, October 7, December 16, 27, 1845; March 8, 9, May 9, July 6, 1846; January 28, February 3, March 25, 1848, in *Chteniya v obshchestve istorii i drevnostei Rossiiskikh* [Proceedings of the Society of History and Antiquities of Russia] (1885–1886, 1892), section entitled "Smyes" [Miscellany] ; hereafter cited as "Patrol Reports," referring in all cases to the Smyes section. These police reports are the most valuable primary source available for the economic activities of the Moscow Old Believers during the reign of Nicholas I. The published collection consists of more than four hundred printed pages of almost daily official observations primarily of the Priestless communities, from 1845 to 1848. Needless to say, the police were hostile to people they considered fanatics and did not always distinguish between fact and rumor. The Soviet scholar Ryndzyundsky, who has had access to the original manuscripts, finds omission and distortion in the Titov edition. The economic history contained in the published documents remains reliable, I have concluded, on the basis of comparison with Ryndzyundsky's own facts, quotes, and interpretation and with the other accounts and sources, as well as on the basis of strong internal evidence. For comparison, see notes 16 and 29 below.

12. V. Kelsiev, *Sbornik pravitelstvennykh svedenii o Raskolnikakh* [Collection of government information on the Schismatics] (London, 1860), I, 55; Patrol Reports, August 5, 1847.

13. Patrol Reports, May 12, 1845.

14. Patrol Reports, May 2, 12, December 7, 29, 1845; Kelsiev, op. cit., I, 9.

15. Rustik, op. cit., 75–76.

16. Patrol Reports, August 1, 1846; also quoted in Ryndzyundsky, 209.

17. Patrol Reports, January 3, 1846.

18. Patrol Reports, July 10, 11, November 27, December 24, 1845; January 16, March 7, 1846.

19. Leroy-Beaulieu, op. cit., III, 154.

20. Patrol Reports, January 21, February 5, 10, July 5, November 29, December 8–10, 20, 1845; March 15, 1847.

21. Ryndzyundsky, op. cit., p. 205.

22. Patrol Reports, March 15, 1845; March 7, July 15, 1846.

23. Patrol Reports, December 19, 1844; Melnikov, op. cit., III, 237–38.

24. Melnikov, op. cit., III, 225–36.

25. "Rogozhskoe kladbishche." In Brokgauz-Efron, *Entsiklopedicheskii slovar* (St. Petersburg, 1899), XXV, 892–93; S. V. Bakhrushin in *Istoriya Moskvy* (Moscow, 1954), III, 295.

26. A. von Haxthausen, *The Russian Empire, Its People, Institutions and Resources* (London, 1856), I, 275–76; Patrol Reports, December 11, 1846; January 20, February 10, June 11, 1947.

27. Ryndzyundsky, 205–206, 209; Rustik, p. 72.

28. Leroy-Beaulieu, III, 354.

29. Patrol Reports, August 1, 1846, see also Ryndzyundsky, 209.

30. Haxthausen, I, 277.

31. Ibid., p. 272: "The Starovertsi in the large cities—Moscow, St. Petersburg and Riga merchants and manufacturers who have grown rich, only remain true to their sect for the first generation; the next cut off their beards, throw off the kaftan, and put on coats; and with the old customs and dress, their religious notions also disappear."

32. Patrol Reports, December 1844; Nikolsky, pp. 237–38.

33. Leroy-Beaulieu, III, 343.

34. Patrol Reports, January 15, 1846.

35. Kelsiev, I, 36–38; Patrol Reports, March 7, 1846.

36. Nikolsky, p. 296.

37. W. Kolarz, *Religion in the Soviet Union* (London, 1961), pp. 140–41.

38. Patrol Reports, 1845–1846, *passim.;* Ryndzyundsky, 204, 208, 214, 218–19.

39. For details on the early Guchkov family history, I am indebted to Mr. Louis Menashe, who has examined a family chronicle, formerly owned and probably authored by the late Aleksander Guchkov and now in the possession of Madame L. Csaszar of Paris. See also Patrol Reports, July 15, 17, August 21, November 5, 23, 1847, for some interesting data on Fedor Guchkov's property and industrial holdings, his factory school, mortgage buying, and serf redeeming. On the Konovalovs, see Roger Portal, *"Du servage a la bourgeoisie: La famille Konovalov,"* Revue des études slaves, XXXVIII (1961), 143–50.

40. Quoted in Leroy-Beaulieu, III, 340. Brief statements of the main interpretations of tsarist times can be found in Milyukov, III, 206, 209–11; and Andreev, pp. 160–61.

41. For the Soviet views, see notes 2 and 10 above, and a discussion in Kolarz, pp. 129–31.

42. Leroy-Beaulieu, III, 338–39; Max Weber, *Wirtschaft und Gesellschaft,* 4th ed. (Tubingen, 1956), I, 292, and *The Protestant Ethic and the Spirit of Capitalism* (New York, 1958), pp. 39, 189–90, 197. Weber also had pertinent observations in his studies of Oriental society and of the city, although no other direct comments on the Russian religious dissenters.

43. Leroy-Beaulieu, III, 339.

VII Muscovite Industrialists: The Cotton Sector (1861–1914)

1. On this point we refer to the very useful collection of articles published under the direction of M. K. Rozhkova: *Ocherki ekonomiceskoi istorii Rossii pervoi poloviny XIX veka* [*Essays on the economic history of Russia in the middle of the nineteenth century*] (Moscow, 1959).

2. On the occasion of the centenary of the suppression of serfdom, the Division of Cultural Areas of the VI section from the Practical School of Higher Studies published (1963) in its *Studies on Economy, History and Sociology of Slavic Countries,* a collection of articles and translated documents in which the following participated: T. Bakounine,

M. Confino, Cl. Kastler, B. Kerblay, P. Pechoux, R. Philippot, and R. Portal: *The Status of Peasants Freed From Serfdom, 1861–1961*.

    3. Exportation of cereal and flour (value in millions of rubles):

1861	70
1870	166
1880	232
1890	341
1900	306
1905	508
1910	746

Source: P. A. Khromov, *Ekonomicheskoe razvitie Rossii v XIX–XX v.* [The economic development of Russia in the nineteenth and twentieth centuries] (Moscow, 1950), supplementary tables, pp. 472–74.

    4. There are, however (see note 11), cotton manufacturers who did not seem to come from the working classes.

    5. The argument found in *Istoriya S.S.S.R.* [*History of the USSR*] II, 508, is, however, contestable, because at the same time agricultural and industrial prices were raised. On this subject see Ya. I. Livsin, *Monopolii v ekonomike Rossi* [Monopoly in the economy of Russia] (Moscow, 1961), pp. 360–62. The rise of prices, moreover, is accentuated after 1910. The author, basing his figures on an index of average prices during the years 1890–1900 as 100, gives the following statistics for two products of basic need:

	1900–1901	*1910*	*1911*	*1912*	*1913*	*1914*
Cereals	120.2	117.2	130.1	147.8	130.1	140.1
Calico	116.4	137	135.7	123.3	124.7	137

    6. With the exception of the fact that 1912 was a bad year for harvests in about twenty districts in the outer Volga and the Siberian regions. The measures taken by the government checked the most outright effects of the famine.

7. R. Portal, "On the Origins of an Industrial Bourgeoisie in Russia," *Revue d'histoire modern contemporaine* (January–March, 1961), pp. 35–60; and similarly, "From Serfdom to the Bourgeoisie; the Konovalov Family," *Melanges Pierre Pascal*, pp. 143–50.

8. Of course the merchants didn't wait until this time to make themselves heard. But their requests for power, for example, those made by the Moscow merchants in 1821 during discussion on tariff rates, did not seem a determining factor even when the decisions made went in their favor.

9. *Istoriya S.S.S.R.*, vol. II, 1861–1917, *Period Kapitalizma* [*History of the USSR*, capitalist period] (Moscow, 1959), p. 222.

10. Distribution of Russian cotton industries around 1880 (in percentages):

	Spinning		Weaving	
Governments	*Spindles*	*Production*	*Looms*	*Production*
Moscow	25	27	23	20
Vladimir	16	20.4	29	31
Kostroma	0.8	0.9	12	12
Yaroslav	0.7	1	1.9	1.7
Ryazan	4.1	5.4	0.6	0.5
Tver	0.6	0.7	6.5	6.8
St. Petersburg	24	16.4	10.3	9.3
Estonia (Narva)	11	8	2.4	2.1
Poland (Petrkov)	6	8.6	2.4	2.1

11. On the repugnance of the first Old Believer manufacturers to participate in administrative functions, cf. R. Portal, "From Serfdom to the Bourgeoisie, op. cit., p. 148. On the relations between economic activity and the religion of the Old Believers, cf. the short Bibliography provided by R. Portal, "On the Origins of an Industrial Bourgeoisie," op. cit., p. 47, footnote, and p. 29, no. 31 (apropos P. G. Ryndzyunsky).

12. A family without male descendants in the twentieth century.

13. R. Portal, *Melanges Pierre Pascal*, p. 147, op. cit.

14. A. P. Polovnikov, *Torgovlya v staroi Rossi* [*Trade in Old Russia*] (Moscow, 1959), p. 50.

15. At Serpukhov, a very great business utilizing some 14,000 workers for the manufacture of printed fabrics and scarves.

16. The name designates a Moscow suburb. It concerns a calico factory specializing in sweaters and scarves. The factory was constructed in 1867 and belonged, from 1880 on, to N. I. Shchukin and to K. T. Soldatenkov. Six thousand workers.

17. A calico factory founded by a Frenchman in 1884, A. O. Hubner, whose successors, after his death, did not reside in Russia any longer. The factory, declining after 1905, was bought by N. A. Vtorov in 1910. Close to 2000 workers.

18. However, this type of weaving continued (for example in the Bogorodsk region, where village artisans were working for the Morozov family) up to the First World War. In the wool industry, the transformation was less rapid; around 1880 handweaving had scarcely ceded to mechanical weaving.

19. *Materialy po istorii Prokhorovskoi Trekhgornoi manufaktury i torgovo promyshlennoi deyatelnosti semi Prokhorovykh, Moskva 1799–1815* [Materials for the history of the Prokhorov factory of the three mountains and the industrial and commercial activity of the Prokhorov family Moscow, 1799–1915].

20. This information can be found in the brochure covering the family history.

21. S. M. Yuksimovich, *Manufakturnaya promyshlennost' v proshlom i nastoyashchem* [The manufacturing industry in the past and present] (Moscow, 1915), I, 134–39.

22. *To bumago-tkachkoi M br. G. i A. Gorbunovykh, 1826–1913* [The cotton weaving manufacturing company, G. and A. Gorvunov Brothers], op. cit., pp. 78–85.

23. Lev Gerasimovich Knoop, son of a small merchant from Bremen, who became a clerk for a commercial English firm. While involved in exporting cotton threads to Russia, he moved into Moscow in 1839 and began an extraordinary career which soon put him in the cen-

ter of all the cotton-thread purchases executed in England by the manufacturers; particularly, he dealt with importations of English threading machines which equipped the Russian factories in the 1840s. The buyer for the accounts of Morozov, Khlyudov, Malyutin, and Baranov, he got rich quickly; as a result of his having shares in more than 100 spinning factories it reached a point where people said: "Not a church without a Pope, not a factory without a Knoop." In 1857, together with the Moscow capitalist Soldatenkov, he created, on the Narova near Narva, the Kregholm spinning factory which, in 1914, employed 10,000 workers. Up till his death in 1894, Knoop, raised in 1877 to the hereditary rank of baron, occupied a dominant position in the textile industry. His son, Andrei Lvovich, managed the Kregholm factory from 1901 on.

24. Of 59 arshins (or 52 meters), especially calicos.

25. The value of factory goods had, between 1892 and 1911, risen from 1,760,000 to nearly 8,000,000 rubles. The purchasing of lands, forests, and peat bogs was carried out between 1897–1902 and 1907–1912; by 1912 the entire value was worth 600,000 rubles. In 1911–1912 the factory schools (270 boys and 140 girls) received a subsidy of 13,000 rubles, the factory hospitals, 52,000 rubles.

26. S. M. Yuksimovich, op. cit., pp. 161–67.

27. *Torgovoe i promyshlennoe delo Ryabushinsky* [The commercial and manufacturing enterprises of the Ryabushinsky family], 1913, edited by the P. P. Ryabushinsky Typographic Workshop.

28. We know, in fact, that with the approach of the Napoleonic armies, Moscow's businessmen hastily evacuated their stores and workshops and took refuge in the provinces. This explains why, in spite of the burning and pillage of Moscow in 1812, the city, once evacuated by the French, rapidly took up its activities again.

29. The fact that a merchant or a manufacturer, whose business was in jeopardy and who could no longer declare the minimum capital necessary to be enrolled in a guild, fell into the category of the *meshchanstvo* was rather frequent, especially in the second half of the nineteenth century and during troubled times.

30. This is a problem which has greatly occupied Soviet historians. Generally speaking, they attribute the development of Russian industry

to capital born from commerce, which allows us to draw an almost perfect analogy between the economic evolution of Russia and that of the West. In reality, however, the industrial development can be attributed only in part to the utilization of commercial capital. A good part of this development was due to the exercising of feudal rights: the utilization of almost free serf labor; the exploitation, cost-free, of resources (forests, and certain types of plants used to manufacture textiles) had a great deal to do with the prosperity of noble entrepreneurs, and also of self-made entrepreneurs who exercised, through tolerance or special privileges, their noble rights.

31. The end of the reign of Nicholas I was thus marked by violent persecution, carried on in Moscow by Governor Zabrevsky; it was at this time that the community archives of the Old Believers, located at the Preobrazhensk Cemetery, were confiscated by the police. These archives permitted the Soviet historian Ryndzyunskii to study in great depth the relations between the sect and industrial development.

32. In spite of the monetary reforms between 1839 and 1843, which reestablished the conversion rate of 3.5 rubles worth of assignats per one silver ruble, and finally replaced the assignats with credit notes (the latter bringing an even exchange), the merchants continued (for about twenty years) to balance their books in assignats.

33. The construction of railroads revolutionized the conditions of circulating goods in the region and brought about the decline of traffic through the canals. Among the three river routes that linked the Moscow Center to St. Petersburg, the Vyshnii-Volochek was the most important until around 1870. The Nicholas Railroad brought the decisive blow, and once the work on the Omega Canal was finished in 1852, the Marya Network, on which steam navigation was developed, slowly but surely dominated. The Tikhvin Route was no longer used except to transport wood.

34. This was also the case with the Naidenov family, owners of certain printing and dyeing factories. Of this family, one of the members, M. Naidenov, created the Commercial Bank of Moscow.

35. See Appendix, p. 40 (not included in this collection—ed.).

36. For the list of factories of the empire, consult: (1) P. A. Orlov, *Ukazatel' fabrik i zavodov Europeiskoi Rossii* [List of manufacturing

enterprises of European Russia] (Moscow, 1881). Figures valued for the year 1879. A second edition gives the foundation dates of the factories (1887). (2) *Fabriki i zavody vsei Rossii, svedeniya o fabrikah i zavodakh* [Industrial firms in Russia: statistical information] (Kiev, 1913). Figures valued for the year 1912.

37. These memoirs scarcely go back beyond the years 1830–1840. Written in the second half of the century, they were not published and were reserved for an elite circle of readers; therefore, they remained unknown for a long time. Cf. B. B. Kafengauz, "Kupecheskie memuary" ["Merchants' Memoirs"], in *Moskovskii Krai i ego proshloe* [The Moscow region and its past], *Ocherki po sotsialnoi i ekonomicheskoi istorii XV–XIX veka* [Essays on the social and economic history of the fifteenth–nineteenth centuries] (Moscow, 1928).

38. P. A. Berlin, *Russkaya burzhuaziya v staroe i novoe vremya* [The Russian bourgeoisie, past and present] (Moscow, 1922).

39. P. A. Buryskin, *Moskva Kupecheskaya* [Merchants Moscow] (New York, 1954).

40. P. Kovalevskii, "The 'Rascol' and His Role in Russia's Industrial Development," The Archives of the Sociology of Religions, 1957, no. 3, pp. 1–6.

41. P. G. Ryndzyundsky, *Gorodskoe grazhdanstvo doreformennoi Rossii* [The urban citizenship in Russia before 1861] (Moscow, 1952).

42. Cf. the Bibliography in Yatsunsky, *Cahiers du Monde russe et sovietique* (Paris), II, 3.

43. I. F. Gindin, *Russkie Kommercheskie banki* [The commercial banks of Russia] (Moscow, 1948), and likewise: *Gosudarstvennii bank i ekonomicheskaya politika Tsarskogo pravitel'stva* [The State Bank and the tsarist economic policy] (Moscow, 1960).

44. *Semeinaya Khronika Krestovnikovykh, 1901–1904* [Chronicles of the Krestonovnikov family] (Moscow).

45. A sign of this reduced economic expansion (always linked, moreover, to consolidation of businesses) is evident in the figures of the proportion of the number of merchants to the total population. In 1913, in a population of 147,000,000 inhabitants, there were 2,222,000 merchants or one merchant for every 66 persons; however, in 1900 the proportion was one merchant for every 78 persons. As to the proportions

of commercial proprietors per store or boutique, in the same time period they dropped from 159 to 129. Of course, such figures only have an indicative value; they do show, however, what authors ironically called, as an antinomy, the "inflation" (*razbukhanie*) of commercial organization in prerevolutionary Russia. A. P. Polovnikov, *Torgovlya v Staroi Rossii* [Commerce in Old Russia] (Moscow, 1958), p. 79, quoting S. G. Strumilin, *Ocherki sovetskoi ekonomiki* [Essays on the Soviet economy] (1930), pp. 230–31. The inadequacies of commercial organization appear in the table below:

Number of Stores and Wholesale Businesses, 1899–1912

1899	157,300	1906	136,800
1900	152,800	1907	140,100
1901	149,700	1908	146,700
1902	145,600	1909	156,700
1903	147,500	1910	162,000
1904	146,000	1911	175,800
1905	142,000	1912	183,200

46. A rather large bibliography on the formation of manufacturing monopolies in the years between 1900–1910 exists. The latest work is that of Ya. I. Livshin, *Monopolii v ekonomike Rossi* [Monopolies in the economy of Russia] (Moscow, 1961).

47. With the exception of some families without male descendants whose businesses were inherited by daughters and brothers-in-law.

VIII The State and the Economy

1. Cited by A. P. Pogrebinsky, *Ocherki istorii finansov dorevoliutsionnoi Rossii* [Essays on the history of Finances in pre-Revolutionary Russia] (*XIX–XX vv.*) [XIX–XX lectures] (Moscow, 1954), p. 98.

2. Between 1862 and 1870, for instance, the deficits amounted to about 300 million rubles (Pogrebinsky, 1888); between 1866 and 1888 the budget was officially balanced only three times (p. 87). Even thereafter deficits prevailed, but were concealed more skillfully.

3. Cited by P. P. Lyashchenko, *Istoriia narodnogo khoziaistva, SSSR* [History of the national economy of the Soviet Union] 2 vols., 3rd ed. (Moscow-Leningrad, 1952), II, 189.

4. One of the better-known examples was Bismarck's action in 1887 which drove the Russian securities from the Berlin stock market; another was the French demand in 1901 that Russia build the Sedlets-Bologoe railway line in return for the granting of a loan.

5. Figures from P. A. Khromov, *Ekonomicheskoe razvitie Rossii v XIX–XX vekakh* (Moscow-Leningrad, 1950), table 14, p. 469.

6. Vyshnegradsky, who otherwise had no prejudice against travel in Europe. The State Council, however, turned down his request. I mention this fact especially in order to underscore a point made about a "materialist interpretation" of the Iron Curtain by Ragnar Nurkse in *Problems of Capital Formation in Underdeveloped Countries* (Oxford, 1955), p. 76.

7. W. L. Langer, *The Franco-Russian Alliance, 1890–1894* (Cambridge, Mass., 1929), p. 228.

8. *"Dokladnaia zapiska Vitte Nikolaiu II," Istorik marksist,* no. 2/3 (1935), p. 130.

9. Ibid.

10. In Witte's letter to Nicholas II on agrarian reform. See Sergei Witte, *Vospominaniia. Tsarstvovanie Nikolaia II,* 2 vols. (Berlin, 1923), I, 467–73.

11. Witte, *Vorlesungen über Volks- und Staatswirtschaft,* 2 vols. (Stuttgart, 1913), I, 140.

12. Witte, *Vospominaniia,* I, 467–73.

13. In Witte's budget report for 1893.

14. Cited in Theodore H. Von Laue, "A Secret Memorandum of Sergei Witte on the Industrialization of Imperial Russia," *Journal of Modern History,* XXVI (March 1954), 65.

15. Witte always spoke of "the protective system," although strictly speaking the motives for the tariff of 1891 were fiscal, that is, designed to prevent imports for the sake of an active balance of payments. The terminology of protectionism, however, was a useful propaganda tool for industrialization.

16. My figures are based on the budgets published in Khromov, pp. 514 ff. For this rough estimate, I have added the expenses listed in the Ordinary Budgets for the service on the government debt, for the Ministries of Finance, Communications, State Domains and Agriculture, State Control, and the Administration of the State Stud-farms, and in the Extraordinary Budgets the funds for the expansion of railroads and ports and for the conversion of loans. This estimate for the economic expenditures of the government is probably slightly high: part of the debt service covered loans which had a military rather than an economic significance.

Total ordinary and extraordinary expenditures (in 1000 rubles):

1861–1870	1894–1902	1908–1914
4,594,000	15,137,000	22,128,000

Total economic expenditures (as itemized above):

2,091,000	10,611,000	12,223,000

17. Cited in Von Laue, pp. 64–74.

18. Von Laue, pp. 67–74.

19. B. F. Brandt, *Innostrannye kapitaly. Ikh vliianie na ekonomicheskoe razvitie strany,* 2 vols. (St. Petersburg, 1898–1899), I, 87.

20. A. V. Pogozhev, *Uchet chislennosti i sostava rabochykh v Rossii* (St. Petersburg, 1906), pp. 80–81.

21. Witte, *Vospominaniia,* I, 467–73.

22. My source for this is Witte's pamphlet, *Samoderzhavie i zemstvo* (Stuttgart, 1903), and his correspondence with Pobedonostsev of that time, published in *Krasnyi arkhiv,* XXX (1928), 89–116.

23. In *"Dokladnaia zapiska,"* cited above.

24. B. A. Romanov's *Rossiia v Manchzhurii* (Leningrad, 1928) gives a very misleading account of Witte's Far Eastern policy.

25. If the government was bad, wrote Witte to Pobedonostsev in 1899, a revolution was fully justified. *Krasnyi arkhiv,* XXX (1928), 104.

26. In the State Council, Nicholas II was likened to the mad Paul for issuing the decisive *ukaz* on the gold standard. See A. A. Polovstov's diary, *Krasnyi arkhiv,* XLVI (1931), 116.

27. Stalin's speech to the business executives of February 4, 1931. *Sochineniia,* XIII, 39. For a theory of "the revolution from without," see my *"Die Revolution von Aussen als erste Phase der russischen Revolution* 1917," *Jahrbücher für Geschichte Osteuropas,* IV (1956), 138–58.

28. There is much good material in an article by Olga Crisp, "Some Problems of French Investment in Russian Joint Stock Companies, 1894–1914," *Slavonic and East European Review,* XXXV (December 1956), 223–40.

29. Lyashchenko, II, 406.

30. For comparative statistics on industrial growth before 1914, see the League of Nations volume, *Industrialization and Foreign Trade* (New York, 1945).

31. Lyashchenko, II, 760.

IX *Stalin's Views on Soviet Economic Development*

1. The author acknowledges gratefully the support of the Russian Research Center of Harvard University in the preparation of this study. He is also indebted to Professor Alexander Gerschenkron and Dr. Joseph S. Berliner for valuable suggestions.

2. It goes without saying that the men who faced this question approached it with some definite, preconceived ideas. All of them were emphatic in recognizing the need for rapid economic development and in taking the latter to be synonymous with industrialization; in this respect they were faithfully following the line of Russian Marxism of the prerevolutionary era. They sharply deviated from the traditional approach by accepting Lenin's view that a proletarian party which succeeded in rising to political power in a backward country had a clear duty not to leave the task of industrialization to the bourgeoisie but to put itself in charge after dislodging the propertied classes from their positions of control. But this amendment, which came in response to the massive *faits accomplis* of the first revolutionary years, could not by itself make the original doctrine grind out solutions which would provide a clear-cut directive for action. The Marxian theory, to be sure, helped

to bring sharply into focus some phenomena and relationships which were of relevance for the impending decisions, like advantages of large-scale production, capital-consuming and labor-displacing effects of technological progress, importance of the relative size of investment and consumers'-goods industries. It was equally categorical in assigning to the transformation of property relationships the key role in the process of social change. But it provided no criterion for optimal solutions within each of these areas, or more particularly, for appropriate speed at which the transition from the existing state of affairs to a more satisfactory one should take place. Moreover, even determined efforts toward establishing such optimum conditions would not change the situation to any substantial extent. They could, at best, lead to a more clear-cut formulation of existing alternatives and, consequently, to elimination of some minor errors and inconsistencies from the judgments: but this would not eliminate the need for choosing nor reduce the formidable risks and uncertainties attendant upon the final decision and due to the nature of the problems involved.

3. *"Ekonomicheskie zametki," Pravda,* December 15, 1925. The notion of "forced sales" referred to the part of the produce sold by the peasant in order to meet such obligations as taxes or (in prerevolutionary Russia) payments to the landlords.

4. Abbreviation for *Osoboe soveshchanie po vosproizvodstvu osnovnogo kapitala promyshlennosti SSSR.*

5. For a more detailed account of the controversy, see Maurice Dobb, *Soviet Economic Development Since 1917* (New York, 1948), chap. VIII, and my *Soviet Industrialization Debate 1924–1928* (Cambridge, Mass., Harvard, 1960).

6. *XIV s"ezd vsesoiuznoi kommunisticheskoi partii (b). Stenograficheskii otchët* (Moscow-Leningrad, 1926), p. 191. In volume VII of Stalin's collected works containing the text of this speech the words "and we shall be" are omitted.

7. I. V. Stalin, *Sochineniia* (Moscow, 1947), VII, 355.

8. Ibid., p. 382.

9. Ibid., p. 153.

10. Ibid., pp. 123, 125.

11. Ibid., p. 29. How seriously Stalin took this idea can be seen from the fact that in the immediately following sentence he expressed grave concern about the situation in which Russia would find itself after her industry had "outgrown" the internal market and had to compete for the foreign markets with the advanced capitalist countries.

12. "Our country depends on other countries just as other countries depend on our national economy; but this does not mean yet that our country has lost, or is going to lose, its sovereignty [*samostoiatel'nost'*], . . . that it will become a little screw [*sic*] of the international capitalist economy" (ibid., IX, 132–133). Contrary to what may be the first impression, this passage is not incompatible either with the above-quoted statements or with Stalin's well-known pronouncements of later years. It does, however, provide an additional indication that Stalin's real long-term goal was superiority and not insularity. Such a policy, and more particularly the high rate of economic growth implied in it, did in fact make it rational to develop the domestic capital-goods industry on a substantial scale, since the demand for the services of this industry was known to be large and sustained and a sizable initial stock was already in existence; but it would also call for making extensive use of the advantages of international division of labor. Still, in the middle twenties, all this sounded rather academic because, as will be shown presently, the decision in favor of the high rate of growth had not yet been made.

13. Ibid., VII, 200.

14. Ibid., p. 131.

15. Ibid., pp. 315–16.

16. Ibid., VIII, 120.

17. Ibid., p. 131.

18. Ibid., p. 132.

19. Ibid., pp. 122–25.

20. Ibid., p. 287.

21. They include (1) improved incentives for peasant saving; (2) reduction in retail prices of industrial goods; (3) orderly amortization policies; (4) building up export reserves; (5) creation of budgetary surplus (ibid., pp. 126–29). In other contexts, elimination of waste and

inefficiency in economic and political administration receives the top billing (ibid., IX, 196, and joint declaration by Stalin, Rykov, and Kuibyshev in *Pravda,* August 17, 1926). Some of these measures, while pointing in the right direction, could hardly be expected to have much effect in the immediate future, and others involved putting the cart before the horse, e.g., price reductions not preceded by substantial expansion in productive capacity.

22. Stalin, *Sochineniia,* IX, 120.

23. Ibid., pp. 288, 352–53.

24. Ibid., X, 300.

25. Ibid., pp. 301–302.

26. Ibid., p. 309.

27. Ibid., p. 225.

28. "There is every indication that we could increase the yield of the peasant farms by 15–20 per cent within a few years. We have now in use about 5 million hoes. The substitution of ploughs for them could alone result in a most substantial increase in the output of grain in the country, not to speak of supplying the peasant farms with a certain minimum of fertilizer, improved seeds, small machinery and the like" (ibid., XI, 92).

29. Ibid., XII, 59.

30. Ibid., XI, 4–5.

31. Ibid., VIII, 291–92.

32. Ibid., XI, 15, 124–25.

33. Ibid., p. 12.

34. Ibid., p. 14.

35. Ibid., p. 267.

36. Ibid., p. 159 (italics in original). It may be worth noting that this speech, which led to the final break between Stalin and the Bukharin-Rykov group, was not published until 1949.

37. Ibid., p. 275.

38. Ibid., pp. 3–4, 235.

39. Ibid., X, 301.

40. Ibid., XI, 252–53.

41. Ibid., p. 40.

42. Ibid., XIII, 29–42, especially 38–40.

43. Ibid., pp. 192–93 and *Voprosy leninizma,* 11th ed. (Moscow, 1947), p. 575.

44. His *"Golovokruzhenie ot uspekhov"* (Stalin, *Sochineniia,* XII, 191–99), which put a temporary halt to the forced collectivization, is, to be sure, the best-known example of this. It may be worthwhile, however, to quote a similar instance from a different area. In 1930, with reports from industrial battlefields claiming big victories, Stalin allowed himself another brief spell of "dizziness with success": he called for raising the 1933 target for pig iron from 10 to 15–17 million tons and used abusive language against the "Trotskyite theory of the leveling-off curve of growth" (ibid., pp. 331, 349–52). In 1933, however, when the actual level of pig iron output fell far short of the initial target and the rate of overall industrial expansion slumped heavily, he did not hesitate to move more than halfway toward this much-detested theory: he argued then that the rate of growth in output had shown a decline as a result of the transition from the "period of restoration" to the "period of reconstruction," and went on to say that there was nothing sinister about it (ibid., pp. 183–85). But in the following years the rate of increase went up again, if not quite to the level of the preceding period, and the unholy distinction between "restoration" and "reconstruction" disappeared from Stalin's vocabulary.

45. Speech to the voters of the Stalin electoral district of Moscow, *Pravda,* February 10, 1946.

46. I. Stalin, *Ekonomicheskie problemy sotsializma v SSSR* (Moscow, 1952), p. 24. It goes without saying that this is much too strong a condition. An "uninterrupted growth of the national economy" is secured whenever the volume of investment exceeds the amount needed to maintain the capital equipment at a level sufficient to keep the income per head of growing population constant. This requirement might indeed involve a "preponderance [for example, more rapid tempo of growth] of the production of the means of production" if at least one of the following assumptions could be taken to hold: (1) abnormally high rate of wear and tear due either to low durability of the average

piece of machinery or to the unusually large share of old-vintage equipment in the existing capital stock; (2) necessity to provide productive facilities for a discontinuously large increase in the total labor force in order to offset the pressure of increasing population on the income-per-capita levels; (3) the capital-goods industry exposed to these pressures being adapted in its capacity to a very limited volume of net capital construction over and above the "normal" replacement levels. It would certainly be bold to argue that any of these assumptions actually prevailed in the Soviet economy of 1952. But it would be even more drastic to assume that when Stalin said "uninterrupted growth" he meant precisely this, and nothing else.

X The Decision to Collectivize Agriculture

1. *History of the Communist Party of the Soviet Union (Bolsheviks)* (New York, 1939), pp. 291–92.

2. Ibid., p. 292.

3. Ibid.

4. Ibid., p. 293.

5. A. M. Pankratova, ed., *Istoriya SSSR* (Moscow, 1946), III, 324.

6. Ibid.

7. *Stenograficheskii otchet XV s"ezda VKP(b)*, p. 56. As quoted in Pankratova, op. cit., p. 325. Italics mine.

8. M. P. Kim, ed., *Istoriya SSSR, Epokha Sotsializma* (Moscow, 1958). See particularly pp. 360–67.

9. Ibid., p. 363.

10. Ibid.

11. Alexander Baykov, *The Development of the Soviet Economic System* (New York, 1947), pp. 138–39, 189–93. Maurice Dobb, *Soviet Economic Development since 1917* (New York, 1948), pp. 215–23.

12. Edward Hallett Carr, *A History of Soviet Russia. Socialism in One Country: 1924–26* (London, 1958), vol. I, chap. V.

13. For an example of this approach, see Harry Schwartz, *Russia's Soviet Economy* (New York, 1954), p. 113. Schwartz offers three fac-

tors which "merged in determining the final outcome of this struggle": (1) the rising need for grain for more rapid industrialization, (2) the tendency of kulak farming to restrict the grain supply, and (3) the fact that the government had long been committed to the objective of socialized agriculture.

14. W. Bowden, M. Karpovich, and A. P. Usher, *An Economic History of Europe since 1750* (New York, 1937), p. 770. Karpovich was commenting on the adoption of the First Five-Year Plan as a whole, though in the context of the comment the decision to socialize agriculture was the main object of attention.

15. Schwartz, op. cit., p. 113.

16. Herbert S. Dinerstein, *Communism and the Russian Peasant* (Glencoe, Ill., 1955), p. 19.

17. For a variety of forms of this particular emphasis see: Donald W. Treadgold, *Twentieth Century Russia* (Chicago, 1959), pp. 225–28; Georg von Rauch, *A History of Soviet Russia* (New York, 1957), pp. 178–81; David Mitrany, *Marx Against the Peasant* (Chapel Hill, N.C., 1951), pp. 70–73.

18. Sidney Harcave, *Russia: A History*, 4th ed. (New York, 1959), pp. 576–79. Dinerstein, op. cit., p. 19; Schwartz, op. cit., pp. 112–13; Georg von Rauch, op. cit., pp. 180–81.

Both Dinerstein and Rauch are critical of these concepts but both employ them in their analysis, even if in inverted commas. There are, of course, many other examples which could be given, especially of the borrowing of the work of Soviet specialists by those who are not specialists.

19. The question is examined from several points of view in Lancelot Lawton, *An Economic History of Soviet Russia* (London, 1932), II, 355–58. It has also been examined more recently (and more systematically) by Donald W. Treadgold, op. cit., pp. 267–69.

20. Naum Jasny, *The Socialized Agriculture of the USSR* (Stanford, 1949), p. 223. Many of the criticisms of the Soviet economic rationalization are taken from Jasny and Lawton. It is indeed surprising how the more significant conclusions of both of these scholars concerning Soviet economic life in the 1920s have been ignored, even by specialists in Soviet economic development.

21. Ibid., pp. 223–27. An exception among government leaders was Bukharin (see below) who did not insist on what he styled the hoarding "fairy tale."

22. On the migration schemes of the 1920s, see Carr, op. cit., pp. 520–29. Plainly the large-scale colonization of the pre-World War I era had been replaced by a colonization program which produced maximum plans and minimum results.

23. The Bolshevik impact upon the cooperative movement was far removed in reality from the promising transformation which Lenin predicted would occur (and later claimed had occurred) with the placing of the "bourgeois" system in a "proletarian" environment. The main historian of cooperation in the early years of Bolshevik power writes: "The Soviet power succeeded in utilizing the co-operative apparatus, but having transformed it into 'Sovietized' machinery of state, co-operation was deprived of the spirit of initiative and thus it became a typical bureaucratic mechanism. After it underwent all the changes demanded by the government, it became a 'living corpse'; the body still remained but the spirit was gone." Elsie T. Blanc, *Co-operative Movement in Russia* (New York, 1924), pp. 197–98.

24. A. Yugoff, *Economic Trends in Soviet Russia* (London, 1930), p. 347.

25. These problems are very interestingly discussed in Jasny, op. cit., pp. 213–31.

26. Dobb, op. cit., p. 222.

27. Ibid.

28. Carr, op. cit., pp. 245–46, 260.

29. Dinerstein, op. cit., p. 18.

30. I. V. Stalin, *"O pravoi opasnosti v VKP* (b)," *Sochineniia* (Moscow, 1949), p. 225.

31. Ibid.

32. Ibid., p. 228.

33. Ibid., p. 227.

34. Ibid.

35. Rykov's views on the important question of the relative em-

phasis of light and heavy industry are discussed in Abdurakhman Avtorkhanov, *Stalin and the Soviet Communist Party* (New York, 1959), pp. 84–85.

36. N. I. Bukharin, *"Zametki ekonomista. (K nachalu novogo khozyaistvennogo goda),"* *Pravda,* September 30, 1928. Quotation taken from the translation in B. D. Wolfe, *Khrushchev and Stalin's Ghost* (New York, 1957), p. 302.

37. Ibid., p. 305.

38. Ibid., p. 309.

39. Ibid., p. 303.

40. Ibid., p. 308.

41. Ibid., pp. 308–309.

42. Though his approach is different from my own, this viewpoint is shared by A. Avtorkhanov when he writes of Stalin: "Those whom he attacked as rightists did not differ from Stalin regarding the need of moving toward socialism, or the need of promoting industrialization, or the need of socializing agriculture, but on the manner and means of doing these things." (Avtorkhanov, op. cit., p. 84.)

43. This view was expounded in detail in Lev Trotskii, *The Real Situation in Russia* (New York, 1928).

XI Financing Soviet Economic Development

1. Before 1930 the transportation and communications systems were included in the budget on a gross basis; this was true of almost all state enterprises during War Communism (1918–1921).

2. Money continues to flow, of course, but the possessor of money has so little option as to its use that the role of money in transaction must be considered trivial.

3. And not only for ideological reasons. Remember that Western investors took a heavy loss when the Bolsheviks refused to honor the very large foreign debts of the Russian imperial government.

4. Amounting to as much as 3 to 4 percent of total budget receipts.

5. Demand deposits pay only 3 percent.

6. Cf. F. D. Holzman, "The Burden of Soviet Taxation," *American Economic Review,* September 1953, table 1.

7. Since the currency reform, consumer-goods prices have declined steadily; this may eventually have a positive effect on the incentive to save. From 1928 to 1947, consumer-goods prices increased, on the average, about twentyfold. Cf. Naum Jasny, *The Soviet Price System* (Stanford University Press, 1951), chap. 2.

8. Perhaps it should also be noted that the Soviet rural population appears to have the usual peasant distrust of banks and prefers to hold a large part of its savings in the form of cash.

9. The Soviet state budget is a consolidated budget consisting of the all-Union, republican, and local budgets. It is equivalent to the sum of the federal, state, and local budgets in the United States.

10. Looked upon as a markup over cost, as is customary in the West, the tax rates are much higher, of course. A 50-percent tax becomes one of 100 percent; a 90-percent tax becomes one of 900 percent.

11. Although for convenience it will be referred to as a profits tax.

12. For incentive reasons, from 1 to 5 percent of planned profits and 15 to 45 percent of overplan profits are deducted into the Directors' Fund. These amounts are disbursed as bonuses to workers and managers, for workers' housing, for cultural projects, and for extra-plan investment in the enterprises.

13. We might also have included in the category of taxes which enter the commodity price structure the incomes of economic organizations which are allocated "to the trade unions and special funds for workers' training and education" (cf. Abram Bergson, "Soviet National Income and Product," *Quarterly Journal of Economics,* May 1950, p. 288).

14. The Soviet income tax on the urban population does not differ substantially from the income taxes in other countries except that different social and economic classes pay according to different rate schedules in application of Soviet "class policy." Thus workers, artists, professionals with private practices (e.g., lawyers and doctors), and private

shopkeepers pay at rapidly ascending rates (on identical money incomes) from left to right. The rural population pays a very different sort of tax (called the agricultural tax) because the bulk of peasant incomes is in kind. This necessitates, among other things, fairly cumbersome methods of assessing personal income and estimating the amount of tax to be paid. The agricultural tax discriminates in favor of the collective farmer and against the private peasant.

15. In fact, for about twenty years they have not referred to it as a tax on the population, but rather as "accumulation of socialized industry," implying that the amounts returned to the budget are a result solely of great increases in productivity.

16. That persons having their incomes reduced by taxes would tend to work harder.

17. Cf. Abram Bergson, *The Structure of Soviet Wages* (Harvard University Press, 1946), chaps. 13 and 14.

18. Joseph Stalin, *Problems of Leninism* (Moscow: Foreign Languages Publishing House, 1940), pp. 371–73.

19. Bergson, *The Structure of Soviet Wages,* as cited.

20. Cf. Holzman, op. cit., table 3.

21. Ibid., Table 3.

22. The Soviet turnover tax appears to have had a somewhat regressive rate structure in the prewar period; the postwar structure seems to be considerably less regressive and may be roughly proportional. The rate structure is much too complex, and the information on income-expenditure patterns much too limited, for us to come to any but the most tentative conclusions on this matter, however. Cf. F. D. Holzman, *Soviet Taxation: The Fiscal and Monetary Problems of a Planned Economy* (Harvard University Press, 1955), chap. 6.

23. This is especially true since the Soviets have virtually no explicit rent payments but include them implicitly in the turnover tax.

24. Also perhaps to extract the "economic rent" from such practices.

25. What we have said of the urban income tax applies also to the agricultural tax. The agricultural tax discriminates against the private farmer and in favor of the collective farmer.

26. Lottery winners have their bonds redeemed at the same time they receive their lottery prizes. At present, one-third of the subscribers to a bond issue eventually win lottery prizes.

27. Of course, very few bonds were ever actually paid off: the conversions put off repayments in the 1930s and the Currency Reform of 1947 eliminated the need for repayment on two-thirds of all outstanding obligations. However, even if there had been no conversions, the real value of ten-year bonds at maturity could hardly ever have amounted to more than about one-quarter of original value, so rapid was the rise in consumer goods prices in the pre-1948 period. Cf. Naum Jasny, *The Soviet Economy During the Plan Era* (Stanford University Press), 1951, p. 58.

28. This is also true of the consumer and producer cooperatives, but the amounts have never been significant.

29. More often than not, the retained profit of a group of enterprises has been redistributed among them for investment purposes by the administrative head of the group (or *glavk*, translated "chief administration"). Recently, the power of the *glavk* to do this was reduced. Cf. *The New York Times*, August 14, 1952, article by Harry Schwartz.

30. This is because the bulk of the deduction into the Directors' Fund is based on overplan profits, and a firm which reduced planned losses by a certain amount would be considered to have exceeded the plan in the same direction as one which increased positive profits.

31. Receipts from sale of surplus property or livestock are also deposited in the "indivisible fund." Initially, this fund is based on the value of the property and money payments of the collective farmers to the collective farm at the time the farm is organized.

32. Cf. Alexander Baykov, *The Development of the Soviet Economic System* (London: Cambridge University Press, 1946), p. 404.

33. L. E. Hubbard, *Soviet Money and Finance* (London: Macmillan, 1936), p. 228.

34. This refers to the well-known "control by the ruble." This is to say, by making state enterprises dependent upon the State Bank for funds, the bank is placed in a position in which it can supervise and check the progress of enterprises, and put pressure on enterprises which are not operating satisfactorily or according to plan.

35. Gregory Grossman, "The Union of Soviet Socialist Republics," in *Comparative Banking Systems,* B. H. Beckhart, ed. (Columbia University Press, 1954), pp. 733–68.

36. The part used for capital repair is deposited in the state bank.

37. If the procurement price of a bushel of grain which cost 40 rubles to produce were only 20 rubles, and the state resold the grain (as bread) for 100 rubles, the turnover tax on a bushel would be 80 rubles, of which it could be said that 20 rubles (40 minus 20) was paid by the producer and 60 (100 minus 40) by the consumer.

38. Bergson, in his famous study of Soviet wages, demonstrated that relative wages in the Soviet Union appear to reflect relative differences in productivity (cf. Bergson, *The Structure of Soviet Wages,* as cited, pp. 207–209). On this basis one can take the free-market wage for a particular job as a rough measure of the value of the job performance to the state.

39. This separation is attempted for grains, on the basis of heroic assumptions, in Holzman, *Soviet Taxation,* as cited, chap. 7.

40. The *sovkhozy,* or state farms, are owned by the state but produce a very small percentage of total agricultural output.

XII The Main Features of Soviet Forced Labor

1. E. H. Carr gives some information about corrective labor in this period in his *Socialism in One Country, 1924–1926* (London, 1958–1959), II, 423–27, 445–47.

2. The official Soviet statistical yearbook for 1928 (TsSU, *Statisticheski spravochnik za 1928* [1929], pp. 900–901) has given 145,600 as the total number of prisoners on January 1, 1928, and 182,600 on January 1, 1929. It is significant, however, that the figure on January 1, 1929, did not include data on the Karelian ASSR, the Murmansk region, and the Tatar ASSR. These were the regions where forced-labor camps were set up.

3. Victor Kravchenko, *I Chose Freedom: The Personal and Political Life of a Soviet Official* (London, 1947), pp. 405–406.

4. For a survey of this literature for the period up to 1945 see

Dallin and Nicolaevsky, *Forced Labour in Soviet Russia* (1948), pp. 309–19. For a later period see Paul Barton, *L'Institution concentrationnaire en Russie: 1930–1957* (Paris, 1959), pp. 501–16.

5. G. Herling, *A World Apart* (1951).

6. P. J. de la F. Wiles, *The Number of Soviet Prisoners* (1953, privately circulated), app. II.

7. UN and ILO, Ad Hoc Committee on Forced Labor, Report [Ad Hoc Committee in subsequent references], *ESCOR,* 16th sess., suppl. no. 13, 1953, pp. 91–92.

8. B. Roeder, *Katorga: An Aspect of Modern Slavery* (1958).

9. See above, p. 18.

10. Cf. the account by Ernst Fallgren in Dallin and Nicolaevsky, pp. 1–19.

11. In 1950–1951, according to a computation by Francis Seton of Nuffield College, Oxford (in a paper read to the American Economic Association in Chicago in 1958), the increase in capital and labor accounted for about 45 percent of the yearly output growth, the other 55 percent being due to innovation, and technical and administrative improvements.

XIII The Great Industrialization Drive

1. Approximately the same period was called the Plan Era, meaning the Era of the Five-Year Plans (FYPs), in this writer's *The Soviet Economy During the Plan Era,* published in 1951. The assignment of so much importance to the FYPs was soon recognized as a deeply regrettable error.

2. *Problems of Leninism,* 11th ed. (Moscow, 1947), p. 369.

3. "The Law of Steady Growth of the National Economy of the USSR," *Communist,* 1952, no. 20, p. 76.

4. See K. V. Ostrovityanov et al., Political Economy (official) textbook (Moscow, 1954), pp. 409–13. The text contains a special chapter, "Basic Economic Law of Socialism," in which the idea of priority of heavy industry is expounded at length.

5. Private trade was already fully prohibited in 1931. In 1957, a boy was put in jail for a week for peddling a book by Fenimore Cooper (obviously his own) in the street. Even this little act of trade is believed incompatible with the Soviet kind of socialism.

6. A person engaged in one of the few permitted handicrafts and not employing hired labor has to pay taxes on an annual income of between 8401 and 12,000 rubles amounting to 1596 rubles on the first 8401 rubles, plus 37.5 percent on the balance. The rate charged for each additional ruble increases beyond 12,000 rubles per year until it reaches 81 percent of the amount over 70,000 rubles per year. See decree of March 21, 1951, in *Reference Book of a Tax Officer* (Moscow: State Publishing Office for Finance, 1951), p. 119.

7. The figure is for net investment. Construction proper may have increased somewhat less.

8. Personal communication from Dr. Clark.

9. "Mineral Consumption and Economic Development in the United States and the Soviet Union," supplement to D. B. Shimkin, "Minerals: A Key to Soviet Power" (Cambridge, Mass.: Russian Research Center, Harvard University, 1952, mimeographed), p. 49.

10. In *Konjunkturpolitik* (Berlin), 1956, no. 2, p. 80, the growth in Soviet national income in 1928–1952 was calculated by the writer at 228 percent at 1926–1927 prices and at 159 percent at 1952 prices. The geometric average for the two percentage rises is 189 (1928 equals 100).

11. Compulsory transfers from one job to another and similar assignments of new jobs were in force from 1940 to about 1953. Since then, the practice seems to have been limited to former students who have to accept jobs assigned them as payment for the tuition and the stipend they were getting while at school.

12. In addition to expenditures earmarked in the budget for the military ministries, expenditures of a military nature are found also in budgetary appropriations for fixed investment, education, and so on.

13. The two items (investment and total military expenditures) should not be added in view of a certain amount of duplication.

14. The average per capita income was estimated at 313.8 rubles

for the nonfarm population and at 116.8 rubles for the farm population. See *1st FYP*, I, 137. The difference was actually not as large as the data indicate in view of the differences in prices at which the incomes of the two great population groups were calculated, but it was large even at equal prices.

15. Real incomes were presumably above the 75-percent mark for both population groups also in 1929 and 1930. It took time to press the consumption level down from that predating the Industrialization Drive to a level more typical of the drive era.

16. Including barter, wages in kind, etc.

17. Colin Clark and Julius Wyler avoided dealing with the effect of the commercialization of consumption and of the transfer of production on the rates of growth of national income by calculating the consumption of households uniformly at retail prices.

18. Fiscal year October–September; the fiscal year was abolished at the end of 1930.

19. By order of May 1955, the idea of planning for a period of ten to fifteen years (the general plan) has been revived. According to the announcement of October 1957, the Soviet Union will have a Seven-Year Plan in 1959–1965.

20. In the summer of 1927, the almost endless upward revisions of the targets set in the draft of the First FYP, known as the *Perspectives*, began. This time might have been another suitable date as the starting point of the *Warming-Up* period and the Great Industrialization Drive as a whole.

21. Peter Wiles of Oxford wants to treat the prewar segment of the period here analyzed as a preliminary stage, with postwar the mature stage. This writer hesitates to accept this subdivision. But Wiles' suggestion contains the relevant observation of the substantial difference between the prewar and postwar economy.

22. *Industry of the USSR*, 1957, pp. 122, 124.

23. Ibid., p. 120.

24. Data from A. A. Chertkova, *Labor Productivity on the Railway Transportation of the USSR* (1957), p. 50.

XIV The Soviet Economy: Performance and Growth

1. Raymond Goldsmith, "The Economic Growth of Tsarist Russia, 1860–1913," *Economic Development and Cultural Change,* Chicago, April 1961, p. 471.

2. Ibid., pp. 453–54.

3. See app. I, table I-1, this study.

4. *Narodnoe khozyaystvo SSSR v 1964 godu* [The economy of the USSR in 1964] (Moscow, 1965), p. 92.

5. There is no overall ranking for industrial output, but the USSR slipped one rank in coal, steel, and electric power, and two ranks in iron ore, between 1913 and 1928. See *Narodnoe khozyaystvo SSSR v 1964 godu,* op. cit., p. 93.

6. G. Warren Nutter, *Growth of Industrial Production in the Soviet Union* (Princeton, N.J.: Princeton University Press, 1962), p. 164.

7. Nicholas DeWitt, *Education and Professional Employment in the USSR* (Washington, D.C.: National Science Foundation, 1961), p. 577.

8. Frederick Harbison and Charles Myers, *Education, Manpower, and Economic Growth* (New York: McGraw-Hill Book Co., 1964), p. 46.

9. Simon Kuznets, "Industrial Distribution of National Product and the Labor Force," *Economic Development and Cultural Change,* July 1957.

10. Abram Bergson, Hans Heymann, and Oleg Hoeffding, *Soviet National Income and Product, 1928–1948, Revised Data* (Santa Monica, Calif.: The RAND Corporation, 1966), p. 13.

11. Stanley H. Cohn, in U.S. Congress, Joint Economic Committee, *Annual Economic Indicators for the USSR,* Washington, D.C., Government Printing Office, 1964, table VIII-6, p. 97.

12. Angus Maddison, *Economic Growth in the West* (New York: Twentieth Century Fund, 1964), pp. 201–202.

13. Michael C. Kaser, "Education and Economic Progress," *The*

Economics of Education, ed. E. A. G. Robinson and J. E. Vaizey (New York: St. Martin's Press, 1966), p. 169.

14. The ability of the Soviet system to survive tremendous wartime losses, sustain a victorious military effort, and support rapid recovery is a theme worthy of detailed, separate analysis. In this study, it will only be noted in summary fashion.

15. Maddison, op. cit., p. 31.

16. Warren W. Eason, "Labor Force," in *Economic Trends in the Soviet Union,* ed. Abram Bergson and Simon Kuznets (Cambridge, Mass.: Harvard University Press, 1963), p. 87.

17. Stanley H. Cohn, "Soviet Growth Retardation: Trends in Resource Availability and Efficiency," in U.S. Congress, Joint Economic Committee, *New Directions in the Soviet Economy,* Washington, D.C., Government Printing Office, 1966, p. 114.

18. Simon S. Kuznets, *Capital in the American Economy,* National Bureau of Economic Research (Princeton, N.J.: Princeton University Press, 1961), p. 80; John W. Kendrick, *Productivity Trends in the United States,* National Bureau of Economic Research (Princeton, N.J.: Princeton University Press, 1961), p. 167. Kendrick's estimates, which exclude housing and government capital, show no negative trends for any decade between 1869 and 1953. Kuznets' estimates, which include both of these factors to the extent that data are available, show a rising ratio of gross capital to GNP through 1919, with a secular decline through 1955. Estimates of United States capital stock based on Bulletin F depreciation rates indicate that the post-1919 trend has persisted into the 1960s. The postwar estimates for Western Europe are preliminary calculations by Edward Denison, as reported in Michael Boretsky, "Comparative Progress in Technology, Productivity, and Economic Efficiency: USSR versus U.S.," *New Directions in the Soviet Economy,* op. cit., p. 212.

19. For a comparison of postwar, fixed, nonresidential output ratios, see Cohn, "Soviet Growth Retardation," *New Directions in the Soviet Economy,* op. cit., p. 120. If historical ratios of investment to output, as computed by Simon Kuznets, are compared with postwar ratios, as computed by this author using techniques and sources described in

the article cited, ratios for Germany and Italy prove to have been at historic lows after World War II and those for Japan at the lowest level in this century.

20. Reliable estimates of capital stock are not available for other major economies for years prior to World War II, thus limiting the comparison to the economy of the United States.

21. Kuznets, op. cit., p. 64.

22. Data suitable for constructing production functions for West European economies are available only for the postwar years and are limited to factors of man-years and business capital investment. In West Germany, France, and Italy, between 1950 and 1962, the preponderant influence on growth was exerted by factor productivity rather than factor inputs. See Boretsky, op. cit.

23. Simon Kuznets, "The Share and Structure of Consumption," *Economic Development and Cultural Change,* January 1962, pp. 72–74. Also see app. I, this study, for estimates on which the choice of analogues is based.

24. Ibid.

25. Simon Kuznets, "Long-Term Trends in Capital Formation Proportions," *Economic Development and Cultural Change,* July 1961, pp. 10–11.

26. Simon Kuznets, *Capital in the American Economy,* op. cit., p. 133.

27. Ibid.

28. *Kapitalnoe stroitelstvo v SSSR* [Capital construction in the USSR], Central Statistical Administration, Moscow, 1961, pp. 39, 187.

29. Simon Kuznets, *Economic Development and Cultural Change,* July 1961, pp. 65, 73, 97, 116.

30. Janet G. Chapman, "Consumption," in *Economic Trends in the Soviet Union,* edited by Abram Bergson and Simon Kuznets, op. cit., p. 238.

31. Timothy Sosnovy, "Housing Conditions and Urban Development in the USSR," *New Directions in the Soviet Economy,* op. cit., 1966, p. 533.

32. Cohn, "Soviet Growth Retardation," *New Directions in the Soviet Economy*, op. cit., p. 118.

33. Ibid., p. 117.

34. Norman M. Kaplan, "Capital Formation and Allocation," *Soviet Economic Growth*, ed. Abram Bergson (Evanston, Ill.: Row and Peterson, 1953), p. 59.

35. Ibid., p. 63.

36. Cohn, "Soviet Growth Retardation," *New Directions in the Soviet Economy*, op. cit., p. 118.

37. Estimates of Raymond Powell, in *Economic Trends in the Soviet Union*, ed. Bergson and Kuznets, op. cit., pp. 88, 178.

38. Estimates of Gale Johnson, in ibid., p. 218.

39. Deborah C. Paige, "Economic Growth: The Last Hundred Years," *National Institute Economic Review*, London, England, July 1961, p. 39.

40. Douglas B. Diamond, "Trends in Output, Inputs, and Factor Productivity in Soviet Agriculture," *New Directions in the Soviet Economy*, op. cit., p. 353.

41. Murray Feshbach, "Manpower in the USSR," *New Directions in the Soviet Economy*, op. cit., 1966, p. 786.

42. Angus Maddison, "Soviet Economic Performance," *Banca Nazionale del Lavoro Quarterly Review*, Rome, Italy, March 1965, p. 13.

43. Diamond, op. cit., pp. 348, 381.

44. Cohn, "Soviet Growth Retardation," *New Directions in the Soviet Economy*, op. cit., p. 115.

45. Ibid., p. 111.

46. More explicitly, each level of attainment is valued as the total cost expended for education per person, including incomes foregone by the students. The procedure is based on the methodology developed by Nicholas DeWitt in "Costs and Returns in Education in the USSR," an unpublished doctoral dissertation of Harvard University, 1962.

47. Theodore W. Schultz, "Reflections on Investment in Men," *Journal of Political Economy*, Supplement, Chicago, October, 1962, p. 6.

48. Simon Kuznets, *Capital in the American Economy,* op. cit., p. 64.

49. Maddison, op. cit., p. 224.

50. Edward F. Denison, *The Sources of Economic Growth in the United States,* Committee for Economic Development, 1962, p. 148.

Appendix II

1. Stanley H. Cohn, *Derivation of 1959 Value-Added Weights for Originating Sectors of Soviet Gross National Product* (McLean, Va.: Research Analysis Corporation, TP-210, 1966), p. 21.

2. Douglas Diamond, "Trends in Output, Inputs, and Factor Productivity in Soviet Agriculture," U.S. Congress, Joint Economic Committee, *New Directions in the Soviet Economy* (Washington, D.C.: Government Printing Office, 1966), p. 373.

3. Nicholas DeWitt, "Costs and Returns in Education in the USSR," unpublished doctoral dissertation (Cambridge, Mass.: Harvard University, 1962), p. 273.

4. Cohn, op. cit., p. 17.

Bibliography

Note: The monographic literature on this subject is enormous, particularly works in the Russian language. The following bibliography is intended as a kind of critical master list. Asterisks placed by certain works indicate that they contain substantial bibliographies of various kinds of sources where more exhaustive bibliographical work can be pursued.

I. General Surveys, Interpretative Works, and Treatments of Particular Periods

Abramov, A. *Prichiny ekonomicheskoi otstalnosti tsarskoi Rossii.* [Causes of the economic backwardness of tsarist Russia.] Leningrad, 1941.

The only Soviet study directed specifically to this problem, with some useful suggestions.

* Blackwell, William L. *The Beginnings of Russian Industrialization 1800–1860*. Princeton, 1968.

A survey of industry, transport, technology, state policy, and private enterprise in the period immediately prior to the Russian Industrial Revolution.

* ————. *The Industrialization of Russia*. New York, 1970.

A short summary of the most important trends and literature with regard to Russian industrial development in the tsarist and Soviet periods.

Dobb, Maurice. *Soviet Economic Development since 1917*. 2d ed. London, 1966.

The oldest (first edition, 1928) and best-known survey of Soviet economic development, written from a Marxist point of view sympathetic to Soviet goals and policies.

Gille, Bertrand. *Histoire économique et sociale de la Russie*. Paris, 1949.

The standard French survey of Russian economic development from medieval times to the present.

Jasny, Naum. *Soviet Industrialization 1928–1952*. Chicago, 1961.

A landmark work by a leading American economist specializing in the Soviet Union, and the first to study the costs and performance as well as the achievements of Stalinist industrialization.

Khromov, Pavel. *Ekonomicheskoe razvitie Rossii*. [The economic development of Russia.] Moscow, 1967.

A leading recent Soviet study, essentially quantitative in its orientation, of the development of agriculture, industry, and banking in tsarist Russia.

* Lyashchenko, Peter. *History of the National Economy of Russia to 1917*. New York, 1949.

This is a translation of the older and best-known Soviet history of the pre-1917 economy. A comprehensive study, parts of which are becoming outdated.

————. *Istoriya narodnovo khozyaistva SSSR*. [History of the national economy of the USSR.] 4th ed. Moscow, 1956.

The third, substantial volume of Lyashchenko's study, not translated.

Nove, Alec. *An Economic History of the USSR*. London, 1969.

The most recent and the best survey of Soviet economic history, the work of a noted economist.

Plekhanov, G. V. *Istoriya Russkoi obshchestvennoi mysli, vvedenie.* [The history of Russian social thought, introduction.] Moscow, 1914. Vol. I.

Plekhanov's great classic, which traces the social and economic foundations of oriental despotism in tsarist Russia.

―――――. *Introduction à l'histoire sociale de la Russie*. Paris, 1926.

A French translation of the above.

Rozhkova, N. K., ed. *Ocherki ekonomicheskoi istorii Rossii, pervoi poloviny XIX veka.* [Essays on the economic history of Russia, the first half of the nineteenth century.] Moscow, 1959.

A first-rate Soviet study, somewhat narrowly conceived.

Schwartz, Harry. *Russia's Soviet Economy*. New York, 1958.

The best known and most readable American survey of the Soviet economy since 1917.

―――――. *The Soviet Economy since Stalin*. New York, 1965.

Economic problems essentially of the Khrushchev era.

Tugan-Baranovsky, Mikhail I. *Russkaya fabrika v proshlom i nastoyashchem.* [The Russian factory in past and present.] 3rd ed. St. Petersburg, 1907.

Another classic from tsarist times, the first important industrial history of Russia, and still very valuable.

―――――. *Geschichte der Russischen Fabrik*. Berlin, 1900.

A German translation of the above.

―――――. *The Russian Factory in the Nineteenth Century.* American Economic Association, 1970.

An English translation of the above.

II. Agriculture

Belov, F. *The History of a Collective Farm*. New York, 1955.

Personal experience of peasants in the Stalin era.

* Blum, Jerome. *Lord and Peasant in Russia from the Ninth to the Nineteenth Century.* Princeton, 1961.

A comprehensive survey of Russian agrarian history and its literature to the 1861 emancipation.

Confino, Michael. *Domaines et seigneurs en Russie vers la fin du xviii siècle.* Institut d'études slaves, Paris, *Collection historique,* vol. XVIII (1963).

Reasons for the economic difficulties of Russian landlords at the end of the eighteenth century.

Jasny, Naum. *The Socialized Agriculture of the U.S.S.R.* Stanford, 1949.

The definitive study of Soviet agriculture in the 1930s and 1940s.

――――. *Khrushchev's Crop Policy.* Glasgow, 1965.

The corn drive and other policies.

Kahan, Arcadius. "The Costs of Westernization in Russia: the Gentry and the Economy in the 18th Century," *Slavic Review,* XXV (1966), 40–46.

Entrepreneurial activities of the Russian gentry on their estates.

* Lewin, Moshe. *Russian Peasants and Soviet Power.* London, 1968.

The most detailed study we have of the economic, and administrative background of the 1929 collectivization drive.

* Robinson, Gerold T. *Rural Russia Under the Old Régime.* New York, 1932.

Definitive on agrarian problems during the reigns of the last three tsars.

Semevsky, V. I. *Krestyanye v tsarstvovanie imperatritsy Yekateriny II.* [The peasants in the reign of Empress Catherine II.] 2 vols. St. Petersburg, 1881–1901.

――――. *Krestyanskii vopros v Rossii v XVIII i pervoi polovinye XIX vyeka.* 2 vols. [The peasant question in Russia in the eighteenth and the first half of the nineteenth centuries.] St. Petersburg, 1888.

Classic studies of the peasants in Russia in the late eighteenth and early nineteenth centuries by one of the best known *narodnik* scholars of tsarist times.

III. Industry

Danilevsky, V. V. *Russkoe zoloto.* [Russian gold.] Moscow, 1959.

Kononenko, K. *Ukraine and Russia, a History of the Economic Relations Between Ukraine and Russia 1654–1917.* Marquette, 1958.

The Ukraine and its economic development in the tsarist period, seen as an exploited Russian colony.

Livshitz, R. S. *Razmeshchenie promyshlennosti v dorevolyutsionnoi Rossii.* [The dispersal of industry in prerevolutionary Russia.] Moscow, 1956.

Lukyanov, P. M. *Istoriya khimicheskikh promyslov i khimicheskoi promyshlennosti Rossii.* [History of the chemical profession and the chemical industry of Russia.] Moscow-Leningrad, 1948.

Obzor razlichnykh otraslei manufakturnoi promyshlennosi Rossii. [Survey of the various branches of the manufacturing industry in Russia.] 3 vols. St. Petersburg, 1863.

A valuable compendium of descriptions and data dealing with nineteenth-century Russian industries.

Pazhitnov, K. A. *Ocherki istorii tekstilnoi promyshlennosti dorevolyutsionnoi Rossii, khlopehatobumazhnaya, l'no-penkovaya i shelkovaya promyshlennost.* [Essays on the history of the textile industry of prerevolutionary Russia, the cotton, linen, and silk industries.] Moscow, 1958.

———. *Sherstyanaya Promyshlennost.* [The woolens industry.] Moscow, 1955.

Ryndzyunsky, P. G. *Krestyanskaya promyshlennost v poreformennoi Rossii.* [Peasant industry in postreform Russia.] Moscow, 1966.

Peasant crafts in the late nineteenth century.

Strumilin, S. G. *Istoriya Chernoi metallurgii v S.S.S.R.* [History of ferrous metallurgy in the USSR.] Moscow, 1954, vol. I.

Tengoborskii, L. *Commentaries on the Productive Forces of Russia.* 2 vols. English ed. London, 1855–56.

Another important nineteenth-century descriptive work.

Vobly, K. G. *Opyt istorii sveklo-sakharnoi promyshlennosti SSSR.*

[An essay on the history of the beet-sugar industry of the USSR.] Moscow, 1928, vol. I.

IV. Transport and Trade

Entner, Marvin. *Russo-Persian Commercial Relations 1828–1914.* University of Florida Monographs; Social Sciences, 1965, no. 28.

Haywood, Richard. *The Beginnings of Railway Development in Russia in the Reign of Nicholas I, 1835–1842.* Duke, 1969.

Hunter, Holland. *Soviet Transportation Policy.* Harvard, 1957.

A comprehensive study of the Stalinist period, with a good historical introduction.

Kirchner, Walter, *Commercial Relations between Russia and Europe, 1400–1800.* Bloomington, Ind., 1966.

Kulisher, Josef. *Ocherk po istorii russkoi torgovli.* [Essay on the history of Russian trade.] Petrograd, 1923.

Lebedev, V. V. *Russko-Amerikanskie ekonomicheskie otnosheniya 1900–1917 gg.* [Russian-American economic relations 1900–1917.] Moscow, 1964.

Pokrovsky, S. A. *Vneshnaya torgovlya i vneshnaya torgovaya politika Rossii.* [The foreign trade and foreign trade policy of Russia.] Moscow, 1947.

Rozhkova, M. K. *Ekonomicheskie svyazi Rossii co Srednei Aziei 40-60-e gody XIX veka.* [The economic ties of Russia with Central Asia, 1840s to 1860s.] Moscow, 1963.

Westwood, John. *History of Russian Railways.* London, 1964.

Zlotnikov, M. F. *Kontinentalnaya blokada i Rossiya.* [The continental blockade and Russia.] Moscow-Leningrad, 1966.

V. Science and Technology

Danilevsky, V. V. *Russkaya Tekhnika.* [Russian technology] 2d ed. Leningrad, 1948.

Figurovsky, N. A., ed. *Istoriya yestestvoznaniya v Rossii* [The history of natural science in Russia.] 2 vols. Moscow, 1957.

This and the Danilevsky work are the standard Soviet histories of Russian science and technology.

Graham, Loren. *The Soviet Academy of Sciences and the Communist Party 1917–1932*. Princeton, 1967.

State mobilization of Russian science for industrialization.

Mendeleyev, D. I. *Problemy ekonomicheskogo razvitiya Rossii*. [Problems of the economic development of Russia.] Moscow, 1960.

Writings of the famous Russian scientist on the late tsarist era on this subject.

Menshutkin, B. *Russia's Lomonosov*. Princeton, 1952.

Translation of the definitive biography of the eighteenth-century scientist.

Virginsky, V. S. *Tvortsy novoi tekhniki v krepostnoi Rossii*. [Creators of new technology in feudal Russia.] 2d ed. Moscow, 1962.

Early Russian inventors.

* Vucinich, Alexander. *Science in Russian Culture*. Stanford, 1963.

* ———. *Science in Russian Culture 1861–1917*. Stanford, 1970.

The first, and an almost encyclopedic survey of science and technology in tsarist Russia.

Zvorikine, A. A. *"Remarques sur l'histoire des inventions et de la pensée scientifique et technique russes des XVIIIe et XIXe siècles."* *Contributions à l'histoire russe, cahiers d'histoire mondiale*, special issue (1958), pp. 183–211.

VI. State Economic Policy: the Tsarist Period

Gerschenkron, Alexander. "Agrarian Policies and Industrialization: Russia 1861–1917," *Cambridge Economic History of Europe*. Cambridge, 1965, VI, 706–800.

An important study of how tsarist agrarian policy impeded an industrial revolution and yet opened a path to industrialization.

Kinyapina, N. S. *Politika Russkogo Samoderzhaviya v oblasti pro-myshlennosti* (20-50-e gody XIX v.). [Policy of the Russian autocracy in the area of industry, 1820s to 1850s.] Moscow University, 1968.

* Pintner, Walter McKenzie, *Russian Economic Policy Under Nicholas I.* Cornell, 1967.

A recent study of tsarist economic policy in the second quarter of the nineteenth century, which complements that of the Soviet scholar, Kinyapina, listed above. Both are based on archival research.

Polyansky, F. Ya. *"Promyshlennaya politika russkogo absolutizma vo vtoroi chetverti XVIII veka* (1725–1740 gg.)." [Industrial policy of the Russian absolutism in the second quarter of the eighteenth century (1725–1740.] I. V. Maevsky and F. Ya. Polyansky, eds. *Voprosy istorii narodnogo khozyaistva SSSR.* [Problems in the history of the national economy of the USSR.] Moscow, 1957, pp. 85–137.

A Soviet discussion of tsarist industrial policy in the post-Petrine period, which comes to conclusions similar to those of the article by Arcadius Kahan in this collection.

* Von Laue, Theodore. *Sergei Witte and the Industrialization of Russia.* New York, 1963.

The tsarist method of industrialization in the late nineteenth century.

Zagorsky, S. O. *State Control of Industry in Russia During the War.* Yale, 1928.

One of several volumes written for the Carnegie Endowment *Economic and Social History of the World War* on the subject of tsarist state economic policy at that time.

VII. Capitalism, Russian and Foreign

Amburger, Eric. *"Der fremde Unternehmer in Russland bis zur Oktoberrevolution im jahre* 1917." *Tradition, Zeitschrift für Firmenge-schichte und Unternehmerbiographie,* 2d year (1957), no. 4, pp. 337–55.

Berlin, Pavl A. *Russkaya burzhuaziya v staroe i novoe vremya.* [The Russian bourgeoisie in old and new times.] Moscow, 1922.

Beskrovny, L. G., ed. *K voprosu pervonachalnom nakoplenii v Rossii (XVII–XVIII v.v.), sbornik statei.* [The question of the primary accumulation in Russia, seventeenth-eighteenth centuries, collection of articles.] Moscow, 1958.

Preindustrial accumulation of capital.

Bill, Valentine. *The Forgotten Class.* New York, 1959.

Both the Bill and the Berlin books deal with social and economic aspects of the Russian middle class in the late tsarist period.

Brandt, B. F. *Inostrannie kapitaly v Rossii.* [Foreign capital in Russia.] St. Petersburg, 1899.

Crihan, Anton. *Le capital étrangere en Russie.* Paris, 1934.

Gerschenkron, Alexander. *Europe in the Russian Mirror: Four Lectures in Economic History.* Cambridge, Mass., 1970.

The Weber thesis and mercantilism examined in light of Russian experience.

Kahan, Arcadius. "The Costs of 'Westernization' in Russia: the Gentry and the Economy in the Eighteenth Century." *Slavic Review,* XXV (1966), 40–66.

Estate industry in the eighteenth century.

* McKay, John P. *Pioneers for Profit, Foreign Entrepreneurship and Russian Industrialization 1885–1913.* Chicago, 1970.

A reappraisal of the role of foreign enterprise in Russia in the last decades of the old regime.

Polyansky, F. Ya *Pervonalchalnoe nakoplenie kapitala v Rossii.* [The primary accumulation of capital in Russia.] Moscow, 1958.

VIII. Labor

Berliner, Joseph. *Factory and Manager in the U.S.S.R.* Harvard, 1957.

* Conquest, Robert, ed. *Industrial Workers in the U.S.S.R.* London, 1967.

Dallin, David, and Nikolaevsky, Boris. *Forced Labor in Soviet Russia.* London, 1948.

Deutscher, Isaac. *Soviet Trade Unions*. New York, 1950.

Pasquier, A. *Le Stakhanovisme*. Paris, 1938.

Pazhitnov, K. A. *Problema remeslennykh tsekov v zakonodatelstva russkago absolutizma*. [The problem of craft guilds in the legislation of Russian absolutism.] Moscow, 1952.

Rashin, A. G. *Formirovanie Rabochego klassa Rossii*. [The formation of the working class of Russia.] Moscow, 1958.

Schwarz, Solomon. *Labor in the Soviet Union. London, 1953*. A good summary of labor problems in the 1930s.

Swianiewicz, Stanislaw. *Forced Labour and Economic Development*. London, 1965.

* Zelnik, Reginald. *Labor and Society in Tsarist Russia 1855–1870*. Stanford, 1971.

IX. State Economic Policy: The Soviet Period

Arnold, Arthur Z. *Banks, Credit and Money in Soviet Russia*. Columbia, 1937.

Davies, Robert W. *The Soviet Budgetary System*. Cambridge, 1958.

Holzman, Franklyn. *Soviet Taxation*. Harvard, 1955. A full analysis of the turnover tax and other sources of Soviet revenue.

Jasny, Naum. *Essays on the Soviet Economy*. New York, 1962. A full discussion of long-range planning.

Sokolnikov, G. Ya. *Soviet Policy in Public Finance 1917–1928*. Stanford, 1931.

Sosnovy, Timothy. *The Housing Problem in the Soviet Union*. New York, 1954.

Zaleski, E. *Planification de la croissance et fluctuations économiques en U.R.S.S.* Paris, 1962. A detailed study of the early ups and downs of the plan era.

X. Measuring Russian Economic Growth

Bergson, Abram. *The Real National Income of Soviet Russia since 1928*. Harvard, 1961.

Chapman, Janet. *Real Wages in the Soviet Union*. Harvard, 1963.

Goldsmith, Raymond. "The Economic Growth of Tsarist Russia 1860–1913." *Economic Development and Cultural Change,* IX (1961), 441–75.

The most up-to-date and detailed estimate we have for the tsarist period.

Grossman, Gregory. *Soviet Statistics of Physical Output*. Princeton, 1960.

Hodgman, Donald. *Soviet Industrial Production 1928–1951*. Harvard, 1954.

Jasny, Naum. *The Soviet Economy in the Plan Era*. Stanford, 1951.

―――. *The Soviet 1956 Statistical Handbook*. Michigan State University Press, 1957.

This book and the work of Grossman cited above are two discussions of Soviet statistics and their pitfalls.

Nutter, Gilbert W. *Growth of Industrial Production in the Soviet Union*. Princeton, 1962.

Seton, Francis. *The Tempo of Soviet Industrial Expansion*. London, 1957.

Strana sovetov za 50 let. [The country of the Soviets for fifty years.] Moscow, 1967.

A recent short collection of official statistics.

XI. Russian Economic Thought Relating to Development

Erlich, Alexander. *The Soviet Industrialization Debates 1924–1928*. Harvard, 1960.

A comprehensive summary of the various views of Russian economic development expanded by Soviet economists in the 1920s.

Mendel, Arthur. *Dilemmas of Progress in Tsarist Russia*. Harvard, 1961.

View and debates of Marxist and Populist writers on the subject of Russian economic development.

Miller, Margaret. *Rise of the Russian Consumer*. London, 1965.

Includes a summary of the views of Soviet economists and planners on reform of the economy.

Preobrazhensky, Ye. *The New Economics*. London, 1965.

The "Left position" argued by one of the leading Soviet economists of the 1920s.

XII. Comparative Dimension

Black, C. E. *The Dynamics of Modernization*. New York, 1966.

Genezis kapitalizma v promyshlennosti. [The genesis of capitalism in industry.] Academy of Sciences, USSR, 1963.

Gerschenkron, Alexander. *Economic Backwardness in Historical Perspective*. New York, 1965.

Maddison, Angus. *Economic Growth in Japan and the U.S.S.R.* London, 1969.

Moore, Barrington. *Social Origins of Dictatorship and Democracy*. Boston, 1967.

Rostow, W. W. *The Stages of Economic Growth*. Cambridge, Mass., 1960.

Wiles, Peter. *The Political Economy of Communism*. Oxford, 1962.

Index